A COMPREHENSIVE INDEX OF
POET LORE

VOLUMES 1 – 58 : 1889 – 1963

COMPILED BY ALICE VERY
WITH AN INTRODUCTION BY MELVIN H. BERNSTEIN

BOSTON
BRANDEN PRESS
PUBLISHERS

THE EARLY YEARS OF POET LORE
1889-1929

By MELVIN H. BERNSTEIN

Since 1889 *Poet Lore* has been edited successively by Helen A. Clarke and Charlotte E. Porter, Ruth Hill, John Heard, Edmund R. Brown and John Williams Andrews. It was the creation of Miss Clarke and Miss Porter, and it is their contribution over three decades that is largely the subject of this prefatory note.[1]

Helen Archibald Clarke (1860-1926) was the granddaughter and daughter of Scotch-Canadian musicians. Her father Dr. (Hon.) Hugh Archibald Clarke (1839-1927), born in Toronto, was an organist, poet, translator, fiction writer, and a composer of music to accompany plays by Euripides and Aristophanes. Starting in 1875 and continuing to serve until 1927, Professor Clarke occupied at the University of Pennsylvania the second chair of academic music in the United States (Harvard had been first). He had married Jane Searle in 1859; Helen was their only child. Mrs. Clarke died in 1906; in 1907 Dr. Clarke remarried. Before the University of Pennsylvania was officially open to women students, Helen entered as a special student in 1881 and under her father's tutelage earned a certificate of proficiency in music in 1883. Although interested in science, particularly physics, she discovered Robert Browning who became the literary inspiration of much of her life's work. She dramatized his poetry, and set his poems, along with poems of Shakespeare, Spenser, Marlowe, and verses of her friends, especially Charlotte's, to music. Her life's work was *Poet Lore* and the publication of dozens of related books that came out of her editorial interests.

Charlotte Endymion Porter (1859-1942) had been born in Towanda, Pennsylvania, the child of Dr. Henry Clinton Porter and Elizabeth Betts Porter. After she was graduated Phi Beta Kappa from Wells College, Aurora, N.Y, in 1875,

9

she went to Europe and briefly studied at the Sorbonne, concentrating on the French theater. Back in Philadelphia Charlotte edited the first five volumes of *Shakesperiana* (1883-1887) in Philadelphia — though it was published by the Shakespeare Society of New York. It led to her meeting with Helen. They became inseparable friends, exchanging token rings and musical compositions for poems. Having started *Poet Lore,* they lived together in Philadelphia, and after 1891 in Boston at 3 Joy Street (subsequently bought by the Boston Authors Club), at 11 Queensberry Street, and summers at "Ardensea," Isle au Haut, Maine. On July 1, 1926, Charlotte, whose love for Helen is commemorated in her book of collected poems, *Lips of Music* (1910), first reading some verses from Emerson and Browning, then scattered Helen's ashes in the sea off Maine. Charlotte lived actively on until January 16, 1942, dying in a nursing home in Melrose, Massachusetts.[2]

The two women were indefatigable literary people, indeed, the very pattern of model late Victorian literary ladies. Helen worked at her music all her life and Charlotte monitored the theater abroad and at home. Perhaps to the harm of their fame, no literary genre was alien to them. Both wrote literary essays, book reviews, study programs, anthologies, original plays, fiction, poetry, and translations; both edited multivolume library and student editions of Robert Browning, Shakespeare, and Elizabeth Barrett Browning. Many of these were elegant editions with expensive covers, illustrations, and mountainous annotations. Helen wrote libretti (*Gethsemane,* music by Gustave Schrube, Schirmer, 1912), children's plays (*Starrylocks in Butterflyland, Hermes at School*), *Browning's Italy* (1907), *A Child's Guide to Mythology* (1908), *Browning's England* (1908), dedicated to Charlotte, *Longfellow's Country* (1909), dedicated to Alice W. Longfellow, *Ancient Myths in Modern Poets* (1910) *Hawthorne's Country* (1910), *Poets' New England* (1911), *Browning and His Century* (1912) and dedicated to the Boston Browning Society in commemoration of the Browning centenary, 1812-1912.

Charlotte wrote a three-act play *Jeanne d'Arc* (1913), and *Shakespeare Study Programs* for the Drama League of America (1915-1916). In 1917 she copyrighted a scale model of "Shakespeare's Globe Theater — 1599 - 1613" for which she did research over nine years; edited a 12-volume edition of Browning with an introductory essay by William Lyon Phelps (Fred De Fau & Co., 1910); edited the Walter Hampden Edition of *The Ring and the Book* (Crowell, 1927) to which Montrose J. Moses wrote the introduction. (Hampden was playing the title role in *Caponsacchi* in the fall of 1926.) Meanwhile, along with Helen, she was almost annually contributing translations of plays to *Poet Lore*.

Established literary clubs were their homes away from home, and away from the editorial offices of *Poet Lore*. In fact, they were charter members of new clubs. In Philadelphia they were members of the Shakespeare and Browning societies. In Boston they in time became officers in the Boston Browning Society (active on the Publications Committee, of course), and the Boston Authors Club, then under the presidency of Julia Ward Howe, T. W. Higginson, vice-president.[3] During 1920-25 Helen held a ladies' tea-table "Symposium" regularly at her home, sometimes teaching versification, other times leading discussions on the progressive movements in philosophy, science, and the arts. After her death, the Symposium continued to meet at the Boston Art Club. At the time of her death, Helen was first vice-president of the American Poetry Association. Charlotte supported the New England Poetry Club, was president of the American Drama Society founded in Boston, November, 1909, to organize a civic theater, and remained active on the executive board. One of her colleagues was Thomas Augustus Watson (1854-1934), telephone man, ship builder, actor, sometime president of the Boston Browning Society, and one of the four vice-presidents of the new drama society.

Charlotte printed many of her own "first" American translations of European plays in *Poet Lore* and initiated the

first American performance of a Lord Dunsany play. With Robert Frost's permission she arranged some of his poems as "folk drama poems." She supported the Allied Arts Association, an enterprise to further the domestic sale of work by American craftsmen.

These, then, are the indicators of the literary sensibilities and gross energies of the two women who in late 1888 from offices at 223 South 38th Street, Philadelphia, planned a January 1889 issue of *Poet Lore,* a new magazine to fill a void.

II

It was a small but intense group out of sixty-two million Americans in the United States in 1889 who were interested in Shakespeare and Browning. Indulged but unassisted by the poet himself, the Browning Society had been started in England in 1881 by Dr. F. J. Furnivall and Miss Emily H. Hickey. J. O. Halliwell-Phillips (1880-89) along with J. Payne Collier in 1841 had founded the old Shakespeare Society in England. Shakespeare adulation was a minor industry on both sides of the Atlantic. To read the club news reported in the early volumes of *Poet Lore* is an exercise in tracking the misty drift of culture across continents.

Shakespeare clubs existed in Hamilton and Melbourne, Australia; Bristol and London, England; Montreal, Canada; Concord, New Hampshire; Natick, Massachusetts; Wellesley College; New York, Philadelphia, Baltimore, Detroit, Grand Rapids; Dubuque, Iowa; Peoria, Illinois; Nicholasville, Kentucky; Springfield, Missouri; Berlin, Wisconsin; Bonham, Texas; and San Francisco, California.

Browning Clubs (which spread to South Africa and Copenhagen) also proliferated in America: Boston; Philadelphia; Meadville, Pennsylvania; Plainfield, New Jersey; Syracuse, New York, "the oldest Browning society in this country"; Rochester, New York; Jacksonville, Illinois. There was an ominous Sordello Club in St. Louis.

In addition, there were miscellaneous clubs that may have

been Shakespeare or Browning clubs, or both. Every so often they sent in reports on the utility of *Poet Lore's* programs of study. The clubs had unusual names and were located in unsuspected cultural El Dorados: The Query Club of Nashville, Tennessee; Miss M. E. Ford's Literary Circle in the same city; The Mutual Club of Woodland, California; The Alcuin Club of Madison, Indiana; The Ebell Society of Oakland "the oldest literary woman's club of California"; The Ladies Literary Club of Grand Rapids, Michigan; Friends in Council, Quincy, Illinois; The Saturday Morning Club in Boston with a membership of seventy young women; the Fellowcraft Club of New York City which had Richard Watson Gilder as toastmaster.[4]

The mauve atmosphere of these clubs seeps through the listing. The Browning Club of Meadville called themselves "Women and Roses," because the members were all women and because "roses almost invariably graced the presence of their meetings."[5] The ladies met in club halls, churches, alumnae libraries, and private homes. They celebrated the birthdays of Shakespeare and Browning—and occasionally Shelley—with talks, impromptus, roundtable discussions of the evolution of Service, Religion and Woman, with vocal and instrumental solos, and with choral groups such as the Orpheus Club of Philadelphia. Presiding chairwomen bravely answered members' on-the-spot queries such as, "Wherein does the fascination of Robert Browning's poetry lie?" Names were dropped with facile grace — Euripides, Goethe, Tennyson, Emerson — but always perspective pointed to Shakespeare and Browning. In the first three volumes of *Poet Lore* there were roughly forty-five articles on Shakespeare, forty-seven on Browning.

Perhaps in those *fin-de-siècle* days of eager literary ladies all was not women, roses, Shakespeare and Browning, as this vignette testifies. A Paris correspondent reported the following to *Poet Lore*:

One of the American colonists — a young lady — said to me recently, "We have a Shakespeare Society in our American circle here; quite a large one." "Ah, I should like to join," I answered at once. "Will you give me some idea of your plan of study?" She hesitated, looked a little disconcerted, then laughed. "We — don't — do much *studying*," she acknowledged. "We meet only once a fortnight, spending an hour on Shakespeare, reading round in turn, you know; the rest of the evening we *dance*."[6]

With their own Anglophiliac interest in Shakespeare and Browning, Helen and Charlotte must have sensed the yeast of interest in a magazine that would raise a breadloaf of culture. The venture would join restless America to the world. Change was everywhere to be seen. Academia was reaching out to the public; colleges were expanding; professors were walking unpushed to the lyceum platform and also mailing regularly acceptable articles to magazines; the magazines themselves were multiplying amoebically.[7] The twentieth century — the American Century — was a decade away. The Western New York spirit of the Reverend John H. Vincent accompanied by the gently provocative breezes from Lake Chautauqua brooded over the land. Andrew Carnegie's bookless libraries (there were to be more than 2500) were punctuating the American Gothic landscape. Surely, literature was more than the ubiquitous, domestic local-color fiction. Surely, the predictions of Herbert Spencer and the outlines of John Fiske's *Cosmic Philosophy* (1874) were manifestly destined to be filled in. To read a monthly magazine, twenty-five cents per copy, which according to its cover page was "devoted to Shakespeare, Browning and the comparative study of literature," was to collaborate toward the creation of the new world of emergent women, positivism, beneficent Social Darwinism, a vague liberalism, and an understanding of the supranational art of literature.. Germany boasted a *Zeitschrift für vergleichende Litteratur-geschichte*. Why not America (I, 52)? The colophon on later covers — a cornucopia from which poured literature and truth — contained all these hopes, and more.

Poet Lore soon broke out of its Anglophile inspiration. Its essays were peppered with French, German, Greek, and Latin phrases.   It reported the eminent American Victorians like Agnes Repplier and Vida D. Scudder; it recorded the triumphs of actors and actresses (Henry Irving, Ellen Terry, Julia Marlowe, Lillie Langtry, Helena Modjeska, Ada Rehan); it celebrated scholars (R. G. Moulton, Sidney Lee, Israel Gollancz, F. J. Furnivall, W. J. Rolfe, George Saintsbury, H. H. Furness, Paul Shorey, Dr. E. Berdoe); it noticed scholarly publications, concordances, and facsimiles; it reproduced pages of musical settings of famous poems; it acknowledged unqualified praise for Shakespeare and reverence for Browning (I, 50), but a reverence that must be treated in "a rational manner. . . by sensible readers." (I, 37).

The reasonableness hoped for by the editors is reflected in the title they made up for their magazine.   Later in 1926 Miss Porter recalled that the first part of the title referred to Browning and Shakespeare.   By the other part they meant "the whole illuminating lore of the art" of poetry, intending to supply in the magazine not Gradgrind facts but explanation, scholarship, criticism, and guided study linking poetry to evolutionist ideals.   Lamentably, they were misconstrued by some, for they did not mean that Browning was the equal of Shakespeare in drama.[8]   In retrospect, the women were sure they were pioneering. No other American periodical regularly published translations, especially of drama.   And the little poetry then published was generally filler, "delegated to chance margins" (XXXVII, 442).   In 1899, the *Magazine of Poetry* did publish quantities of verse along with pictures of the poets and short autobiographical-biographical sketches.   The editors were certain that the reading of poetry was a more important index to a nation's civilization than its annual consumption of soap.[9]

Poet Lore did not immediately fulfill its prospectus nor did it right off hit upon its most useful work of discovering world literature to readers at home and, through Brentano's

in London and Paris, abroad.   International encouragement it
had from Halliwell-Phillips in England; Browning himself
acknowledged the magazine.   With sincere grief the editors
memorialized the death of Browning and his burial in West-
minister Abbey, December 31, 1889. At home, E. C. Stedman
applauded them, as did H. H. Furness in Philadelphia, and
W. J. Rolfe in Boston.   From Camden Walt Whitman, despite
his reservations about Shakespeare, solicitously wrote them two
or three times.   The prevailing tone of its essays was historicist,
and defensive of Victorian values.   Too many of its earliest
contributors could barely distinguish between criticism and
appreciation, between explanation and adulation.   Criticism
would never pierce, so many of them wrote, to the heart of
the mystery of beauty that stirred "every fibre of one's soul."
Yet its essays did have a vaunted purpose: to undercut academic "old fogeyism" that was then allegedly blighting college
instruction and the educational snobbism — "upperclass phi-
lanthropy," they called it — of professional literary special-
ists.[10]   This, then, was the editorial ladies' critical populism
which positively recorded the imperishable moments of "appreciation" but negatively yielded little of enduring, reprint-
able, critical insight.   Fortunately, *Poet Lore* was shifting in
another, more valuable direction.

The Charleston *News,* the Springfield *Republican,* the Ken-
nebec *Journal,* and the *Popular Science Monthly* which by
1891 had noticed *Poet Lore,* had found the inclusion of Russian and Norwegian fiction incongruent with its title.   The
editors defended the variance by assuring their friendly critics
that the scope of the magazine was wider than its title.[11]   And
Volume III was different: for the first time it contained translations of foreign fiction and a complete text of a foreign play.
The Elizabethan-Victorian crown jewels of poetry were still
there but also therein were essays on Hafiz and Firdausi;
Nathan Haskell Dole's critical précis of Pushkin's *Boris Godu-
nov;* a Russian short story by Vsevolod Garshin (1855-88);
a short story by the Norwegian Alexander Kielland (1849-

1906); allusions to Sidney Lanier; a book review of Whitman's recent *Good-bye My Fancy;* and an essay on Moricz Jokai (1825-1904) by John Heard, Jr., later to be an editor of *Poet Lore.* There were numerous defensive references to Ibsen gleaned from Edmund Gosse's *Northern Studies* (1890).[12] Two issues that year supplied a complete serialized text of *Harold,* a three-act play by Ernst von Wildenbruch (1845-1909), translated from the German by Otto Heller but done into English verse by — of all people — Dr. Hugh Archibald Clarke. (Charlotte's father, Dr. Henry Porter, over the years also assisted in translations and advice.)

Thus was the pattern set. It had taken time; in fact, thirty-six monthly issues. The visible straws in the wind of direction were now indicated in the three volumes: Shakespeare, yes, but in Holland, in Japan, in Russia, in Paris; also an Arabic version of *Macbeth's* "moving wood" by Morris Jastrow, Jr.; and Emerson and the *Bhagavad-Gita.* Volume IV (1892) reinforced the pattern; it contained the first English translation of Jakub Arbes (1840-1914), a liberal, anticlerical Czech novelist and patriot; a sensitive essay, "Hamlet and Don Quixote," by Turgenev; *Karen,* a Norwegian novelette by Kielland; and Björnson's pro-feminist *A Glove.* (Björnson had been in America in 1880-81 and received the Nobel Prize in 1903.)[13]

The shift in contents of the magazine may have been hastened by its remove from Philadelphia. In 1891 Dana Estes, then beginning his own publishing firm, invited *Poet Lore* to Boston where it has since remained. His offer of free office space for three pages per issue of free advertising was accepted. There were other sad excitements in 1892. Tennyson, whom Whitman had called "Boss of us all," died, as did Whittier and Whitman himself.[14] Horace Traubel had brought Whitman's last greeting from Camden to Philadelphia where the two editors were packing to go to Boston. "God bless them, and may they be prospered wherever they go!"[15] Yet there were consolations. That year women students were

admitted to Edinburgh University on the same terms and conditions as men, and the University of Chicago was founded.

In Volume V (1893) *Poet Lore* celebrated soberly a domestic delight, the World's Columbian Exposition in Chicago. In its pages, Horace Traubel and Oscar L. Triggs mournfully praised Whitman; Miss Clarke and Miss Porter consistently praised Emma Lazarus and Emerson and had a good word for James Herne's *Shore Acres;* and an essayist celebrated America's women poets from Anne Bradstreet to Sarah Wentworth Morton, omitting Emily Dickinson.[16] But it turned its attention abroad in an essay on Giacomo Leopardi by Gamaliel Bradford, Jr., then thirty years old. Bradford's prose, incidentally, is a stylistic delight amid the carbuncular prose of Traubel, Triggs, and the small, determined squad of scribbling women who regularly infiltrated the pages of the magazine.[17] It did have a new enthusiasm — Maeterlinck.

In espousing Maeterlinck barely two years after the first French performance of his plays, *Poet Lore* applied adventurously its potentially debilitating critical test—the Browning-Shakespeare touchstone. In Maeterlinck Miss Clarke and Miss Porter correctly saw symbolism and poetry joined; they linked his theatricality with the excitement supplied by Ibsen — all ushering in a new age of drama. In four issues were printed the editor's own new translation of *Les Aveugles* (The Sightless). During the years that followed they added more translations, supplementing them with editorial comments defending Maeterlinck against charges of *Yellow Book* decadence made by critics like Symons and Nordau.[18] No attempt was made by the editors to account for their ambivalence in at once championing a vigorous Whitman, a bouncing Browning, and a morbid Maeterlinck, whose plays projected a universe of futility, old age, sickness, deafness, blindness and will-less sleep, doors that don't open, pools that stagnate, and forests into which even the powerful sun cannot penetrate.

By Volume VI (1894) the reports of literary society activity decline noticeably, but the editors' study programs on

the great English and American poets of the nineteenth century are available for purchase in book form. A circulation jolter was introduced. A symposium on how literature may best be taught brought Professors F. I. Carpenter and Oscar L. Triggs (Chicago), L. A. Sherman (Nebraska), Katharine Lee Bates (Wellesley), and Hiram Corson (Cornell) into public discussion, incidentally eliciting from them commendation for *Poet Lore's* high purpose.[19] Significantly, the magazine began to reach out for new literary excitements in addition to slight notices of Garland, Santayana, Fenollosa, Frazer's *The Golden Bough,* and Henry James. These included introducing Danish Holger Drachmann (1846-1908); recommending Dostoievski; printing the editors' translations of short stories by Strindberg, a Villiers de L'Isle-Adam (1838-89) short story, and the Portuguese sonnets of Antero de Quental (1842-91). Villiers remained the enthusiasm of the editors for several years thereafter especially because of his influence upon Maeterlinck. From Villiers Edmund Wilson took the title of his study of the imaginative literature of 1870-1930, *Axel's Castle* (1931).

More and more *Poet Lore* felt itself embracing the literature of all nations, acting as mediator in disseminating in America that shock of recognition we call genius. The new cover of Volume VII (1895) featured a lyre, bays and laurel, and superscribed were dozens of writers' names from Aeschylus to Firdausi, from Ariosto to Lanier. To be sure, Shakespeare was accorded an anniversary issue in April, and Browning in May that year. But the other issues continued to reprint translations of Villiers, Maeterlinck, Drachmann, Richard Hovey's translation of Karl Gutzkow's (1811-78) *Uriel Acosta* (1847), and more Gamaliel Bradford. In *Uriel Acosta* the many allusions to Socrates, Jesus, Galileo, and Spinoza critical of tyranny and religious zealousness accorded well with *Poet Lore's* liberalism.

Publication difficulties developed in 1896. The subscription price remaining at $2.50 per year, *Poet Lore* became a quarterly with its October issue and moved from 196 Summer

Street to 18 Pemberton Square, Boston. It seemed to grasp its own new idea more firmly, called itself a "New Series," and promised longer articles, more rare classics and original native work. It observed its promise by printing Richard Hovey's *Taliesin: A Masque,* invested erringly in stories by Walter Blackburn Harte, supplied more Villiers and Von Wildenbruch, praised Sudermann and Yeats, and expressed displeasure with the social sewers opened by Zola and the ephemera in the *Chap-Book* of Chicago and in the *Lark* of San Francisco.[20]

In 1897 *Poet Lore* confessed to being unable to keep up with the plethora of new fiction. It ignored Twain, Howells, and James and took long, wrong chances on newer writers. Its ability to spot the best of the emerging poets was dubious. It paid negligible attention to Stephen Crane and liked Bliss Carman, Paul Lawrence Dunbar, and Edward Rowland Sill. When Miss Clarke read E. A. Robinson's *The Torrent and the Night Before* (1896), she was reminded of Browning's dramatic monologues and Gabriele D'Annunzio.[21] The point is that D'Annunzio was on the editors' minds, not Robinson. Readers of *Poet Lore* were going to get a lot of D'Annunzio, hardly any more Robinson.

The editors did much homework in foreign periodicals such as the Parisian *L'Humanité Nouvelle* and *Le Magazine International.* In them they found major source material for their curiosity about foreign writers, national movements, and what must have seemed knowledge exotic to many but agreeably cosmopolitan to a few. The editors wanted to make the few into the many. They, for instance, translated from *Le Magazine International* an essay by Chaken Garo, "Modern Armenian Literature."[22] They introduced examples of folksongs and tales from modern Greece,[23] and a novella, *A Village Romeo and Juliet,* by the Swiss writer, Gottfried Keller (1819-90).[24]

The presidencies of Harrison and Cleveland, the Gold Panic, Coxey's Army, the Pullman Strike, and the Gold Rush had elicited no comment from *Poet Lore.* But the Spanish-

American War made the editors in 1898 sympathize with James Russell Lowell's line: "Gutenberg's gun has the longest range." The sonnet of Florence Earle Coates (1850-1927), "Dreyfus," was another profession of *Poet Lore's* liberal sympathies.[25] More to its concern in 1898 was some fiction of J. H. Rosny and Edouard Rod (contemporaries of J. K. Huysmans), Maeterlinck's neglected essay on Emerson, Fred Lewis Pattee's analytical essay, "Fear in *Macbeth*," an essay on the Spanish poet, José Zorilla (1817-93), and Mary Harned's translation of *The Sunken Bell*, a most romantic play by Gerhart Hauptmann (1862-1946). In addition there was a delightful, symbolic story by Adachi Kinnosuki, "A Japanese Garden."

New translations of Björnson, Anatole France, Paul Bourget (then, perhaps, at the height of his fame), Sudermann's play *Johannes*, and Selma Lagerlöf's story, "It," were the major contributions in Volume XI (1899). Domestic writers were represented by Ferris Greenslet and a reprint of the famous San Francisco *Examiner* poem by Edwin Markham, "The Man with the Hoe."[26]

III

Swedish and Finnish fiction mingled cheek by jowl with dismay about the Boer War and the Boxer Rebellion, along with articles on Emerson, Browning, Ruskin, Poe, and Louise Chandler Moulton in Volume XII (1900). There were other plays by Sudermann and Hauptmann, more fiction by Garshin, recognition five years before his Nobel Prize for José Echegaray (1832-1916), another essay by Bradford, a correct estimate of Richard Hovey whose "promise was greater than his achievement," and a short verse drama by Harriet Monroe.[27]

In content, Volume XIII (1901) faltered, printing some dreadful original verse tales, fiction, and plays, some translations of Ibsen and the Danish Jens Johannes Jorgensen (1866-1956), and pointed to the poetry of the Canadian, Isabella Valancy Crawford (1850-87). The "Life and Letters" de-

partments of the several issues, usually the work of both Miss Porter and Miss Clarke, were more interesting, more contentious, than usual. They criticized the prevailing Utilitarianism without its correlative social conscience ideals; they regretted the tendency of magazines — so pronounced today as to be fixed policy — to compete with newspapers for topicality; without comment they announced a new edition of the *Index Expurgatorius* containing a reduction of former sentences — an *adoucissement* in the words of Pope Leo XIII; and joined with Bliss Perry in defending Poe against the Puritan critics like T. W. Higginson who damned Poe's poetry because Poe was less than a gentleman: he didn't pay his debts. Noting that at an auction a first edition of *Tamerlane* recently brought $2,050, *Poet Lore* commented:

If Poe himself had been paid for his manuscripts in some such ratio as this . . . he would become very nearly respectable enough to associate with John D. Rockefeller, who doubtless pays his own bills, but frequently makes it impossible for others to pay theirs in the process of crushing out the small manufacturers — the process recently described by his son as akin to the florist's nipping many buds in order to produce "The American Beauty Rose," or "The Standard Oil Trust."[28]

In the same issue, by the way, *Poet Lore* printed a poem by one Charles James that it thought was acceptable to "liberal parents" for an equivalent to prayer:

Now I lie down to sleep;
Softly may slumber creep
    over my eyes.
May I be true and pure,
May I of love be sure
When I arise.[29]

For the next four years (1902-06), *Poet Lore* experienced publishing problems. The pagination is disordered. For a while it called itself the *American Quarterly*. Its issues were now sewed, not bound together with wire staples and were named after the seasons. It moved to 194 Boylston Street, raised its subscription to $3.00 in 1903 and to $4.00 in 1906, and increased its book advertising — all reflecting its change

to a new publisher, Richard G. Badger. Besides, after 1904 *Poet Lore* was not for sale by booksellers or newsdealers but only by subscription. Editorially its "Life and Letters" department grew skimpier and skimpier. After 1905 old contributors now became editorial advisors: W. J. Rolfe, Hiram Corson, and George Willis Cooke. For about half a dozen years after 1906 Professor Paul H. Grummann, German Department, University of Nebraska, and Professor Curtis Hidden Page, Romance Languages Department, Columbia University, were associate editors. In 1905 the printers' strike delayed issues long beyond their due seasons.

Volume XIV, which covered the issues from October 1902 through December 1903, published the realistic German play by Max Dreyer, *On Probation* (an early analogue to *The Male Animal*), some more Maeterlinck, praised Japanese poetry, commended Willa Cather's poetry, agreed to the desirability of an American national theater only if it did not boycott the dramas of other countries and times, and began a protracted but mixed enthusiasm for publishing plays by D'Annunzio (1863-1938).

Badger's new face on *Poet Lore* in 1904 made it sprightlier, easier to read. The font was changed, the margins were narrower, and for a brief time somewhat Pre-Raphaelitish illustrations and some photographs were added. The world literature accent of Volume XV was discernibly loud: more plays of D'Annunzio, Arthur Schnitzler (1862-1931), and Maeterlinck; fiction by Sienkiewicz, and Gorki; Greek fiction and a Japanese farce translated by Yone Noguchi, essays on Paul Hervieu, Icelandic literature, Andalusian lyrics; and a slender, negligible notice of Yeats. The book reviews too heavily attending to Badger's Gorham Press series blighted *Poet Lore's* subsequent criticism. Although book reviewing in *Poet Lore* had never been very valuable critically, in this department of the magazine the connection with Badger exacted literally a killing price.

There was more Gorki in Volume XVI (1905) and more

Hauptmann, Schnitzler, and Strindberg in Volume XVII (1906). A Badger-inspired offer of a $100 prize poem competition in 1905 did not yield anything; apparently people were more interested in innovations such as typewriters and bicycles then becoming popular, the latter cited in the literature of the day as a threat to the persistence of culture, if not to civilization itself.

Andreyev's play *To the Stars* and Oscar Wilde's *Salome* translated from the French distinguished Volume XVIII (1907). The next year essays on the biblical Song of Songs considered as a play and the literature of Portugal, the Spanish Echegaray, the Bulgarian Ivan Vazov (1850-1921), and a German peace play, *The Wages of War,* were included in Volume XIX (1908), as was a translation of a Danish essay on the American novelist Robert Herrick that had appeared in a leading Copenhagen review. Volume XX (1909) in addition to plays by Frederick Hebbel and Paul Hervieu (1857-1915) contained early essays by Henry Seidel Canby and Louis Untermeyer. Benito Pérez Galdos (1843-1920) appeared in Volume XXI (1910) along with more poetry of Nietzsche, who had first appeared in *Poet Lore* as early as 1905.

In 1911, Volume XXII was a small library of European drama: plays by Björnson, two by Strindberg, including *Miss Julie,* Schnitzler, and Andreyev. Volume XXIII (1912) applauded the American Drama Society (Boston, 1909), the American Drama League (Chicago, 1910), and the Drama League of Boston (1911) — all reflections of earlier German and English excitement in civic, local, little theaters and endowed theaters. (The motion picture was by 1910 a distinct competitor.) In editorial pleas for serious playreading, *Poet Lore* countered the rising consumption of novels.[30] Regrettably the American theater had in the meantime, in the eyes of many, changed its character. If Augustin Daly had produced in the late 1880's and early '90's elaborate revivals of Shakespeare, they were not equally available twenty years later. Drama had become, William Winter lamented in *Other Days*

(1908), "the Amusement Business," and theater had taken on a bazaar atmosphere.[31]   In the 1911 volume the play by Stanislav Pshibishevsky [Przybyszewski] (1868-1927), and a classical 15th century Japanese play were not Amusement Business pieces.

Chekhov's *The Sea Gull* appeared in Volume XXIV (1913) along with poems by Jules Romains, William Rose Benét, Frederick Louis Pattee, and Joseph Warren Beach (the latter two going on to distinction in American scholarship and teaching); a story by Lermontov; and an essay, "Twilight of the Arts," by Van Wyck Brooks. Rabindranath Tagore, a defense of the Futurist F. T. Marinetti against charges of pornography, and a five-act Christian Friedrich Hebbell (1813-1863) play *Judith*, translated by Carl Van Doren were in Volume XXV (1914).

World War I did not give *Poet Lore* the jingoistic jitters. In Volume XXVI (1915) the world was not fragmented by national rivalries but rather brought together in reprints of folksongs of Greece under the Turk; Ukrainian folksongs; translations of Rainer Maria Rilke (by Sasha Best),[32] of Paul Fort and Verlaine; the five-act play *The Combat* by Georges Duhamel; Barrett H. Clark's essay, "Latest Tendencies in German Drama"; and a notice of O'Neill's volume of one-act plays, *Thirst*, probably because it had appeared in Badger's American Dramatist's Series.

Poet Lore over the years interlaced its volumes with essays on classical poetry and Ibsen, but its recurrent editorial talent was for exploring the new, the unfamiliar, the unpublished, the faraway, and the foreign writer who in unilingual America was unapproachable.   The war which delayed issues of Volume XXIX (1918) because many printers had enlisted did not diminish the energy of the editors in the interests of comparative literature.   They tried to keep aloof from "the turmoil of the times," which had more pity than glory in their events.   H. G. Montillon in an essay, "Some Modern War Dramas," regretted the poor caliber of war plays: "We have

not heard from the Germans. Doubtless they have been affected with as many and as poor plays as we have."[33] *Poet Lore* merely listed MacLeish's *The Tower of Ivory* and Ezra Pound's *Lustra* but accorded eighteen pages in Volume XXIX (1918) to Yone Noguchi's hokku poems and selections from Noh drama. Volume XXX (1919) was dull despite its potpourri of Danish, Hungarian, Belgian, and Mexican contents.

IV

It remains to survey the issues of the 1920's. The war over, *Poet Lore* perked up. The price per issue went up to $1.50, $6.00 per year. Poet and playwright Ruth Hill began to assist the two editors, now aging, enduring illness, yet still active as officers in artistic societies. *Poet Lore* reached out in new directions.

Volume XXXI (1920) was notable for its inclusion in a developing American atmosphere of anti-Russianism of plays by Chekhov and Pushkin;[34] of an essay on Ford Madox Hueffer by Lawrence M. Price, in which he predicted that the novelist's "poetry is most surely immortal"; and of an analysis of *Hiawatha,* drawing on Frazer's *Golden Bough.* More irregular in *Poet Lore's* remarkable publishing record but characteristic of its awareness of deep tides in contemporary literature is its reprint of a complete Ph.D. dissertation that had been approved by G. Stanley Hall of Clark University. It was Axel Johan Uppvall's *August Strindberg,* A Psychoanalytical Study with Special Reference to the Oedipus Complex.[35]

Volume XXXII (1921) featured a realistic Chinese play by Shen Hung, then at Harvard, and introduced the first of a series of articles on Yiddish writers. Deeply insinuated in the pages of *Poet Lore* ever since its founding was an unqualified confidence in intelligent, self-conscious Americanism able to assimilate the foreign to Whitman's dream of comrades. All along, its tables of contents had invoked a literate democracy. It had expressed a dislike for Coventry Patmore's anti-democratic ideas (VI, 270). It had expressed alarm "to learn that

[Nietzsche's Over-Man] was the most popular philosophy in Germany" (XI, 623). It had been consistently against censorship. And just as it without argument published Russian literature in a decade of mounting Red fear, so in the same decade of anti-immigrant feeling, 100 per cent Americanism, anti-Semitism, and anti-Negroism, *Poet Lore* published work on and by Yiddish writers, work on and by Negro writers. The former are illustrated by Charles A. Madison's series of eight essays 1921-26 on: the Yiddish theater, Mendele, Shalom Aleichem, Shalom Asch, Abraham Reisen, David Pinski, Isaac Leib Peretz, and Solomon Bloomgarden ("Yehoash").[36] To be added to this were J. C. Augenlicht's translation of H. Leivick's *The Golem*, a dramatic poem in eight scenes,[37] and the translation by S. K. Padover and Chasye Cooperman of a four-act play by L. Miller, *Mr. Man*.[38] More than praising faintly Negro writers like W. E. B. DuBois and Paul Lawrence Dunbar, *Poet Lore* printed four plays by one of Frederick H. Koch's distinguished Carolina playmakers, Paul Green, including *The Lord's Will* and *Sam Tucker*.[39]

During the 1920's *Poet Lore* continued to point in compass directions both tried and adventurous. It published a score of famous poets — Leopardi, Carducci, Laforgue, Rémy de Gourmont, Baudelaire, Gautier, Verlaine — and poets not since heard from. It published early critical essays and translations by Joseph T. Shipley, Charles Putnam, and Margaret Schlauch (a poem by Franz Werfel). It reproduced a play by Georg Kaiser, 1878-1944 (Vol. XXXI), a play by Ford Madox Ford (Vol. XXXIV), plays by Karel Capek, 1890-1938 (Vols. XXXIV, XXXV), Alois Jirasek, 1851-1930 (Vol. XXXVI), and seven one-act plays by Von Kotzebue, 1761-1819 (Vol. XXXVIII). It reported on symbolist drama, Moslem sources of Dante's *Divine Comedy*, Arabic poetry, the poems of the Welsh poet, Dafydd ab Gwilym, the Irish Literary Theatre, Philippine poetry, Ezra Pound's "Ballad of the Goodly Fere," the latest Pirandello, and "The Classical in Robert Frost" — the last four items in Vol. XL (1929).

V

Readers of the *Comprehensive Index to Poet Lore* can go on to discover its rich, neglected contents. Neither any individual volume index which *Poet Lore* occasionally printed, nor Frank R. Holmes' *A Complete Index Volumes 1-25 of Poet Lore* published by Richard G. Badger in 1916, nor Miss Porter's memoir of *Poet Lore* in 1926, and certainly not Frank Luther Mott's two-paragraph summary of the magazine in Volume IV of his *History of American Magazines* — not any one of these is as useful as this *Index* and a perusal of the volumes one-by-one to sense the significance of one of the earliest magazines of comparative literature in the United States. Over the years subscribers to *Poet Lore* did not live in that "Sahara of the Bozarts" that men like H. L. Mencken and James Huneker complained America was in the early decades of the twentieth century.[40]

By 1930 — where this study arbitarily concludes — the schools, magazines, newspapers, films, and radio extended their task of informing millions of educable Americans, many of whom had been to Europe, courtesy of the A.E.F. The 1920's had seen a proliferation of little magazines intending severally to do much of what *Poet Lore* within its covers had been doing singly and valiantly since 1889. Consistently it had opted for evolution, change, progress, truth through literature, cosmopolitanism, and internationalism. It had been — and has continued to be — liberal. It had been — and has continued to take — the long chances of fame on new writers: from all over this scribbling globe, now hugely modified by T.V. images.

Poet Lore showed a commendable flexibility to change. It did not, however, fall easily to the seduction of novelty. It early freed itself from any quasi-official connections with Browning and Shakespeare societies. It innovated, doggedly trying to catch the scent of modernism. The Transcendentalist *Dial* back in 1840-44, for example, had a publishing pro-

gram marked by an international literary sensibility; but it burned itself out like a lucifer match in four years.

In another metaphor, *Poet Lore* had not two Janus-faces but three faces (like the seal of The City College of New York): at its inception it looked backward and forward from Shakespeare and Browning to the twentieth century a decade away; and it also looked at the contemporary. True, it later slighted Joyce, Gide, Hemingway, Anderson, and Dreiser, even as it earlier had slighted Twain, James ("the greyhound of literature," *Poet Lore* called him in 1928), Howells and Wharton. Yet *Poet Lore* retained its modernist flavor by being contemporary, risking the publication of mediocre work while trying to rescue the American reader's imagination from the parochialism of both modernism and nativism. For that matter, to skim the volumes of Harriet Monroe's *Poetry* will also yield a long list of the published obscure. By printing the substantive artistic texts themselves, the literary one-world idea immanent in *Poet Lore* is its undeniable signature and colophon. Materials for doctoral dissertations of intrinsic value to our cultural history lie imbedded in its collected volumes.[41]

Ending this study with the year of the Big Crash coincides with a contemporary observation in a 1929 issue of *Poetry*. Some distinguished literary magazines had also crashed. Morton D. Zabel wrote an obituary of The *Dial* and the *Little Review*, magazines that had found themselves unable to survive without readers and contributors. He noted that they had gone, alas, the way of *Broom, Others, The Egoist, Wheels, S4N,* and *Secession:* "The way of periodicals is strange. By them we trace the ebb and flow of ideas and literary manners."[42]

Indeed, the way is strange. It applies to *Poet Lore,* too — which survives.

1. For assistance in assembling this material, thanks are due to the Alfred University Research Foundation, the College Center of the Finger Lakes, Miss Frances Hepinstall, Herrick Memorial Library, Alfred University; Mr. John Alden, Rare Book Room, Boston Public Library, Copley Square; archi-

vists of the libraries of the University of Pennsylvania, Wells College, and Princeton University; and the present Editors of *Poet Lore.*

2 Biographical data from the archives of the University of Pennsylvania and Wells College; "Helen A. Clarke," *Dictionary of American Biography,* IV (1930), 152-153; C. E. Porter, "A Story of *Poet Lore,*" *Poet Lore,* XXXVII (1926), 432-453; newspaper obituaries. *Lips of Music* (N.Y., Thomas Y. Crowell, 1910), collected poems from *Ainsley's, The Atlantic Monthly, The Century, The Christian Register, Lippincott's, The Outlook, The Pathfinder,* and *Poet Lore.* See *Shakesperiana*, II (1884) for Miss Porter's essay on a Paris production of "Macbeth" and V (1886) for Miss Clarke's essay on "Shakespeare's Music." Miss Porter's biography is missing from *DAB.*

3.   Minute books of the Boston Authors Club are in the Rare Book Room, Boston Public Library. Miss Porter's letter of reply to an invitation to join is dated December 21, 1899. One of her editorial jobs was *The Boston Browning Society Papers,* Selected to Represent the Work of the Society from 1886-1897 (N.Y., Macmillan Co., 1897). In it Higginson wrote: "In case I was going to prison and could have but one book, I should think it a calamity to have Tennyson offered me instead of Browning. . . " (p.5). See also *The Year Book of the Golden Anniversary of the Boston Browning Society* 1885-1935 (n.p., Boston, 1937, esp. pp. 9-10), for the executive dramatic activities of the two women on behalf of the Society.

4.   See *Poet Lore,* Volumes I-III, *passim.*

5.   *Poet Lore,* III (1901), 539.

6.   *Poet Lore,* II (1890), 224.

7.   According to F. L. Mott, *A History of American Magazines,* (Cambridge, Mass., Harvard University Press, 1957), IV, 11, *Poet Lore* was one of 4,400 magazines published in 1889.

8.   *Poet Lore,* XXXVII (1926), 432-453. Her essay, "A Story of *Poet Lore,*" is a bit deformed in writing style, reflecting her grief for the recent death of Miss Clarke. One sees in it also her disengagement from the magazine. She was then sixty-seven; she had done a small mountain of writing and editing; she was interested in new literary and artistic associations; and Ruth Hill was managing editor. See also II (1900), 337.

9.   *Poet Lore,* I (1889), 333. Alexander von Humboldt had insisted it was soap consumption. The *Magazine of Poetry,* a quarterly, was published by Charles Wells Moulton in Buffalo, N.Y. It was an undiscriminating magazine, printing both T. B. Aldrich and W. B. Yeats. Enlivened by photographs or sketches, the poetry was particularly suitable for a minister's sermons, for the excerpts were arranged under headings such as "Religion," "Failure," "Sin," and "Love." Editorially it sounded its death rattle by pointing to Edward Bok whose bargain counter methods to advance the national literature was making for mediocrity (*Magazine of Poetry,* VII (1895), 326). F. L. Mott was in error when he put the two magazines in the same class. The *Magazine* was born of the marriage of scissors and paste pot, and died of inanity. *Poet Lore* announced the merger in VIII (1896), 465.

10.   *Poet Lore,* I (1889), 50, 52; II (1890), 667-668; 337; III (1891), 43.

11.   *Poet Lore,* III (1891), Vol. III, printed by J. B. Lippincott Company, listed its office at 1602 Chestnut Street, Philadelphia.

12.   Helena Modjeska had introduced Ibsen on the American stage in 1883. See Arthur Hornblow, *A History of the Theater in America* (N.Y., Benjamin Blom, reissue 1965), II, 234.

13.   *Poet Lore* was not without some editorial gaucheries. Though using double summer numbers — two issues in four months — it serialized Björnson's play in a tantalizing fashion. It broke off in the middle of a character's conversation.

14. *Poet Lore,* IV (1892), 589.

15. *Poet Lore,* IV (1892), 229-230. It printed excerpts from the Whitman graveside service in Harleigh Cemetery, Camden, N.J. See IV, 461ff.; also 22-31.

16. Miss Clarke had paid Emily Dickinson a nebulous fifty-word compliment the year before, IV (1892), 580-581.

17. Occasionally the early writing in *Poet Lore* was graceless. For example: speaking of R. C. Jebb's *The Growth and Influence of Classical Greek Poetry* (1893) the reviewer wrote: "These pages exhibit the progression of tragedy as growing from Homer's loins and under Pindar's fluent touch. . ." VI (1894), 43.

18. See *Poet Lore,* VII (1895), 466. What the two editors sensed is contained in Alan S. Downer's statement about the importance of symbolism. "It is through symbolism, of course, that the realistic drama achieves universality, the status of art." *American Drama* (N.Y., Thomas Y. Crowell Co., 1960), 9.

19. The subject was reopened in VIII (1896).

20. Foreign magazines picked up enthusiasm from *Poet Lore.* For instance, *Le Magazine International* (Paris) printed in September, 1896, French translations of Hovey's work first printed in *Poet Lore. Poet Lore,* though, published work by Yone Noguchi, Carolyn Wells, and Walter Blackburn Harte who contributed heavily to the *Lark.*

21. *Poet Lore,* IX (1897), 448-449; X (1898), 597. The editors issued an anthology, *Clever Tales* (Boston, Copeland and Day, 1897) with twelve short stories culled from *Poet Lore.* Eight of them by Halevy, Strindberg, and Villiers they translated; the other authors were Garshin, Kielland, and Arbes.

22. IX (1897), 122-126.

23. IX (1897), 353-366.

24. IX 1897), 498-540. It became the basis of an opera by Delius.

25. X (1898), 335.

26. Amid these real nuggets was fool's gold. A Miss Gertrude Withington in an essay, "Motherless Heroines in English Classics," wrote: "I believe women are not supposed to read Fielding's *Tom Jones.* Being a woman, of course I cannot say I have; but . . . " XI (1899), 261.

27. For Hovey, XII (1900), 459, for Harriet Monroe, pp. 321-6.

28. XIII (1901), 602.

29. XIII (1901), 604-5. In 1901, averaging 150 pages per issue, *Poet Lore* sold for 65c per issue and could be bought in London from Gay and Bird, 22 Bedford Street, Strand.

30. XXIII (1912), 155-6.

31. Quoted in Hornblow, II, 319.

32. More Rilke poems appeared in XXX (1919).

33. XXVIII (1917), 607.

34. More Chekhov translated by N. Bryllion Fagin appeared in XXXII (1921); *Uncle Vanya* in XXXIII (1922); more Lermontov in XXXIV (1923); another essay on Garshin by Virgil Geddes, XXXV (1924); plays by Alexander Ostrovsky in XXXVI (1925) and XXXIX (1928).

35. XXXI (1920). 69-156. Badger published it later as a book ($2.50), even as he also published S. Ferenczi's *Sex in Psycho-analysis,* translated by Ernest Jones ($5.00).

36. See XXXII (1921), 497-519; XXXIII (1922), 255-267; 563-594; XXXIV (1923), 524-531; XXXV (1924), 210-231; 562-568; XXXVII (1926), 73-106; 537-550. Madison later wrote the influential *Critics and Crusaders.* The Yiddish Art Theater on the East Side of New York was then in its heyday. Mendele, pseud., Shalom Abramowitsch (1836-1917);

Shalom Aleichem, pseud., Shalom Rabinovich (1859-1916); Shalom Asch (1880-1957); Abraham Reisin (1876-1953); Isaac Leib Peretz (1852-1915); Solomon Bloomgarden (1870-1927).

37. XXXIX (1928), 159-287. H. Leivick, pseud., Leivick Halper, b. 1888.

38. XL (1929), 475-543. As early as the 1890s *Poet Lore* had been hospitable to discussions of the Jew in fiction and drama. Essays in *Browning Studies* (N.Y., Macmillan, 1895) contained an essay "Browning's Jews and Shakespeare's Jews." According to *Poet Lore*, II (1890), 327-328, the Baltimore Shakespeare Club, December 17, 1889, heard a motion for a new trial on the case of "Shylock vs. Antonio." It was argued before distinguished jurists, but "judgment was reserved." Its philo-Semitism led *Poet Lore* to protest the pogroms in Russia, II (1890), 661.

39. XXXIII (1922), 366-384; XXXIV (1923), 220-246; XXXV (1924), 232-270; also XXXIX (1928), 431-5. Another of Koch's Carolina playmakers was. Thomas Wolfe.

40. See Walter Pritchard Eaton's essay, "Our Infant Industry" (1908), in Alan S. Downer's *American Drama and its Critics* (Gemini Books, University of Chicago Press, 1965), 18.

41. At least one is in progress by Miss Judith Oloskey who is examining the Slavic content of *Poet Lore* in fulfillment of a degree from the University of Pennsylvania.

42. *Poetry*, XXXIV, No. 6 (Sept. 1929), 332.

A Comprehensive Index of Poet Lore

NOTE

For four years, 1903–1906, the Editors of *Poet Lore* tried the experiment of numbering the volumes by separate issues, each issue beginning with "page 1."

In the "Compiler's Note." included in the *Index* for *Poet Lore's* first twenty-five years, is the following explanation:

"In order that there may be no confusion in the reference to these volumes, we designate first the volume, second the issue of the volume by a letter, and third the page of the issue on which the reference appears.

"For example, *Aglavaine and Selysette* XIV D 11 . . . appears on page eleven of the fourth issue of Volume XIV."

Apparently, the Editors did not find this system satisfactory, for in subsequent issues they returned to the usual method of numbering the pages consecutively through each volume, and this is the method followed at the present time.

Abbott, Anne — *Enduring as the Sun*   50:266
Abbott, Avery — *Mr. Enright Entertains, a Possibility*   34:127
Abbott, Celinda Bishoprick —
   To a Contemptuous Chinese Camel   41:131
Abbott, Frances M. —
   Shakespeare's Birthday in Concord, N. H.   1:274
Abendfeier — E. Ziel   27:707
Abnormal Poets and Abnormal Poetry — Cullen Jones   56:228
Above the Gaspereau — Bliss Carman   9:321
Abraham — Hrotsvitha — Translated by John Heard   42:299
Abraham Raisen — Charles A. Madison   35:210
"Abt Vogler" — *Query and Answer*   11: 28
"Abt Vogler" — *Study Program*   10:288
Abydos: A Fragment —   20:192
A Cassandre — Pierre de Ronsard —
   Translated by Beatrice M. Riedel   44:181
Achtenhagen, Olga — *In a Far Country*   43:361
Ackerman, Phyllis — *Our Moribund Verse*   29:356
Ackerson, John — *Two Poems*   49:371
Acting in Tents in Chautauqua — Arthur William Row   36:222
Ad Una Cantate — Albert Edmund Trombly   32:618
Adam and Eve — Antonio Porras — Translated by
   Willis Knapp Jones and Glenn Barr   41: 1
"Adam, Lilith, and Eve" — C. R. Corson   8:278
Adam, Villiers de l'Isle — *Best Love, The*   8:281
   — *Elect of Dreams, The*   8:286
   — *Love of the Natural*   7:388
   — *Milton's Daughters*   7:601
   — *Torture by Hope, The*   6:303
Adams, Marguerite Janvrin —
   In the Beginning Was the Word   55: 20
Adee, Lucy A. K. — *Among the White Hills*   48:358
   — *His Mother in the Home of the*
    Beloved Disciple   55: 79
   — *Jimmie*   53:279
   — *Meditation*   52:279
   — *Poems*   47:191
   — *Poems*   51:170
   — *Spring Song*   46:149
   — *The Thorn Tree*   49:359
   — *Valley Slumber Song*   48: 58
   — *Wild Roses*   54:372
Adieu, Suzon! — Alfred de Musset —
   Translated by Richard Eldridge   44:182
Admonition to a Poet — Patrick De Cesare   48:275
Adventures of Ernest Alembert: A Fairy Tale —
   Charlotte Brontë   12: 22

Ady, Endre — *Poems*   58: 90
Ady, A Hungarian Genius — Cornel Lengyel   48:238
"A. E.," The Neo--Celtic Mystic —
    Julia Ellsworth Ford   16D: 82
A. E., Poet and Man — J. Patrick Byrne   47:240
Aeschylus, The Religious Teachings of —
    Mary Taylor Blauvelt   4:415
Aesthetics, May There Be a Science of? —
    L. A. Sherman   6:323
Aesthetics: Two Moods — Treadwell Cleveland, Jr.   10:235
Aesthetics: Syllabus for Study of —
    Oscar Lowell Triggs   9:281
Africa (Reprint) — Maria Lowell   10: 19
After — Leonora Speyer   32:148
After All — Harriet Monroe   12:321
After-Glow, The — Elizabeth F. Corbett   36:311
After Moonlight — Charles Vildrac   22:399
After Reading The Notes in the Furness Variorum
    "Macbeth" — Julia B. Anthony   13:608
After the Rain — Richard Dehmel   55:339
After the Storm — Hannah Parker Kimball   9:477
Aftermath, The — H. Glynn Ward   37:501
Afternoon Walk, The — Henri Lavédan   28:403
Afterward — Isla Paschal Richardson   40:118
Agard, Arthur F. — *Poetic Personifications of Evil*   9:206
Age of Accountability, The — Mody C. Boatright   40:295
Aglavaine and Selysette — Maurice Maeterlinck   14D: 11
Agnes Bernauer — Frederick Hebbel   20: 1
Agony — Sully Prud'Homme   22:400
"Ah! Happy Boughs, That Cannot Lose Your Leaves"   10:526
Ai Ching — *He Died the Second Time*   53:119
"Aims of Literary Study, The" — P. A. C.   7:270
Air Cadet, To an — Sophie Himmell   50: 2
Airships — Camille Fairchild   27:711
Alarçon, Mariano —
    Benavente as an Interpreter of Woman   29:201
Alarçon, D. Juan Ruiz de — *The Truth Suspected* —
    Translated by Julio de Toro and Robert V. Finney   38:475
Alas, Claudio de, Poet of Gloom — Willis K. Jones   35:456
Albanese, Margaret Lewis — *Villanelle of the Guignol*   48:253
Albatross, The — Charles Baudelaire   36:625
Albee, John — *Letter from an Athenian Physician to*
    His Patient, Telesilla, a Maiden of Argos, and
    Her Reply   11: 20
    — *Virgil's Art*   7:306
Albert, Irene Holt — *To the Dark Water*   58: 64
Alcman — *Night*   54: 70

Aldrich, Thomas Bailey — *In Present Day Poets*   12:306
Alençar José de — *Jesuit, The* —
    Translated by Edgardo de Britto   30:475
Alexander, Grace — *Art for Man's Sake*   6:605
Alexander the Great — Herbert Edward Mierow   55: 99
Alfred Noyes in Retrospect — Mabel Vincent   41:293
Alger, Esther Marion — *In'ependence*   41:140
Alger, George W. — *In Memoriam, Shelley, 1792-1892*   4:315
    — *Tennyson as Poet of the English People*   8:325
Alice in Everydayland: A Fantasy —
    Egbert H. Van Delden   38: 96
Alien Singer, The — Delina Margot-Parle   54:269
"Alkestis" of Euripides and of Browning —
    C. A. Wurtzburg   2:345
All-Embracing, The — Ingram Crockett   17D: 74
All Things Considered — Roland English Hartley   42:165
All This I Know When Sounds the Chinese Lute —
    Dan Norton   37:575
"Alladine and Palomides" — Maurice Maeterlinck   7:281
Allegorical Sonnet — David Stacton   55:135
Allen, Genieve M. — *The Problem of Individualism in
    Relation to Society in Ibsen, Materlinck, and
    Hauptmann*   32:262
Allen, Harrison — *Poetry and Science*   3:233
Allen, Joseph C. — *Julius Caesar of Shakespeare and of
    History, The*   13:560
Allen, Katharine — *Lucretius the Poet, and Tennyson's
    Poem, "Lucretius"*   11:529
Allen, Margaret F. and Lou Wall Moore, Dramatisers of
    The Happy Prince, by Oscar Wilde   27:406
Allison, Susan Whally — *The Stronghold*   10:491
Along the Quays — Henri Lavédan   28:385
Alper, Benedict S. — *The Mysticism of William Blake*   44:344
Altrocchi, Julia Cooley — *Black Boat*   53:310
    — *To a Bleak Young Man of Today*   58:271
Altrocchi, Rudolph, Translator — *The Little Soldier
    Unknown* — by Ada Negri   28:476
    — *The Sowers,* by Gabriele D'Annunzio   33:137
Always Ridiculous — José Echegaray   27:233
Always You — Nathan I. Fine   46:156
Alysoun, Song to: Early English Lyric   6: 62
Ambassador, The Turkish — August Von Kotzebue —
    Translated by Beatrice B. Beebe   38:192
Amber of Koenigsberg — Margaret Ward   43:228
Ambroise — *History of the Holy War*   50:259
America and Her Intellectuals — Leo Ferrero   45:210
America: A Prophecy — William Blake   5:363

37

America: A Prophecy of   5: 93
America: Parley on   5:383
America's First Epic — Willis Knapp Jones   48:256
American Aeschylus, The — Abraham Feldman   52:149
American Anthology — H. A. C.   12:606
American Brother of the Poet Keats — Felix J. Koch   17C: 97
American Drama Society   23:152
American Fiction of Today, Realism in —
    Irving Wilson Voorhees   17C: 76
American Grandfather, An — Marian Spencer Smith   35:443
American Literature, An Introduction to —
    Helena Knorr   10:587
American Music Society   17A:139
American Notes and Queries   1:147
American Patriotic Poems, A Talk on —
    Charlotte Porter   5:342
American Poem, A Great — William Benjamin Smith   17A:124
American Poets, Glimpses of Present Day   13:527
American Poetry of the Past Year — H. A. C.   13:123
American Poetry, Recent   11:129
American Symphony — Florence Crocker Comfort   50: 27
Americans, French Writers on   1:396
Americanization of "Das Verlorene Paradies" —
    Ellery Lothrop Davis   16D:149
Ames, Charles G. — *The Democracy of Aprile*   5: 27
Amiel's Garden — Gertrude Huntington McGiffert   17B:117
Amnon and Tamar — I. L. Peretz   48:149
A Modern Richard — Charlotte Porter   2: 30
Among Friends   27:721; 28:121, 252, 378, 490, 622, 749;
        29:122, 246, 376, 497, 640; 30:310, 617;
        31:309, 470
Among the White Hills — Lucy A. K. Adee   48:358
Anacreon, Some Lyrics of — John Patterson   9:400
Anacreontics — Jacopo Vittorelli   27:709
Anarchy in the Theatre — Alfred Capus   27:180
Anatole France Reminiscent — S. M. Delson   31:261
Ancient Lament, An — Giosue Carducci —
    Translated by William A. Drake   35:158
Ancient Love Letter, An — Gimil Marduk   16C:157
"Ancient Mariner," The Artistic Devices of The —
    Eleanor P. Hammond   10:425
Ancient Realist, An — George Norlin   27:417
And Pippa Dances: A Mystical Tale —
    Gerhart Hauptmann   18:289
Andalusian Love Songs — Ameen Rihani   15B: 74
Anderson, Dorothy — *Some Troubadours of Province*   38:473

38

Anderson, Dorothy Wheless, Translator — *Ecstasy* —
    Hugo   45:226
    — *In This Belated Twilight* —
      Comtesse de Noailes   45:226
Anderson, Jessie M. — *Humor in Carlyle and Browning*   2:421
Anderson, Lilian M. — *Christmas Roses*   28:460
    — *Regina, A Poem of 1910*   29:609
Anderson, Margaret Steele — *Dante's "Beatrice"*   15A: 45
Anderson, Mary, in "Winter's Tale"   1: 92
Anderson, Mrs. Louis Francis — See Bennett
Anderson, M. S. — *The Color Element in Keats "Eve of*
    St. Agnes"   8: 84
Anderson, W. H. — *Browning, The Poet of the People*   6:244
Andrea, Marianne — *A Chess Game*   53: 65
"Andrea Del Sarto" —
    Charlotte Porter and Helen A. Clarke   8:586
"Andrea Del Sarto": A Painter's Poem —
    Harriet Ford   4:144
Andreieff — See Andreyev
Andrew Jackson — Ellery H. Clark   51:174
Andrew Jackson Refuses — Helen von Kolnitz Hyer   37:623
Andrews, George Furman — *Evening Prayer*   48: 83
Andrews, Irene Dwen — *The Irish Literary Theatre*   39: 94
Andrews, John Williams — *Four Antarctica*   52: 99
    — *He is Something*   58:258
    — *Poetry and the Radio*   52:261
Andrews, Nancy — *Early Oceans*   57:367
    — *Harbor Sounds*   57:370
Andreyev, Leonid — *Incident, An*   27:121
    — *King Hunger*   22:401
    — *To the Stars*   18:417
Andrzij Strug — Sophia L. Corson   30: 35
Angelico's, Doctor, Manuscripts   24:268
Angeline, Sister M. — *Two Poems*   47:284
Angermann, William G. — *What Will You Bring Me*   53:164
Anglo-Saxon Poems   1:577
Angoff, Charles — *To a Little Girl*   47:262
    — *Group of Poems, A*   58:312
    — *Worn Steps*   48:266
Anguish — Stephane Mallarmé   50: 24
Angus, Francis R. — *Two Poems*   47:321
Ankenbrand, Frank, Jr. — *A Group of Poems*   43:186
Anna Amelia Queiroz Carneira de Mendoca —
    Marie Pope Wallis   58: 45
Annals of a Quiet Browning Club   7:225, 356, 436, 556, 619
Annals of Shakespeare's "Fellow," Robert Armin —
    Frederick Gard Fleay   1:507

Annunzio, Gabriele d' — *Consolation*   56:174
  — *"Daughter of Joria, The"*   18: 1
  — *"Dithgramb"*   14C: 40
  — *Dream of a Spring Morning, The*   14A: 6
  — *Dream of an Autumn Sunset, The*   15A: 6
  — *From "Elegie Romane"*   27:662
  — *Italian Landscape, An*   16C:110
  — *On a Figure of France Crucified*   27:111
  — *Sowers, The* —
    Translated by Rudolph Altrocchi   33:137
Annunzio, d', The Imagery of — Frank Crane   26:488
Annunzio's, d', Dramas — Pietro Isola   19:111, 215
Anonymous — *A Soldier — His Prayer*   51:149
  — *Let Me Grow Lovely*   48:194
  — *Old Gaelic Rune of Hospitality*   46: 2
Another Complaint of Lord Pierrot — Jules Laforgue —
    Translated by William A. Drake   34: 46
Anselm, Felix — *Hermann Hesse*   53:353
Answer — Lyra Lu Vaile   53:160
Antecedents of Longfellow's "King Robert of Sicily" —
    Hjalmar Edgren   14B:127
Anthony, Julia B. — *After Reading the Notes in the*
    Furness Variorum Macbeth   13:608
Antigone of Sophocles and Shakespeare's Isabel —
    W. L. Sheldon   4:609
Antigone of Sophocles in Boston — O. M.   2:263
"Antonio's Revenge" and Hamlet —
    L. M. Griffiths   2:414
Antonius Stradivarius, Cremonenlis Faciebat Anno
    MCVIIXII — Harold Davis   33:308
Antony and Cleopatra —
    Oliver Farrar Emerson   2:516
Antony and Cleopatra — José Maria de Heredia   52: 68
Antony and Cleopatra and Octavius —
    Oliver Farrar Emerson   2:516
Antony and Cleopatra, Comradeship of, The —
    S. E. Peart   4:217
Antony and Cleopatra, Moral Proportion and Fatalism
    in — Ella Adams Moore   7:613
Antony and Cleopatra: Study Program   12:97; 20:315
Apgar, Genevieve —
    Morris's *"The Lady of the Land"*   33:274
Apparitions — Robert Browning —
    Music by Helen A. Clarke   2:288
Applegate, Allita E. — *The Choice of Gianetta*   36:405
Appointment, The — Melvin Irving Weisburd   57: 61
"Appreciations," Pater — Talcott Williams   2:326

Après-Midi d'un Faune, L' — Stéphane Mallarmé   31:305
April Dreaming — Ruth McEnery Stuart   25:611
April Nights — James Meagher   39:472
Aprile, The Democracy of — Charles G. Ames   5: 27
Approaching Spring — Joseph Upper   33:151
Apulius, Introducing — Elizabeth Hazelton Haight   26:694
Apulius' Story of Cupid and Psyche in English Literature, — *On Certain Uses of*
   Elizabeth Hazelton Haight   26:744
Aquatint — Nellie Baxter   48:163
Aquinas, Sister Mary — *The Clock*   55: 64
   — *Two Sonnets for One Lately Dead*   55: 38
A Quoi Bon Entendre — Victor Hugo —
   Translated by Beatrice M. Riedel   42:190
Arabesque — Edith Lombard Squires   39:454
Arabesque, An — Jens Peter Jacobsen   31:467
Arabian Night — Paul J. Ketrick   40:316
Arabic Poetry Before and After Islam —
   A. E. Khuri   36:200
Arabic Version of Macbeth's "Moving Wood," An —
   Morris Jastrow, Jr.   2:247
Aragon, Louis — *May Night*   57:194
   — *Zone Libre*   57: 80
Araña, Juanita — *Gift of Persia*   51:269
Arauco Tamed — Pedro de Ona   49: 41
Araujo Murillo — *Poems*   58:367
Arbes, Jakub — *Newton's Brain*   4:429, 511, 569, 616
   — *Under a Bush of Lilacs*   4:318
Arbes, Jakub: A Modern Bohemian Novelist —
   Joseph Kràl   4: 1
Archer, Ruby — *Idyl of Israel Known as "The Song of Solomon" or "Song of Songs," The*   18: 97
Archer, William — *The Dying Drama*   1:527
Are We Approaching a Dark Age?   4:637
Argo, De Maris — *Sleep*   49:322
Arguimbau, Elinor — *Snow*   57:217
Arias-Laretta, Abraham — *Inca Literature*   55: 21
Ariel — Charlotte Porter   25:217
Arion, A Tale of — Elizabeth Taylor   10: 8
Aristophanes' Apology   5:237
Arlett, Vera — *Gardener, The*   41:305
   — *Last Man In*   41:410
Armenian Literature, Modern — Chahen Garo   9:122
Armenian Poet: Siamanto, An —
   Alice Stone Blackwell   28: 23
Armin, Robert — *Annals of Shakespeare's "Fellow,"* —
   Fleay   1:507

41

Arms, Milo — *A Poet of Italy: An Appreciation of Giosue Carducci* 16B: 67

Armstrong, A. Joseph — *The Browning Pilgrimage* 41: 72

Armstrong, Agnes — *Evening Vestment* 48:178

— *Poetry* 48:175

Arnault, Antoine-Vincent — *The Snail* — Translated by William A. Drake 36:146

Arnold, Matthew — A Bit of Art from — Lucy Allen Paton 8:134

Arnold, Matthew, and The Spirit of the Age — Jane Lane Boulder 10:589

Arnold, Matthew: Personalia — P. 8:100

Arnold, Matthew, Poetic Characteristics of — Clara C. Barnard 6: 76

Arnold's "Sohrab and Rustum," Blank Verse of — H. E. Coblentz 7:497

Arnold, Morris Le Roy — *To Be or Not to Be — Again* 27: 81

Arnold, Walter G. — *Two Poems* 47:347

Arnoux, C. E. — Translator — *The Djinns* — Hugo 22:146

"Aroint Thee, Witch, Aroint Thee" — George Hempl 13:425

Around My Portrait — Jens Peter Jacobsen 30:411

Arrow, The — June E. Downey 38:297

Art — Charlotte F. Myers 54:353

Art, Beginnings of 9:615

Art for God's Sake: The Secret Problems of a Little Theatre — Paul Green 34:220

Art for Man's Sake — Grace Alexander 6:605

Art of Humilis, The — Maurice Saint-Chamarand 25:572

Art of Lionel Johnson, The — A. Bronson Feldman 57:140

Art of Play Interpretation, The — G. F. Reynolds 27: 91

Art of the Future, The — Park Barnitz 13:357

Art, Use of the Ugly in, The — Katharine Merrill 13:251

Art Works, Duty on — Frank Folio 1:298

Arthur and Beowulf as English Ideals 6:529

Artistic Possibilities of Indian Myths, The — Arthur Farwell 15A: 46

Artists — Dorothy Marie Davis 46:249

A. S. — Harold Davis 33:308

As an Aeolian Harp — Gerhart Hauptmann 26:402

As Shadows on the Waves — Herder 53: 59

As to Differences — May Harris 30:428

— *As to Foreign Criticism* 33:138

As You Like It — Character in: An Inductive Study — C. A. Wurtzburg 4:31, 81

— *Ethics of, The* 4:498

— *Furness Variorium* — C. P. 2:270

— *Plot of, The: An Inductive Study*   3:341, 4:31, 81
— *Study Program* — Oscar Lovell Triggs   9:275
Asckenasy, Ysidor, Translator — *In Chains* —
    Hervieu   20:. 81
Ashes — Eleanor Curtis Whiting   33:423
Ashmead, Mary A. — *Hathaway Club*   1:326
Ashurst, Richard L. — *Prolegomena to "Henry IV"* 1:367
Aspinwall, Dorothy, Translator — *Two Poems*   54:220
Aspinwall, Dorothy Brown, Translator —
    For the Gate of Exiles — de Regnier   52: 80
Assumption of Hannele — Gerhart Hauptmann   20:161
Astorg, Bertrand d' — *Itinerary and Litany for Oradour* 55: 18
Astronomy in the Divine Comedy — Paul S. Dwyer 39:530
"Astrophel and Stella," Sidney's — T. G. Marquis 8:570
At a Factory Door — Glenn Ward Dresbach   28:367
At Dawn — Elizabeth Hazelton Haight   27:405
At Inspection — Dorothy Lundt   5:305
At Ravello — Elizabeth Hazelton Haight   26:111
At The Chasm — Jaroslav Vrchlicky   24:289
At the Jolly Spot: A Comedy in Three Acts —
    Alexander Ostrovsky — Translated by June
    Paxton Campbell and George Rapall Noyes   36: 1
At the Little Pipe — Lillian Sutton Pelée   31:422
At the Stork Lake — Richard Dehmel   55:339
At the Waking of Helgi — Anna Robertson Brown   2: 18
At Versailles (In the Hall of Mirrors) — A. B. Leigh 33:156
Athenaeum Press Series, The   10:436
Atlantic, The — Jean Kendall   49:320
Atmosphere of Obstacle, The —   7: 96
Atonement: A Tragedy in One Act — James H. Parke 41: 59
Attack, The — Andre Lamandé   33:474
Attar and Sanai — Ameen Rihani, after Shams u'Tabriz 16D: 87
Aubade — Stanley Kauffman   46: 98
Audience, The — Philip B. Goetz   7:472
Augenlicht, J. C., Translator — *The Golem* —
    H. Leivick   39:159
August Night — Charles Ballard   42:266
August Strindberg — Axel Uppvall   31: 69
Aunt Lasmi — Sree Basudeb   35:101
Auslander, Joseph, with Gustav Davidson —
    One Man Escapes   44:97, 193
Austin, Alfred   8:53, 110, 111
Authors and Books   26:122, 526
Authorship of "The Nut-Brown Maid" —
    Eugene C. Dolson   20:387
*Auto de los Reyes Magos: A Spanish Mystery Play of the Twelfth
    Century* — Translated by Willis Knapp Jones 39:306

Autumn — Carrie C. Taylor   49:354
Autumn — Gorden E. Peterson   43:362
Autumn — Louis Bartlett Chace   55:271
Autumn Coquetry — Salibelle Royster   47:367
Autumn Day — Rainer Maria Rilke   55: 78
Autumn Evening — David Berenberg   33:524
Autumn Fire — Edythe Hope Genee   47:288
Autumn Longing — Zoola Young   47:358
Autumn Picture — Translated by Alma Ellis Hoernicke   52:352
Autumn Song — Paul Verlaine —
    Translated by William A. Drake   36:199
Autumn Twilight — Henri de Regnier   54:167
Autumnal Dusk — Sophie Himmel   48:267
Ave Post Saecula — Laurens Maynard   28:745
Avenger, The — Richard Dehmel   55:345
Avon Club, The — Fanny E. Minot   1:321
Avrett, Robert — *Two Poems*   55:270
Avril — Gerard de Nerval   54:176
Awakening, The — Francis Adolf Subert —
    Translated by Beatrice M. Mekota   33:159
Aykroyd, George O. — *The Classical in Robert Frost*   40:610
Aza, Vital, and Miguel Ramos Carrion — *Zaragueta* —
    Translated by Stephen Scatori and Roy Temple
    House   33: 1
Babcock, Emma D. — *Perfect Rose, The*   54:183
Bacchanalia — Glenn Ward Dresbach   28:365
Backward Lady, The — Margaret Mauton   53:291
Backward Thoughts — Narcisse Quellien   30:614
Backwaters — Cleon Marquis   56:360
Bacon: A Forgotten Estimate —
    Charlotte Carmichael Stopes   7:185
Bacon, Delia — *Reminiscences*   3:593
Bacon, How Shakespeare Illustrates —
    Henry M. Hugunin   4:200
Bacon, Roger, Unwilling Cause of Baconianism   4: 53
Bacon-Shakespeare: Circular Letter — Pott on Bacon's
    Chipher — (Notes and News)   1:155
Bacon-Shakespeare Controversy — (Notes and News)   1:151
Bacon-Shakespeare: Recent Literature —
    W. H. Wyman   1:69, 2:613
Bacon-Shakespeare: Questions Answered   1:289, 383
Bacon-Shakespeare: Resemblance Between Bacon and
    Shakespeare   1: 98
Baconianism, Main Source of Recent   5:226
Bad Grammar, Our Inherited — A. M. Spence   7:450
Baez, Edmundo — *In Praise of Solitude*   55:130
Bagatelle au Clichage — Robert Beloof   56: 98

44

Bagstad, Anna E. — *Voltaire*   32:519
Bagstad, Anna E., Translator — *The Romancers* —
    Edmond Rostand   33:520
Bagstad, Anna Emilia, Translator —
    The Blockhead — Ludwig Fulda   39: 1
    — *Fanny's Consent* — José Moratin   40:159
Bagwell, Henry — *Two Poems*   47:380
Bailey, Louis, Translator, with Anne Kildal —
    New Letters of Henrik Ibsen   19:420
Bailey, Wilhelmina K. — *Nightfall*   21: 96
Bain, Read — *On Poetry*   45:307
    — *Preface for Critics, A*   51: 67
    — *Three Poems*   58: 77
Bair, Caroline Henning — *On a River*   48:335
Baker, Harry T. — *Two Sonnets*   18:412
Baker, Henry L. — *Genesis*   19:317
Baker, Louise S. — *What Has Poetry Done for the World*   8:145
Bakshy, Alexander — *Russian Theatre and "Le Coq
    d'Or," The Path of the*   27:164
Balade of Charitie, An Excelente — Thomas Rowley   9:181
Balakian, Anna, Translator — *Two Sonnets*   46:183
Balaustion's Euripedes — Helen Archibald Clarke   26: 1
Balaustion's Euripedes, Note to —
    Helen Archibald Clarke   26: 38
Balch, Elizabeth — *Japanese Poetry*   14C:91; 14D:83; 16B: 94
Balcony, The — Gunnar Heiberg —
    Translated by Edwin John Vickner and Glenn
    Hughes   33:475
Baldwin, Eleanor — *Is Chaucer Irreligious?*   4:537
Baldwin, Mary E. — *Browning's "Jules" and
    Du Maurier's "Little Billee"*   9:575
Baldwin, Mary R. — *Nature and Humanity*   33:148
Balfe, Helen Rose — *Federico de Roberto*   37:565
    — *Grazia Dledda, Winner of the Nobel Prize*   39:449
Balkan Poet and Novelist: Ivan Vazoff —
    Radoslav A. Tsanoff   19: 98
Ballad Imitations of Swinbune, The —
    Constance Rummons   33: 58
Ballad of Queen Ysabeau's Hunting —
    Mary Eleanor Roberts   17B: 88
Ballad of San Graal, The — Robert P. Tristram Coffin   33:464
Ballad of Two Knights — Sara Teasdale   22: 78
Ballade — François Villon   52: 67
Ballade — Martha Hart Bliss   32:496
Ballade of Lost Youth, The — S. Griswold Morley   51: 98
Ballade of the Ladyes of Lang Syne — François Villon —
    Translated by Stephen Temple   1:548

Ballade of the One Penny Boy — Isabel Dudley   49: 82
Ballads and Rhymes — Robert L. Smith   58:182
Ballads, Old English — P.   6:563
Ballard, Charles — *August Night*   42:266
     — *Birds' Eggs*   39:572
     — *Dog in a Crate, A*   53:276
     — *My Little Shop Window*   37:501
     — *On Letters*   53:350
     — *Thoughts in World Darkness*   52:271
     — *Two Poems*   44:186
     — *Two Poems*   49:182
Ballet of the Red Shoes, The — Eileen Putt   55:234
Baltimore Shakespeare Club, The — Henry P. Goddard   1:274
Banfield, Edith Colby — *Indian Names*   15A: 61
Banks, G. L. — *Note*   2:607
Banks, Isabella — *The True History of the London Shakespeare Tercentenary*   3:201
Bankside's Shakespeare   1:439
Banquo, A Study in Macbeth — Colin S. Buell   11: 81
Banquo: Was He Bad? — W. J. Rolfe   11:396
Banville, Théodore de — *Gringoire*   27:129
Barbados — Richard Butler Glaenzer   28:457
Barber, Francis — *Two Dreams*   20: 68
Barclay, Aura Lee — *Two Poems*   47:374
Barnard, Clara C. —
     Poetic Characteristics of Matthew Arnold   6: 76
Barnes, Eleanor — *Close to the Wind*   40:588
Barnes, Gladys Wolcott — *Five-Fold Prayers, The*   29: 73
     — *Francis Thompson*   26:229
Barnett, Mavis C. — *The Return*   35:129
Barnitz, Park — *The Art of the Future*   13:357
Baron, Lucille — *Stanislav Pshibishevsky*   23:111
     — Translator — *For Happiness* — Pshibishevsky   23: 81
Barr, Glenn, Translator — *Adam and Eve* — Porras   41: 1
Barr, Ronald Walker — *Love's Bitter Cup*   53: 78
     — *When Evening Comes*   53:194
Barrie's "Peter Pan" — H. A. C.   17D:121
Barrier — Frances Ruth Davidson   38:311
Barrios, Eduardo — *Papa and Mamma* —
     Translated by Willis Knapp Jones   33:286
Barrows, Sarah T., Translator — *Three Songs from "Buch der Lieder"* — Rainer Maria Rilke   27:714
Bartholomew, Julia Hall — *Bazaar, In The*   29:631
     — *Garden, The*   29:632
     — *Lotus, The*   29: 496
     — *Oriental Shop, The*   30:473
     — *Romany Quest, The*   29:630

— *Rug Market, The*	29:628
Bartlett, Elizabeth — *Challenge!*	58:285
Bartlett, Paul Alexander — *On Walking Wings*	52: 30
Baruch of Mayence — Saul Tchemikovsky	54:139
Bas, Joaquin Gomez — *Poema de la Nueble Ciudadana*	53:154
Bass, Althea — *Leaves From a Lesson-Book*	43: 64
Bass, Irene Willis — *Empty Dreams*	53:142
Basudeb, Sree — *"Still It Is Spring"*	42:364
— *Aunt Lasmi*	35:101
Bataille, Frédéric — *It Is Cold Tonight*	28:119
Bates, Edith C. — *Haunting Road, The*	28:482
— *Vagabond, The*	28:485
Bates, Ernest S. and Gladys Chandler Graham —	
Pierre Louys and the Songs of Bilitis	32:562
Bates, Katharine Lee — *Knowledge Versus Feeling*	6:383
Batistich, John J., Translator —	
A Trilogy of Dubrovnik — Ivo Vojnovich	56:195
— *The Resurrection of Lazarus* — Ivo Vojnovich	37:317
Batt, Max — *Feeling for Nature, The*	18:259
— Translator — *Death and the Fool* —	
Von Hoffmannsthal	24:253
— *New Star, The* — Fuchs	20:479
Battey, Adrienne — *Broadway's Beloved Vagabond:*	
Joseph Schildkraut	35: 43
Battle Hymn of the Republic, The: How Written	11:448
Battle With the Water Sprite — *Beowulf* — A. R. Brown	2:185
Battles — Glenn Ward Dresbach	28:366
Baudelaire, Charles — *Albatross, The* —	
Translated by Joseph T. Shipley	36:626
— *From Sad Madrigal* —	
Translated by Joseph T. Shipley	36:625
— *Hymn* —	
Translated by Charlotte Prentiss Hardin	28:118
— *Two Sonnets*	46:183
Baudelaire, To — Pauline Dillingham	38:316
Baum, Bernard — *Sarcels*	57:268
Baxter, Nellie — *Aquatint*	48:163
Baxter, Nelly — *Reverberation in Crystal*	47: 75
Baxter, Sylvester, Translator — *Das Trunkne Lied* —	
Nietzsche	21:416
Bayedère, The — Rabindranath Tagore	25: 61
Bazaar, In The — Julia Hall Bartholomew	29:631
Beach, Joseph Warren — *The Testing of Phaeton*	24:361
Bean, Joseph Herbert — *Two Thousand A.D.*	52:173
Beard, Patten — *Sea Fog, The*	26:776
Beasts, The — Cecil Clayton Sargent	51:167
Beat of a Wing — Charlotte Porter	19:234

47

Beat of the Wing, The — François de Curel —
    Translated by Alice Van Kaathoven   20:321
Beauduin, Nicolas — *Poetry of the Epoch, The*   25:336
  — *Town in Me, The*   25:348
Beauty Lovers — Hannah Parker Kimball   17C: 68
Beaux of Yesterday — Anna Maude Stewart   41:105
Beck, Richard — *Einar H. Kvaren*   43: 56
  — *Salute to Norway*   49: 2
  — *Sillanpää*   46:358
Becker, Edna — *Patience*   42:290
Beckmann, J. H. — *Hauptmann and Shakespeare*   23: 56
Beckner, Lucien — *Eeny Meeny Miny Mo*   53:273
Becquer, Gustavo Adolfo — George H. Daugherty, Jr.   45:127
Becquer, Gustavo Adolfo, Spanish Romanticist —
    L. E. Woodman   26:512
Becquer, Gustavo Adolfo — *Creation, The*   45:139
  — *Dry Leaves, The*   46:246
  — *Jealousy*   45:326
  — *Rimas* — Translated by Marion Lee Reynolds
    Numero   I   32:157
    Numero   IX   34:138
    Numero   LIII   31:158
    Numero   LIV   34:153
    Numero   LV   32:158
    Numero LVIII   32:139
    Numero LXII   33: 96
  — *Rime* — Translated by Ina Duvall Singleton   30:303
Becquer — *El Miserere* —
    Translated by Alice Gray Cowan   15B: 25
Bedts Ruth Brandes de — *These Sudden Stars*   47:314
Bee in Shakespeare, The — Clement A. Harris   43:328
Bee Tender, The — Margaret Adelaide Wilson   19: 86
Beebe, Beatrice B., Translator —
    Seven One-Act Dramas — August Von Kotzebue   38:159
  — *New Pirandello, The in "Diana e la Tuda"* —
    Fredericka Blankner   46:215
  — *Nightcap of the Prophet Elias, The* —
    August Von Kotzebue   40:391
Beer, Taco H.de — *Shakespeare in Dutch*   1:259
Beer-Hoffmann, Richard — *Lullaby for Miriam*   47:290
Beethoven, Poem Translations from — Sara de Ford   54:291
Before a Poem Is — Mary Gould Ogilvie   48:179
Before Dawn — Gerhardt Hauptmann   20:241
Beggar's Harp — Virginia Woodward Cloud   15C: 92
Being Mostly The Early Morning Meditations —
    Mariana Scott   58:146

Belated Appreciation: A Study of Hilda Coukling —
    Hoxie Neale Fairchild   42:167
Belgian Poets, Some Modern — Federico Olivero   31:364
Bell, Clair Hayden —
    Frankfurt's Dialect Author, Friedrich Scholtze   35:612
Bell, Helen — *Sunken Bell, The*   10:161
    — *Sunken Bell, The, Another Interpretation of*   10:452
    — *Sunken Bell, The, Symbolism of*   10:312
Bell, Helen, In Memoriam — E. E. M.   7:277
Bell Ringer, The — Gino Bonola   58: 54
Bellamann, Henry — *Three Men, A Triptych*   35:148
Bellman: The Swedish Poet of Native Romance —
    P. H. Pearson   11:251
Bellows, Isabella Francis — *Actor in Shakespeare, The*   5:589
    — *Love's Dwelling*   17A: 93
    — *Pippa Passes*   6:133
Bellows, Silence Buck — *Surrender*   44:188
Beloof, Robert — *Bagatelle au Clichage*   56: 98
    — *War*   56: 2
Beloved Hedgerose, The — John T. Krumpelmann —
    Translated by Andreas Gryphius   39:544
Beloved, It Is Morn — Adelaide C. Rowell   36:101
Benavente, Jacinto — *Governor's Wife, The* —
    Translated by John Garrett Underhill   29: 1
    — *Prince Who Learned Everything out of Books,*
       The — Translated by John Garrett Underhill   29:505
    — *Saturday Night* —
       Translated by John Garrett Underhill   29:127
Benavente as a Modern — John Garrett Underhill   29:194
Benavente as an Interpreter of Woman —
    Mariano Alarçon   29:201
Benedetti, Anna —
    Giovanni Alfredo Cesareo, The Sicilian Poet   35:529
Benét, William Rose — *No More Fear*   24:119
Bengough, S. E. —
    Music of Language in Venus and Adonis, The   4:562
    — *Use of Alliteration in Shakespeare's Poems,*
       The   5:190
Bennett, Anna Elizabeth — *My Hills*   45:113
Bennett, Florence M. — *Syrian Vignettes*   37:486
Bennett, Florence Mary — *Contemporary Renaissance* 36:126
    — *Laboratory Experiment in Poetry, A*   33:537
    — *Some Thoughts on the Poetic Drama*   30:265
Bennett, Jesse Lee — *Binet-Valmer*   27:591
    — *Three New French Novelists*   27:591
Benton, Joy Kime — *In a Deserted Garden*   33:316
Beowulf and Arthur as English Ideals —
    Sarah J. McNary   6:529

Beowulf, "Battle with the Water Sprite" — A. R. Brown   2:185
Beowulf, "Passing of Scyld" — A. R. Brown   2:133
Berdoe, Edward — Browning and the Christian Faith   8:265
— Browning's Science   1:353
— Browning's Science as Shown in
    "Numpholeptos"   2:617
Berenberg, David — Autumn Evening   33:524
Berenberg, David P. — Exiled   33:506
— Macedon Road, The   37:631
— Revelation   34:472
Bergen, Thomas D. —
    Paesisti of the Nineteenth Century, The   19:235
— Songs of Naples, The   21:152
Berlin Stage During the Past Season — H. S. O.   12:570
Berman, Rosalie —
    Prayer Against Falling in Love in Spring   39:131
Bermuda Churchyard, A — Agnes Carruth   44:189
Bernard Shaw and His Critics (1892-1938) —
    Winifred Smith   47: 76
Bernetta, Sister, O.S.F. — Galere for Shoppers   53:244
Bernhard, Robert — Last Will and Testament   50:261
Bernhardt, Sarah, The Great Lover of the Century —
    Arthur Row   29:606
Bernhardt's "Hamlet"   12:148
Beside the Road — Mabel Holmes Parsons   30:460
Beskin, Murry — Vision   53: 47
Bessey, Rafael M. Saavedra y — La Chinita —
    Translated by Lilian Saunders   37:107
Best Love, The — Villiers de l'Isle Adam   8:281
Best of the New Books   27:125, 452
Best, Sasha — Georges Duhamel   25:204
Best, Sasha, Translator — After Midnight — Vildrac   22:399
— Book of the Hours, The — Rilke   26:121
— Combat, The — Georges Duhamel   26:409
— Great White Bird, The — Vildrac   25:228
— Heights — Goetze   25: 1
— I Am Seeking — Romains   24:350
— In a Large City — Detlev von Liliencron   26:117
— In the Shadow of the Statues — Duhamel   25:371
— It Is Not in Vain that I Have Been Seeking —
    Romains   24:351
— Light, The — Duhamel   25:161
— Life Unanimous — Romains   24:112
— Mill, The — Detlev von Liliencron   26:117
— My Battle Cry — Rainer Maria Rilke   26:274
— Prison in Spring, The — Duhamel   25:460
— Spring — Vildrac   25:137

— *Those There Are* — Vildrac   25:139
— *Visions* — Albert Samain   26:275
Bethesda — Mary Brent Whiteside   36:472
Between Daylight and Dream — Rainer Maria Rilke   30:355
Between the Battles — B. Björnson   47:291
Beyond — A. H. Ware   35:527
Beyond the Gate: De Quincey and Kipling's
    "Misquitta" — Eugene M. Fryer   22:317
Beyond Time and Space — Stanton A. Coblentz   53:245
"Bhagavad Gita," The, and Emerson's "Brahma" —
    W. T. Harris   1:253
"Bhagavad Gita," The: Goetha's "World Spirit" and the
    Vishnu of — W. T. Harris   1:401
Bibliography of Publications in English Literature   3:541, 597
Big Carousel, The — Richard Dehmel   55:340
Bijou, The (Boston) — Homer H. Howard   23:290
Binet-Valmer — Jesse Lee Bennett   27:591
Bingey, M. R. —
    Questions on Tennyson's "Idylls of the King"   8:592
Brinkley, C. A. — *Poetic Interpretation of Nature*   13: 53
Binnacle and Compass — Cleon Marquis   57:492
Bird, Nickels Walker — *Morning*   30:137
Bird of Loveliness — Ruth L. Edgerton   52:194
Bird of Time, The   24:204
Bird Songs — Elizabeth Hazelton Haight   27:405
Birds — Louis A. Shaw, II   56:276
Birds' Eggs — Charles Ballard   39:572
Birds of Pray — Leconte de Lisle   17D: 89
Birthday Poems to Mr. Trowbridge — Alicia Van Buren,
    Nixon Waterman, Nathan Haskell Dole, Finlay
    Ferguson Bush, Mary Louise Keisker, Caroline
    Ticknor, Oscar Fay Adams, Abbie Farwell Brown,
    George F. Smith, Hyacinth Smith, Martha Fletch-
    er Bellinger, Ethel S. Ticknor, Helen A. Clarke,
    Charlotte Porter, Colonna Murray Dallin, and
    Ethel B. Howard   17C:117
Bishop, Beth — *Song for Lost Years*   54:282
    — *Two Poems*   54:360
"Bishop Blougram," Extract from —
    William G. Kingsland   1:444
Bit of Art from Matthew Arnold, A — Lucy Allen Paton   8:134
Bitterly Reviled, The — Lucy Lowe   33:300
Björnson, Björnstjerne — *Between the Battles*   47:291
    — *Beyond Human Strength*   13:543
    — *Glove, A*   4:7, 70, 128, 204, 254, 332
    — *Norwegian Peasant Lad and His Dream Tune,*
    The   5: 52

51

— *Thrond, My First Story* 11: 1
— *When the New Wine Blooms* 22: 1
Björnson's Last Drama, "When the New Wine Blooms" 22: 70
Björnson's Politics — Thyge Sógàrd 4:285
Black Boat — Julia Cooley Altrocchi 53:310
Black Death, The — M. E. Lee 28:691
Black Lambs — Ruth Setterberg 52:126
Black Magic — Pierre Emmanuel 57:368
Blackburne, H. — *"Book of Future"* 2:610
Blackman, Carrie Horton, Translator —
    Eternal Presence, The — André Dumas 29:459
    — *Serbian Poet: Miloutine Boitch, A* — Dorius 30:356
Blackwell, Alice Stone — *Armenian Poet: Siamento, An* 28:231
    — *Hungarian Poet, An* 27:204
    — *Mexico's Most Beloved Poet* 30: 81
Blackwell, Alice Stone, Translator —
    Mass at Dawn, The — Urbina 24:312
Blake, Anne — *"Measure for Measure"* 3:538
Blake, Katharine G. —
    Characters of Othello and Lago, The 18:236
    — *Short Story of Richard III, A* 16A: 80
Blake, William — *Ah, Sunflower* 11: 25
    — *America: A Prophecy* 5:363
    — *Clod and the Pebble, The* 11: 26
    — *Garden of Love, The* 11: 26
    — *Marriage of Heaven and Hell:* — *The Voice of the Devil* 11: 28
    — *Proverbs of Hell* 11: 27
Blake, William, A Phase of Romanticism —
    Lucy Allen Paton 5:481
Blanc, Maurice Le — *She Who Waits* 16A: 36
Blanchard, Ames —
    To One Contemplating the Lyric Route 31:252
Blauvelt, Mary Taylor —
    The Religious Teachings of Aeschylus 4:415
Bleak Young Man of Today, To a —
    Julia Cooley Altrocchi 58:271
Blind Church, The — Charlotte F. Myers 54:359
Bliss, Martha Hart — *Ballade* 32:496
Bloch, Bertram — *Humpty Dumpty* 32: 76
Block, Louis James —
    Dramatic Sentiment and Tennyson's Plays, The 8:512
    — *Loin du Bal* 12: 17
    — *Poetry* 18:224
    — *Sonnets, The Orient, Judea, The Occident* 9:473
    — *Tennyson's Songs* 7:127
    — *Walt Whitman* 5:422

Blockhead, The — Ludwig Fulda —
    Translated by Anna Emilia Bagstad   39: 1
Blok, Alexander — *Love, Poetry, and Civic Service*   57: 99
    — *Song of Fate, The* — Translated by Oleta Joan
      O'Connor and George Rapall Noyes   44: 1
Blood — Mary Carolyn Davies   27:226
Bloomfield, Leonard, Translator —
    Before Dawn — Hauptmann   20:241
Bloomgarden, Solomon: Yehoash — Charles Madison   37:537
Blossoming — Rainer Maria Rilke   36:445
Blowing Sand — John Richard Moreland   41:456
Blue — Grace Evelyn Brown   52:148
Blue Eyes and Others in Shakespeare — W. J. Rolfe   1:479
Blue Mystery — Mildred Ferguson Cousins   41:402
Blue Saltcellar — Willis Eberman   57:489
"*Bluebird," Significance of Maeterlinck's, The* —
    Emily S. Hamblen   22:460
Boat of Love, The — Ralph Adams Cram   46:165
Boatright, Mody C. — *Age of Accountability, The*   40:295
    — *C. C.*   41:124
Bohn, Lewis — *Bibliography of New Publications in*
    English Literature   3:541, 597
Boie, Mildred — *Three Poems*   44: 92
    — *Seven Poems*   44:376
Boitch, Miloutine — Carrie Horton Blackman   30:356
Bolshevist Theory of Art, A — Geraldine P. Dilla   31:454
Bonds of Interest, The — Everett Glass   32:244
Bondwomen — Alexander Ostrovsky — Translated by
    Schöne Charlotte Kurlandzek and George Rapall
    Noyes   36:475
Bonola, Gino — *Bell Ringer, The*   58: 54
    — *Positive Science and Positive Ignorance*   58: 88
Book, The — Florence Brooks   16C:111
"*Book of Job, The*" — Study Program —
    Charlotte Porter   15B:140
Books of Praises — John L. Patterson   43:281
Book of the Hours, The — Rainer Maria Rilke   26:121
Books, and Authors   26:122, 526
Books of the Season, Best New —   6:620; 10:604
    — *New Editions*   10:140, 604
    — *Relating to Poetry and Drama in All*
      Languages   25:160
Books Received   48:183, 276, 366; 49:93, 190, 287, 383; 50:187,
    282, 380; 51:91, 187, 280, 375; 52:87, 181, 280, 377; 53:89,
    186, 283, 377; 54:92, 186, 283, 378; 55:89, 185, 379; 56:92,
    187, 284; 57:91, 189, 285
Bookish Bits   1:246, 298, 392, 445, 587; 2:160, 389; 3:98

Booth's, Edwin, Motto — (Notes and News)   1:155
Borga Gard — Tor Hedberg —
    Translated by Helga Colquist   32:317
Boris Godunof, Pushkin's   3:551
Born, Helena — *Whitman's Ideal Democracy*   11:569
Borradaile, H. Ernst —
    Clowns and Fools of Shakespeare's Time   8:206
Bosi, P. E. — *Here Below*   17A:133
Bos'n — Dorothy Kaucher   36:583
"Bossism," An Aristocratic Survival   4:158
Botrel, Theodore — *By the Little Finger*   53:277
    — *Du Guesclin* —
       Translated by Elisabeth S. Dickerman   30:159
    — *Mass on the Sea, The*   55:266
Boulder, Jane Lane —
    Another Interpretation of "The Sunken Bell"   10:452
    — *Matthew Arnold and the Spirit of the Age*   10:589
Bourget, Paul — *Payment Time*   11:479
Bovshover, Joseph — *A Group of Poems*   56:365
Bowles, Janet Payne —
    Plato as a Literary School for Writers   17D: 90
Boyden, George — *The Shakespeare Memorial Plays*   2:320
Bracco, Roberto — *Phantasms*   19:240
    — *Hidden Spring, The*   18:143
Bradford, Gamaliel, Jr. — *Elizabethan Women*   12:392
    — *Nature in the Elizabethan Poets*   7:529
    — *Pessimist Poet, A, Giocomo Leopardi*   5:385
    — *The Serpent of Old Nile: A Study of the*
       Cleopatra of Tragedy   10:514
Brady, Jack, and Oscar Williams —
    The King Who Scoffed   34:139
"Brahma" and the "Bhagavod Gita" — W. T. Harris   1:253
Brainerd, Gertrude Gardner —
    Paolo and Francesca Theme in Modern Drama,
    The   27:390
Braithwaite, William Stanley — *Four Lyrics*   25:254
    — *Rest Thee! In Thy April Bed*   25:142
    — *Some Recent Verse*   22:223
Brandes, Stella — *Covenant*   50: 73
Brandt, W. R., Translator — *Links* —
    Herman Heijermans   38: 1
Brantôme, Shakespeare's Compliment to —
    Charles Hugh Hinton   4:449
Bratt, Max — *The German Fairy Tale Contest*   17D:109
Brausewetter, Ernst —
    News from the Scandinavian Book Market   8:601
Bray, J. W. —
    — *Literary Democracy of William Wordsworth*   8:306

— Shakespeare as a Critic	9:238
Break-Up — Don Geiger	57:356
Breadth of Feudal Romances, The —	
Charles Maxwell Lancaster	51:138
Bredesen, Inga — *Jon Norstog, The Bookmaker*	30:112
Brent, Imogen, Translator — *Ballade*	52: 67
Brick-Red Steeds — Ruth Setterberg	53:370
Bride of Kossovo, The (Serb Hero Songs) —	
Translated by Abraham Yarmolinsky	27:441
Bride of the Moor — August Stramm —	
Authorized Translation	25:499
Bride of the Sea — Edythe Hope Genee	54:168
Bride's Crown, The — Z. Topelius	28:595
Bride's Night Prayer — Richard Dehmel	55:343
Bridegroom's Songs, A — Portia Martin	31:463
Brief for Ophelia, A — Crane Walton	3:569
Bright Morning, A —	
Serafin and Joaquin Alvarez Quintero	27:669
Brinton, Daniel G. —	
Aims and Traits of a World Language	1:580
— Browning, Addresses on	
Browning on Unconventional Relations	4:266
— Epilogues of Browning:	
Their Artistic Significance, The	4: 57
— Facettes of Love: From Browning	1: 1
— Idea of God in "The Sun," The	3:254
— New Poetic Form as Shown in Browning	2:234
— Primitive American Poetry	4:329
— On Art Poems of Browning	2:146
— Suggestions for Browning Study	8: 51
— Traces of Shelley in Browning	2:662
Bristol, Augusta Cooper, Sketch of the Life of	14D:126
British Verse, Recent — P.	7:366
Britto, Edgardo R. de — Translator —	
Jesuit, The — José de Alençar	30:475
Britton, J. J. — *Browning's "Mildred"*	5:266
— By June Seas	13:348
Broadway's Beloved Vagabond: Joseph Schildkraut —	
Adrienne Battey	35: 43
Brock, David — *For the Dead on the Mountains*	44:231
Broderick, Edwin — *Letters to Sadie, The*	12:347
— Price of Sight, The	13:354
Brodie, Hugh — *A Prayer for Courage*	51: 2
Broken Jug, The — Heinrich von Kleist	45:146
Broken Pines — Charles Hilton	40:461; 42:276

Broken Vase, The — Edith E. King-Fisher   51:268
Bronner, Milton — Cult of Pierrot, The   19:318
    — Sarojini Naidu: The New Hindu Poetess   20: 61
    — William Ernest Henley, The Innovator   15D: 74
Brontë, Charlotte —
    Adventures of Ernest Alembert, The   12: 22
    — Green Dwarf, The   9:479
    — Leaf from an Unopened Volume, A   9:169
Bronte, Emily: A Modern Stoic — Arthur L. Salmon   4: 64
Brood of Aesop, The — Felix Sper   34:271
Brooding Calves — Hans Sachs   38:435
Brookman, Katharine B. — Interpolated   35: 78
Brooks, Edward — Magic in Poetry   4:109
Brooks, Florence — Book, The   16C:111
    — Symbolism of the "Flame of Life," The   16C:112
Brooks, M. Sears — Browning's "Childe Roland" and Its
    Danish Source   4:425
Brooks, Sarah W. — Some Predecessors of Spenser   1:214
Brooks, Van Tyne — The Lyric Origins of Swinburne   18:486
Brooks, Van Wyck — Twilight of the Arts, The 14:322
Brothers — Ricardo Weeks   48:358
Brotherton, Alice Williams — Real Hamlet and the
    Hamlet Oldest of All, The   16D:110
    — Seacoast of Bohemia, The   20:159
    — Shakespeare   5: 81
    — Talisman, The   40:153
Brown, May Heywood, Translator —
Dragon's Head, The —
    Don Ramon del Valle Inclán   29:531
Brow Toward the Stars — Pierre Emmanuel   57:368
Brown, Anna Robertson — Anglo-Saxon Poems   1:577
    — At the Waking of Helgi   2: 18
    — Battle of Brunanbush, The:
      (Early English Chronicle)   3: 20
    — Battle with the Water Spirits, The: —
      Beowulf   2:185
    — Celtic Element in Tennyson's "Lady of
      Shalott," The   4:408
    — Dream of the Holy Road, The — Cynewulf   2: 37
    — Fall of the Angels, The — Caedmon   2:251
    — Happy Land, The — Cynewulf's Phoenix   2:523
    — James M. Garnett, "Elene"   1:577
    — Lotus Symbolism in Homer, Theocritus, Mos-
      chus, Tennyson, and Browning, The   2:625
    — Passing of Scyld: Beowulf   2:133
    — Pearl, The — (Early English Poem)   5:434
    — Song of Alysoun (modernized)   6: 62

— *Wanderer's Lament, The*
  (Early English Lyric)   3:140
— *Wheel of Fortune, The:* Morte d'Arthur   5: 25
Brown, Anna Robertson, Translator —
  King Lier and Cordoille — Layamon's *Brut*   4: 19
— *Song to Alysoun*   6: 62
Brown, Anne Van Ness — *Supremacy*   48:310
Brown Bird, The Little — Grace Shoup   38:158
Brown, Ellen Chantal — *Poems*   47: 73
Brown, Grace Evelyn — *Blue*   52:148
— *Two Poems*   49:372
— *Two Poems*   50: 77
Brown, Lawrence Parmly —
  Foretaste of the Fruit, The   33:621
Brown, Mabel Edna — *Inn by the River Road, The*   57:266
Brown, Sydney Barlow — *In the Heart of a Tree*   40:442
— *La Pluie dans la Nuit*   40:460
Browne, Nelly — *Testament*   45:219
Brownell, Florence Kerr — *Cradle Song*   51:156
— *Let the Wind*   49:365
Browning, Elizabeth B. — *Account of Her Husband's*
  Courtship   10:315
— *Birthday* (Browning Memorial Notes)   2:112
— *First Editions*   4:471
— *"Flush"*   13:607
— *Her Nickname*   10:628
— *Life* — Anne H. Wharton   2: 35
— *On Carlyle*   10:612
— *Opinions of Tennyson*   8: 23
— *Rare Poems* — William G. Kingsland   4: 46
— *Unknown Poem, An*   3:281
Browning Pilgrimage, The — A. Joseph Armstrong   41: 72
Browning, Robert, — *and His Critics*   5:142, 207
— *and Mrs. Orr's "Life"*   3:522
— *and Whitman*   5:277
— *Art Poems*   2:145
— *as a Dramatic Poet* — Henry Jones   6: 13
— *as a Letter Writer* —
  William G. Kingsland   8:78, 225
— *as Others See Him: Berdoe, Jones, and*
  Nettleship — C.   8:265
— *as the Poet of Democracy* — Oscar L. Triggs   4:481
— *Auction Sale of First Editions of*   13:315
— *Books*   3:366
— *Books of the Year* — C.   5:277
— *Cambridge Edition of, The* — C.   8:271
— *"Chief Poet of the Age"* — *Kingsland*   2:208

— *Criticism of*   3: 43
— *Defense of Later Works* — Helen A. Clarke   12:284
— *Definitive Edition of, The*   7:102
— *Does "Alkestis" Interpret Euripides Fairly?* — Philip S. Moxom   8:425
— *Dramatic Lyrics*   2:35, 281
— *English and American Appreciation of* (Notes and News)   1:494
— *Epilogues of: Their Artistic Significance* — D. G. Brinton   4: 57
— *Error of* — Mary M. Barclay   1:300
— *Excerpts from a Sheaf of Letters of* — William G. Kingsland   4:233
— *First American Works (Reprint):* (*First Illustrated Edition*)   3: 95
— *First Editions*   4:471
— *Fitzgerald Affair, The* (Notes and News)   1:400, 447, 448
— *Folk Poems: Study Program* — Charlotte Porter and Helen A. Clarke   12:105
— *French Enthusiasms Satirized in "Two Poets of Croisic"* — Herbert Ernest Cushman   11:382
— *Group of Music Poems, A: Study Program*   10:288
— *Group of Religious Poems: Study Program*   10:103
— *Human Brotherhood in* — P.   10:421
— *Idea of Love* (Notes and News)   1:153
— *Ideals of Beauty in Keats and* — Alice Groff   5:247
— *Is He a Legitimate Member of the Victorian School?* — Mary M. Cohen   12:317
— *Joy — Element of, The* — Mary Phelps   15B: 95
— *Letters by* — William G. Kingsland   9: 83
— *List of Musical Settings* — (The Study)   1:430
— *Love and Duty in Tennyson and* — E. F. R. Stitt   4:271
— *Love Letters* — P.   11:301
— *Macready and* (The Study)   1:138
— *Man, The* — William G. Kingsland   5:229
— *Mastery of Rhyme*   5:258
— *Memorial Meetings* — A. K. Robertson   2:39, 152
— *Memorial Notes*   2:100
— *Memorial Poem*   1: Facing 400
— *Memorial Publications*   2:326
— *Memory of, The* — Geraldine P. Dilla   37:120
— *Mistaken by Boyesen*   10:461
— *Musical Query and Answer* — W. J. Rolfe   5:48, 49
— *Musical Symbolism in*   3:260

— *My Star* — Robert Browning —
Music by Helen A. Clarke   1:349
— *New Letters*   3:522
— *On Unconventional Relations* —
Daniel G. Brinton   4:266
— *Paradoxical Ethics of, The*   23:348
— *Paris Notes on His Death*
(Browning Memorial Notes) — J. Charlton 2:111
— *Personal Recollections of* — W. G. Kingsland 2:130
— *Poet of the People, The* — W. H. Anderson 6:244
— *Poetic Expression*   5:87, 89
— *Poetic Form* — Daniel G. Brinton 2:234
— *Poetic Structure of Shorter Lyrics, The* 5:436
— *Queries and Answers* 3:521, 588, 637
— *Rarities*   6:264
— *Recent Books* — P.   4:276
— *Reference List* (The Library)   1:531
— *Relation of Nature to Man in* —
Francis Howard Williams   4:238
— *Religious Teacher, A* (Department of the
Browning Society, Philadelphia) 2:333
— *Reminiscences of* — William G. Kingsland 5:229, 286
— *Representative of the Times* — Prof. Barnett 1: 31
— *Riccardi Palaces and* — W. S. Rolfe 4: 52
— *Santayana on: A Pessimistic Criticism* —
Helena Dryer Woodard   13: 97
— *Scandinavian on, A*   3:589
— *Science* — Edward Berdoe   1:353
— *Science in "Numpholeptos"* — Edward Berdoe 2:617
— *Scientific Allusions* (The Study) 2:137
— *Secret of Pippa's Power, The*   3:350
— *Shelley's Influence on* —   7: 18
— *Source of Optimism, The* — Mary M. Cohen 4:567
— *Study Hints* 3:521, 588, 637
— *"Colombe's Birthday"*   4: 39
— *Three Poems Relating to Married Life* 5:453
— *Study of Rhymes in* — Elizabeth M. Clark 2:480
— *Study Programs* 8:272, 586; 11:289, 403, 608
— *Suggestions for Study* — D. G. Brinton 8: 51
— *Sun Symbolism in* — Helen A. Clarke 11: 55
— *The Bird, The Star, and The Circle as Used
by* — Esther Matson   31:284
— *Three Types Illustrated:*
Aristocratic, Obsequious, Fraternal —
Charles Fleischer   14B:133
— *True Greatness of* — Alice Groff 1:470
— *Unpublished Letters of*   3:524

— *Varients of "Pietro of Albano"*   3:577
— *Versus Browning* — Harrison S. Morris   1:408
— *Whitman and: Reading Course* —
    Eleanor P. Hammond   10:421
Browning's Kinship of   15C:106
— *French Appreciation of, The*   3:288
Browning's "Andrea del Sarto," a Comparative Study,
    Wordsworth's "Michael," and Tennyson's "Enoch
    Arden" — Vida D. Scudder   3: 87
— *"Andrea del Sarto," A Painter's Poem* —
    Harriet Ford   4:144
— *And Whitman's Democracy, The Purpose of*   7:556
— *"Ask Not One Least Word of Praise"* (Song)   3:258
— *"A Soul's Tragedy"* — Ella Goodenow Wilcox   13:411
— *Authorship of Forster's "Strafford"*   6:555
— *"Bishop Blougram,"* Gertrude Darling on   16A:136
— *"Blot in the Scutcheon,"* Production of   16C:152
— *Caliban: An Objection to, Considered* —
    Maude Wilkinson   5:562
— *"Childe Roland"* —
    Thomas Wentworth Higginson   13:262; 24: 53
— *"Childe Roland" and Its Danish Source* —
    M. Sears Brooks   4:425
— *"Childe Roland" and Tennyson's "Vision of*
    Sin" — Theophilus Parsons Sawin   9:256
— *Courtship*   5:166, 477
— *Evolution of Religion Suggested in Poems* —
    Emma Lightner Hellings   17B:113
— *Facettes of Love, From*   1: 1
— *"Flight of the Duchess," The Art Spirit* —
    Charlotte Moore   11:266
— *Folk Poems* — Charlotte Porter and
    Helen A. Clarke   11:608; 12:105
— *Form*   2:300
— *Funeral*   2: 55
— *Hebraic Sympathies*   3:250
— *Humor*   2:421
— *Interpretation of Romantic Love* —
    George Willis Cook   6:225
— *"Ixion," An Interpretation of* —
    Helen A. Clarke   5:626
— *Jews*   1: 53
— *Jewish Affinities*   2:109
— *"Jules" and Du Maurier's "Little Billee"* —
    Mary E. Baldwin   9:575
— *"Luria"* — John White Chadwick   6:251
— *"Luria," Its Story and Its Motive*   2: 19

— *Lyrics, Structure of* — Ethel Davis   5:436
— *Mesmerism from a Scientific Point of View*   4:261
— *"Mildred"*   5:266
— *Musical Erudition* — Hugh A. Clarke   12:151
— *"One Way of Love"* (Song)
    Music by Helen A. Clarke   4: Facing, 288
— *"One Word More," Dante's Allusions in*   3:533
— *Pictures of Chivalry* — Helen Leah Reed   11:588
— *"Pippa Passes," Performance of by Chicago
    Musical College School of Acting*   16A:142
— *Plays, Stage Production of* —
    Elizabeth McCracken   14C:115
— *Poems of Adventure and Heroism:
    Study Program* —
    Charlotte Porter and Helen A. Clarke   11:403
— *Portrait of Napoleon III* — Charlotte Porter   12: 80
— *Renaissance Pictures in [His] Poetry* —
    Richard Burton   10: 66
— *"Return of the Druses" in Lyric Form* —
    Charlotte Porter   16A: 23
— *"Ring and the Book," Study Program* —
    Charlotte Porter and Helen A. Clarke   10:569
— *"Sagacious Swede"* — Hiram Carson   6:373
— *Science* — Edward Berdoe, L. R. C. P.   1:353
— *Socialism in Literature*   11:418
— *"Sordello," Study in the Psychology of
    Childhood* — A. Tolman Smith   6:238
— *"Statue and the Bust:" A Parable* —
    Prentiss Cummings   10:397
— *"Strafford" Bearing on a Letter to Lord
    Carlisle from Lord Wentworth*   16B:139
— *"Strafford," Dramatic Motive in*   5:515
— *Tablet*   2:611
— *Theology*   12:417
— *Tribute to Shakespeare*   3:213, 216
Brownlow, E. B. — *Curiosities in Sonnet Literature*   3:545
— *Sonnets of Sir Thomas Wyatt*   3: 44, 127
— *Structure of the Sonnet, The*   8:593
— *Tailed Sonnet, The*   4:454
Browsings in Shakespeare —
    William Sloane Kennedy   15C: 70
Brunanburh, Battle of — *Old English Chronicle* —
    Anna Robertson Brown   3: 20
Brunetiére's French Literature — C.   11:138
Bryan, G. S. — *Pliny's Authors*   18:519
— *Translator* — *The Assumption of Hannele*   20:161
Bryant, Frank E. — *Thrymskwitha*   14A: 36

Bryant, William Cullen — *A Forgotten Chapter in The*
  Life of — Robert B. Buckham   11:606
  — *"Thanatopsis," Study Program*   6:520
Bryden, George — *The Shakespeare Anniversary at*
  Stratford-on-Avon   1:286
Buben, Zdenka, Translator — *The Lantern* —
  Alois Jirasek   36:317
"Buch der Lieder," Three Songs from —
  Rainer Maria Rilke   27:714
Buckham, James — *An Elizabethan Lyrist:*
  Thomas Lodge   3:601
  — *Some Characteristics of Persian Poetry*   3: 1
Buckham, Robert B. — *A Case with a Sequel: A*
  Forgotten Chapter in Bryant's Life   11:606
Buddhism and Some Buddhist Poetry —
  Mildred Douthitt Hiers   33: 97
Buell, Colin S. — *Banquo, a Study in "Macbeth"*   11: 81
Buirgy, Mary — *When You Are Gone*   53:170
Bulbs in Water — Ethel Standish Woods   46: 94
Bulleit, Clarence J. — *The Wanderer* (Anglo-Saxon)   17D: 96
Bullies, The — Javier de Burgos —
  Translated by Willis Knapp Jones   43:339
Bullock, Amy H. W. — *The Wooing of Damayanti*   16B: 51
Bulthanpte's Interpretation of Hauptmann —
  Paul H. Grummann   16B:117
Bungalow, Six Rooms, Modern, A — Ida Lowry Sinclair   41:451
Burden of Babylon, The — William Force Stead   29:369
Burden of Lost Prophets — Edward J. O'Brien   35:370
Burgoda, Serviliana Guanes —
  Feast of the Kings in Paraguay   55:274
Burgos, Javier de — *The Bullies* —
  Translated by Willis Knapp Jones   43:339
Burke, Marjorie —
  Meeting of Odysseus and Nausicaa, The   48: 87
Burke, Roydon — *Four Poems*   42:188
Burling, Lancaster — *I Tried to Make a Violin*   41:457
Burne-Jones on Humanity   16A:135
Burnet, F. D., Translator with E. W. Olmstead —
  Fountain of the Satyr, The — de Castro   21: 88
Burns, Irene — *Fear*   48:357
Burns, Robert, Dream Craft of —
  Lewis Worthington Smith   8:233
  — *"Mary in Heaven," Study Program*   6:213
  — *Religion of, The* — Walter Walsh   7: 57
Burns, Winifred — *Certain Women Characters of*
  Pinero's Serious Drama   54:195
  — *Character of Marcus Coriolanus, The*   52: 31

— *Edwin Arlington Robinson in the Hands of the Reviewers*   48:164

Burpee, Lawrence J. —
    Isabella Valancy Crawford: A Canadian Poet   13:575

Burr, Charles H., Jr. — *"Hamlet" Once More*   3:615

Burr, Winifred Adams — *Three Poems*   55:179
    — *Three Poems*   55:372

Burroughs, John — *A Boston Criticism of Whitman*   4:392
    — *Whitman and His Art*   5: 63

Burroughs, Leland M. — *I Shall Never See*   53:161
    — *Is Work Your God?*   53:178

Burton, Richard —
    Democratic and Aristocratic in Literature, The   8:57, 129
    — *Oldest English Lyric, The: Deor's Lament*   5: 57
    — *Quest of Summer, The*   9: 1
    — *Renaissance Pictures in Browning's Poetry*   6: 66
    — *Soubrette, The*   11: 13

But on the Other Hand — Carl Glick   36: 96

Butler, Cora C. — *Pillage*   39:529

Butterfield, Frances Westgate — *Winter Scene*   50: 36

Butterflies, The — Willis Eberman   57:489

Butterfly, The: — Lucine Finch   21:401

Buxbaum, Katherine —
    Ezra Pound's "Ballad of the Goodly Fere"   40:142

Buxton, John — *Flowers*   49:177
    — *Poems*   48:160

By June Seas — Edward Broderick   13:348

By Ourselves — Ludwig Fulda   23: 1

By the Fireside   8:272

By the Light of the Moon —
    Serafin and Joaquin Alvarez Quintero   48: 99

By the Little Finger — Theodore Botrel — Harriet
    Webster Marr, Translator   53:277

By the Sumida River — Colin C. Clements   31:166

Byers, Velma — *Change*   34:301

Byrne, J. Patrick — *A. E., Poet and Man*   47:240
    — *Innocence*   49:300
    — *Rann of the Burning*   46:256
    — *Roots of Magic*   48:231

Byron and Shelley in Italy — Ruth M. Stauffer   28:554, 703

Byron, Lord, Dream Craft of —
    Lewis Worthington Smith   8:233

Byron of the Brush, A — Felix Sper   40:597

C. C., Tragedy in One Act, A — Mody C. Boatright   41:124

Ça Ira Sonnets — Giósue Carducci   27:343

Cabell, Mrs. W. D., Translator —
    Payment Time — Bourget   11:479
Caedmon, "Fall of Angels" — A. R. Brown   2:251
Caesar, Shakespeare's, Is He Ignoble? —
    Annie Russell Wall   4:191
Caine, Hall, 's — *Christian, The* — C.   9:606
Caldron, The, Pélléas and Melisande in Boston
    (*New Drama*)   23:302
Caldwell, Eleanor B. — *Pulse of Spring*   13:321
Caldwell, Mary Grace — *Study of the Sense Epithets of*
    Shelley and Keats, The   10:573
Calendar of Poets, The — Ethel King   51: 59
Caliban and Ariel   3:190
Caliban upon Sétebos — Study Program — The Editors   10:103
"Call Me" — Lieutenant H — M —   47:375
Call of Modern Tragedy, The — Robert Iphys Everett   15A:130
Calling the Bravest — Richard Dehmel   55:350
Calm after Tempest — Giacomo Leopardi — Translated
    by Hattie M. Finlay   42: 92
Calves of Gold — Laura Lourene Le Gear   53: 75
Campbell, Jane Paxton, Translator with George Rapell
    Noyes — *Cat Has Not Always Carnival, A* —
    Alexander Ostrovsky   40:317
    — *At the Jolly Spot*   36: 1
Campbell, Mabel — *In a Cafeteria*   37:550
Campbell, Marjorie Freeman — *Humpty Dumpty*   51:118
Campo-Amor — *Renderings from the Verse of* —
    Olga Marx   31:157
Canadian Poet, A — *Isabella Valencey Crawford* —
    Lawrence J. Burpee   13:575
Canary, The — Josephine Henry Whitehouse   37:589
Canby, Henry Seidel — *Myths of Mary, The*   20:146
"Cantaro Fresco," Selections from —
    Juana de Ibarbourou   56:148
Cape Cod Pictures — Helen Freeman Stevens   43: 94
Capek, K. M. — *Pistol of the Beg, The* —
    Translated by E. D. Schönberger   34:475
Caponsacchi — Henry G. Spaulding   1:269
Caprice, A — Alfred De Musset —
    Translated by Anne-Grace Wirt   33:395
Captain's Walk, The — Elizabeth Alsop Shepard   57:265
Capus, Alfred — *Anarchy in the Theatre*   27:180
Carbery, Ethna, Poetry of, The — William J. Merrill   19:225
Carducci, Giosué, A Poet of Italy: An Appreciation —
    M. W. Arms   16B: 67
Carducci, Giósue — *Ancient Lament* —
    Translated by William A. Drake   35:158

— *Ça Ira Sonnets* 27:343
— *Congedo* 26:114
— *Dante* 35:157
— *Funere Mersit Acerbo* 35:157
— *Morning Song* 35:117
— *Ox, The* 35:113
— *Pantheism* 35: 99
— *White Cross of Savoy, To The* —
　*Translated by Irene Sargent 32:454
— *Winter Weariness* —
　Translated by William A. Drake 35: 88
Cardwill, Mary E. — *Hecate in "Macbeth"* 10:532
Cargill, Asenath — *Three Poems* 44:250
Carlyle, Thomas, Centenary of — W. G. K. 8: 54
— *Unpublished Letter of* 3: 48
Carman, Bliss — *Above the Gaspereau* 9:321
— *At the Road House* 7:397
— *Collected Works* 17D:124
— *Deserted Inn, The* 13:129
— *In Grand Pré Garden* 14A: 1
— *In Present-Day Poets* 12:307
Caro, Alexander — *Vast Domain, The* —
　Translated by Arthur Schnitzler 34:317
Carpenter, Frank Ives — *Study of Literature* 6:279
Carr, Miriam — *Poems* 46:337
Carrier, Warren, Translator — *Chilean Poems* 56:224
Carriere, Warren, Translator — *Roman de la Tardecita* 52:359
Carrington, Hereward — *Omar Khayyam and Mysticism* 19:458
Carrión, Migual Ramos, and Vital Aza — *Zaragueta:*
　Comedy in Two Acts, A — Translated by Stephen
　Scatori and Roy Temple House 33: 1
Carruth, Agnes — *Bermuda Churchyard, A* 44:189
Carruth, W. H. — *Great Poets or Great Poems* 17:378
— *Nibelungenlied, The* 17A:119
Carthage — Mavis Clare Barnett 34:523
Cary, F. M. — *"Timon of Athens"* 3:539
Caryl, Warren — *Hands* 47:281
Casey, John — *From the Book of Visions* 25:251
Caskey, J. Homer — *Grave of Keats, The* 35:622
— *My Trees* 35:632
Cash, Thelma — *Mark Twain Goes West* 52:256
Casson, Lewis — *Steps Towards a Civic Theatre* 22:212
Castello, Carlos C., Translator (with E. L. Overman) —
　Bright Morning, A —
　Serafin and Joaquin Alvarez Quintero 27:669
Castro, Eugenio de — *Fountain of the Satyr, The* 21: 88
Casualty Between Wars — Dorothy Cowles Pinkney 56:219

Cat Has Not Always Carnival, A —
    Alexander Ostrovsky — Translated by June
    Paxton Campbell and George Rapall Noyes   40:317
Catalog of Joys, A — Harriet Plimpton   44:184
Cathedral Imagery in Poetry — Albert J. Edmunds   6:279
Cather, Willa Sibert —
    I Have No House for Love to Shelter Him   16B: 50
    — *Sketch of Life*   14D:113
Catullus — *Two Translations from*   53: 82
Causality — Stanton A. Coblentz   55:184
Cavallotti, Felice — *Quel Che So* (*What I Know*)   26:118
    — *Thou Shalt Not Pass*   27:122
Cawein, Madison — *Elfin Garden, The*   25:602
    — *Iron Crags of Death, The*   26:775
    — *Sketch of Life*   14D:115
Cech, Svatopluk — *Songs of the Slave*   27:114
Celestial Symphony, A — Robert Wood Clack   57:119
Celtic Treasure House, A — Amanda M. Ellis   40:237
Cenas, Héloise, Translator — *To My Reader:* —
    Sully-Prud'homme   15B:139
Cenobite Muses on His Mistress, A — Robert Avrett   55:270
Centaur, The Song of the — Blanche Mary Channing   13:248
Centurions of France — Elizabeth S. Dickerman   31:243
Century's St. Martin's Summer, The   5:456
Certain Women Characters of Pinero's Serious Drama —
    Winifred Burns   54:195
Cervantes, Miguel de Saavedra — Carl T. Keller   44:265
    — *Entremes of the Cave of Salamanca, The*   39:120
Cervantes, Miguel de Saavedra — *Faithful Dog, The*   46:195
    — *Judge of the Divorce Court, The*   45:117
    — *Magic Theatre, The* — Translated by Edith
    Fahnstock and Florence Donnell White   32:234
Cesare, Patrick de — *Admonition to a Poet*   48:275
    — *Poems*   48:120
Cesareo, Giovanni Alfredo — Anna Benedetti   35:528
Cetina, Gutierre de — *Madrigal* —
    Translated by Ina Duvall Singleton   30:470
Chace, Louis Bartlett — *Autumn*   55:271
    — *Death of a Song*   54:171
    — *Elegy to a Fallen Comrade*   57:380
    — *In the Garden*   53:177
    — *My Broken Dream*   53:144
    — *November Bluebird*   53:144
    — *Pines That Forever Dream*   56:223
    — *Two Bay Horses*   56:177
    — *Wild Wind, The*   56:237
    — *Winter Swamp-Meadow Nocturne*   53:145

Chadwick, John White — *Browning's Luria*   6:251
Chaillie, Jean Humphrey — *Prelude to Death*   55:248
Chains of Gold, With — José Andres Vazquez   34:417
Chains, The — Sully-Prud'homme —
    Translated by Curtis Hidden Page   16D: 78
Chaitkin, Jacob, Translator — *Fairy Tale, A* —
    Ilya Erenburg   33:618
Challenge! — Elizabeth Bartlett   58:285
Chambered Nautilus, The   6:570
Chamberlayne, E. S. — *Mr. Howell's Philosophy and*
    "The Son of Royal Langbrith"   16C:144
Chance, William W. — *Poems*   55:352
Change — Velma Byers   34:301
Change, The — Vigiliano Zullo   43:135
Changeling, The — Barbara Hollis   35:568
Channing, Blanche Mary — *Song of the Centaur, The*   13:248
    — *Thought-Bearing*   14B:113
Chanson du Coeur Brisé — Virginia Scott   36:100
Chanson of Henry IV — Francis Howard Williams   1:547
Chansonne of the Lonely Heart — Donald E. Sutcliffe   53:166
Chapel Bells at Eventide — Carl Marton   47:283
Char, Réné — *Edge of Confusion, The*   57:483
    — *Fever of la Petite Pierre d'Alsace* 57:483
    — *Invitation*   57:485
    — *Lyon Pass*   57:484
    — *Muttering*   57:484
    — *Tide Tale*   57:485
    — *To Resume*   57:484
Character in "As You Like It" — C. A. Wurzburg   4:31, 81
Character Writing in English Literature —
    Thomas Ernest Rankin   23: 42
Character of Marcus Coriolanus, The — Winifred Burns   52: 31
Characteristics of Philosophy and Literature —
    Emil C. Wilm   24:122
Chariot of Fire — James Edgar Smith   13: 1
Charles Pelham, Sportsman: His Holiday —
    Grace Louise Cook   7:491
Charlton, J. — *Browning Memorial Notes*   2:100
Charon and the Souls — Modern Greek Folk Tale   9:353
Chat about Boston Writers — W. G. K.   14B: 17
Chat with Madame Modjeska, A — Charlotte Porter   1:524
Chatterton — Arthur L. Salmon   4:593
Chaucer, Geoffrey — *An Unknown Poem*   3:276
    — *Chaucer, Ballade to* — Eustache Deschamps 3:349
    — *Is [he] Irreligious?* — Eleanor Baldwin   4:537
    — *Questions* — M. Lloyd   2:136
    — *Six Weeks With*   3:630

Chaucer's Good Counsel — Addison Leroy Phillips 48:268
Chekhov, Anton — *Sea Gull, The* 24: 1
   — *Tragedian in Spite of Himself, The*
     Translated by Olive Frances Murphy 33:268
   — *Uncle Vanya* —
     Translated by Frances Arno Saphro 33:317
Chekhov, Anton, The Master of the Grey Short Story —
   N. Bryllion Fagin 32:416
Chen, Chin Lin — *Son Left in a Plantation of Mulberry*
   Trees, The 33:595
Cheney, Anne Cleveland — *Clasped Hands* 17D:102
   — *My Dream* 17D:102
Chenku — *Well of Sacrifice* — Gertrude May Lutz 57: 57
Chenot, Anna Adele — *Marie de Gournay* 34: 63
Cherwinski, Joseph — *Lilac and Bronze* 58:172
Chesley, Claire Vincent — *Eugene Labiche, Vaudevillist*
   Member of the Academy 28: 55
Chesley, Claire Vincent, Translator — *A Leghorn Hat* —
   Eugene Labiche and Marc Michel 28: 1
Chesley, Martin — *Regions of Wizadry* 49:180
   — *Windcraft* 51: 47
Chess Game, A — Marianne Andrea 53: 65
Chicago vs New York as a Dramatic Center —
   Arthur Row 22:151
Child by the Sea — Charlotte Porter 16B: 46
Child Cried at Night, A — Ernst Wiechert 45:352
Child in the House, The — Homer Hildreth Howard 24:433
Child of Today, The, His Book 25:160 (insert after)
Child, The — Clotilde de Surville —
   Translated by William A. Drake 34:473
Child, Theodore — *French Version of the Willow Song* 1:172
   — *Hamlet in Paris* 2:557
   — *Othello in Paris* 1:301, 362
Child Verses — Anne Murray Larned 28: 54
Child's Spring Song — Rainer Maria Rilke 58:290
"*Childe Roland*" 2:578
   — *Its Danish Source* — M. Sears Brooks 4:425
   — *Mood of, The* 9:626
   — *Queries Answered* 1:91, 140
   — "*To the Dark Tower Came*" —
     Thomas Wentworth Higginson 13:262
Childhood — Enid Morgan 46:250
Children — Charlotte F. Myers 54:355
Children of Homer, The 24:338
Children of the Sun, The — Maxim Gorki —
   Translated by Archibald John Wolfe 17B: 1
Children of the Sunrise — Julia P. Dabney 26:653

Chilean Poems — Translated by Warren Carrier   56:224
Chimères, Les — Gerard de Nerval   51: 54
Chimpanzee Farce — Franz Werfel —
    Translated by Margaret Schlauch   37:627
China Pig, The — Evelyn Emig   33:439
Chinese Bazaar — Kay de Bard Hall   54:166
    — Chinese Restaurant — Kay de Bard Hall   54:165
Chinese Sappho, A. — Laura Hibbard Loomis, with
    Translations by Wan Ying Hsieh   41:132
Chintamini — Girish P. Ghose   25:144
Chipmunk, The — Albert Edmund Trombly   29:633
Chivalry, Browning's Pictures of — Helen Leah Reed   11:588
Chivalry, Days of   1:583
Choice — Alice Yale Diehl   41:158
Choice of Subject Matter in the Poets: Chaucer,
    Spenser, Tennyson, Browning — "Miss Ariel" —
    A. N. Cog   7:356
Chopin Opus 27, No. 2 — John Alan Haughton   37:292
"Christabel" Contrasted with "Lamia"   6: 32
Christiansen, Einar: A Modern Danish Romantic
    Poet — Daniel Kilham Dodge   6:301
Christmas — Charlotte F. Myers   54:355
Christmas Carol, A — Robert Herrick   9: 33
Christmas Eve — Henrik Wergeland   49:355
Christmas Greeting, A — William G. Kingsland   12: 41
Christmas Magazines and Literary Decay   5: 39
Christmas Orgy, The   4: 49
Christmas Roses — Lilian M. Anderson   28:460
Christmastide Poems   9: 31
Chronicle, A — William Stanley Braithwaite   25:255
Chrysalis — Robert K. Rosenberg   54:276
Chubb, Bronwin — The Folk Song   29:469
Chubb, Edwin Watts —
    Shakespeare's Influence on Goethe   16A: 65
Church, William Pennance — Hills, The   37:253
    — Magic of Love   37: 23
    — Your Gift   37:152
Churchgoers, The — Dorothy Cowles Pinkney   55:240
Churchill — Margaret Fuller   53:166
Cigarette — De Witt Yelton   49:354
Cipher in Shakespeare, No   1:291
City, The — Francisco Navarro   54: 71
City, The: A Grotesque Adventure — David Novak   36:208
City Market Place, The — Edna Wahlert McCourt   27:353
City of the Heart's Desire — William Mountain   17A: 94
Civic Theatre, The — James Platt White   23:320

Civic Theatre: Experiments in Massachusetts —
Charlotte Porter   23:294
Clack, Robert Wood — *A Celestial Symphony*   57:119
Clark, Barrett H. — *Latest Tendencies in German Drama* 26: 72
    — *Plays of Oskar Kokoschka, The*   35:522
Clark, Bertha W. and Luka Djurichich, Translators —
    The Troop — Ivan Mazuranci   34:294
Clark, Charles Badger — *Old Cow Man, The*   28:742
Clark, David R. — *No Sound of a Door*   58:181
Clark, Elizabeth M. — *Study of Rhymes in Browning* 2:481
Clark, Ellery H. — *Andrew Jackson*   51:174
    — *De Lady Who Went to de Dogs*   55: 68
    — *De Lawd Gives Jonah a Whalin'*   53:143
    — *De Man Dat Brought Down de House* 55: 65
    — *Haman Rides High*   54: 81
    — *Kingdom of God*   50: 26
    — *Sacrifice, The*   51:168
Clark, Robert Wood —
Some Remarks on Verse Techniques   56: 76
Clarke, C. Cowden, Letter of   1:446
Clarke, Helen Archibald —
    "Abt Vogler" Query and Answer, An   2: 28
    — *American Poetry of the Past Year*   13:299
    — *"Analytics of Literature" Again, The*   5:529
    — *Antony and Cleopatra: Study Program* 20:315
    — *Apparitions* (Music)   2:288
    — *Ask Not One Least Word of Praise* (Music) 3:258
    — *Asolando*   2: 94
    — *Athenaeum Reviews*   3:528
    — *Barrie's "Peter Pan"*   17D: 21
    — *Banlastion's Euripedes: A Play*   26: 1
    — *Beginnings of Art, The*   9:615
    — *Books Here and There*   13:299
    — *Books: Literary and Artistic Criticism* 6:362
    — *Books of Criticism*   5:469
    — *Books on Tennyson* — C.   5:630; 9:138
    — *Browning as Others See Him*   8:265
    — *Browning Books*   3:366
    — *Browning: The Cambridge Edition*   8:271
    — *Brunetiére's "French Literature"*   11:138
    — *Charlotte Perkins Stetson as a Philosopher
    and Poet*   11:124
    — *Choice Books of the Years: A Group of Essays* 12:586
    — *"Come Away Death"* (Music)   3:212
    — *"Come Live With Me"* (Music)   2:532
    — *Course in Shakespeare, A*   14A:117; 14B:151

— *Courthope's Latest Contribution to Poetical Criticism:* Part I   13:590
— Part II   14A:122
— *Defense of Browning's Later Works*   12:284
— *Emerson as an Exponent of the Beautiful in Poetry*   5:353
— *Emerson's Last Volume*   6: 93
— *Enterprises Private and Public for Improving the American Stage*   17A:135
— *Essays*   7:625
— *Gosse's Personalia*   2:321
— *Griffith's "Evenings with Shakespeare"*   2:376
— *Hall Caine's Last Book*   9:606
— *If I Were God*   10:139
— *"In Memoriam" Study Program*   5:574
— *Interpretation of Browning's "Ixion"*   5:626
— *Ixion*   37:454
— *Januarie*   Frontispiece, 4
— *"King Lear" Study Program*   16B:127
— *Life and Letters*   14B:1; 18:414, 534
— *Life of the Spirit in the Modern English Poet, The*   7:455
— *"Loves Labors Lost": Study Program*   14B:151
— *"Lowly" Poets*   9:298
— *"Macbeth": Study Program*   20:229
— *Maeterlinck and Sharp*   7:157
— *Meditations in Motley*   7: 34
— *Modern Apollo and the Fates, A*   3:518
— *Mr. Dodge's Mystery of the West*   17D:112
— *Mr. Newell's "The Table Round"*   10:309
— *Mrs. Moulton's O'Shaughnessy*   7:211
— *Music Lover's Calendar, The*   17D:122
— *Musical Symbolism in Browning*   3:260
— *My Star* (Music for)   1:349
— *New Books of the Season: American Verse*   6:620
— *New Edition of Poe*   7:519
— *New Volumes of Literary Essays*   7:625
— *New Willow Song, A*   1: 27
— *Notable American Verse*   4:580
— *Note to Baulastion's Euripedes*   26: 38
— *Notes on American Verse*   9:126, 445; 10:134
— *Notes on New Editions*   8:611
— *Notes on Recent Fiction*   8:41, 457, 617
— *One Way of Love* (Music)   4; Facing, 288
— *"Othello": Study Program*   20:394
— *"Paracelsus" and "The Data of Ethics"*   1:117
— *"Pippa Passes" and "Pippa Dances"*   20:122

71

— *Playreader, The*   23:155, 30(
— *Poetry of Louise Chandler Moulton, The*   12:11-
— *Reading Course for a Young Poet*   9:11%
— *Recent American Poetry*   2:427; 3:63%
— *Recent American Verse*   5:375; 6:204; 8:95, 370
                                                  16D:15%
— *Recent Books on Classical Subjects*   6: 4%
— *Recent Books on Classical Stories*   10:13%
— *Repetition and Parallelism in English Verse*   7:45%
— *Review of American Verse*   7:56(
— *Review of Three Dramas by American Writers*   5: 9%
— *Rossettis, The*   10:29%
— *Scientist's Arguments for the Infinite, A*   11:30%
— *Sketch of the Prometheus Myth in Poetry, A*   4:13%
— *Some American Poets*   10:59%
— *Some Modern Portuguese Sonnets*   6:51%
— *Stedman's American Anthology*   12:60(
— *Sun Symbolism in Browning*   11: 5%
— *Survival of the Essay*   9:43%
— *Temple Gate, The*   37:45(
— *Throstle Song, The* (Music)   1:51(
— *"Twelfth Night": Study Program*   16A:124
— *Two Volumes of American Verse*   6:46%
— *Value of Contemporary Judgment*   5:20%
— *Victor Hugo's Letters*   9:141
— *Wordsworth and the Coleridges, Lowell and
  Tolstoy*   11:425
— Also Contributor to *Life and Letters, Notes,
  The Library, Study, Study Programs, Trans-
  lations,* etc.
Clarke, Helen Archibald, Tributes to   37:315
Clarke, Hugh A. — *Browning's Music Poems*   2:278
— *Browning's Musical Erudition*   12:151
— *"Caliban"*   3:292
— *Hamilton's Virgil*   2: 49
— *"Harold," Verse Translation of*   3:393
— *Music: Song of Prometheus*   4; Facing, 384
Clarke, John Henrik — *Poem*   47:288
Clarke, Madge Sutherland — *To an Old Persian Rug*   39: 93
Clarke, Mary Cowden — Letters of   1:445
Clasped Hands — Anne Cleveland Cheney   17D:102
Classical in Robert Frost, The — George O. Aykroyd 40:610
Classical Subjects, Recent Books on — P.   6: 43
Claude Lorraine, A — Camille Fairchild   27:600
Clandel, Paul — *Crusts*   50:195
— *Federico Olivero*   29:110
— *Hostage, The*   50:100

72

 — *Humiliation of the Father*   50:291
 — *Hymn of St. Benoit*   53: 70
 — *Jesus Stripped*   58: 98
Claudia's Garden — Ernst von Wildenbruch —
 Translated by H. C. P. and The Editors 8:478
Claudio de Alas, Poet of Gloom — Willis K. Jones 35:456
Clausen, Wendell — *Life*   53:151
Claytor, Helen Barton — *Dreams*   47: 58
Cleaveland, Treadwell, Jr. — *Two Aesthetic Moods:*
 1. The Ephemeral, 2. The Eternal   10:235
"Clematis and Ivy" — *Extracts from Unpublished Let-*
 ters of George Eliot — William G. Kingsland 6:1, 57, 182
Clemens, Cyril — *Housman in America*   49:266
 — *John Boyle O'Reilly: Neglected New England*
  Poet   54:361
 — *Some Unpublished Housman Letters* 53:255
Clements, Colin Campbell — *By the Sumida River* 31:166
 — *Cherry Blossom River, The*   31:159
 — *Columbine*   31:589
 — *Father, The*   31:187
 — *Growing Old Together*   31:176
 — *Life Is a Dream*   31:204
 — *Man and His Wife*   31:197
 — *Modern Harlequinade*   31:579
 — *Return of Harlequin, The*   31:596
 — *Seven Plays of Old Japan*   31:159
 — *Star Dust Path, The*   31:181
 — *You*   29:472
Clements, Colin C., Translator —
 Love in a French Kitchen   28:722
Clements, Colin C. — Margaret Wright 31:576
"Cleon": Discussion of   3:294
 — *Study Program* — The Editors   10:103
"Cleopatra": A Criticism   2:655
Cleopatra Dramas   1:489
Cleopatra of Tragedy, The — Gamaliel Bradford, Jr. 10:514
Cleveland, Lucy — *The Egyptian Girl*   11:237
Cline, Julia — *Opera in America*   41:239
Cline, Leonard Lauson — *Factory, The*   29:636
 — *Leman, The*   28:105
 — *Love*   30:451
 — *Titan, The*   29:486
Clock, The — Sister Mary Aquinas   55: 64
Clock Replies, The — Blanche Rucker Martin 33:624
Clocks — Emile Verhaeren   55: 83
Clod and the Pebble, The — William Blake 11: 26
Close to the Wind — Eleanor Barnes   40:588

Cloud — Rainer Maria Rilke 30:468

Cloud, Virginia Woodward — *Beggar's Harp, The* 15C: 92

— *Love Looked Back* 16B: 66

Clouds — Donald Richman 49: 76

Clouds of the Sun — Isabella Howe Fiske 15B: 52

Clouds, The 21:417

Cloud Woman, The — Edna Wahlert McCourt 28:470

Clough and Emerson — Francis Howard Williams 6:348

Clowns and Fools of Shakespeare's Time 8:206

Coates, Florence Earle — *Persephone* 13:313

Cobanks, Alvena Martine — *Contrast* 56: 75

— *Lunacy* 56:235

Coblentz, H. E. —

Blank Verse of Sohrab and Rustram, The 7:497

Coblentz, Stanton A. — *Beyond Time and Space* 53:245

— *Causality* 55:184

— *Death of the Tyrant, The* 51:173

— *Fame* 53: 78

— *Four Poems* 44: 89

— *Group of Poems, A* 57:218

— *Literary Style: Must It Join the Dodo?* 52:156

— *Poems* 55:374

— *Poetry in the Doldrums* 48:221

— *This Soft Brown Dust* 47:234

— *Three Poems* 49:321

— *Two Poems* 45:228

— *Visitors* 46:357

Cockcrow — L. M. Taylor 33:118

Coddington, Hester — *Alvilde Prydz* 25:245

Coddington, Hester, Translator — *A Meeting* — Prydz 25:498

— *From the Mountain Top* — Prydz 25:459

— *He is Coming* — Prydz 25:230

Codicil, The — Paul Ferrier —

Translated by Elizabeth Lester Mullin 19:193

Coffin, Robert P. Tristram — *Ballad of San Graal, The* 33:464

— *Four Fishermen, The* 33:157

— *King David's Harp* 34:471

— *In Viis* 34:152

— *Via Cruciata* 33:608

Cog, I. N. — *Annals of a Quiet Browning Club* 7:225, 356, 436, 556

Cohen, Mary M. — *Browning* 2: 39

— *Browning as a Member of the Victorian School* 12:317

— *Browning's Hebraic Sympathies* 3:250

— *Emma Lazerus, Woman, Poet, Patriot* 5:320

— *"Pietro of Abano" and "Paracelsus"* 3: 53

— *Source of Browning's Optimism, The* 4:567

Colby, Inez Sachs, Translator —
    Wolves and Sheep — Alexander Ostrovsky   37:159
Cole, Madeleine Burch — *Golden Bird*   56:363
    — *Love Has No Coat of Mail*   56:362
    — *Stairway's End*   56:363
Coleman, Dorothy — *A Thought*   47: 85
Coleman, Lucille — *From Where I Sit*   56:345
Coleridge, Samuel Taylor — *Personalia*   8:100
Coleridges, The — C.   11:425
Coleridge's "Ancient Mariner," The Artistic Devices
    of — Eleanor P. Hammond   10:425
Coleridge's "Christabel" Contrasted with Keats' "Lamia"
    — Charlotte Porter   6: 12
Collaci, Mario — *Ming-Y*   44:160
Collar, Mary Evelyn —
    A Layman's Impression of Pélléas et Mélisande   23:158
Collar, William C. — *New Ideas in Teaching Literature*   8:449
Collins, Leslie — *I Sing of New Orleans*   46:353
    — *Jungle Saga*   52:127
Colloque Sentimental — Paul Verlaine   53:161
"Colombe's Birthday" by The Julia Marlowe-Taber
    Company   7: 32
Colonial Poets, Early — A. Kingsley Glover   13: 80
Colonial Prose and Poetry   13:597
Colophon — Raymond Morse Herrick   32:250
Color Element in Keats' "Eve of St. Agnes," The —
    M. S. Anderson   8: 84
Colquist, Helga, Translator — Borga Gard —
    Tor Hedberg   32:317
    — *John Ulfstjerna* — Tor Hedberg   32: 1
Colton, Arthur W. —
    First English Essayist, The: Walter Map   5:537
    — *Saturnalia, The*   19: 90
Columbine — Colin C. Clements   31:589
Columbine Wants Flowers — Adolfo Prago-Bracco   55:144
Colwell, Lewis — *Death*   42:264
    — *To John*   42:275
    — *Two Papers a Day*   42:382
Combat, The — Georges Duhamel   26:409
"Come Away, Death" (Song) —
    Music by Helen A. Clarke   3:212
"Come Live With Me" — Music by Helen A. Clarke   2:532
Comedy of Death, A — G. Edward Harris   36: 63
Comedy of Errors, Modern   1:203
Comedy of the Exile — Isabella Howe Fiske   17A: 51
Comfort, Florence Crocker — *American Symphony*   50: 27
    — *Time Turns Under*   48:290

75

Comic in German Folk-Christmas Plays, The —
    F. G. Jenney   27:680
Comic Shillelagh, The — Clifford Montague   57:114
Coming of Age — Marion Conger   56:362
Comitatus with Heroes — A. J. Shelton   55:260
Common Ground — Eleanor Whiting   32:140
Common Street, The — Helen Gray Cone   22:160
Communion — Gertrude B. Gunderson   36:551
Communion of Saints, The — Fréderic Mistral   26:355
Comparative Drama: Chekhov, Shaw, Odets —
    Charles W. Meister   55:249
Comparative Studies — P. A. C.   4:91, 148, 516
Conant, Lucy Scarborough — *Group of Sea Poems*   8:476
    — *In Asolo*   18:247
Conant, Martha Pike —
    Giordano Bruno, Martyr and Idealist   17B: 91
Concert on the Common — Stephan B. Stanton   38:400
Concord School of Dramatic Art   13:457
Condon, Emilie Honzik, Translator —
    The Princess Pampeliska   54: 3
Condor — José Eustasio Rivera   55:132
Condor's Sleep, The — Leconte de Lisle   54:250
Cone, Helen Gray — *Common Street, The*   22:160
Confession — Blanche Yvonne Mosler   47: 64
Confessions of an Erratic Reader — Felix Sper   35: 89
Congedo — Giosué Carducci   26:114
Conger, Marion — *Coming of Age*   56:362
    — *Reflection*   56:361
Conklin, Viola — *Contrition*   53: 35
    — *Mother's Jewel*   53: 77
Conquistador's Song of Freedom, A —
    Charles M. Lancaster and Paul T. Manchester   52: 49
Conservative's Creed — Temple Hollcroft   47:377
Consolation — Gabriele d'Annunzio   56:174
Constance, Jennie M. —
    Some Tendencies of the English Speaking Drama   33:385
Consummation — Hannah Parker Kimball   7:453
Contemporary Brazilian Poet, A: Adalgisa Nery —
    Mary Pope Wallis   55: 51
Contemporary Catholic Theatre, A Note on the —
    Anthony J. Klančar   50:371
Contemporary French Novelists — P.   11:431
Contemporary Judgment, The Value of   5:201
Contemporary Poetry in Spain — John Crow   46:178
Contemporary Renaissance, A — Florence Mary Bennett   36:126
Contemporary Women Poets in Italy   16A:141
Contemporary Women Poets of Spanish America —
    Sidonia C. Rosenbaum   52:133

Contemporary Writers Series:
    1. *Louise Chandler Moulton* — H. A. C.   12:114
    2. *Louise Imogen Guiney* — Helen Tracy Porter   13:287
    3. *Rudyard Kipling* — Benjamin A. Heydrick   14A: 84
Contrast — Alvena Martine Cobanks   56: 75
Contrition — Viola Conklin   53: 35
Converse, Florence — *Shelley's Influence on Browning*   7: 18
Cook, Albert S. —
    Literary Factors in Tennyson's "St. Agnes' Eve"   3: 10
    — *Literary Genealogy of Tennyson's "Ulysses"*   3:499
    — *New Ideas in Teaching Literature*   8:567
Cook, Alice Carter — *Komateekay*   43:151
Cook, Grace Louise —
    Charles Pelham, Sportsman: His Holiday   7:491
Cook, Leroy James, Translator — *Peace at Home* —
    Georges Courteline   29:331
Cooke, George Willis —   14A, Facing 1
    — *Browning as a Religious Teacher*   2:333
    — *Browning's Interpretation of Romantic Love*
        Compared with Plato, Dante, Petrarch   6:225
    — *Future Is Better than the Past, The*   14A:105
    — *Poetic Limitations of "Sordello," The*   4:612
    — *Queries*   2:591
Cooksley, S. Bert — *Shattuck Forest*   37:153
Cooper, S. — *Browning's Poems*   2:283
Cooperman, Chasye, Translator — *Mr. Man* — L. Miller   40:475
Copeland, F. S., Translator — *Passion's Furnace* —
    Josip Kosor   41:459
Coppee, François — *The Passerby* —
    Translated by L. Dora   34:461
Copplestone, Edward — *Dawn*   51:147
Copy Money, First   2:446
Copyright Law, Our So-Called — Charlotte Porter   4:155
'Coq d'Or, Le" — *The Path of the Russian Theatre and*
    Alexander Bakshy   27:164
Corbett, Elizabeth F. — *After-Glow, The*   36:311
    — *Hanger Back, The*   41: 91
Cordia — Hyacinth Stoddart Smith   19:165
Corel, Leona — *Three Poems*   46:190
'Corinne:" Study Program —
    Charlotte Porter and Helen A. Clarke   13:430
'Coriolanus": Moral Proportion and Fatalism in —
    Ella Adams Moore   8: 86
Coristine, Alwyn — *Impregnation*   53:140
    — *Three Poems*   50: 25
    — *When*   51:117
Corkery, Daniel, The Short Stories of —
    George Brandon Saul   58:118

Cornell, Agnes — *Song of Drought, The*   37:274
Corson, C. R. — *Adam, Lilith, and Eve*   8:278
    — *Browning Note, A*   7:223
Corson, Hiram —
    Aims of Literary Study, The   6:386, 473, 536
    — *Browning's "Sagacious Swede"*   6:373
    — *Cost of a Poet, The*   7:259
    — *Light on a Curious Allusion in "The Ring and
      The Book"*   6:248
Corwin, Sophia L. — *Andrzej Strug*   30: 35
Corwin, Sophia L., Translator —
    Last Letters by Andrzej Strug   30: 36
Cossa, Pietro — C. Sadakichi Hartmann   2:595
Cossack Prisoner, The — Mikhail Lermontov —
    Translated by G. G. Lake   34:158
Cost of a Poet, The — Hiram Corson   7:259
Cosulich, Gilbert — *Tito, The Unresisting*   24:339
"Count Gismond" — P. A. C.   8:272
Country Girl — Froylan Turcios   54:185
Country Ramble, A — J. Wiseman   13:355
Courage — Marion Dorothy Hermes   50: 33
Courteline, George — *Peace at Home* —
    Translated by Leroy James Cook   29:331
    — *Pitless Policeman, The*   28:217
Course of True Love, The — Roland English Hartley   55:163
Courthope's Last Contribution to Poetical Criticism —
    Helen A. Clarke   13:590
    — *Courthope's Latest Contribution to Literary
      Criticism* — Helen A. Clarke   14A:122
Cousens, Mildred Ferguson — *Blue Mystery*   41:402
Covenant — Stella Brandes   50: 73
Cowan, Alice Gray, Translator — *El Miserere* —
    Becczner   15B: 25
Coward — William E. Onions   34:428
Cowards All — Frances Avery Faunce   33:622
Cowell, Harry — *San Francisco Under Stress*   17C: 73
Cowles, Florence Earle — *Dreyfus*   10:335
    — *Longing*   10: 25
Cox, George J. — *Immortelle*   49:106
Cradle Song — Florence Kerr Brownell   51:156
Cradle Song, The — Gregorio Martinez Sierra   28:625
Craig, Anne Throop — *Fortune Teller, The*   29:494
    — *Hidden Word, The*   28:248
    — *Sound Magic in Poetry*   29:596
    — *Well of Hazels, The*   34:429
Cram, Ralph Adams — *Boat of Love, The*   46:165
    — *Excalibur*   44:351

Cramp, Helen —
    Social Theories and Art in Modern Drama   22:141
Crane, Frank — *Imagery of d'Annunzio, The*   26:488
Crane, Frank Dougall — *Purple Cobwebs*   43:372
Crane, William Ward — *Allegory in "Hamlet", The*   3:565
Crawford, Isabella Valency: A Canadian Poet —
    Lawrence J. Burpee   13:575
Crazy Mary — John Casey   25:252
Cream of Conrad, The — Felix Sper   38:422
Creation, The — Gustavo Adolfo Becquer   45:139
Creative Writing — Frances Robinson   50:271
Creditor, The — August Strindberg —
    Translated by Mary Harned   22: 81
Credos for the Critics — Clifford M. Montague   46:371
Creighton, Gerald — *Poems*   48:235
Crew, Helen Coale — *Twilight in Ireland*   22:150
Criminals — Gustav of Geijerstam —
    Translated by Roy W. Swanson   34:186
Cristina's Journey Home — Hugo von Hofmannsthal   28:129
Critical Canons of Ezra Pound, The —
    A. Bronson Feldman   57:226
Criticism and Decadence — Samuel Putnam   34:408
Criticism, Books of — C.   5:469; 6:362
Criticism, A Brief Defense of — Carolyn B. La Monte   6:332
Criticism, New — H. A. Clarke   2:598
Criticism, Poetic — P.   5: 43
Crittenden, C. L., Translator —
    Birds of Prey — De Lisle   17D: 89
    — *Fall of the Stars, The*   17D: 88
    — *Lamp of Heaven, The*   20:158
    — *Moonlight*   17D: 87
    — *Prairie, The*   19: 89
    — *Red Star, The*   19:292
    — *Secret of Life, The*   20: 80
Crittenton, Celia Louise, Translator —
    For the Monument of Leconte de Lisle by Pierre
    Louys   28:481
    — *Heart of Hialmar, The* — Leconte de Lisle   28:479
    — *In Excelsis*   28:478
    — *In the Soft Air*   27:700
    — *It Is Cold Tonight* — Bataille   28:119
Crockett, Ingram — *All Embracing, The*   17D: 74
Crop of Dreams — Rafael Solana   55:129
Cros, Charles Guy — *Prayer* —
    Translated by Edward H. Pfeiffer   32:315
Cross, Allen Eastman — *Sonnets from the Portuguese*   1:172

Cross, Samuel Hazard —
    Introductory Note to Lyrics from the Russian   44:277
Crow, John — *Contemporary Poetry in Spain*   46:178
Crowell, Ella —
    Shakespeare's "Katharine" and Ibsen's "Nora"   8:192
Crowned Poetess of Brazil, The — Ignatius Phayre   40:110
Cruciata, Via — Robert P. Tristram Coffin   33:608
Crusts — Paul Claudel   50:195
Cruz, Juana Ines de la — *Elusive Shadow*   53:352
    — *Redondillas*   53: 66
Cry of Today — Gilean Douglas   54:219
Cuckolds Go to Heaven — Lope de Rueda   46:208
Cuevas, Ester Valiz — *Untouchable*   56:224
Cult of Pierrot, The — Milton Bronner   19:318
Cummings, Franklin — *European Memories*   50: 98
    — *Sonnet of a New Year*   50:381
Cummings, Prentiss —
    Browning's "The Statue and the Bust:" A Parable   10:397
Cunningham, Leon — *Dralda Bloom, The*   30:553
    — *Wondership, The*   30:363
Cunningham, Will J. — *Matron of Ephesus*   46:258
Cups Break — Mary Carolyn Davies   40:143
Curel, François de — *Beat of the Wing, The*   20:321
Curious Allusion in "The Ring and the Book" —
    Hiram Corson   6:248
Curtis, Christine Turner — *Songs of the Gitanos*   47:350
Cushman, Herbert Ernest — *French Enthusiasms*
    Satirized in Browning's "Two Poets of Croisic"   11:382
Cydalises, Les — Gerard de Nerval   54:176
"Cymbeline": Lesson of, The — Henry P. Goddard   3:572
    — *Study Program* — The Editors   10:276
Cynewulf — Anna Robertson Brown   2:371, 523
Cypress Swamp — Mary Willis Shelburne   53:367
"Cyrano de Bergerac": What It Is and What It Is Not —
    P.   11:118

Dabney, Julia P. — *Children of the Sunrise*   26:653
Dabney, O. Frederica —
    A Son of Spain: José de Espronceda   7:546
Dagger of the Goth, The — José Zorrilla —
    Translated by Willis Knapp Jones   40:426
Daily Bread — Josephine Henry Whitehouse   40:129
Dall, Caroline A. — *Comments on Maria Lowell's Poem*   10: 22
    — *Harriet Beecher Stowe's Life and Letters*   10:579
    — *Roger Bacon,*
    The Unwilling Cause of Baconianism   4: 53
Dam, The — Albert E. Trombly   31:465

Dalliance — Geoffrey Johnson   52:272
Dalton, Dorothy — *Desolation*   49:134
Dame Care — Heinrich Heine   55: 17
Damon, Lindsay Todd — *The Devil Inspires the Monk*   7:301
Dandridge, Danske — *Poe on Happiness*   15D:108
— *Wild Asters*   13:357
Dandridge, Danske   14D:120
Dangerous Desire for Growth in a Glass House, The —
     Vsevolod Garshin   12:327
Daniel — B. Cyril Windeler   45: 49
Daniel, Patricia — *Marriage*   58:384
Daniel, Samuel — *Sonnets to Delia*   2:473; 8:473
Daniel White — Stanley Kauffmann   44:136
Daniels, Camilla Chapin, Translator — *Fairy Gold* —
     Alexander Ostrovsky   40: 1
Daniels, E. D. — *Cursory Review of Symbolism in
     Maeterlinck's "The Blind," A*   13:554
D'Annunzio — *See* Annunzio, d'
Dante — Giosué Carducci —
     Translated by William A. Drake   35:157
Dante in the Drama Class — Lucy Lockwood Hazard   33:228
Dante's Beatrice — Margaret Steele Anderson   15A: 45
Dante's Claim to Poetic Eminence — Samuel D. Davies   4:490
Dante's Dwina Commedia: Its Moslem Sources and
     Parallels — Charlotte Brewster Jordan   32:375
Dante's Imperialism — Annie Russell Wall   2:501
Dante's Rejected Canto — Albert E. Trombly   27:446
Darcy, Louise — *Minutiae*   44: 86
Dario, Ruben — *Sonatina*   45:353
Dark Halls of Maldane, The — A. J. Shelton   55:258
Dark Window — Harriet Plimpton   48:336
Darkness Will Go, The — Carol Foster   46:286
Das Trunkne Lied — Friedrich Nietzsche —
     Translated by Sylvester Baxter   21:416
D'Astorg — *See* Astorg, d'
Daudet, Alphonse — *The Bluebird*   53:171
Daugherty, George H., Jr. — *Gustavo Adolfo Becquer*   45:127
— Translator — *Creation, The*   45:139
— Translator — *Jealousy*   45:326
Daughter Mine — Camille Mauclair —
     Translated by Joseph T. Shipley   36:624
Daughter of Joria — Gabriele d'Annunzio   18: 1
David Pinski, The Dramatist — Charles A. Madison   35:562
Davidson, Frances Ruth — *Barrier*   38:311
— *Precious*   38:425
— *Singing Things*   38:290

Davidson, Gustav — *Dead Profounds*   35:147
— *Dependence*   29:200
— *Eternals*   33:611
— *Great Adventure, The*   51:195
— *I Said When I First Saw You*   28:621
— *Missing on Camelot and Avalon*   33:552
— *New Star*   33:617
— *"One Man Escapes"*   54:97, 193
— *Planet Home*   45:350
— *Rencontre*   29:205
— *Response*   27:701
— *Responses*   29:634
— *Serpent*   38:421
— *Somewhere I Chanced to Read*   33:155
— *Stream of Time*   33:594
Davidson, Gustav, Adaptor — *Wasted Lives* —
   Antonio de Lezama and Enrique de Meueses   41:159
Davidson, Gustav, Translator —
   The Glittering Highway — Enrique de Meneses   38:317
Davidson, Sam E. — *"Stream of Consciousness," Drama*
   — *An Introduction to the, "To Damascus,"*
   Trilogy of Strindberg   42: 71
Davidson, Sam E., Translator — *To Damascus* —
   Part I — August Strindberg   42: 1
— Part II   42: 99
— Part III   42:195
Davie, G. — *Persian Poetry*   3:153
Davies, Mary Carolyn — *Blood*   27:226
— *Cups Break*   40:143
— *Makers, The*   27:110
— *Reform*   27:110
Davis, Dorothy Marie — *Artists*   46:249
— *Time and Space*   56:143
Davis, Ethel — *The Poetic Structure of Browning's*
   Shorter Lyrics   5:436
Davis, Harold A. S. — *Antonius Stradivarius Cremonen-*
   lis, Faciebat Anno MCVIIXII   33:308
Davis, Hazel Griffith — *Down the Path*   47:383
— *I Could Have Gone*   53: 59
— *Let Me Forget*   53:169
— *No Tears*   56:378
— *Untimely Death*   56:364
— *We Will Not Ask*   56:359
— *Winter*   50:258
Davis, Horace — *Shakespeare and Lyly*   5:177
Daw, Beatrice — *For C — Sailing for France*   29:471
— *Madrigal Sans Politesse*   29:121

— *Mentem Mortalia Tangent*   29:468
— *Verses For My Friends*   29:595
Dawn — Dorothy Wilkey Frey   44: 87
Dawn — Edward Copplestone   51:147
Dawson, Grace Strickler — *The Transient*   41:447
Day Dreams — A. H. Ware   33:267
Day Dreams — Robert L. Morgan   53:169
Day Has Passed, The — Edward T. Lewis   58:170
Day, Varnishing — Frederick J. Pohl   38:128
de Alas — *See* Alas, de
de Alençar — *See* Alençar, de
d'Annunzio — *See* Annunzio, d'
d'Astorg — *See* Astorg, d'
de Banville — *See* Banville, de
De Beer, Taco H. — *Shakespeare in Dutch*   1:259
De Besa, Violet S., Translator — *Memories* —
    Helene Picard   31:242
de Britto — *See* Britto, de
de Burgoda — *See* Burgoda, de
de Castro — *See* Castro, de
de Cetina — *See* Cetina, de
de Espronceda — *See* Espronceda, de
De Ford, Sara — *Poem Translations from the Symphon-*
    ies of Beethoven   54:291
    — *Screw, The*   57: 60
    — *St. Francis*   57:276
de France — *See* France, de
de Gourmont — *See* Gourmont, de
de Gournay — *See* Gournay, de
de la Monnoye — *See* Monnoye, de la
De Lady Who Went to de Dogs — Ellery H. Clark   55: 68
de Larmandie — *See* Larmandie, de
de Larra — *See* Larra, de
De Lattie, Louis — *A Little Sentimental Voyage*   9:186
De Lawd Gives Jonah a Whalin' — Ellery H. Clark   53:143
de Lezama — *See* Lezama, de
de Lisle, *or* de l'Isle — *See* Lisle
De Man Dat Brought Down de House — Ellery H. Clark   55: 65
de Marivaux — *See* Marivaux, de
de Mendoza — *See* Mendoza, de
de Meneses — *See* Meneses, de
de Menocal — *See* Menocal, de
de Musset — *See* Musset, de
de Nerval — *See* Nerval, de
d'Orleans — *See* Orleans, de
De Porte, J. Vital (with Roy Temple House) Translator
    — *The Nymph* — Gorki   24:368

De Quincey's Dream Fugue — Lucille Price Leonard   28:680

de Regnier — *See* Regnier, de

de Solenni — *See* Solenni, de

de Stael — *See* Stael, de

de Undurruga — *See* Undurruga, de

de Vega — *See* Vega, de

de Vellio — *See* Vellio, de

Dead Dreams — Kathryn Worth   30:465

Dead Friend, A — William Stanley Braithwaite   25:254

Dead in Time — Roque Esteban Scarpa   56:220

Dead Maiden, The — Paul Fort   26:522

Dead Minstrel, The (Richard Hovey) — Anonymous   12:464

Dead Nephew, The — August von Kotzebue —
Translated by Beatrice B. Beebe   38:160

Dead Profounds — Gustav Davidson   35:147

Dearborn-Detroit — Lewis Worthington Smith   53: 38

Death — Charlotte W. Stephens   46:290

Death — Hugo von Hofmannsthal   29:245

Death — Lewis Colwell   42:264

Death, A Comedy of — G. Edward Harris   36: 63

Death and the Fool — Hugo von Hofmannsthal   24:353; 45: 5

Death in the Desert, The — *Study Program* —
The Editors   10:103

Death Is Great — Rainer Maria Rilke   56:173

Death of a Song — Louis Bartlett Chace   54:171

Death of the Beloved — Rainer Maria Rilke   55: 79

Death of the Duc d'Enghien — Leon Hennique —
Translated by F. Gridland Evans   20:401

Death of the Tyrant, The — Stanton A. Coblentz   51:173

Decadence of American Culture — *Why?* —
Florence E. Hyde   23: 64

Deed Forborne, A — Louise Collier Willcox   15A: 30

Dehmel, Richard — *After the Rain*   55:339

     — *Avenger, The*   55:345

     — *Fifteen Poems*   55:338

     — *Harvest Song*   26:498

     — *Longing*   24:200

     — *Many a Night*   24:125

     — *Self-Culture*   24: 58

     — *Song Before Night* —
Translated by Leonora Speyer   30:264

     — *Song to My Son*   26:652

     — *Venus-Madonna*   24: 64

Dehmel, Richard — Edwin H. Zeydel   31:393

Delano, Aline, Translator — *Hindu Legend, A.* —
Sienkewicz   15B: 48

     — *Summer Folk* — Gorki   16C: 1

Delden, Egbert H. Van —
    Alice in Everydayland: A Fantasy   38: 96
Delfica — Gerard de Nerval   26:113
Delia, Sonnets to — S. Daniel   8:473
Delson, S. M. — *Anatole France Reminiscent*   31:261
Delusion of a Human Cup, The — Translated from the
    Japanese Noh Play by Yone Noguchi   33:152
Democracy of Aprile, The — Charles G. Ames   5: 27
Democracy, Whitman's Ideal — Helena Born   11:569
Democratic Vagaries —   4:100
Demon's Shell, The — From the Japanese —
    Translated by Yone Noguchi   17C: 44
Deor's Lament: The Oldest English Lyric —
    Richard Burton   5: 60
Densmore, L. C., Translator — *The Last Day* —
    Jorgensen   13:484
"Der Rote Hahn" — Paul H. Grummann   14B:114
Derelict, The — Clarendon Ross   30:601
Derleth, August — *Every Man Is An Inlet*   55: 74
    — *Snow Legend*   43:338
Deschamps, Eustache —
    Ballad Addressed to Geoffrey Chancer   3:349
Deseo, Lydia Grover — *Never the Twain*   41:272
Desert, The — Edna Wahlert McCourt   28:475
Deserted — Robert C. Francis   41:314
Deserted Inn, The — Bliss Carman   13:129
Desire — Janice Meredith Goodrich   39:414
Desire — Joseph Bovshover   56:369
Desolation — Dorothy Dalton   49:134
Deus Benignus et Natura — Frederic Hunter   25:497
Deutsches Künstler Theatre, The — James Platt White   23:303
Devil Inspires the Monk, The — Lindsay Todd Damon   7:301
Devil's Doll, The — Mary Margaret Russell-Basedou —
    A Mirror for Witches — by permission of the
    Author, Esther Forbes   42:338
Devotee of Grief — Mary Willis Shelburne   48:334
Devotee of Molière, A — Paul Ginistry —
    Translated by H. Schnurer   34:426
Dew — Gabriela Mistral   57:160
Diamonds That Fell, The — Charles Randall Murphee   58:279
Diarmuid and Grainne — Julius Zeyer — Translated
    from the Bohemian by George Rapall Noyes and
    Vera Mezirka   44:289
Dias, A. Gonclaves — *Maraba*   15A: 43
Dickerman, Elizabeth S. — *Centurions of France*   31:243
    — *Emile Marechal, A Soldier Poet of Belgium*   32:136
    — *Four Poems of Chang Won-Kien, 1879* —
    Tranlsated in "La Flute de Jade"   33:158

Dickermann, Elizabeth S., Translator —
  — *Du Guesclin* —
    Dramatic Poem by Theodore Botrel   30:15!
  — *Madelon*   30:46!
  — *Sainte Genevieve* — Charles Péguy   28:24(
  — *Song of the Blowing Wind, The*   27:357
  — *Those Who Sleep Beneath the Cross: Elegies*
    of the Soldier-Priest — J. Bellouard   30:14!
Diehl, Alice Yale — *Choice*   41:15!
Dies Irae — William Mountain   12:237
Difficulties of Henry James, The — J. H. Lewis   39:117
Dilla Geraldine P. — *Bolshevist Theory of Art, A*   31:454
  — *Memory of Robert Browning, The*   37:12(
  — *Principal Tones of Arnold's Poetry, The*   32:27!
Dillingham, Pauline — *To Baudelaire*   38:31(
Dillman, Willard — *Complaint of the Times, A*   13:60!
Dimick, Katherine — *Group of Poems, A*   43:27!
Dimmock, Ann — *Rapport*   53: !
Disappointment — Virginia Lee   47:37!
Disciples in the Boat, The — Louis A. Shaw, II   56:27(
Discouragement — Nathan Haskell Dole   4:39(
Disenchantment — Evelyn Vermillion Glied   46:24!
Disinherited — Joseph Upper   36:57(
Disloyal Wife in Literature —
    Charlotte Porter and Helen A. Clarke   9:26!
Dissolution — Joseph Uber   36:60!
Distance — Hazel Hall   33: 57
Dithyramb — Gabriele Annunzio   14C: 4(
Divided — Ursula Tannenforst   2:19!
Divine Trust — King James I of Scotland   47: !
Dix, Bealah Marie — *Legend of St. Nicholas, A*   25:47!
Dizaino — From the Verse of the Duchesse de Roche-
    Guyon — Translated by Edith M. Thomas   19:47!
Djinns, The — Victor Hugo —
    Translated by C. E. Arnoux   22:14(
Djurichich, Luka and Bertha W. Clark, Translators —
  Prince of Samberia, The — Braiuslav Nooshich   33: 8!
  — *Troop, The* — Ivan Mazuranic   34:29!
Dledda, Grazia, Winner of the Nobel Prize —
    Helen Rose Balfe   39:44!
Dobromila Rettig — Alois Jirásek   31:47!
Doctor Praying for Prayer, A — Cecil Clayton Sargent   48:18!
Doctor's Duty, The — Luigi Pirandello   48:29
Dodge, Daniel Kilham — *Discouragement*   4:39(
  — *Modern Danish Romantic Poet, A:* —
    Einar Christiansen   6:30.
Dodson, Dorothy — *Fog*   52:16!

oes Alcohol Stimulate Poetic Inspiration? —
   C. E. Graves   35:271
og in a Crate, A — Charles Ballard   53:276
ole, Nathan Haskell — *Discouragement*   4:396
   — *Electric Light Station, The*   6:463
   — *Emendation of Pope*   8:635
   — *Love at First Sight*   10:627
   — *New Renderings of Omar Khayyam* 10:293
   — *Pope's "Essay on Man"*   8:635
   — *Pushkin's "Boris Godunof": The Closing*
     Episode   3:551
   — *Russian Drama*   2:113
   — *Spanish Origin of Shakespeare's "Patines"* 8:224
   — *Stephen Phillips' Rhymes*   10:448
   — *To a Beautiful Nun*   5:149
   — *What Is the Rank of Journalism in Compari-*
     son with Other Literary Work?   14C: 14
ole, Nathan Haskell, Translator — *Four Days* —
   Garshin   3:297
Doll's House, The": First Translation, and
   Mr. Stedman's Opinion of It   16A:135
olson, Eugene C. —
   Authorship of "The Nut Brown Maid   20: 38
omesticity — Eunice V. Redden   52:267
ominica — Richard Butler Glaenzer   28:459
on Juan's Women — Armando Moock   46: 45
ondo, Mathurin M. — *Two Blind Men and a Donkey* 32:391
onkey Boy of Haifa, The — Mary Brent Whiteside 36:471
onnelly, Ignatius: Letter from   1:586
onner, Herman Montague — *Sketch of Life* 15A:140
oole, Delia — *Upon the Death of My Father* 48:271
oor Mats — Stella Dunaway Whipkey   40: 92
ora, Lucile, Translator — *The Passer-By*   34:461
orchester, D., Jr. — *Nature of Poetic Expression, The* 5: 81
ornis, Jean — *Serbian Poet, A: Miloutine Boitch* —
   Translated by Carrie Horton Blackman   30:356
orr, Julia C. R. — *When Spenser Died*   7:183
ostoyevski, Feodor: A Russian Pietist —
   Arthur L. Salmon   6:309
ouglas, Gilean — *Eternal*   47:259
   — *For Poets*   53: 84
   — *I Am a Realist*   47:257
   — *In This Light*   46: 96
   — *Songs*   49:181
   — *We, the Occupied*   51:148
ove, The — Willis Eberman   57:490
oves, The — Theophile Gautier —
   Translated by William A. Drake   36:310

Dower Rug, The — Maud Murat O'Dair 36:46
Down on the East Side — Oscar C. Williams 36:63
Down the Path — Hazel Griffith Davis 47:38
Downey, Harris —
    To a Mother Who Lost Her Son in the War 55:23
Downey, June E. — Arrow, The 38:29
    — Gold Hunting 28:11
    — Old Earth 11:35
    — Study in the Nude, A 31:25
Drachmann, Holger — Present Day Saga, A 6:39
    — "Renaissance" 19:36
    — Whitsunday Fight, The 7:40
Drago-Bracco, Adolfo — Columbine Wants Flowers 55:14
Dragon Boat Festival — Kay De Bard Hall 54:16
Dragon's Head, The — Don Ramon Del Valle Inclán 29:53
Drake, Rose — Trilogy, A 43:18
Drake, William A., Translator —
    — Ancient Lament — Giosué Carducci 35:15
    — Another Complaint of Lord Pierrot 34:46
    — Autumn Song — Paul Verlaine 36:19
    — Child, The — Clotilde de Surville 34:47
    — Dante — Giosué Carducci 35:15
    — Doves, The — Theophile Gautier 36:31
    — Funere Mersit Acerbo — Giosué Carducci 35:15
    — Giocomo Leopardi 34:61
    — Group of Poems, A — Paul Verlaine 33:45
    — Life and Deeds of Dada 33:49
    — Morning Song — Giosué Carducci 35:11
    — Ox, The — Giosué Carducci 35:11
    — Pantheism — Giosué Carducci 35: 9
    — Pastel — Theophile Gautier 36:24
    — Rising Moon, The — Gustave Kahn 34:44
    — Snail, The — Antoine Vincent Arnault 36:14
    — Winter Weariness — Giosué Carducci 35: 8
Dralda Bloom, The — Leon Cunningham 30:55
Drama and Poetry, Recent German — Amelia von Ende 18:12
Drama, Dying, The 1:52
Drama, German, and Pippa Dances — Hauptmann 18:28
Drama in Relation to Truth — Helen Abbott Michael 7:14
Drama, The Irish Literary — Vida D. Scudder 16A: 40
Drama League of America 23:14
Drama, Origin of 13:60
Drama, Realistic — George Moore 2: 35
Drama: Taliesin: A Mosque — Richard Hovey 8:1, 63, 29
Drama, Technique of the, The 7:21
Dramas by American Writers, A Review of Three — C. 5: 97
Dramas of d'Annunzio — Pietro Isola 19:111, 21

Dramas of New England   5:371
Dramas of Paul Hervieu — James Platt White   14C:79; 15A: 77
Dramas, Recent Poetic: Phillips' "Ulysses" —
    Charlotte Porter   14A:128
Dramas, Seven One Act — August Von Kotzebue —
    Translated by Beatrice B. Beebe   38:159
Dramatic Ability, Do Women Possess Any?   7:512
Dramatic Criticism — Arthur Swan   24:201
Dramatic Literature of Jugoslavia — Anthony J. Klançar   48:305
Dramatic Sentiment and Tennyson's Plays   8:512
Dransfield, Jane — Now Let Me Hasten   46: 82
Dream, The — Herbert Edward Mierow   58:123
Dream and the Business, The — Laura Simmons   24:126
Dream for Tomorrow — Kunigunde Duncan   58:320
Dream Nuptials — Campo-Amor   31:157
Dream of a Spring Morning, The — Gabriele d'Annunzio   14A: 6
Dream of a Tourney, A — E. K. Herron   11:476
Dream of an Autumn Sunset — Gabriele d'Annunzio   15A: 6
Dream of the Holy Rood   2:371
Dreams — Helen Barton Claytor   47: 58
Dreams, The Elect of — Villiers de l'Isle Adam —
    Translated by the Editors   8:281
Dreams, The Literature of: A Study in the Dream-
    Craft of Holmes, Burns, Lamb, Hood, Lowell,
    Tennyson and Others — Lewis Worthington
    Smith   8:233
Drennan, Marie — Valley of Gloom, The   34:449
Dresbach, Glen Ward — At a Factory Door   28:367
    — Bacchanalia   28:365
    — Battles   28:366
Drewry, Carleton — Poems   57:221
Dreyer, Max — On Probation   14B: 40
Dreyfus — Florence Earle Coates   10:335
Droste-Hülshoff, Annette von — Pool, The   27:229
Drury, Mary R. — Fable, A   14D: 65
Dry Leaves, The — Gustavo Adolfo Becquer   46:246
Dryfus, R. — Titus Andronicus   3:539
Du Guesclin — Theodore Botrel   30:159
Dual Standard — Campo-Amor   31:157
D'Ucel, Jeanne — Songs of Arab and Moor   38:447
Dudley, Isabel — Ballade of the One Penny Boy   49: 82
Duffield, C. W. — "Unreason of a She-Intelligence"   3: 45
Dugdale, Jennie Bard — Grave of Edgar Allan Poe, The   11:583
Duhamel, Georges — Combat, The   26:409
    — In the Shadow of the Statues   25:371
    — Light, The   25:161
    — Prison in Spring, The   25:460

Duhamel, Georges — Sasha Best   25:204
Duke and the Actress, The — Arthur Schnitzler —
    Translated by Hans Weysz   25:257
Dukes, Ashley, Translator — *From Morn to Midnight*   31:317
Dulakis, Carrie C. —
    Klephtic Folk Songs of Modern Greece   53:222
Du Maurier's "Little Billee" and Browning's "Jules" —
    Mary R. Baldwin   9:575
Dumas, André — *The Eternal Presence* —
    Translated by Carrie Horton Blackman   29:459
Dumas Fils, Alexandre — *Money Question, The*   26:129
Dumas the Younger and French Dramatic Forms Exist-
    ing in 1850 — Charles Maxwell Lancaster   51:345
Dunbar, Mary Louise — *Pastoral Poetry*   18:265
    — Translator — *Noon* — De Lisle   24:332
Duncan, Isadora, Priestess — Shaemus O'Sheel   21:480
Duncan, Kunigunde — *Dream for Tomorrow*   58:320
Dunning, Homer N., Translator — *Enchanted Garden,*
    The — From the Siegried Saga   22:319
Dupuis, Ethel Paclin — *Pain of Beauty, The*   50:188
Durand — *Fabliau of the Three Hunchbacks*   24:333
Durdik, Pavel, with Josef Jiri Kral, Translators —
    "Hamlet and Don Quixote" — Turgeniev   4:169
During the Riot — Ludovic Halévy   5:603
Duse's Magda — P.   8:557
Dusk — Oscar C. Williams   32:287
Dutch and Flemish Poets, Modern — Sipko Rederus   13:386
Dutch, Elizabeth, *Hands*   46:287
Du Val, Marita — *"Here's to the Little Gentleman in*
    Black Velvet"   16A: 56
"Dwarf, The Green" — William G. Kingsland   9:479
Dwyer, Paul S. — *Astronomy in "The Divine Comedy"*   39:530
Dying Drama, The — William Archer   1:527
Dyk, Victor — *Ninth Night, The* —
    Translated by Cyril Jeffrey Horbek   29: 90

"Each and All": Study Program   6:273
Earll, M. A. —
    Faust Problem: What Was the Homunculus?   13:269
Early English, Prize for the Study of   1:154
Early Oceans — Nancy Andrews   57:367
Early Women Poets of America — Mary Harned   5:332
Earth Lover — Edith Lombard Squires   46:194
Easton, Morton W. — *Tendencies of English and French*
    Literature during the Elizabethan Period   1:157
Eaton, Burnham — *The Lost and the Not Lost*   55: 35
Eaton, Charles Edward — *Puerto Rican Peasant Song*   45:351

Eberman, Willis — *Blue Saltcellar*   57:489
 — *Butterflies, The*   57:489
 — *Dove, The*   57:490
 — *Smile, The*   57:490
 — *Sonnets*   49:276
 — *Spring Snow*   57:491
Ebner-Eschenbach, Marie von — *Man of the World, A*   22:128
Echegaray, José — *Always Ridiculous*   27:233
 — *Madman Divine, The*   19: 1
 — *Madman or Saint*   23:161
Echagaray, José — *Samper's Sonnet on*   20:228
Echagaray, José — *Some Aspects of* —
   Katharine A. Graham   21:234
Echagaray, José — *Spanish Statesman, Dramatist, Poet*   12:405
Eckert, Lawrence Ida — *Louisiana Purchase, The:*
   Exposition Ode   15C:113
Eclipse of Seriousness in Contemporary Literature —
   Walter Blackburn Harte   9: 36
Ecstasy — Mana Willis Fisher   49:247
Ecstasy — Victor Hugo   45:226
Edgar Hating — Robert S. Lehman   48: 84
Edge of Confusion, The — René Char   57:483
Edgerton, Ruth L. — *Bird of Loveliness*   52:194
Edgren, Hjalmar —
   Antecedents of Longfellow's "Robert of Sicily"   14B:127
 — *Translator* — *On the Highlands* — Ibsen   13:335
Edinburgh University and Women —
   Charlotte Carmichael Stopes   4:635
Editions, New   8:611
Editorial Note   49:299
Editor's Note   50: 99
Editors of Shakespeare, The — J. O. Halliwell —
   Phillipps — J. Parker Norris   1: 64
Edmunds-Hemingway, Clara — *Use of Imagery, The*   50: 34
Edwards, Richard — *Street Light in the Rain, The*   58:311
 — *When the World Is October Yellow*   58:355
Edwin Arlington Robinson — Allen E. Woodall   43:363
Edwin Arlington Robinson in the Hands of the Review-
   ers — Winifred Burns   48:164
Eeny Meeny Miny Mo — Lucian Beckner   53:273
Egge, Albert E., Translator — *The Lay of Thrym:*
   From the Old Norse of the *Elder Edda*   22:309
Egyptian Girl, The — Lucy Cleveland   11:237
Eight Poems — Alice Very   43: 84
Eighth Circle of Gehenna, The — J. L. Perez   30:436
Einar H. Kvaran — Richard Beck   43: 56
Einarsson, Indridi — *Sword and Crozier*   23:225

Einarsson, Indridi: Icelandic Dramatist and His Saga Drama   23:284
Eiseman, Fred, Translator — *Sea Gull, The* — Chekhov   24: 1
Eisenberg, Emanuel, Translator —
    Pleasant Evening, The — Theophile Gautier   36:462
    — *Posthumous Coquetry* — Theophile Gautier   36:460
    — *Smoke* — Theophile Gautier   36:462
    — *To a Pink Gown* — Theophile Gautier   36:462
Elaine — Mildred Weinberger   34: 72
Elder, L. W. — *Philosophical Note on "King John", A*   22:314
    — *Shakespeare's Political Philosophy*   21:483
Eldridge, Elisabeth — *Truth about Negro Poetry, The*   43:183
Eldridge, Richard Burdick — *Of One Most Beautiful*   47:349
    — *Slumber Song for Maria*   47:194
Eldridge, Richard, Translator — *Adieu, Suzon!* —
    Alfred de Musset   44:182
    — *Antony and Cleopatra*   52: 68
Elect of Dreams, The — Villiers de Lisle Adam   8:286
Election of the Roulette — William Byron Mowery   33:525
Electric Light Station, The — Nathan Haskell Dole   6:463
Elegie Romane — Gabriele d'Annunzio   27:662
Elegy to a Fallen Comrade — Louis B. Chace   57:380
Elenáki — Modern Greek Folksong   9:355
Elephants, The — Leconte de Lisle   54:250
Elévation — Raymond Morse Herrick   29:639
Eleven Pines — S. Griswold Mosley   49: 40
Elfin Garden, The — Madison Cawein   25:602
Elga — Gerhart Hauptmann —
    Translated by Mary Harned   17A: 1
Eliot, George — *Extracts from "Clematis and Ivy":* —
    Unpublished Letters   6:1, 57, 182
Eliza's Golden Time, "In Great" —
    Archibald MacMechan   5:431
Elizabeth — Olga Marx   30:578
Elizabethan Literature   1:101
    — *Lyrics*   7:213
    — *Novelist, An* — Leon H. Vincent   9: 47
    — *Women* — Gamaliel Bradford, Jr.   12:392
Ellis, Amanda M. — *Celtic Treasure House, A*   40:237
Elmendorf, Marion L. — *Recent Renaissance, A*   2:401, 449
Elmquist, A. Louis, Translator — *Song* — Topelius   24:207
Elusive Shadow — Sor Ines de la Cruz   53:352
Ely, Catherine Beach — *Philosophy of Balzac, The*   30:381
"Emanuel Quint," Hauptmann's — Paul H. Grummann   27:430
Emerson, Oliver F. — *Antony and Cleopatra*   2:71, 125, 188
    — *Antony and Octavius*   2:516

Emerson, Ralph Waldo — Maurice Maeterlinck   10: 76
— And Clough   6:348
— As an Exponent of the Beautiful in Poetry —
Helen A. Clarke   5:353
— Friend of, A. — Antonia C. de P. P. Maury   26:357
— Friendship of Whitman and, The —
William Sloane Kennedy   7: 71
— Poem in Honor of, A — Charles Malloy   14C: 19
— Sterling Letters — P.   10:143
— Two Unpublished Letters by —
George Willis Cooke   14A:104
Emerson's "Brahma" and the "Bhagavad Gita" —
W. T. Harris   1:253
— "Circles": Study Program   10:284
— "Each and All" Study Program   6:273
— Last Volume — C.   6: 93
— Mystic Verse: Clews to   11:243; 12:71, 270
— Poems, What Bearing Have Their Titles on? —
Charles Malloy   14C: 65
— "Self Reliance:" Study Program —
Charlotte Porter and Helen A. Clarke   14A:111
— "World Soul" — Francis Howard Williams   6:348
Emig, Evelyn — China Pig, The   33:439
— Old Order, The   32:586
Emile Maréchal, A Soldier Poet of Belgium —
Elizabeth S. Dickerman   32:136
Emilia Viviani — Charmion von Wiegand   36:552
Emily Is in the House — Flora Rheta Schreiber   46: 76
Emmanuel, Pierre — Black Magic   57:368
— Brow Toward the Stars   57:368
— Only Fools Understand   57:369
Empty Dreams — Irene Willis   53:142
Enamel — José Maria de Heredia —
Translated by Cammie H. Lamy   34:293
Enchanted Garden, The — From the Siegfried Saga —
Translated by Homer N. Dunning   22:319
Enchanted Wood, The — Minna Irving   30:126
End of the Row — Paul Green   35: 58
Ende, Amelia von — Among the German Writers   18:481
— Ethical Message of Richard Hovey's Poem in
Dramas   20: 69
— German-American Literature   17C:108
— German Book World, The   18:280
— German Drama, Poetry, and Fiction   19:120
— Recent Poetry and Drama   18:123
— Recent Works by German Writers   18:404
— Translator — Dawn, The — Viele-Griffin   22:398

93

— *Wages of War, The* —
Wiegand and Scharrelmann   19:129
— *Walt Whitman and Arno Holz*   16B: 61
Enduring as the Sun — Anne Abbott   50:266
England, George Allan — *Feministic and Literary Influ-*
ences of Petrarchism   28:187
— *Gandolfo*   48: 59
English and German Literature of the Eighteenth Cen-
tury — Oswald Seidensticker   2: 57, 169
English Hexameter — H. W. Boyd Mackay   23:139
English Life and Literature: Study Program   2:489
English Literature:
Bibliography of New Publications   3:541, 597
— *Character Writing in* —
Thomas Ernest Rankin   23: 42
— *During the Elizabethan Period*   1:157
— *Evolution of Woman in, The* — Alice Groff   10:242
— *In America, A Word on*   1:210
English of Lafcadio Hearn, The —
Charles Woodward Hutson   16A: 53
Enigma — Evarts Scudder   30: 34
Enna, A. Alexander — *Was Ibsen Original?*   40:420
Enright, Mr., Entertains — Avery Abbott   34:127
Enrique Gonzales Martinez — Edna Lue Furness   58:282
Enterprises, Private and Public, for Improving the
American Stage   17A:135
Entertainment, Folk, in England the Latter Years of the
Reign of Elizabeth — Philip George Neserius   38:141
Entremes of the Cave of Salamanca, The —
Miguel de Cervantes Saavedra   39:120
Ephraim's Breite — Carl Hauptmann   12:465
Epic, Our Anglo-Saxon — P.   6:565
Epigram and Its Greatest Master: Martial, The —
F. B. R. Hellems   16D: 67
Epigram: Life — Schaukal —
Translated by Charles Wharton Stork   23: 79
Epigrams — Translated by Oliver W. Evans   48: 98
Epilogues of Browning — D. G. Brinton   4: 57
"Epistle," Spider Allusions in   1:518
Epitaph — Thor Hrolf Wisby   10:629
Erbes, Philip H. — *Essence of Goethe's "Faust," The*   4:504
Erenburg, Ilya — *Fairy Tale, A* —
Translated by Jacob Chaitkin   33:618
Erickson, Edwin M. — *Frosted Glass*   46:189
Erinna to Sappho — Mörike —
Translated by Charles Wharton Stork   24:199
Ernest Lacy: Forgotten Immortal — Abraham Feldman   47: 86

Ernst, Alice Hanson — *Nightingale*   37:293
Ernst, Jessie, Translator — *The Sheriff and His Son*   48:311
Ernst Possart as Shylock — Otto Heller   1:571
Errant Heart — Kathryn Evans McKay   56:377
Errilla, Tom T. — *Waiting Till You Come*   46:338
"Es Lebe das Leben" — Paul H. Grummann   14B:114
Escendero, Carlos, Translator —   51:353
   — *Tragic Song, The*   50: 3
   — *You Can't Fool with Love*   49:107
Espronceda, José de, and Gustavo Adolfo Becquer —
   Fragments from the Spanish —
   Translated by Ina Duvall Singleton   30:464
Essay, The Survival of the — C.   9:431
Essayist, The First English: Walter Map —
   Arthur W. Colton   5:537
Essays   7:625
Essentials of Literary Appreciation, Some —
   Ethel Allen Murphy   20:390
Ester, Irene M. — *Sequel*   52:369
Etching — Murray Skinner   49:367
Eternal — Gilean Douglas   47:259
Eternal Presence, The — André Dumas   29:459
Eternals — Gustav Davidson   33:611
Eugene O'Neill in Russia — Horst Frenz   49:241
Euripides, Does Browning's "Alkestis" Interpret [It]
   Fairly?   8:425
European Memories — Franklin Cummings   50: 98
"Evangeline" a Product of Swedish Influence, Is? —
   Edward Thostenberg   19:301
"Evangeline," An Unpublished Letter from Longfellow
   on — Henry C. Warnack   14A:108
Evans, F. C., Translator — *Art* — Gautier   20:399
   — *Death of the Duc d'Englien, The* — Hennique 20:461
   — *Songs from "La Bonne Chanson"* — Verlaine 16D: 80
Evans, Gladys La Due — *The Little Mortal Child*   32:409
Evans, Margaret — *Faith*   33:132
Evans, Oliver W. — *Truant*   49: 83
Evans, Oliver W., Translator — *Doctor's Duty, The*   48:291
   — *Epigrams*   48: 98
Eve Has Seven Faces — Eisig Silberschlag   49: 50
Evenfall — Adolf Wenig   46:282
Evening Memory — Celia Keegan   46:191
Evening Prayer — George Furman Andrews   48: 83
Evening Songs — Vitezlav Hálek   27:716
Evening Sonnet — Juan Lozano y Lozano   54:185
Evening Vestment — Agnes Armstrong   48:178

Eventide — Paul Verlaine —
    Translated by William Raleigh Price   23:368
Ever Present Dream — Gwynnedd Gruffydd   44:180
Everett, Charles Carroll — *"Sordello": The Hero as Man*   8:313
    — *The Hero as Poet*   8:243
Everett, Robert Iphys — *Call of Modern Tragedy, The*   15A:130
    — *Hushed Strain, The*   15A: 39
    — *Icarus*   15D: 71
    — *Love's Banquet*   15B, Facing 18
Every Man Is an Inlet — August Derleth   55: 74
Everydayland, Alice in — Egbert H. Van Delden   38: 96
Eviction — Jessie A. Swigart   53: 79
Evolution of "Hamlet" Criticism, The — Walter Libby   15A: 87
Evolution of Religion as Suggested in Browning's Poems
    — Emma Lightner Hellings   17B:113
Ewing, Thomas, Jr., Translator — Horace — *Epode XI*   21:415
    — *Ode I:5*   22:222
    — *Ode II:16*   22:145
    — *Ode IV:7*   23: 80
    — *Satire I, IX*   21:149
    — *To His Wine Jug*   21:487
Ex Libris — Everett Gillis   46:282
Exchange — Virginia Irene Sullivan   46:370
Exile, The — Amy Josephine Klauber   33:246
Exiled — David Berenberg   33:506
Expressionism in Germany — Edwin H. Zeydel   36:399
Eyes in Shakespeare — W. J. Rolfe   1:479
Ezra Pound's "Ballad of the Goodly Fere" —
    Katherine Buxbaum   40:142

Fable, A — Mary R. Drury   14D: 65
Fabliau of the Three Hunchbacks, The — Durand —
    Translated by Frederick Bliss Luquiens   24:333
Facettes of Love from Browning — Daniel G. Brinton   1: 1
Facing Reality — Floy Pascal   33:451
Factory, The — Leonard Lanson Cline   29:636
Faded Leaves — From the Norse of Alexander Kielland
    — Translated by C. Sadakichi Hartmann   3:311
Fagin, Mary — *Room 226*   36:610
Fagin, N. Bryllion — *Anton Chekhov, The Master of the
    Gray Short-Story*   32:416
    — *Sidney Lanier*   43:161
Fahnstock, Edith, with Florence Donnell White, Transla-
    tors — *The Magic Theatre* — Cervantes   32:234
Failure — Theodore Roberts   10:234
Fair Exchange — John Robert Quinn   56:375
Fair Rohtraut — Edward Mörike   27:227

Fairchild, Camille — *Airships*   27:711
   — *Claude Lorraine, A*   27:600
   — *Ride on Air, A*   27:448
   — *Song of the Stars*   27:706
Fairchild, Hoxie Neele —
   Belated Appreciation: A Study of Hilda Conkling   42:267
Fairy-Dream — Alexander Petöfi   48:112
Fairy Gold — Alexander Ostrovsky — Translated by
   Camilla Chapin Daniels and George Rapall Noyes   40: 1
Fairy Rhythms, Shakespeare's   1: 30
Fairy Tale, A — Ilya Erenburg —
   Translated by Jacob Chaitkin   33:618
Faith — Edward F. Jackman   29:485
Faith — Margaret Evans   33:132
Faithful Dog, The — Cervantes   46:195
Faithless, The — Sully Prud'homme —
   Translated by Edith Summers   18:533
Falke, Gustav — *Grave, The*   53:147
   — *Thistle on the Beach*   53:148
Fall of Stars — Leconte de Lisle   54:255
"Fall of the Angels," Caedmon — Anna Robertson Brown   2:251
Fall of the Stars, The — Leconte de Lisle   17D: 88
Fallen, The — Stephen Berrien Stanton   36:398
Falstaff, Was He Immoral? — L. D. Lawhead   2:142
Falstaff, Why He Dies in "Henry V"   8:330
Falstaff's Death   1:346
Fame — Stanton A. Coblentz   53: 78
Family of My Heart, The — Humphrey F. Noyes   52:175
Fanning, Cecil —
   Recent Progress in Community Music and Drama   32:149
Fanny's Consent — José Moratin —
   Translated by Anna Emilia Bagstad   40:159
Fantaisie — Gerard de Nerval —
   Translated by Frances Taylor   35:379
Fantaisie — Gerard de Nerval   54:177
Fantasy of Life, The — Mabel Holmes Parsons   28:368
Farber, Charles — *Patience of Li Po, The*   58:158
Farber, Marjorie E., Translator —
   Lyrics from the Russian   44:277
Farce of the Worthy Master Pierre Patelin the Lawyer —
   Transcribed from the Mediaeval French by Maur-
   ice Relonde   28:343
Farmer's Wife — Ursula Wadleigh   50: 78
Farquahar, Gentle George — Louise Imogen Guiney   6:406
Farrere — Jesse Lee Bennett   27:591
Farwell, Arthur —
   Artistic Possibilities of Indian Myths, The   15A: 46

Fate: A Parable — Charlotte Porter   17C:103
Father, The — Colin C. Clements   31:187
Father's God, My — James Meaghar   39:473
Fatherly Feelings — Joseph Bovshover   56:369
Faunce, Frances Avery — *Cowards All*   33:622
     — *Sunset Down Mt. Vernon Street*   34: 62
Faust, A. B. — *Friedrich Spielhagen:*
     The Veteran German Novelist   16D:131
"Faust" Problem, A: What Was the Homunculus? —
     M. Earll   13:269
"Faust," Essence of Goethe's, The — Philip H. Erbes   4:504
"Faust": Study Program — Charlotte Porter   15B:140
Favorable Moment, The — Paul Verlaine   56:194
Favorites of Fortune, The — Walter Blackburn Harte   8:377
Fawcett, Edgar — *Lincoln Loquitur*   11:528
Fay, Frances C., Translator — *Forgiveness* — Lemaître   24:209
Fear — Irene Burns   48:357
Feast of the Kings in Paraguay —
     Serviliana Guanes de Burgoda   55:274
Federico de Roberto — Helen Rose Balfe   37:565
Feet — A. E. Hammond   51: 83
Feinberg, Elihu T. — *June Landscape*   57:113
Feipel, Louis N. —
     A Perennial Witticism vs a Shakespearan Crux   23:341
Feldman, A. Bronson — *Art of Lionel Johnson, The*   57:140
     — *Critical Canons of Ezra Pound*   57:226
Feldman, Abraham — *American Aeschylus, The*   52:149
     — *Ernest Lacy: Forgotten Immortal*   47: 86
     — *To François Rabelais*   52:290
"Félibrige," The — Maria Lefferts Elmendorf   2: 32
Felim's Daughter — George Brandon Saul   58:291
Felipe, Leon: Spanish War Poet — Willis Knapp Jones   47:263
Feministic and Literary Influences of Petrarchism —
     George Allan England   28:187
Femme Qui Rit, La — Dora N. Raymond   31:392
Ferber, Maurice — *Wanderers, The*   43:364
Ferishtah's Fancies   3:379
Fermer, A. — *Poems*   46: 95
Fernan, Silva Valdes — Willis Knapp Jones   47:352
Ferrero, Leo — *America and Her Intellectuals*   45:210
Ferrier, Paul — *Codicil, The*   19:193
Ferrill, Thomas H. — *Portraits*   33:131
Ferrill, Thomas Hornsby — *Morning*   34:246
     — *Return*   36:474
Festival for Spring — Kay De Bard Hall   54:162
     — *Festival of Flowers*   54:163
     — *Lyrics of China, Old and New*   54:162

"Festspiel," Hauptmann's — Paul H. Grummann   26: 68
Feud of the Schroffensteins, The — Heinrich von Kleist   27:457
Fever of La Petite d'Alsace — Réné Char   57:483
Few Donkeys, A — Francis Jammes   49:360
Ficke, Arthur Davidson, Translator —
     Stormbird, The — Roelvink   24: 65
Fiction, Notes on Recent   8:41, 617, 657
Fiction, The Primitive Man in Modern — Hilda Ridley   19:212
Fidelity — Catulle Mendes — Translated by R. T. House   18:413
Field, Louise Maunsell — Happy Ending, The   17A: 97
     — Motherless Heroine, The   17D: 99
Field of Enchantment, The — Z. Topelius   28:584
Fiet, Afanasiy — Night — Translated by George G. Lake   34:309
Fifteen Poems — Richard Dehmel   55:338
Figs from Asphalt — Christabel F. Fiske   32:596
Figueira, Gaston — Edna Lue Furness   53:362
Figueira, Gaston: Poet of America — Jones   47: 65
Figueroa, Francesco P. — Marimba   49:368
Fillmore, J. E. — War   25:523
Filpus, Paula S. — Song of the Blood-Red Sun, The   53: 72
Finch, Lucine — Butterfly, The   21:401
Fine, Nathan I. — Always You   46:156
Finlay, Hattie M., Translator — Calm after Tempest —
     Giacomo Leopardi   42: 92
Fire of Earth, The — Asher Gerecht   50: 79
Fireflies: A Little Reverie — Mary Harned   8:376
Firing Squad — Elva June Stark   50:267
Firkins, O. W. — Unbidden Guest, The   35:276
     — Paradoxical Ethics of Browning, The   23:348
     — Poetry and Prose in Life and Literature   15C: 77
     — Supernatural in Two Recent Plays, The   20:438
First American Shakespeare Society — Albert R. Frey   2:534
First Argentine Gaucho Drama, The —
     Eduardo Guttierez and José J. Podesta   51: 99
First Black World Poet, The — Thomas Millard Henry   40:303
First Born — Louise Louis   53:159
First of the Moderns — Joseph T. Shipley   35:626
First Star, The — Ruth E. Hopkins   35:532
Fisher, Betty — Prayer   46:257
Fisher, Katharine Rolston —
     Woman Egoist: Meredith's "Cecilia," The   24:113
Fisher, Mana Willis — Ecstasy   49:247
     — Nostalgia   49:164
Fishers — Harold R. Hardin   53:173
Fishing at Dawn — Marcia Nichols Holden   51:368
Fiske, Christabel F. — Figs from Asphalt   32:596
     — Mercerized Folklore   31:538

— *Painted Legends*	35:380
— *Reflection of the Bible in Early English Literature*	30:208
— *Saneness of George Gifford, The*	31:210
— *Scott of Buccleugh Clan*	37: 24
— *Sixteenth Century Garden, A, or the Adventure of the Advised Eye*	29:565
Fiske, Isabella Howe — *Clouds of the Sun*	15B: 52
— *Comedy of the Exile*	17A: 51
— *Flame*	17C: 94
— *Justice*	17C: 95
— *Life of the Bee, The*	14C: 59
— *Poetry and a Courageous Publisher*	15A:113
— *Stirrups of Eros, The*	16B: 76
— *To a Child*	17C: 96
— *What Flush Might Have Said*	13:607
Fitzgerald, Caroline — *"Venetia Victrix"*	1:379
Fitzgerald, Edward — *Letters and Literary Remains of*	1.447
Five-Fold Prayers, The — Gladys Wolcott Barnes	29: 73
Five Lyrics from the German — Alberta Robison	53:147
Five Medieval Latin Lyrics — Translated by George Frisbie Whicher	49:165
Five Poems — Kathryn Evans McKay	56:376
Five Poems — Ralph Friedrich	46:252
Flame — Isabella Howe Fiske	17C: 94
Flame of Life, The Symbolism of the — Florence Brooks	16C:112
"Flammantia Moenia Mundi" — Walter S. Hinchman	17B: 86
Fleay, F. G. — *Annals of Shakespeare's "Fellow": Robert Armin*	1:507
— *Gentle Will, Our Fellow* 5:7, 72, 129, 183, 254, 414,	
	505, 564, 612
— *Story of Shelley's Life in His "Epipsichidion"*	2:225
Fleischer, Charles — *Leadership — Autocratic, Obsequious, Fraternal*	14B:133
Flemish and Dutch Poets, Modern — Sipko Rederus	13:386
Flemish Poet: Karel van de Woestijne, The — Clark Stillman	47:274
Flight and the Passing, The — Marion Couthouy Smith	27:102
"Flight of the Duchess," Art Spirit in Browning's — Charlotte Moore	11:266
Flokos, N. G. — *Hippocrates Dying*	58:328
Florer, Warren Washburn — *Herman Sudermann*	16C:116
— *Hillingenlei*	18:377
Florizel to Fiametta — Dora N. Raymond	31:469
Flowering Althaea — Laura Lourene Le Gear	51: 82
Flowering Althaea — Laura Lourene Le Gear	53:153
Flowers, Priscilla — *May Night*	37:551

Flying the Kites — Kay De Bard Hall   54:165
Fog — Dorothy Dodson   52:162
Fog-Bound — Marion Sinclair Walker   47: 95
Fogazzaro, Antonio — *Italian Literature*   18:133
Folio, Frank — *Bookish Bits* 1:160; 2:246, 298, 392, 445, 587,
                                                      389; 3: 98
    — *First Performance of "King John"*   3:487
Folk Entertainment in England in the Latter Years of
    the Reign of Elizabeth — Philip George Neserius   38:141
Folk Poems, Browning's: Study Program —
    Charlotte Porter and Helen A. Clarke   12:105
Folk-Song, The — Bronwin Chubb   29:469
Folk Songs of Greece under the Turk — Perikles Mellon   26: 47
Fool on a Roof, A — Jean Wright   25: 53
Fool Who Lives Contentedly, The — D. McVickar   32:109
Foote, A. A. — *Two Poems*   51:267
For a Friend — A. Wilber Stevens   55:263
For C — Sailing for France — Beatricce Daw   29:471
For Ever and Ever — Henri Lavédan   28:391
For Green Is Hope — From the Norse of Alexander
    Kielland — Translated by C. Sadakichi Hartmann   3:315
For Happiness — Stanislav Pshibishevsky —
    Translated by Lucille Baron   23: 81
For Helen — Pierre de Ronsard   53:174
For Poets — Gilean Douglas   53: 84
For Such Great Glory! — John Laurence Gilmartin   47:239
For the Dead on the Mountains — David Brock   44:231
For the Gate of Exiles — Henri de Regnier —
    Translated by Dorothy Brown Aspinwall   52: 80
For the Return — Ora Mary Hulli   51:272
For What Is Given — Helen J. Goede   51:178
For Whom Does the Poet Write? —
    Harry Elmore Hurd   47:252
Forbes, Giralda — *Lover's Fancy, A*   53:309
Ford, Ford Madox — *Mister Bosphorus and the Muses*   34:532
Ford, Harriet — *"Andrea del Sarto," a Painter's Poem*   4:144
    — *Browning Right about the Riccardi Palace*   3:648
Ford, Julia Ellsworth — *"A. E..," the Neo-Celtic Mystic* 16D: 82
Ford Madox Hueffer — Lawrence Marsden Price   31:432
Forest-Moment — J. Corson Miller   56:344
Forest Warden, The — Otto Ludwig —
    Translated by Paula Green   24:129
Forfeit, The — Corrie Crandall Howell   36:136
Forgiveness — Jules Lemaître —
    Translated by Frances C. Fay   24:209
Forgiveness, A   8:272
Forgotten Art, A — Jeanette Marks   19:488

Forsaken — Eduard Mörike   27:230
Forsberg, Laura, Translator — *Sonatina*   45:353
Forsslund, Karl-Erik — *Wanderer's Song*   51: 79
"Forster's" Life of Strafford: Is It Forster's or Brownings?   6:555
Fort, Paul — *Dead Maiden, The*   26:522
Fortune Favors Fools — Ivan Narodny —
    Translated by Maria Ossipovna Mieler   23:305
Fortune Teller, The — Anne Throop Craig   29:494
Foster, Carol — *Darkness Will Go, The*   46:286
Foster, Mary Salinda — *Springtime in the Ozarks*   53:348
Foster, Nancy K. — *Word for Rossetti, A*   21:322
Fouchaux, Madeleine — *Song for Women*   53: 80
Foulke, Adrienne, Translator — *Rude Awakening* —
    Sarment   45:231
Found — Goethe   54:239
Fountain of the Satyr — Eugenio de Castro —
    Translated by E. W. Olmstead and F. D. Burnet   21: 88
Four Ages, The: Indian Symbols —
    Marcia Nichols Holden   49:181
Four Antarctica — John W. Andrews   52: 99
Four Bare Walls, The — Francis Adolf Subert   28:497
Four Bare Walls, The Message of —
    Beatrice M. Mekota and Francis Haffkine Snow   28:553
Four Days — Vasevold Garshin —
    Translated by Nathan Haskell Dole   3:297
Four Fairy Plays — Z. Topelius   28:567
Four Legends of Brittany — John Heard   43: 99
Four Lyrics — William Stanley Braithwaite   25:254
Four Poems — Amy Lee Spencer   53:271
Four Poems — Barbara True   51:176
Four Poems — Clare Shelley   55:336
Four Poems from the Korean — Grace W. Mitchell   47:269
Four Poems — John Robert Quinn   57:279
Four Poems — Kathleen Sutton   44: 82
Four Poems — Roydon Burke   42:188
Four Poems — Stanton A. Coblentz   44: 89
Four Quatrains for November — Una W. Harsen   47:273
Four Translations from Theophile Gautier —
    Emanuel Eisenberg   36:460
Four Triolets to a Garden — Ruth H. Ward   44: 84
Foxglove, The — Claire Shelley   55:337
"Fra Lippo Lippi"   8:586
Fragile Shell, The — James Meagher   39:473
Fragments — Jean Mitchell Lawrence   44: 47
Fragments from the Spanish — José de Espronceda and
    Gustavo Adolfo Becquer —
    Translated by Ina Duvall Singleton   30:464

ragments of a Play — Kate Douglas Wiggin   40:281
'rance, Anatole —
   M. Pigeonneau's Inadvertent Romance   11:128
'rance, Anatole, Reminiscent — S. M. Delson   31:261
'rance, Marie de — *Lay of the Honeysuckle*   54:272
   — *Prologue to the Lays*   54: 86
'rance, Travel in Old — Helen Tracy Porter   11:436
'rancis, Adelaide — *Gray Mists*   38:608
   — *Deserted*   41:314
'rancis, Helen M. — *Yesterday*   35:270
'rancis, Robert C. — *They Were All Young Once*   39:290
'rançon, Marcel — *Ideal of Feminine Beauty at the Time
   of Ronsard, The*   46:157
   — *Remy de Gourmont's "Lilith"* — A Critique   51:291
'ranck, Inez E. — *Cloud of Black Wings*   48:243
'rank, Florence Kiper —
   "O When Will God Come as a Mighty Flood"   26:649
   — *Three Sonnets*   26:401
'rank, John Geisenberger, Translator —
   Tristan and Isolde   49:301
'rank, Our — August Von Kotzebue —
   Translated by Beatrice B. Beebe   38:206
'rankfurt's Dialect Author, Friedrich Scholze —
   Clair Hayden Bell   35:612
'ray Luis De Leon to His Pupil, Juan de Grial —
   Translated by Thomas Walsh   22: 79
'razer, Margaret E. N., Translator —
   Thou Shalt Not Pass — Felice Cavallotti   27:122
'rederick, John Towner — *Weaving, The*   30:607
'reedom, A Dream of —
   From *Poets' Parleys* — The Editors   5:382
'reedom to Write and to Print — Horace L. Traubel   2:529
'reedom's Muscles — Charles Maxwell Lancaster   50:290
'reeman, A. E. — *Psychological Basis of Swinburne's
   Convictions, The*   38:579
'reeman, Joseph L. — *Mood*   33:623
'rench Curio, A.   13:459
'rench Enthusiasm Satirized in Browning's "Two Poets
   of Croisic" — Herbert Ernest Cushman   11:382
'rench Literature During the Elizabethan Period   1:157
'rench Lyrics, Three Old — Henry Clinton Hutchins   27:597
'rench Poets and Novelists, Current —
   Curtis Hidden Page   18:113
'rench Writers on Americans   1:396
'renz, Horst — *Eugene O'Neill in Russia*   49:241
   — *Georg Kaiser*   52:363
'renzel, Karl — *On the Berlin Theatre*   12:571

Freund, Yvonne A. — *Weary Black* 58:19
Frey, A. R. — *First Shakespeare Society Records* 2:53
Frey, Dorothy Wilkey — *Dawn* 44: 8
Freybe, C. E. — *In Garrison* — (*Leave of Absence*) 26:49
Freyre, Gilberto — *Generation d'Apresguerre: Bourne and Psichari, The* — Translated by Robert White Linker and Francis Simkins 41:43
Friedrich, Gerhard — *Two Poems* 54: 8
— *Two Poems* 54:37
Friedrich, Ralph — *Five Poems* 46:25
— *Two Poems* 45:35
French Versions of the Willow Song, With Music by J. J. Rousseau — Théodore Child 1:17
Frey, Albert R. — *First Shakespeare Society Records* 2:53
Friend of Emerson, A — Antonia C. de P. P. Maury 26:35
Friend of His Youth, A — Edmund See — Translated by M. E. Brandon 36:15
Frier Bacon and Frier Bungay, Performance of by University of Illinois 16B:14
Frierson, Anne — *"Wheels ob de Human Chariot"* 41:45
Frithiof the Bold, Story of — William Morris 12:35
From an Unpublished Sequence — Frederic Hunter 25:22
From Morn to Midnight — Georg Kaiser 31:31
From Sad Madrigal — Charles Baudelaire — Translated by Joseph T. Shipley 36:62
From the Book of Visions — John Casey 25:25
From the Mountain Top — Alvilde Prydz 25:45
From the "Nomad Palaces" — Gustave Kahn — Translated by Curtis Hidden Page 16D: 7
From the Prayers of the Maidens to Mary — Rainer Maria Rilke 30:20
From the Roman de la Rosè — Charlotte Pendleton 1:54
From the Sanskrit — Lucille M. Hein 44:12
From Where I Sit — Lucille Coleman 56:34
Froome, John Redhead, Jr. — *Listening* 28:42
Frost, Frances M. — *Transformation* 37:51
Frost, Robert, The Classical in — George Aykroyd 40:61
Frosted Glass — Edwin M. Erickson 46:18
Fruchter, M. J. — *Rats* 37:15
Fruit, John Phelps —
Destiny of Marriage, The: Portia and the Caskets 3: 6
— *Obsession of Edgar Allan Poe, The* 12: 4
— *Rationale of the Short Story according to Poe* 16A: 5
— *Shakespeare's Egoism* 1:40
Frustration — Kingsley Tufts 47:28
Fryer, Eugene M. — *Beyond the Gate: DeQuincey and Kipling's Misquitta* 22:31
— *Hewlett and Hearn: Two Types of Orientalists* 18:47

Frygyes Karinthy, Hungarian Humorist —
    Joseph Remenyi   52: 69
Fuchs, Reinhold — *New Star, The*   20:479
Fucini, Renato — *Night* —
    Translated by Herbert King Stone   32:390
Fulda, Ludwig — *Blockhead, The* —
        Translated by Anna Emilia Bagstad   39: 1
    — *By Ourselves*   23: 1
Full Many a Flower — Robert R. Rosenburg   52:163
Full of the Moon — Gertrude Herrick   31:379
Fuller, Margaret — *Churchill*   53:166
    — *To Peter Short, Aged Five*   53: 80
Fuller, Margaret, and Her Friends — P.   8:155
Fuller, Margaret, Critical Work of, The —
    Carolyn B. La Monte   7:477
Fuller, Margaret, Memorial, The   13:457
Fuller, Margaret, Permanent Influence of —
    Kenyon West   7:377
Funeral March of a Marionette, The —
    Arthur H. Nethercot   31:232
Furness, Edna Lue — *Enrique Gonzales Martinez*   58:282
    — *Gaston Figueira*   53:362
    — *Group of Latin American Poets, A*   58:356
    — *Juana de Ibarbourou*   54:242
Furness, Edna L., Translator — *Selections from*
    "Cantaro Fresco" — Juana de Ibarbourou   56:148
    — *Two Poems* — Gabriela Mistral   55: 36
    — *You Were Mine* — Gabriela Mistral   57: 98
Furness, Horace Howard — *"Hamlet" Prize Questions*   3:153
    — *"Hanging a Wolf" (The Merchant of Venice)*   3:655
    — *Meaning of "Talents" in "A Lover's Com-*
        plaint," The   3:196
    — *Study of Shakespeare, The*   1:109
    — *Text of Shakespeare*   3:335
    — *Variorum Shakespeare*   1:249
Furrows — Virginia Stait   36:157
Further Comment, A — John Heard   48:227
Future is Better than the Past — Eliza Thayer Clapp   14A:105

G. I. Bread — John L. Stewart   52: 2
G. W. C. — *Social Tendencies*   14B:27; 14C: 23
Gabriela Mistral — A. Ortiz-Vargas   46:339
Gaelic, Three Songs from the —
    Translated by John J. Savage   25:140
Galatea Wakes — Edith Lombard Squires   38:105
Galbraith, Georgie Starbuck — *Testament*   50:267
    — *Three Poems*   48:272
    — *Two Poems*   49:278

Galdos, Perez — *Grandfather, The*   21:16

Gale, Jane Winsor — *Victoria*   26: 7

Galère for Shoppers — Sister M. Bernetta, O.S.F.   53:24

Gallagher, Kate L. — *Browning and Ibsen*   3:10

   — *"Julius Caesar" and "Strafford"*   2:21

   — *Shakespeare Society of the New Century Guild*   1:27

Gallant Cassian — A. Schnitzler —

   Translated by Moritz A. Jagendorf   33:50

Gallicanus — Hrotvitha — Translated by John Heard   42:31

Game, The — Marvin Davis Winsett   58:36

Gammon, Margaret Henry — *Mirage*   39:10

Gandolfo — George Allan England   48: 5

Gannett, William Channing — *"Idylls of the King":*

   Suggestions to Study   13:58

   — *"In Memoriam": Suggestions to Study*   13:28

Garborg, Arne: Scandinavian Author   3: 3

"Garden is a Lovesome Thing, A" — Ella Kirk Jelliffe   40:11

Garden, The — Julia Hall Bartholomew   29:63

Garden of Love, The — William Blake   11: 2

Garden, The Elfin — Madison Cawein   25:60

Gardens and the English Poets — J. C. Wright   29:34

Gardener, The — Vera I. Arlett   41:30

Gardiner, Fanny Hale — *Echegaray: Spanish States-*

   man, Dramatist, Poet   12:40

   — *Spanish Poet Laureate, A: José Zorilla*   10:50

Gardner, Emelyn E. — *Raising the Devil, A Snap-Shot*

   of Mountain Life   39:13

Gargoyles of Notre Dame: 1942 — Lirrel Starling   49:35

Garland of Brickbats, A — Charles C. Sellars   37:39

Garratt, Grace Edith — *Travail*   53: 8

Garrett, Harriet — *If We Forget*   53:16

Garshin, Vasevold — *Dangerous Desire for Growth in*

   a Glass House, The   12:32

   — *Four Days*   3:29

Garshin's Malady: Words on a Neglected Master —

   Virgil Geddes   35: 7

Gary, Lorena M. — *Into the Known-Unknown*   45: 4

   — *Poet Who Dwells in "The Valley Nis," The*   47: 5

   — *Rose and Red Wine, The*   54:31

   — *Stained Glass Window*   58:31

   — *Sunset at Gettysburg*   48: 8

   — *Tiger Lilies*   58:17

   — *Value — Per Se*   46:37

   — *Walt Whitman's Imagery*   52:36

Gaston Figueira — Edna Lue Furness   53:36

Gaston Figueira: Poet of America — *Willis Knapp Jones*   47: 6

Gates of Wishes — Mary MacMillan   22:46

Gautier, Theophile — *Art* 20:399
— *Poems* — Translated by Emanuel Eisenberg 36:460
Gaw, Chaken — *Modern American Literature* 9:122
Geddes, Virgil — *De Gourmont and the Idea* 33:362
— *Garshin's Malady: Words on a Neglected Master* 35: 75
— *Huysmans, Trappist and Litterateur* 33:521
Geiger, Don — *Break-Up* 57:356
— *On Rate of Learning Our Missions* 57:355
— *Power Almighty* 57:354
Geijerstam, Gustavof — *Criminals* —
Translated by Roy W. Swanson 34:186
Genee, Edythe Hope — *Autumn Fire* 47:288
— *Bride of the Sea* 54:168
Generation d'Apresguerre: Bourne and Psichari —
Gilberto Freyre — Translated from the Portuguese by Robert White Linker and Francis Simkins 41:433
Genesis — Henry L. Baker 19:317
Gentle George Farquhar — Louise Imogen Guiney 6:406
Gentle Will, Our Fellow — F. G. Fleay 5:7, 72, 129, 183, 254, 414, 505, 564, 612
Georg Kaiser — Horst Frenz 52:363
George, Ruth — *Spring* 49: 79
George, Stefan — *Ten Poems* 45:343
George Washington Speaks — C. B. Carlaw 34:531
Georges Duhamel: A Study — Frank C. Hanighen 41:150
Gerecht, Asher — *Fire of Earth, The* 50: 79
Germ of the Domestic Drama, The — Felix Sper 40:544
Germain, André — *The Traveler* —
Translated by Joseph T. Shipley 36:624
German-American Literature — Amelia von Ende 17C:108
— *German Book World, The* 18:280
German Criticism, Recent: Hermann Sudermann —
Warren Washburn Florer 16C:116
German Criticisms, Recent — Paul H. Grummann 16B:117
German Drama, Latest Tendencies in — Barrett H. Clark 26: 72
German Drama, Poetry, and Fiction — Amelia von Ende 19:120
German Fairytale Contest, The — Max Bratt 17D:109
German Literature During the Past Year — Mary Harned 9:284
German Literature, Ibsen's Influence Upon —
F. G. G. Schmidt 17A:112
German Literature in the Eighteenth Century —
Oswald Seidensticker 2:57, 169
German Literature, Modern — John Scholte Noller 16C:127
German Poetry and Criticism — Otto Heller 2:266
German Poetry and Drama — Amelia von Ende 18:123
German Romance and Longfellow — Fred Lewis Pattee 17A: 59

107

German Writers, Among the — Amelia von Ende   18:481
German Writers of America — Amelia von Ende   17C:108
German Writers, Recent Works by — Amelia von Ende   18:404
Germanic Myths, Hauptmann's Treatment of —
    Paul H. Grummann   18: 89
Germond, George —
    Lines Sent with a Copy of the Rubaiyat   17C:116
    — *Songs of the Wilderness*   15D: 72
Gertha's Lovers — William Morris   10:337
Gesture — Elizabeth J. Savage   47:382
Ghose, Girish C. — *Chintamini*   25:144
Ghosts at First Nights in Italy — Winifred Smith   33:114
Giacomo Leopardi — William A. Drake   34:614
Giacoso, Guiseppe — *Unhappy Love*   27:601
Gibson, Catherine B. — *Sky's Veil*   46:283
Gideon, Donna Lois — *Wild Wind*   47:287
Gideon, Henry L. —
    Caldron, The — *Pélléas and Mélisande in Boston* 23:157
Gideon, Richard W. — *Songs of Sunrise*   9:407
Giffard, George, The Saneness of — Christabel F. Fiske   31:210
Gift, The — Silne Kayrd   40:109
Gift of Persia — Juanita de Araña   51:269
Gilbert, Helen — *Good Sainte Anne, The*   35:576
    — *Spot on the Porch, The*   42: 81
Gilbert, Laura Fullerton, Translator —
    — *Ca Ira Sonnets* — Carducci   27:243
    — *On a Figure of France Crucified* — d'Annunzio   27:111
Gilkyson, T. Walter, Translator —
    — *Always Ridiculous* — José Echegaray   27:233
Gillis, Everett — *Ex Libris*   46:282
    — *Triolet Nocturne*   45:114
Gillis, H. R. — *Revelations in an Empty Rooming House*   53: 60
Gilmartin, John Laurence — *For Such Great Glory!*   47:239
Gilt Edges — Russell Speirs   41:525
Ginistry, Paul — *Devotee of Moliére, A* —
    Translated by H. Schnurer   34:426
Gink, Peter — Arthur H. Nethercot   35:118

Girdlestone, E. D., Translator of *The Norwegian Peasant*
    Lad and His Dream-Tune — Björnson   5: 52
Giordano Bruno, Martyr and Idealist —
    Martha Pike Conant   17B: 91
Giovanni Alfredo Cesareo: The Sicilian Poet —
    Anna Benedetti   35:529
Giuffré — *Thee Only*   17A:134
Glaenzer, Richard Butler — *Golden Plover, The*   27:117
    — *Last Crusade, The*   29:363

108

— *Letter from Lovelace, A*   28:250
— *Old Jake*   30:467
— *Roses Three*   28:117
— *Shafts from a Carib Bow*   28:459
— *St. George o'Dreams*   29:365
— *Thanks to a Fruit Shop*   29:366
Glance at "Lord Ormont and His Aminta," —
Louise Cann Ranum   22:137
Glass, Everett — *Bonds of Interest, The*   32:244
— *Tumbler*   37:516
Gleaner of Sapri, The — Luigi Mercantini   27:712
Gleason, Harold Willard — *William Shakespeare* 39:289
Gleim, Miss — *Strafford*   2:212
Glennie, J. S. Stuart — *Chivalry and Woman*   1:583
— *Greene Entries*   2:341
— *Shakespeare as a Citizen*   2: 1
— *True Character of Chivalry, The*   1:583
Glick, Carl — *Art for God's Sake: The Secret Problems*
of a Little Theatre   34:247
— *But on the Other Hand*   36: 96
— *Prologue*   33:553
— *Suncold*   36:280
Glick, Carl, with Bernard Sobel — *The Immortal* 32:441
Glied, Evelyn Vermillion — *Disenchantment*   46:245
Glimpse of a Childhood — Rainer Maria Rilke   27:120
Glimpses of Present Day Poets   11:610; 12:305; 13:527;
                14D:113; 15A:131; 15B:149
Glittering Highway, The — Enrique de Meneses —
Translated by Gustav Davidson   38:317
Glove, A — Björnstjerne Björnson   4:7, 70, 128, 204, 254, 332
Glover, A. Kingsley — *Early Colonial Poets*   13: 80
Glover, Gertrude Clarke — *Song in My Heart, A* 54:290
Glynn-Ward, H. — *Aftermath, The*   37:501
Goblins! — Alfred J. Wright, Jr.   57:136
God, The Idea of, in "The Sun" — David G. Brinton 3:254
God, If I Were — C.   10:139
God, My Father's — James Meagher   39:473
God Speaks to Travelers — Hal S. White   35:156
God to a Tired Mother — Cecil Clayton Sargent 46:286
God's Nod — Charles Hugh Richardson Harper 53:162
Goddard, Henry P. — *Baltimore Shakespeare Club, The* 1:273
— *Horatio as a Friend*   7:203
— *Lesson of "Cymbeline", The*   3:572
Goede, Helen J. — *For What is Given*   51:178
— *Sonnets on Separation*   47: 56
Goethe, An Appeal to Celebrate His 150th Birthday —
Kuno Francke   11:159

Goethe, Shakespeare's Influence on —
    Edwin Watts Chubb   16A: 6£
Goethe's "Faust" and the Book of Job: Study Program —
    Charlotte Porter   15B:14(
Goethe's "Faust": Disputed Authorship   1:15£
Goethe's "Faust": Essence of — Philip H. Erbes   4:50₄
Goethe's "Faust": Relations to Russian Writers —
    Otto Harnack   2:57£
Goethe's "World Spirit" and the Vishnu of the "Bhaga-
    vad Gita" — W. T. Harris   1:40₹
Goetz, Philip B. — Audience, The   7:47£
    — Books   7:47£
Goetze, A. — Heights   25: 1
Gogol, Nicolai — Sheriff and His Son, The   48:311
Going — John Nixon, Jr.   57:167
Going after Rubber — José Verissimo — Translated by
    Bob White Linker and Francis Simkins   39:154
Gold — Oscar C. Williams   32:306
Gold-Hunting — June E. Downey   28:112
Golden Bird — Madeleine Burch Cole   56:363
Golden Bough, The — Edith M. Thomas   18:277
Golden Plover, The — Richard Butler Glaenzer 27:117
Golden Wedding, A — Edouard Rod —
    Translated by the Editors   10:483
Golden Wedding, The — Dorothy E. Reid   38:155
Goldfinch Back, The — Elizabeth Hazelton Haight 27:405
Golem, The — H. Lewick —
    Translated by J. C. Augenlicht   39:159
Gonzales, Angel Custodio —
    So Many Wounded Words Without Sound 56:227
Good Sainte Anne, The — Helen Gilbert   35:576
Goodlet, I. — New Word on Shakespeare's Sonnets, A 3:505
Goodman, Riah Tomarkin — Three Poems   57:111
Goodrich, Janice Meredith — Desire   39:414
Goodson, Louise — Three Prayers   55: 64
Goodwin, Frederick Day —
    He Did the Murder in a Dozen Words   36:577
Goodwin, Grace Duffield —
    Two Singers of Sunrise: Lanier and Gilder 9:407
Godwin, Shelley and — William G. Kingsland 10:389
Gorki, Maxim — Children of the Sun, The 17B: 1
    — Nymph, The   24:368
    — Reader, The   15B: 33
    — Smug Citizen, The   17D: 1
    — Summer Folk   16C: 1
    — Summer Lodging, A   16D: 1
Gosse's Northern Studies — P.   3: 93

Gottschalk, Laura R. — *Fallacies*   35:153
Goudiss, A., Translator — *To the Stars* — Andreyev   18:417
Gourmont, Remy de — *Lilith*   51:298
— *Litanies of the Rose* —
        Translated by George Williamson   33:469
— *Shadow of a Woman, The*   55: 3
— *She Has a Body* —
        Translated by George Williamson   34:302
Gourmont, Remy de, and the Idea — Virgil Geddes   33:362
Gournay, Marie de, Feministe and Friend of Montaigne —
        Anna Adele Chenot   34: 63
Governor Lenhard, — Einar H. Kvaren —
        Translated by Jakobina Johnson   43: 3
Grace after Beauty — Joseph Upper   39:314
Grafe, Frances Barbara — *Overlooking the Dyke*   53:165
Graham, Gladys C., with Ernest S. Bates —
        Pierre Louys and the Songs of Bilitis   32:562
Graham, H. L. — *Bird Anthology from Sill, A*   9:566
— *Some Aspects of Echegaray*   21:234
Grand Pré Garden, In a — Bliss Carman   14A: 1
Grandfather, The — Perez Galdós —
        Translated by Elizabeth Wallace   21:161
Gratz, R. J. — *Journey of "Childe Roland"*   2:578
Grave of Keats, The — J. Homer Caskey   35:622
Grave, The — Russell Speirs   40:113
Graves, C. E. —
        Does Alcohol Stimulate Poetic Inspiration?   35:271
Gray, Elizabeth Jordan — *Realization*   44:286
Gray Mists — Adelaide Francis   38:608
Gray's Elegy   1:246, 248
Grazia Dledda, Winner of the Nobel Prize —
        Helen Rose Balfe   38:449
Grazyna — Adam Mieckiewicz   46: 3
Great Adventure, The — Gustav Davidson   51:195
Great American Poem, A — William Benjamin Smith   17A:124
Great Freeholder, The — Frantisek Adolf Subert —
        Translated by Beatrice M. Mekota   35:318
Great Moments in Great Acting — Arthur Row   29:358
Great Poets or Great Poems — W. H. Carruth   17B: 78
Great White Bird, The — Charles Vildrac —
        Translated by Sasha Best   25:228
Greater Courage in Ibsen's "Hedda", The —
        Anton Hellman   22:134
Greatest Stage Success in History, The —
        Roy Temple House   31:629
Greece — Jens Peter Jacobsen   30:474
Greece, Modern Folk Songs and Tales from Modern   9:253

111

Grecian Urn, The — Arthur N. Nethercot 33:142
Greek Impressions — Mariana Scott 58:332
Greek Literature, The Oedipus Myth in 11:102
Greek Way, The — Frederick Locke 47: 63
Green, Paul — *Art for God's Sake, The Secret Problems
 of a Little Theatre* 34:220
 — *End of the Row, The* 35: 58
 — *Hot Iron, The* 35: 48
 — *Old Wash Lucas* 35:254
 — *Prayer Meeting, The* 35:232
 — *Sam Tucker* 34:220
Green, Paula — *Christian Friedrich Hebbel* 25:123
Green, Paula, Translator — *Forest Warden, The* —
 Ludwig 24:129
 — *Maria Magdalena* — Hebbel 25: 81
Greene Entries — William Clarke Robinson 2:221
 — J. S. Stuart Glennie 2:341
Greene, Paul — *Lord's Will, The* 33:366
Greenslet, Ferris — *Propaganda for Poetry, A* 9: 41
Greenwood, Julia Wickham — *Woodlands, The* 27:342
Grendon, Felix —
 Some Misconceptions Concerning Shaw 20:376
Gresser, Seymour — *Simple Destiny, A* 58: 93
Gridlestone, E. D., Translator — *Norwegian Peasant
 Lad and His Dream Tune, The* — Björnson 5: 52
Grief — Serafin and Alvarez Quintero — Authorized
 Translation by Ana Lee Utt 41:391
Griffith, Alice Mary M. — *Whither* 35:140
Griffiths, L. M. — *Antonio's Revenge and Hamlet* 2:414
 — *Marston's Shakespearianisms* 2:289, 360
 — *Romeo and Rosaline* 1:205
 — *Shakespearian Qualities of "A Kingdom and
  No King"* 3:169
Grillo, Giacomo — *D'Annunzio's Prophetic Vision of
 America's Mission* 54:312
Gringoire — Theodore de Banville 27:129
Groff, Alice — *Evolution of Women in English Litera-
 ture, The* 10:242
 — *Ideals of Beauty in Keats and Browning* 5:247
 — *Paris Letter, A* 2:222
 — *True Greatness of Browning, The* 1:470
Grosse, Anna — *Progress* 58: 79
Group of Latin American Poems, A — Renée Tallantyre 54:184
Group of Latin American Poets, A — Edna Lue Furness 58:356
Group of Poems, A 17C:94; 17D: 87
Group of Poems, A — Charles Angoff 58:312
Group of Poems, A — Frank Ankenbrand, Jr. 43:186

Group of Poems, A — Joseph Bovshover   56:365
Group of Poems, A — Katherine Dimick   43:279
Group of Poems, A — Paul Verlaine —
    Translated by William Drake   33:458
Group of Poems, A — Stanton A. Coblentz   57:218
Group of Poems, A: Verse from the Italian —
    Translated by Louise W. Kidder   17A:133
Group of Poems, A — Vigliano Zullo   42:356
Group of Poems, A — Warren Heinrich   57:247
Group of Translations, A — Charles J. Guenther   51: 42
Growing Old Together — Colin C. Clements   31:176
Grown-Up Children — Mattie F. Simonds   36:434
Gruffydd, Gwynnedd — *Ever-Present Dream*   44:180
Grummann, Paul H. — *Gerhart Hauptmann's "Des Aüe*
    Heinrich"   16D:145
  — *Gerhart Hauptmann's Dramas*   21:285
  — *Gerhart Hauptmann's Treatment of Germanic*
    Myths   18: 89
  — *Gerhart Hauptmann's Viewpoint in "Und*
    Pippa Tanzt"   20:129
  — *Hauptmann's "Emanuel Quint"*   27:430
  — *Hauptmann's "Festspiel"*   26: 68
  — *Ibsen in His Maturity*   28:432, 609, 730; 29:229
  — *Modern European Dramatists:*
    I   *Gerhart Hauptmann*   22:117
    II *Herman Sudermann*   29:195
    III *Arthur Schnitzler*   23: 25
    IV *Max Halbe*   23:125
    V *August Strindberg*   24: 42
  — *Motivation of Wagner's "Parsifal"*   16C:123
  — *Pessimism of the Ring of the Nibelung, The*   26:258
  — *Recent German Criticism*   16B:117
  — *Suderman and Hauptmann and Their Latest*
    Plays: "Es Lebe das Leben" and "Der Rote
    Hahn"   14B:114
Grumman, Paul H., Translator — *"Longing"* — Dehmel   24:200
  — *"Many a Night"* — Dehmel   24:125
  — *Rosenhagens, The* — Halbe   21: 1
  — *Self Culture* — Dehmel   24: 58
  — *Twilight* — Rosmer   23:369
  — *Venus-Madonna* — Dehmel   24: 64
Guardian, The — Henri de Regnier   46:291
Guillermo Valencia, Colombia's Master Poet —
    A. Ortiz Vargas   41:419
Guiney, Louise Imogen — *Gentle George Farquhar*   6:406
Guiney, Louise Imogen — *In Present Day Poets* —
    The Editors   12:306

Guiney, Louise Imogen, Characteristics of the Work of   13:287
Gunderson, Gertrude B. — *Communion*   36:551
Gützkow, Karl — *Uriel Acosta*   7:6, 83, 140, 198, 263, 333
Guy Upstairs, The — Egbert H. Van Delden   40:251
Gyp — *Little Blue Guinea Hen, The* —
     Translated by Roy Temple House   30: 60

H. F. G. — *Oscar Wilde, Fifteen Years After*   27:411
H. Leivick, Poet and Playwright — Aaron Schmuller   53: 43
Haber, Tom Burns — *Housman's Poetic Ear*   54:257
Hafiz: Two Translations — Edna Worthley Underwood   21:467
Hafiz, The Modernism of — P.   7:516
Haight, Elizabeth Hazelton — *At Dawn*   27:405
     — *At Ravello*   26:111
     — *Bird Songs*   27:405
     — *Introducing Apulius*   26:694
     — *Masaevsis' "Hero and Leander", A Greek Sea
       Idyll*   20:449
     — *On Certain Uses of Apuleius' Story of Cupid
       and Psyche in English Literature*   26:744
     — *Roman Advocate of the Simple Life, A*   17A: 78
     — *Tennyson's Use of Homeric Material*   12:541
     — *What is Love*   14D: 66
Haiku, A — Gordon Lockhart   57:356
Halbe, Max — Paul H. Grummann   23:125
Halbe, Max — *Rosenhagens, The*   21: 1
Halek, Vetezslav — *Evening Songs*   27:716
Halevy, Ludovic — *During the Riot*   5:603
Haley, Albert W., Jr. — *Poems*   58: 94
     — Translator — *The Wanderer*   58:352
Half a Loaf — Peggy Kniskern James   44: 91
Hall, A. — *Welcombe Enclosures, The*   2:159
Hall, Amanda Benjamin — *White Water Man*   49: 3
Hall, Cathy — *Just You and I*   53:177
Hall, Clarissa — *Warning*   48:273
Hall, Gertrude —
     Legends of Saint Cariberte des Ois, The   14D: 1
Hall, Hazel — *Distance*   33: 57
     — *Things That Grow*   32:152
Hall, Kay De Bard — *Chinese Bazaar*   54:166
     — *Chinese Restaurant*   54:165
     — *Dragon Boat Festival*   54:163
     — *Festival for Spring*   54:162
     — *Festival of Flowers*   54:163
     — *Flying the Kites*   54:165
     — *Lyrics of China, Old and New*   54:162
     — *New Year's Festival*   54:162
     — *Unquiet Warriors, The*   53:111

Hallam, Arthur Henry, Letters of, on the Tennysons   8: 27
Halliwell-Phillipps, J. O. — Biography of   1: 64
  — Funeral and Will of   1:105
Halvosa, Gwen — Petals   58:370
  — Ready?   58:149
  — Starlings   58:145
Haman Rides High — Ellery H. Clark   54: 88
Hamblen, Emily S. — Kindliness as an Element of Faith;
  Illustrated in Literature   10: 85
  — Significance of Maeterlinck's "Blue Bird"   22:460
Hamilton, Horace E. — Poems   57:270
Hamilton, John Andrew — "The Pearl of Princesses"   44:240
Hamlet: A Greek   3: 38
Hamlet: A New Query — James M. Street   20:468
Hamlet and Antonio's Revenge — L. M. Griffiths   2:414
Hamlet and Don Quixote — Ivan Turgeniev —   4:169
  Translated by Josef Jiri Kral and Pavel Durdik
Hamlet and Ophelia (A Brief for Ophelia)   3:569
Hamlet as a Solar Myth   3:214
Hamlet at the Comédie Française — Charles Seymour   1:571
Hamlet, Bernhardt's   12:148
Hamlet, Browsings in — William Sloane Kennedy   9:376
Hamlet: Human Mystery in (The Library)   1:100
Hamlet in Greek   1:54, 151
Hamlet in Modern Dress — Dr. Max Huhner   37:254
Hamlet in Paris — Theodore Child   2:557
Hamlet: Moral Proportion and Fatalism —
  Ella Adams Moore   7:191
Hamlet Once More   3:615
Hamlet: Prize Questions   3:153
Hamlet, The Real, and the Hamlet Oldest of All —
  Alice Williams Brotherton   16D:110
Hamlet's Criticism, The Evolution of   15A: 87
Hammond, A. E. — Feet   51: 83
Hammond, Eleanor P. — Artistic Devices of Coleridge's
  "Ancient Mariner," The   10:425
  — Lear and His Daughters   24:110
Hands — Elizabeth Dutch   46:287
Hands — Warren Caryl   47:281
Handcart Expeditions, The — Edward Nehls   47:315
Hanger Back, The — Elizabeth F. Corbett   41: 91
Hanighen, Frank C. — Georges Duhamel: A Study   41:150
Hanna Jagert — Otto Erich Hartleben   24:369
Hanrahan, Agnes L. — Maureen   25: 59
  — Roses   25: 58
Hansen, Jean Crosse — To a Violinist   53:174
Hansson, Ola: Scandinavian Author   3: 37

115

Hapgood, Norman — *Philosophy and Poetry*   8:47

Happiness — Pauline Bridge Henderson   53:15

Happy Ending, The — Louise Maunsell Field   17A: 9

"Happy Land," Cynewulf — Anna Robertson Brown   2:52

Happy Prince, The — Oscar Wilde — Dramatized by
    Margaret F. Allen and Lou Wall Moore   27:40

Harbor Sounds — Nancy Andrews   57:37

Hardin, Charlotte Prentiss, Translator — *Hymn* —
    Charles Baudelaire   28:11

Hardin, Harold R. — *Fishers*   53:17

    — *I Shall Remember*   53:17

Hardt, Erich — *To a Crocus*   48: 4

Hardt, Ernst — *Tristram the Jester* — Adapted and Trans-
    lated by John Heard   Part I 43:229; Part II 43:28

Hardy, Irene — *Browning's "Childe Roland"; A Literary
    Parallel and Something More*   24: 5

Harnack, Otto — *Goethe's Relations to Russian Writers*   2:57

Harned, Mary — *Early Women Poets of America*   5:33

    — *Fireflies, A Little Reverie*   8:37

    — *Glance at German Literature, A*   9:28

Harned, Mary, Translator — *And Pippa Dances* —
    Hauptmann   18:28

    — *Creditor, The* — Strindberg   22: 8

    — *Debit and Credit* — Strindberg   17C: 28

    — *Elga* — Hauptmann   17A:

    — *Ephraim's Breite* — Hauptmann   12:46

    — *John Herkner* — Rosmer   22:32

    — *Morituri: Teias* — Sudermann   9:33

    — *On Probation* — Dreyer   14B: 4

    — *Outcast, The* — Strindberg   17: 6

    — *Shakespeare in Japan* — Hausknecht   1:46

    — *Simoon* — Strindberg   17C: 2

    — *Sunken Bell, The* — Hauptmann   10:16

Harned, Mary, Translator, with W. H. Harned —
    Johannes — Sudermann   11:16

Harned, W. H., Translator, with Mary Harned —
    Johannes — Sudermann   11:16

Harold — Ernst von Wildenbruch —
    Translated by Otto Heller and Hugh A. Clarke   3:39

Harper, Charles Hugh Richardson — *God's Nod*   53:16

Harris, Clement A. — *Bee in Shakespeare, The*   43:32

Harris, Edna M. — *Windblown*   38:42

Harris, G. Edward — *Comedy of Death, A*   36: 6

Harris, Hazel Harper — *When a Man Wanders*   40:60

Harris, Lillian — *Marriage is so Difficult*   38:45

    — *Publicity*   38:59

Harris, May — *As to Differences*   30:42

— *As to Foreign Criticism* 33:138
— *Gossip and Gossipers* 33:291
Harris, Rose Madeline — *Twilight Lullaby* 50: 76
Harris, Rosemary — *Raindrops* 52:155
Harris, W. T. — *Emerson's "Brahma" and the Bhaga-*
    vad Gita 1:253
— *Goethe's "World Spirit" and the "Vishnu" of*
    the Bhagavad Gita 1:401
Harrison, Margaret H., Translator —
    Feast of the Kings in Paraguay 55:274
— *Inca Highway, The* 55:273
Harry — Jesse Lee Bennett 27:591
Harsen, Una W. — *Four Quatrains for November* 47:273
— *Literary Legacy* 53:172
— *Two Poems* 48:265
Hart, Charles R. — *Intimations of Immortality* 47: 39
Hart, Katherine — *Such Sarcenet Security* 3:113
Harte, Walter Blackburn — *Eclipse of Seriousness, in*
    Contemporary Literature, The 9: 36
— *Favorites of Fortune, The* 8:377
— *Irony of Progress, The* 8:113
Hartleben, Otto Erich — *Hanna Jagert* 24:369
Hartley, Roland English — *All Things Considered* 42:165
— *Course of True Love, The* 55:163
— *Hour at Noon, An* 42:176
— *Other Side of the Door, The* 41:223
— *Portrait of the Artist's Wife* 48:121
— *Two One-Act Plays* 42:165
— *What's Right* 43:169
Hartman, Herbert — *Distances* 39:731
Hartmann, C. Sadakichi —
    Modern Scandinavian Authors 3: 33
— *Recent Italian Writers* 2:595
Hartmann, C. Sadakichi, Translator — *Faded Leaves* —
    Kielland 3:311
— *For Green is Hope* — Kielland 3:315
Harvest Refrain — Emory E. Petho 51:155
Hastings, Alison — *L'Envoi* 29:330
Hatfield, Ellen Lown — *Her Bit of the Desert* 50:268
Hatfield, Myrtle Margaret, Translator —
    Favorable Moment, The — Verlaine 56:194
Hathaway Club — Mary A. Ashmead 1:326
Hatto the Hermit: A Legend — Selma Lagerlöf 11:348
Haughton, John Alan — *Chopin Opus 27, No. 2* 37:292
Haunting Road, The — Edith C. Bates 28:482
Haunts of Paul Scarron, The — Katherine Stanley-Brown 35:569
Hauptmann, Carl — *Ephraim's Breite* 12:465

117

Hauptmann, Gerhart — *And Pippa Dances*   18:289
  — *As an Aeolian Harp*   26:402
  — *Assumption of Hannele, The*   20:161
  — *Before the Dawn*   20:241
  — *Elga*   7A: 1
  — *Poet, The*   27:103
  — *Reconciliation, The*   21:337
  — *Sunken Bell, The*   10:161
Hauptmann, Gerhart — Paul H. Grummann   22:117
Hauptmann, Gerhart, and Shakespeare —
    J. H. Beckmann   23: 56
Hauptmann, Gerhart, and the Nietzschean Philosophy —
    Anton Hellmann   24:341
Hauptmann, Gerhart, Bulthaupt's Interpretation of —
    Paul H. Grummann   16B:117
Hauptmann, Sudermann, and Their Latest Plays —
    Paul H. Grummann   14B:114
Hauptmann's "Der Arme Heinrich" —
    Paul H. Grummann   16D:145
Hauptmann's Dramas — Paul H. Grummann   21:285
Hauptmann's "Emanuel Quint" — Paul H. Grummann   27:430
Hauptmann's Treatment of Germanic Myths —
    Paul H. Grummann   18: 89
Hauptmann's Viewpoints in "Und Pippa Tanzt" —
    — Paul H. Grummann   20:129
Hausknecht, Emil — *Shakespeare in Japan*   1:466
Hausman, Jay, Translator — *Few Donkeys, A*   49:360
  — *Jean de Noarrieli*   50:362
  — *Poems*   46:185
  — *Poems*   50: 68
  — *Shadow of a Woman, The*   55: 3
  — *Two Poems*   50:264
Hawaiian Pantheon — Beatrice Ayer Patton   47:177
Hawks, Josephine — *On Past the Bars*   46:283
Hawthorne on Delia Bacon   3:592
Hawthorne's "Marble Faun," Readings from —
    Charlotte Porter and Helen A. Clarke   13:433
Hayes, Bridget T. — *Winter Bloom*   30:385
Hayward, Ira N. —
    Strindberg's Influence on Eugene O'Neill   39:596
Hazard, Lucy Lockwood — *Dante in the Drama Class*   33:228
Hazlitt, William: Man and Critic — Charles A. Madison   40:373
He Did the Murder in a Dozen Words —
    Frederick Day Goodwin   36:577
He Died the Second Time — Ai Ch'ing   53:119
He is Coming — Alvilde Prydz —
    Translated by Hester Coddington   25:230

He is Something — John Williams Andrews 58:258
He Lives — A. Holdas 52:117
He Who Visions — Rainer Maria Rilke —
    Translated by Jessie Lemont 34:157
Heal, Edith — *Into the Everywhere* 38:466
Heard, John — *Four Legends of Brittany* 43: 99
    — *Further Comment, A* 48:227
    — *Hrotsvitha, the Nun of Gandersheim* 42:291
    — *Louise Labé, La Belle Cordière de Lyons* 42:151
    — *Marriage of Tristram, The* 48: 72
    — *White Wolves, The* 47:368
    — *Whom God Hath Joined* 44:232
Heard, John, Jr. —
    Jokai: The Father of Hungarian Literature 3:135
Heard, John, Rephraser — *Divine Trust* 47: 2
Heard, John, Translator — *Abraham* — Hrotsvitha 42:299
    — *Crusts* — Claudel 50:195
    — *Death and the Fool* — von Hoffmannsthal 45: 5
    — *Gallicanus* — Hrotsvitha 42:314
    — *Hostage, The* — Claudel 50:100
    — *Humiliation of the Father, The* — Claudel 50:291
    — *In the City* 47: 99
    — *Lilith* 51:298
    — *Our Lady of Past Empires* 51: 48
    — *Peace at Home* — *at Any Price* 47:195
    — *Prayer, A* — Francis Jammes 42:265
    — *Prayers* — Francis Jammes 44:363
    — *Selected Poems of Louise Labé* 42:160
    — *Tristram the Jester* — Ernst Hardt — Part I 43:229
    Part II 43:289
    — *You Can't Live Just as You Please* —
    Ostrovsky 49:203
Hearn, Lafcadio, The English of —
    Charles Woodward Hutson 16A: 53
Heart of Hjalmar — Leconte de Lisle 54:252
Hearth, Fire, The — Charlotte Porter 20:155
Heaven's Blue — Victor Rydberg 27:356
Heavenly Drinker, The — Alfred Mombert 26:396
Hebbel, Christian Friedrich — *Agnes Bernauer* 20: 1
    — *Judith* 25:257
    — *Maria Magdalena* 25: 81
Hebbel, Christian Friedrich 25:123
Hecate in Macbeth — Mary E. Cardwill 10:532
Hecate: Is It Shakespeare's? — W. J. Rolfe 11:602
Hedberg, Tor — *Borga Gard* —
    Translated by Helga Colquist 32:317
    — *John Ulfstjerna* —
    Translated by Helga Colquist 32: 1

Heedless — Jennie M. Palen   53:17
Heiberg, Gunnar — *Balcony, The* — Translated by
    Edwin Johan Vickner and Glenn Hughes   33:47
Heiby, Walter — *Tall Jew, The*   46:36
Height, Joseph Stuart, Translator — *Fifteen Poems*   55:33
Heights — A. Goetze — Translated by Sasha Best   25:
Heijermans, Herman — *Links* —
    Translated by Howard Peacey and W. R. Brandt   38:
Heil Hitler! — Harriet Rukenbrod   47:37
Hein, Lucille E., Translator — *Poems by Arno Holz*   48: 9
Hein, Lucille M., Translator — *From the Sanskrit*   44:12
Heine, Heinrich — *Dame Care*   55: 1
Heine, Heinrich, A Letter From — Nathan Rosenbaum   58:18
Helen — Kenneth Mélançon-Dubuys   58:31
Hellems, F. B. R. — *Epigram and Its Greatest Master* —
    Martial, The   16D: 6
    — *Some Recent Poetry and the Emotionalizing
    of Evolution*   20:11
Heller, Otto — *Ernst Possant as Shylock*   1:57
    — *German Poetry and Criticism*   2:26
Heller, Otto, Translator — *Harold* — Von Wildenbruch   3:39
Heller, Samuel — *Lesbian*   36:20
Hellings, Emma Lightner — *Evolution of Religion as
    Suggested in Browning's Poems*   17B:11
    — *Rossetti's Treatment of Love*   16A: 7
Hellman, Anton —
    Greater Courage in Ibsen's "Hedda," The   22:134
    — *Hauptmann and the Nietzschean Philosophy*   24:341
Hello — Edmond Rostand —
    Translated by Mrs. Richard Mansfield   32:155
Heloise to Abelard — Marian C. Stanley   20:156
Heloise to Abelard — Clyde Robertson   36:158
Hemenway, Daniel — *Two Haiku*   57:495
Hemple, George — *"Aroint Thee, Witch, Aroint Thee"*   13:425
Hendee, Russell W. — *Old Song, An*   38:296
Henderson, C. Harford —
    Browning's "Hervé Riel" and "The Patriot"   3:110
Henderson, Pauline Bridge — *Happiness*   53:156
Henley, William Ernest, The Innovator: An Estimate
    — Milton Bronner   15D: 74
Hennique, Leon — *Death of the Duc d'Enghien, The*   20:401
Hennrich, Warren — *Group of Poems, A*   57:247
"Henry IV," — *Apostrophe to Sleep in* —
    Charles W. Hodell   13:309
    — *Prolegomena to*   1:367
    — *Study Program* —
    Charlotte Porter and Helen A. Clarke   11:94, 283

"Henry VIII" — *Study Program* —
    Charlotte Porter and Helen A. Clarke   14D: 95
Henry James, The Difficulties of — J. H. Lewis   39:117
Henry, Thomas Millard — *First Black World Poet, The*   40:303
Her Bit of the Desert — Ellen Lown Hatfield   50:268
Herder — *As Shadows on the Waves*   53: 59
Here Below — P. E. Bosi —
    Translated by Louise W. Kidder   17A:133
Here's to the Little Gentleman in Black Velvet —
    Marita Du Val   16A: 56
Heredia, José-Maria de — *Antony and Cleopatra*   52: 68
    — *Enamel* — Translated by Cammie H. Lamy   34:293
    — *La Belle Viole* —
    Translated by Cammie H. Lamy   34:282
Herman, Bernice, Translator — *Dobromila Rettig* —
    Alois Jirasek   31:475
Hermann Hesse — Felix Anselm   53:353
Hermes, Marion Dorothy — *Courage*   50: 33
    — *Woman's Way, A*   47:288
Herodiade — Mallarmé —
    Translated by Joseph Twadell Shipley   32:458
Herrick, Gertrude — *Full of the Moon, The*   31:379
Herrick, Raymond Morse — *Colophon*   32:250
    — *Elévation*   29:639
Herrick, Robert   19:337
Herron, E. K. — *Dream of a Tourney, A*   11:476
    — *Limitations*   11:477
    — *Music*   19:110
    — *Sleep*   11:478
Herron, E. K., Translator — *Anacreontics* —
    Jacopo Vittorelli   27:709
    — *Gleaner of Sapri, The* — Luigi Mercantini   27:712
Hertel, François — *Poems*   53:130
Hertzberg, M. J. — *Translations from the Greek Songs*
    from Plato and Ptolemaeus   19:438
Hervieu, Paul — *In Chains* —
    Translated by Ysador Asckenasy   20: 81
Hervieu, Paul — Dramas of, The —
    James Platt White   14C:79; 15A: 77
Hesse, Hermann — *He Walked in Darkness*   53:147
Hesse, Hermann — Felix Anselm   53:353
Hester, William — *Sea-Trove*   48: 91
Hewlett and Hearn: Two Types of Orientalists —
    Eugenie M. Fryer   18:478
Hexameter, English — H. W. Boyd Mackay   23:139
Heydrick, Benjamin A.
    Echoes and Growth in Rudyard Kipling   14A: 84
    — *Shakespeare Quotes Spenser*   3:102

Heyse, Paul — *On the Death of a Child*   26:279

Hidden Memory — Helen Douglas Thomas   58: 93

Hidden Spring, The — Roberto Bracco —
    Translated by Dirce St. Cyr   18:143

Hidden Word, The — Anne Throop Craig   28:248

Hiers, Mildred Douthitt —
    Buddhism and Some Buddhist Poetry   33: 9?

Higbee, Alma Robison — *I Love These Things*   45:114
    — *My Love Came Riding*   52:171
    — *Rogue's Treasure*   51: 6?

Higgins, John Lee — *To the Poet*   38:472

Higginson, Thomas Wentworth —
    "Childe Roland to the Dark Tower Came"   13:263

Higginson's "Cheerful Yesterday" — P.   10:440

Higginson's "Contemporaries" — Helen Tracy Porter   12:311

High Tide — Lilian Saunders   36:630

Hilarion — Josephine Howell-Carter   26:374

Hilbert, Jaroslav — *Whom the Gods Destroy*   27:361

Hildreth, Earl W. — *Other Blind Man of Jericho, The*   37:512

Hill, The — Herbert Edward Mierow   52: ?

Hills, The — William Pennance Church   37:255

Hilligenlei — Warren Washburn Florer   18:377

Hilton, Charles — *Broken Pines*   42:270

Himmell, Sophie — *Autumnal Dusk*   48:267
    — *Joy*   49: 49
    — *Poems*   46:255
    — *To an Air Cadet*   50: 2
    — *Two Poems*   47:382

Himwich, Alfred — *Stéphane Mallarmé*   35:621

Hinchman, Walter S. — *"Flammantia Moenia Mundi"*   17B: 86

Hindoo Legend, A — Henrik Sienkiewicz —
    Translated by Aline Delano   15B: 48

Hindu Poetess Sarojini Naidu, The New —
    Milton Bronner   20: 61

Hinton, Mary Boole — *Sonnet on the Petrarchan*   14A:152

Hippocrates Dying — N. G. Flokos   58:328

Hirschbein, Peretz — Charles A. Madison   38:106

Hirschfeld, Georg — *Second Life, The* —
    Translated by Mary L. Stephenson   39:475

His Mother in the Home of the Beloved Disciple —
    Lucy A. K. Adee   55: 79

His Son — Tracy D. Mygatt   39:605

Historical Allusions in "Strafford" — P. A. C.   1:280, 332, 372
                                       426, 511, 562

History of the Holy War: A Selection from the —
    Ambroise   50:259

History, Shakespeare's Fidelity to — Talcott Williams   13: 91

122

Iobo's Song of Praise, The — Richard Dehmel 55:347
Iobson, Dorothy — *Let There Be Light* 49:135
Iodell, Charles W. — *Apostrophe to Sleep in "Henry IV"* 13:309
 — *Shakespeare's Clownery* 17D:113
 — *Shakespeare's Opening Scenes as Striking the
  Keynote of Dramatic Action and Motive* 6:169, 337, 452
 — *Three Christmases in "In Memoriam," The* 11:451
Iodgson, Ralph — See *Merlin's Flight* 56:263
Ioernecke, Alma Ellis, Translator — *Autumn Picture* 52:352
 — *Christina's Journey Home* 28:129
Ioffmannsthal, Hugo von — *Death* —
  Translated by C. N. Stork 29:245
 — *Death and the Fool* 24:253
  Translated by John Heard 45: 5
 — *Idyl* 52:141
 — *The Two* 23:444
 — *Venice Preserved* 26:529
 — *White Fan, The* 54:120
Ioffmannsthal, Hugo von, Neo-Romanticist —
  Elizabeth Walter 26:644
Iolbrook, Mary Sibyl, Translator —
  Sunday on Sunday Goes By — Henri Lavédan 27:185
Iolbrook, Sibyl Collar, Translator —
  Five Little Dramas — Lavédan 28:385
 — *Lavédan's Little Dramas* 28:414
Ioldas, A. — *He Lives* 52:117
Iolden, Marcia Nichols — *Fishing at Dawn* 51:368
Iollander, Lee M. — *Björnstjerne Björnson's Last
  Drama, "When the New Wine Blooms"* 22: 70
 — *Indridi Einarsson: Icelandic Dramatist and
  His Saga Drama* 23:284
Iollander, Lee M., Translator — *"Robert Herrick"* —
  Nielsen 19:337
 — *Souls Exchanged* 52:195, 291
 — *Sword and Crozier* — Einarsson 23:225
 — *When the New Wine Blooms* — Björnson 22: 1
Iollcroft, Temple — *Conservative's Creed* 47:377
Iollis, Barbara — *Changeling, The* 35:568
 — *Regeneration* 35:209
 — *Sunset* 33:141
Iolmes, Oliver Wendell, Dream Craft of 8:233
Iolmes, Oliver Wendell: Life and Letters — P. 8:608
Iolmes, Sarah Elizabeth, Translator — *Hanna Jagert* —
  Hartleben 24:369
Ioly Day Prayers — Charlotte Porter 17B:117
"Holy Grail," The Symbolism of the — Eugene Parsons 16B: 86

123

Holy Night — Richard Dehmel   55:349

"Holy Rood," Cynewulf — Anna Robertson Brown   2:371

Holy War, A Selection from the History of the —
Ambroise   50:259

Holz, Arno, and Walt Whitman — Amelia von Ende   16B: 61

Holz, Arno — *Poems*   48: 92

    — *Poems* — Translated by Nesta M. Thompson   34:154

    — *Song, The*   27:231

Home — Grace Shoup   41:369

Home as the Root of All Evil — Arthur William Row   35:623

Home of Love — Miriam H. Krarup   45:219

Homer, The Troy Myth After —
William Cranston Lawton   8: 14

Homeric Material, Tennyson's Use of —
Elizabeth Hazelton Haight   12:541

Homunculus, What Was the? A Faust Problem   13:269

Honor Cross, The — M. E. Lee   27:702

Hood, Tom — W. J. Rolfe   8:535

Hood, Tom, Dream Craft of — Lewis Worthington Smith   8:233

Hooker, Emily G. —
George Meredith on the Source of Destiny   12:238

Hooley, Teresa — *In a Wild Garden*   31:308

    — *Inheritance*   32:617

    — *Rain in Poetry*   30:412

    — *Stars of Poetry*   34:445

Hope, Edythe — *Who is There to Say*   55:230

Hopkins, Edwin, Translator — *Night's Lodging, A* —
Gorki   16D: 1

    — *Smug Citizen, The* — Gorki   17D: 1

Hopkins, P. T. — *On a Popular Poet*   32:581

Hopkins, Percie Trowbridge — *On Female Poets*   30:588

Hopkins, Ruth E. — *First Star, The*   35:532

Horace — *Epode XI* — Translated by Thomas Ewing, Jr.   21:415

    — *To His Wine Jug* —
Translated by Thomas Ewing, Jr.   21:487

Horace's *Odes I:5* — Translated by Thomas Ewing, Jr.   22:222

    — *II:16* — Translated by Thomas Ewing, Jr.   22:145

    — *IV:7* — Translated by Thomas Ewing, Jr.   23: 80

    — *Satire I, IX* —
Translated by Thomas Ewing, Jr.   21:149

Horatio as a Friend — Henry P. Goddard   7:203

Hornbrooke, Francis B. — *"Mr. Sludge, the Medium"*   7:240

    — *Some of the Teachings of "The Ring and the
Book"*   1:314

    — *What Should Be the Poet's Attitude Towards
His Critics?*   5:135

Horniman, A. E. F. — *Manchester Players, The*   25:210

Horniman's, Miss, Players — Homer H. Howard   23:292
Horse Inoue, The — Wilhelm von Scholz   58:150
Horses of Paradise — Helene Magaret   40:452
Hosokawa, Lady — Kido Okomoto —
    Translated by Asatoro Miyameri   37: 1
Hospital, To a — Maxine Prockter   50:186
Hostage, The — Paul Claudel   50:100
Hosting of the Sidhe — Edward J. O'Brien   26:399
Hot Iron, The — Paul Green   35: 48
Hotel Room — Marguerite Walbridge Truslow   56:146
Hour at Noon, An — Roland English Hartley   42:176
Hour Before Dawn, The — Gordon Lockhart   58: 88
Hour, The — Cleon Marquis   57:493
House, Boyce — Mesquite, The   43:360
"House of the Wolfings" — F. S. Ellis   1:583
House, Roy Temple —
    Greatest Stage Success in History, The   31:629
    — Life and Poetry of Richard Dehmel, The   38:264
    — Richard Hovey: His Work   12:608
House, Roy Temple, Translator — Bayadère, The —
    Tagore   25: 61
    — Cristina's Journey Home —
    Hugo von Hofmannsthal   28:129
    — Fidelity — Mendes   18:413
    — Legend from the Talmud, A — Salus   24:348
    — Little Blue Guinea-Hen, The — Gyp   30: 60
    — Man of the World, A — Von Ebner-Eschenbach   22:128
    — Reconciliation, The — Hauptmann   21:337
    — Tears — Mendes   21: 95
    — Two Husbands — Lavédan   19:207
House, Roy Temple, Translator, with J. Vital DePorte —
    Nymph, The — Gorki   24:368
    — With Stephen Scatori — Zaragüeta — Miguel
    Ramos Carrion and Vital Aza   33: 1
Housekeeping — John Nixon, Jr.   57:139
Housman in America — Cyril Clemens   49:266
Housman: Some Unpublished Letters —
    Cyril Clemens   53:255
Housman's Poetic Ear — Tom Burns Faber   54:257
Hovey, Richard — Impressions of Maurice Maeterlinck
    and the Théatre d l'Oeuvre   7:446
    — In Present Day Poets   12:306
    — Letters from   12:620
    — Promise and Work   12:436
    — Spring (an Ode)   10: 1
    — Taliesin   8:1, 63, 292
    — Verses On   12:464

Hovey, Richard, Translator, with F. S. Jones —
   Uriel Acosta — Gützkow   7:6, 83, 140, 198, 263, 33:
Hovey's Poems, Ethical Message of, in Dramas —
   Amelie von Ende   20: 6§
How My Lord, El Cid, Defied the Pope —
   George H. Daugherty, Jr.   54:17§
Howard, Homer Hildreth — *American Drama Society*   23:15§
   — *Bijou, The* (Boston)   23:29(
   — *Child in the House, The*   24:43§
   — *Drama League of America, The*   23:14§
   — *Horniman's, Miss, Players*   23:29§
   — *Little Theatre* (New York)   23:29§
   — *Playfarer, The*   23:145, 29(
   — *Sumurûn*   23:29§
   — *Toy Theatre, The*   23:14§
Howard, L. — *Where Shakespeare Critics Disagree*   5:14§
Howe's, Julia Ward, Reminiscences —
   Helen Tracy Porter   12:31§
Howell, Corrie Crandall — *Forfeit, The*   36:13(
Howell-Carter, Josephine — *Hilarion*   26:374
Howell's Philosophy and "The Son of Royal Langbrith"   16C:144
Hrbek, Cyril Jeffrey, Translator — *Ninth Night, The* —
   Victor Dyk   29: 9(
Hrbkova, Sarka B., Translator — *Jan Vyrava* —
   Frantisek Adolf Subert   26:28§
Hrotsvitha — *Abraham* — Translated by John Heard   42:29§
   — *Gallicanus*   42:314
Hrotsvitha, the Nun of Gandersheim — John Heard   42:29§
Hsieh, Wan Ying, Translator — *Chinese Sappho, A*   41:132
Hsing, C. C. —
   Marvellous Romance of Wen Chun-Chin, The   35:29§
Hudson, Ruby — *Little Song, A*   44: 9§
Hudson, William Henry —
   Early Mutilators of Shakespeare   4:36(
   — *Love Drama of the Tenth Century, A*   3:48§
Hueffer, Ford Madox — Lawrence M. Price   31:43§
Huger, R. D. — *Rust of Unused Powers, The*   26:27§
Hughes, Dorothy Berry — *Salisbury Cathedral*   55:247
Hughes, Glenn, Translator, with Edwin Johan Vickner —
   Balcony, The — Gunnar Heiberg   33:47§
Huglins, Ida, Translator — *Wanderer's Song*   51: 7§
Hugo, Victor — *A Quoi Bon Entendre* —
   Translated by Beatrix M. Riedel   42:19(
   — *Djinns, The*   22:14(
   — *Ecstasy* —
      Translated by Dorothy Wheless Anderson   45:22(
Hugo, Victor, Talent of, The   1: 9§
Hugo's Letters — C.   9:14§

Hugunin, Henry M. —
    How Shakespeare Illustrates Bacon   4 :200
Huhner, Dr. Max — *Hamlet in Modern Dress*   37 :254
    — *New Aspect of Shakespeare's Conception of*
        Woman, A   32: 98
Huidobro, Vicente — *Mill, The*   58: 76
    — *Relativity of Spring*   58: 87
Hujas, The Meditations of   19 :469
Hull, William D., II, Translator — *Ode in Miniature*   45 :349
    — *Odelette*   45 :348
Hulli, Ora Mary — *For the Return*   51 :272
Hülshoff, Annette von Droste — *The Pool*   27 :229
Human Ecstasy — E. Pedio —
    Translated by Louise W. Kidder   17A :133
Humiliation of the Father — Paul Claudel   50 :291
Humilis, Art of, The — Maurice Saint Chamarand   25 :572
    — *Study of J. G. N. Called*   25 :576
Humilis — *Body and Soul*   25 :594
    — *Four Poems*   25 :593
    — *Hands, The*   25 :593
    — *Invocation*   25 :499
    — *Love of Love*   25 :600
    — *Predestined Couples*   25 :597
Humor: Carlyle and Browning — Jessie M. Anderson   2 :421
Humpty Dumpty — Marjorie Freeman Campbell   51 :118
Humpty Dumpty, A Fantasy — Bertram Bloch   32: 76
Hung, Shen — *Wedded Husband, The*   32 :110
Hunt, Leigh — *Estimate of His Poetry*   1 :308
Hunter, Frederic — *Deus Benignus et Natura*   25 :497
Huntingdon, Harriet L. — *Tuley Francis: Note*   8 :375
    — *Wisdom of Nichette, The*   16A: 28
Hunton, Charles Hugh —
    Shakespeare's Compliment to Brantôme   4 :449
Hurd, Harry Elmore — *For Whom Does the Poet Write?*   47 :252
Hurll, Estelle M. — *Study of Poetry from the Standpoint*
    of Aesthetics, The   6 :546
Hushed Strain, The — Robert Iphys Everett   15A: 39
Husks — Carrie Wood Lyon   56 :236
Hutchins, Hazel — *Variations on an Old Theme*   41 :455
Hutchins, Will — *Jeanne D'Arc at Vancouleurs*   21: 97
Hutson, Charles Woodward —
    English of Lafcadio Hearn, The   16A: 53
Huysmans, Trappist and Litterateur — Virgil Geddes   33 :521
Hyde, Douglas — *Marriage, The*   20 :135
    — *Twisting of the Rope, The*   16A: 12
Hyde, Florence E. —
    Decadence of American Culture — Why?   23: 64
Hyer, Helen von Kolnitz — *Andrew Jackson Refuses*   37 :623

Hymn — Baudelaire   28:118
Hymn of Saint Benoit — Paul Claudel   53: 70
Hymn to the Winged Niké — Florence Kiper   18:402

I Am a Realist — Gilean Douglas   47:257
I Am Not Alone — Gabriela Mistral   57:381
"I Am Seeking" — Jules Romains —
     Translated by Sasha Best   24:350
I Bore a Son — Donna Nichols   53: 69
I Climbed a Pinnacle — Noel Jordan   51:352
I Could Have Gone — Hazel Griffith Davis   53: 59
I Did but Jest — Godfrey P. Schmidt, Jr.   35:130
I Go on Tour with the Miracle — Arthur William Row   38:291
I Have No House for Love to Shelter Him —
     Willa Cather   16B: 50
I Hung My Heart to the Wind —
     Albert Edmund Trombly   29:109
I Love These Things — Alma Robison Higbee   45:114
I Puritani — A. Palacio Valdés   16D: 97
I Said When First I Saw You — Gustav Davidson   28:621
I Shall Forgive — Helen A. Mulhall   38:607
I Shall Never See — Leland M. Burroughs   53:161
I Shall Remember — Harold R. Hardin   53:173
I Sing of a Maiden — Old English   9: 31
I Sing of New Orleans — Leslie Collins   46:353
I Travel on the Broad Highway — Ina Duval Singleton   30:472
I Tried to Make a Violin — Lancaster Burling   41:457
I Want to Hide — Freda Lillian Presser   51:255
I Want to Hide — Freda Lillian Presser   53: 75
"I Will Not Have it So" — Harriet Plimpton   46:213
I Wonder (From the German) —
     Louise Chandler Moulton   9:367
Iago and Othello, The Characters of —
     Katherine G. Blake   18:236
Iago's Conscience — A. M. Spence   5:194
Ibarbourou, Juana de —
     Selections from "Cantaro Fresco"   56:148
     — Two Poems   58:286
Ibsen, Henrik — *"Abydos," a Fragment*   20:192
Ibsen, Henrik — *Early Architectural Schemes* —
     Translated by Philip H. Wicksteed   3:656
Ibsen, Henrik — *On the Highlands* —
     Translated by Hjalmar Edgren   13:335
Ibsen, Henrik — Owen Wister   2:338
*Ibsen, Henrik, and the Ethical Drama of the Nineteenth
     Century* — Helena Knorr   10: 49
Ibsen, Henrik, New Letters of —
     Translated by Arne Kildal and Louïs J. Bailey   19:420

bsen in His Maturity — Paul H. Grummann   28:432, 609, 730;
                                                          29:229
bsen's "Börkman" —
    Charlotte Porter and Helen A. Clarke   11:102
bsen's "Brand," An Interpretation —
    Jane Dransfield Stone   17C: 60
bsen's "Doll's House" in Cairo   4:528
bsen's "Doll's House" in London   1:378, 528
bsen's "Doll's House" in St. Petersburg   4:528
bsen's Dramas — Otto Heller   1:337
bsen's "Ghosts" in Milan   4:286
bsen's "Ghosts," The Art and Moral of   6:356
bsen's Hedda, The Greater Courage in —
    Anton Hellmann   22:134
bsen's Influence Upon German Literature —
    F. G. G. Schmidt   17A:112
bsen's "Little Eyolf" — P.   7: 99
bsen's "Masterbuilder" in New York — Helena Knorr   12: 95
bsen's Nora and Shakespeare's Katharine —
    Ella Crowell   8:192
bsen's "Peer Gynt"   4:592
bsen's "When We Dead Awaken" —
    Tollet B. Thompson   20:201
carus — Robert Iphys Everett   15D: 71
ce Dragon and the Sun God, The — Isabel Moore   19: 87
celand, Newer Literature of, The —
    Vilhjalmur Stefansson   15A: 62
celand, Present Day Literature of —
    Vilhjalmur Stefansson   15B:126
ci-Bas — Sully-Prudhomme   53:171
dea of God in "The Sun," The — Daniel G. Brinton 3:254
deas of the Soul in English and Scottish Popular
    Ballads — Lowry Charles Wimberly   36:542
deal of Feminine Beauty at the Time of Ronsard, The —
    Marcel Françon   46:157
deals and Danger of the Dawning Century   13:150
diot, The — Cesare Lodovici   30:317
dyl — Hugo von Hoffmansthal   52:141
dyl of Israel Known as the Song of Solomon —
    Ruby Archer   18: 97
dyll — Martinez Sierra —
    Translated by Charlotte M. Lorenz   37: 63
dyll of a Northern River, The —
    Archibald MacMechan   6:299
Idylls of the King" — Study Program —
    William Channing Gannett   13:588
ère — Richard Butler Glaenzer   28:458

If I Knew — Cheryl Mason   53:158

If Life Were a Dance on Roses — T. Christian Thomsen   53:231

If Once, Just Once — Louise Chandler Moulton   15B: 18

If She Had Been — Kathryn Evans McKay   56:377

If We Forget — Harriet Garrett   53:165

Image — Gladys Merrifield   55:243

Imagery of d'Annunzio, The — Frank Crane   26:488

Imagery, The Use of — Clara Edmunds-Hemingway   50: 34

Imagery, Walt Whitman's — Lorena M. Gary   52:360

Imaginary Patteran — Hildegarde Walls Johnson   49:277

Imitation d'une Ode d'Anacreon —
Bernard de la Monnoye   51: 76

Immortal, The — Carl Glick and Bernard Sobel   32:441

Immortality — Sara Perry   57:494

Immortality as a Motive in Poetry —
Francis Howard Williams   9:367

Immortelle — George J. Cox   49:100

Immune — Nora Archibald Smith   37:473

Impetuous Angel, An —Emma F. Sahler   14A: 46

Impregnation — Alwyn Coristine   53:140

Imprint — Bess Foster Smith   56:181

"In a Balcony" — Alice Kent Robertson   2:310

In a Cafeteria — Mabel Campbell   37:550

In a Deserted Garden — Joy Kime Benton   33:316

In a Far Country — Olga Achtenhagen   43:361

"In a Gondola"   8:272

In a Large City — Detlev von Liliencron   26:117

In a Wild Garden — Teresa Hooley   31:308

In All Fairness — A. S. Johanneson   44: 91

In an Orient Barge — Charles Van Lerberghe —
Translated by Joseph T. Shipley   36:627

In Asolo — Lucy S. Conant   18:247

In Brittany — Paul Scott Mowrer   28:483

In Chains — Paul Hervieu —
Translated by Ysidor Asckenasy   20: 81

In Delos — *In the Drifting Isle* —
Mildred McNeal Sweeney   21:240

In Excelsis — Leconte de Lisle   28:478

In Garrison (Leave of Absence) — C. E. Freybe   26:499

In God's Hand — Anthero de Quental   29:627

In His Honor — Nina Willis Walter   50:360

In Memoriam: A. H. Ware   35:575

"In Memoriam" and Other Tennysonia — W. J. Rolfe   8: 90

In Memoriam: Charlotte E. Porter   48: 2

"In Memoriam:" Notes on   7:428

In Memoriam: Shelley, 1792-1892 — George W. Alger   4:315

"In Memoriam:" Study Programs   5:574;13:284

"In Memoriam," The Christmases of   13:151
"In Memoriam," The Three Christmases in —
    Charles W. Hodell   11:451
n Memoriam to Anne Simon   27:660
n Muscovy — Edith M. Thomas   16D: 65
n Praise of Solitude — Edmundo Baez   55:130
n Praise of the Morn — Miriam Solomon   53:307
n Present Day Poets — Thomas Bailey Aldrich —
    The Editors   12:306
n Re Caliban — Oscar Lovell Triggs   17D: 76
n Switzerland — Juluisg Sowacki —
    Translated by Vladyslaus Jarzemski   24: 59
n the Bazaar — Julia Hall Bartholomew   29:631
n the Beginning Was the Word —
    Margaret Janvrin Adams   55: 20
n the City — Semen Yushkevich   47: 99
n the Garden — Esther Matson   35:114
n the Garden — Louis Bartlett Chace   53:177
n the Heart of a Tree — Sydney Barlow Brown   40:442
n the Hunger after the Perfect — Helen Gilbert   36:294
n the Manner of "The Quair" — Harrison S. Morris   1:545
n the Shadow of the Statues — Georges Duhamel —
    Translated by Sasha Best   25:371
n the Soft Air — Leconte de Lisle   27:700
n the Tents of the Shepherd Prince —
    Nellie Burget Miller   53:232
n the Workshop — Lewis Worthington Smith   24:365
n This Belated Twilight — Comtesse de Noailles   45:226
n This Light — Gilean Douglas   46: 96
n Viis — Robert P. Tristram Coffin   34:152
n What Alembic — Nina Willis Walter   58:331
nadvertant Romance, M. Pigeonneau's —
    Anatole France   11: 28
narticulate — Helen Genevieve Jefferson   53:368
ncident, An — Leonid Andreyev   27:171
nca Highway, The — Juan Draghi Lucero de Mendoza   55:273
nca Literature — Abraham Arias-Laretta   55: 21
ndian Myths, The Artistic Possibilities of —
    Arthur Farwell   15A: 46
ndian Names — Edith Colby Banfield   15A: 61
ndian Summer — Josephine Henry Whitehouse   39:455
ndian's Last Dream, The — Cecil Cobb Wesley   55:176
ndo-China — Louis A. Shaw II   56:276
n 'ependence — Esther Marion Alger   41:140
nfidelity? — Doryll Winter   47: 72
nfinite, The — Giacomo Leopardi   47:370
ngraham, Charles A. — Literary Cookery   35:471

Inheritance — Teresa Hooley 32:61'
Initiation — Frances Beveridge Sydnor 55:26
Inscription on a Stone at Corinth —
    Edith E. King-Fisher 54: 7
Inscription on a Spring — Wilhelm von Scholz 58: 8
Inn by the River Road, The — Mabel Edna Brown 57:26
Innocence — J. Patrick Byrne 49:30'
Interference — Maryon Langbell 48: 6'
Institutionalized — Helene Mullins 58:11'
Interlude — Janet Preston 36: 7'
Interlude — M. E. Grenander 49: 2'
Interpolated — A One-Act Play of King Tut's Time 35: 7'
"Intimations of Immortality" 8:45'
Intimations of Immortality — Charles R. Hart 47: 3'
Into the Everywhere — Edith Heal 38:46'
Into the Known-Unknown — Lorena M. Gary 45: 4'
Into the Tents of Men — M. G. Jacobs 58:33'
Introducing Apuleius — Elizabeth Hazelton Haight 26:69'
Invention, A Night Song of 4:52'
Inventory — Joseph Upper 37:47'
Invitation — René Char 57:48'
Invocation — "Humilis" 25:49'
Irish Literary Drama — Vida D. Scudder 16A: 4'
Irish Literary Theatre, The — Irene Dwen Andrews 39: 9'
Irish Players in Philadelphia, The — C. P. 23:15'
Iron Crags of Death, The — Madison Cawein 26:77'
Iron Hive, The — George Turpin 25:61'
Irony of Progress, The — Walter Blackburn Harte 8:11'
Irving's, Henry, Macbeth — A. G. L. 1: 4'
Irving, Maria — *Enchanted Wood, The* 30:12'
    — *Sleeping Beauty, The* 30:56'
Is Work Your God? — Leland M. Burroughs 53:17'
Isaak Loeb Peretz — Charles A. Madison 37: 7'
Isadora Duncan, Priestess — Shaemus O'Sheel 21:48'
Isola, Pietro Gabrele —
    Current Italian Literature — Fagazzaro 18:13'
    — *d'Annunzio* 18:48'
    — *d'Annunzio's Dramas* 19:111, 21'
Israel, The Idyl of — Ruby Archer 18: 9'
"It," a Love Story — Selma Lagerlöf 11:32'
It is Cold Tonight — Frédéric Bataille 28:11'
It is Going to Snow — Francis Jammes 51:29'
It is Not in Vain I Have Been Seeking —
    Jules Romains — Translated by Sasha Best 24:35'
Italian Art, Study Program —
    Charlotte Porter and Helen A. Clarke 13:42'
Italian Landscape, An — Gabriele d'Annunzio 16C:11'

Italian Literature, Current, Fogazzara — Pietro Isola   18:133
Italian Poetry and Pascoli —
    Gertrude E. T. Slaughter   18:501
Italian Writers — C. Sadakichi Hartmann   2:595
Itinerary and Litany for Oradour — Bertrand d'Astorg   55: 18
Ivory Tower, The —
    Elizabeth Macintire and Colin Clements   30:127
Ixion — Helen Archibald Clarke   37:454
"Ixion," A Study of — George Dimmick Latimer   4:243
"Ixion," An Interpretation of Browning's —
    Helen A. Clarke   5:626

Jack's Later Beanstalk — Albert Edmund Trombly   29:638
Jackman, Edward F. — Faith   29:485
Jackson, Esther — "Such a Commonplace Man"   7:210
Jacobi, Elizabeth — Parable and a Prophecy, A   34:458
Jacobs, M. G. — Into the Tents of Men   58:336
Jacobsen, Jens Peter — Arabesque, An   31:467
    — Around My Portrait —
    Translated by Jeannette Kiekintveld   30:411
    — Greece — Translated by Jeannette Kiekintveld   30:474
    — Hour of Meeting Strikes, The —
    Translated by Jeannette Kiekintveld   30:309
    — My Thoughts Name You —
    Translated by Jeannette Kiekintveld   30:376
    — Nameless   31:363
    — Where the Low Borderland Rises   31:615
Jagendorf, Moritz A., Translator — Gallant Cassian:
    A Puppet Play, by A. Schnitzler   33:507
James I of Scotland, King — Divine Trust   47: 2
James, Henry, Artist — Anne Blanche McGill   16D: 90
James, Henry, The Difficulties of — J. H. Lewis   39:117
James, Peggy Kniskern — Half a Loaf   44: 91
James R. Garnett, "Elene" — Anna R. Brown   1:577
Jameson, Edward A. — Juxtaposition   55: 73
Jammes, Francis — Federico Olivero   34:177
Jammes, Francis — Few Donkeys, A   49:360
    — It is Going to Snow   51:290
    — Jean de Noarrieli   50:362
    — Poems   46:185
    — Poems   50: 68
    — Prayer, A — Translated by John Heard   42:265
    — Prayers — Translated by John Heard   44:363
    — Two Poems   50:264
Jan Vyrava — Frantisek Adolf Subert   26:281
Janssen, Helen Carson — Requiem   55: 98
Januarie," A Song from Spenser with Music —
    Helen A. Clarke   Frontispiece 4

133

January Thaw — Leslie Dae Lindon .... 51:16!

Japan, Popular Songs of — Yone Noguchi .... 15B: 7?

Japanese Garden, A — Adachi Kinnosuki .... 10:32]

Japanese Hokku Poems — Yone Noguchi .... 29:10?

Japanese Poetry — Elizabeth Balch   14C:91; 14D:83; 16B: 9·

Japanese Print, To a — Mary Colby Thresher .... 24:41?

Japanese Theme, Variations on a — Bell Thurnbull ...... 34:41(

Japanese Women in Literature — Yone Noguchi .... 15C: 8?

Jarzembski, Vladyslaus, Translator — In Switzerland —
    Sowacki .... 24: 5?

Jasmine and the Poet — Charmion Von Wiegand .... 37:41?

Jastrow, Morris, Jr. — Arabic Version of Macbeth's
    "Moving Wood" .... 2:24'
    — Magic and Prodigy in the East .... 4:11?
    — "Mr. Sludge" and Modern Spiritualism .... 3: 7?
    — On Browning's Poems .... 2:28?

Jealousy — Gustavo Adolfo Becquer .... 45:32(

Jean D'Arc at Vaucouleurs — Will Hutchins .... 21: 9'

Jean de Noarrieli — Francis Jammes .... 50:36?

Jean-Desthieux, F. — Nicolas Beauduin .... 25:32?

Jefferson, Helen Genevieve — Inarticulate .... 53:36?

Jelliffe, Ella K. — "A Garden is a Lovesome Thing" ...... 40:11?
    — Lamb and Hogarth 39:41
    — Random Recollections of Brothers in Fiction ...... 41: 5(
    — Some Husbands and Wives of Fiction .... 41:40?
    — Some Storied Parents 40: 8
    — Letters in English Fiction .... 41:51'
    — Priests and Prayers in Literature 41:26

Jenney, F. G. —
    The Comic in German Folk-Christmas Plays .... 27:68(

"Jenny" — Extracts from a Hitherto Unpublished Ver-
    sion of the Poem 7:

Jephthah's Daughter — Mildred C. Wood .... 48:14'

Jerusalem — Mary Brent Whiteside 36:47

Jessop, Alexander —
    The Poetry of Robert Louis Stevenson 18:39

Jessamine Shakespeare Society, The —
    Josephine Mann 1:32

Jesuit, The — José de Alençar 30:47

Jesus Stripped — Paul Claudel 58: 9

Jew and the Star Moon — Charlotte F. Myers 54:35

Jew of Constance, The — Wilhelm von Scholtz 57:38

Jews of Browning and Shakespeare 1: 5

Jimenez, Juan Ramon — Perfumed Thorns —
    Translated by Herbert King Stone 32:37
    — Weariness from Suffering —
    Translated by Herbert King Stone 32:43

134

Jimmie — Lucy A. K. Adee 53:279
Jirásek, Alois — *Dobromila Rettig* 31:475
— *The Lantern* — Translated by Zdenka Ruben
and George Rapall Noyes 36:317
Johan Sigurjonsson — Jacobina Johnson 46:147
Johannes 11:161
Johanneson, A. S. — *In All Fairness* 44: 91
Johansson, Albert Edward — *Villon's Last Rondeau* 53: 81
John Boyle O'Reilly, Neglected New England Poet —
Cyril Clemens 54:361
John Herkner — Elsa Porges Bernstein (Ernst Rosmer)
— Translated by Mary Harned 22:321
John Masefield's First Reading — Lawrence Stuckey 38:312
John Muir, Prophet, Naturalist — L. E. Pearson 36: 45
John Ulfstjerna — Tor Hedberg —
Translated by Helga Colquist 32: 1
Johnson, A. E. — *The Pond* 44:251
Johnson, Arthur Franklin — *Ode on the Heights* 15D: 95
— *Poetry of Louise Chandler Moulton* 19:473
Johnson, Charles F. —
Peculiarity of Shakespeare's Phrasing, A 7:527
Johnson, Geoffrey — *Dalliance* 52:272
Johnson, Hildegarde Walls — *Imaginary Patteran* 49:277
— *Scarlet Slippers, The* 49:179
Johnson, Jakobina — *Johan Sigurjonsson* 46:147
Johnson, Jakobina, Translator — *Governor Lenhard* —
Einar H. Kvaran 43: 3
— *Loft's Wish* 46: 99
Johnson, Lionel — Edward J. O'Brien 26:405
Johnson, Siddie Joe — *Solitude* 40:390
Johnston, Charles — *Yeats in the Making* 17B:102
Jokaï, The Father of Hungarian Literature —
John Heard, Jr. 3:135
Jon Norstog, The Bookmaker — Inge M. Bredeson 30:112
Jonaitis, Demie —
Lithuanian Folk Song — *The Daina, The* 47:322
Jonaitis, Demie, Translator — *Lithuanian Folk Songs* 47:329
Jones, Cullen — *Abnormal Poets and Abnormal Poetry* 56:228
Jones, Francois Stewart, Translator (with Richard
Hovey) — *Uriel Acosta* 7:6, 83, 140, 198, 263, 333
Jones, Henry — *Browning as a Dramatic Poet* 6: 13
— *Browning as a Philosophical and Religious
Teacher* 8:265
Jones, Ruth Lambert — *Lacrimae Rerum* 42:185
— *Letter, The* 30:147
— *Our Trust* 30: 80
— *Paradox* 30:552

135

Jones, Dr. Thomas S. — *Piper, The*   15C: 7
Jones, Willis K. — *Poetry in Chile*   32:40
Jones, Willis Knapp — *America's First Epic*   48:25
  — *Claudio de Alas: Poet of Gloom*   35:45
  — *Fernan Silva Valdes*   47:35
  — *Gaston Figueira: Poet of America*   47: 6
  — *Leon Felipe: Spanish War Poet*   47:26
  — *Mermaid Tavern in Fact and Fiction, The*   36:44
  — *Miller of Ancos, The*   58: 6
  — *Spiced Wine*   36: 8
Jones, Willis Knapp, Translator —, *Adam and Eve* —
  Antonio Porras   41:
  — *Auto de Los Reyes Magos*   39:30
  — *Bullies, The* — Javier de Burgos   43:33
  — *City, The*   54: 7
  — *Columbine Wants Flowers* — Zorilla   55:14
  — *Dagger of the Goth* — José Zorilla   40:42
  — *Don Juan's Women*   46: 4
  — *Moonlight Sonata*   51:35
  — *Olives, The* — Lope de Ruida   39:31
  — *Papa and Mamma* — Eduardo Barrios   33:28
  — *Rural Justice of the Peace, A*   54: 9
  — *Test, The* — Pierre Chamblain de Marivaux   35:53
  — *Tragic Song, The*   50:
  — *With Chains of Gold* — José Andres Vazques   34:41
  — *You Can't Fool with Love*   49:10
Jonson, Ben, Swinburne's Study — Mary Lloyd   2:32
Jordan, Charlotte Brewster — *Dante's Divine Comedy:*
  Its Moslem Sources and Parallels   32:37
Jordan, Noel — *I Climbed a Pinnacle*   51:35
  — *Logistics*   51:15
Jorge Guillen — Eleanor L. Turnbull   48:15
Jorgensen — *The Last Day*   13:48
José de Espronceda — *A Song of Spain* —
  O. Frederica Dabney   7:54
José Echegaray — Nora Archibald Smith   20:21
Joseph Rodman Drake: Keats' "Twin Spirit" —
  Helen J. McCormack   38:53
Journalism in Comparison with Other Literary Work —
  Nathan Haskell Dole   14C: 1
Journey of Childe Roland — R. J. Gratz   2:57
Journey, The — Joseph Upper   36:46
Journey to Bikini — Frank James Singer   53:21
Joy — Sophie Himmell   49: 4
Joy Element of Browning, The — Mary Phelps   15B: 9
Joy of Poetry, The — C. H. Williamson   43:13
Joyzelle — Maurice Maeterlinck —
  Translated by Clarence Stratton   16B:

136

Juana de Ibarbourou — Edna Lue Furness   54:242
Jubilee, The — Anton Chekhov   31:616
Judas, The Saving of — Hannah Parker Kimball   9:161
Judea — Louis J. Block   9:474
Judith — Friedrich Hebbel —
      Translated by Carl Van Doren   25:257
Judkins, Esther — Lost Lilacs   53:290
Julie — August Strindberg —
      Translated by Arthur Swan   22:161
Juliet's Runaway Once More — Edmund C. Stedman   4: 14
Julio Herre Y Reissig — Thomas Walsh   33:601
"Julius Caesar" and "Strafford" — Kate L. Gallagher   2:214;
                                                       4:148
"Julius Caesar" Contrasted with "Strafford"   5:518
"Julius Caesar," Falling Sickness in, The —
      C. Alphonso Smith   6:469
"Julius Caesar" of Shakespeare and of History, The —
      Joseph C. Allen   13:560
"Julius Caesar," Shakespeare's — W. J. Rolfe   5:169, 424
"Julius Caesar," Shakespeare's, Is [Ite] Ignoble? —
      Annie Russell Wall   4:191
"Julius Caesar," Shakespeare's, Is [He] Ignoble? —
      in   11:276
"Julius Caesar:" Study Program —
      Charlotte Porter and Helen A. Clarke   10:564
"Julius Caesar," Supernatural in — Annie Russell Wall 5:620
June Landscape — Elihu T. Feinberg   57:113
Jungle Saga — Leslie Collins   52:127
Just One, The — Modern Greek Folk Tale   9:363
Just You and I — Cathy Hall   53:177
Justice — Herbert Spencer   2:344
Juxtaposition — Edward A. Jameson   55: 73

Kaathoven, Alice Van, Translator —
      Beat of the Wing, The — De Curel   20:321
Kadison, Alexander — Ovid as a Short Story Writer in
      the Light of Modern Technique   29:206
Kafka, Andrew — Prayer Meeting   56:176
Kahn, Gustave — "From the Nomad Palaces"   16D: 78
      — Rising Moon, The —
      Translated by William A. Drake   34:444
Kahn, Hannah — Two Poems   47:190
Kahn, Sholem J., Translator — Baruch of Mayence   54:139
Kahns, Oscar —
      Literary Influence of Medieval Zoology, The   11: 73
Kaiser, Georg — From Morn to Midnight   31:317
Kalidasa's Masterpiece — P.   8: 35

137

Kanawa: A Japanese Classical Drama —
    Translated by T. Ochiai   23:222
Kaplan, De Witte — *Madonna and the Scarecrow, The*   34:254
Kaplan, Ysabel 'De Witte —
    Princess Weaver of the Skies, The   32:267
Karen — Alexander Kielland —
    Translated by Thyge Sógàrd   4:385
Karpova, Susan — *My School Days in Old Russia*   38:551
    — *Story of the Russian Theatre, The*   38: 77
Katouc, Otto, Translator — *On Golgotha* — J. S. Machar   28:485
Kaucher, Dorothy — *Bos'n*   36:585
    — *My Father* — *An American*   57:486
Kaufman, Kenneth C., Translator — *Quitting Business*
    Mariano José de Larra   35:159
Kauffmann, Stanley — *Aubade*   46: 98
    — *Daniel White*   44:136
    — *Matthew Beloved*   44: 48
Kayden, Eugene M., Translator — *King Hunger* —
    Andreyev   22:401
    — *Mothers* — Nikolai A. Nekrassov   26:278
    — *Song of Tzar Ivan Vasiljevich: His Young*
        Lifeguardsman, and the Valiant Merchant,
        Kalashnikov — Lermontov   24:278
Kayrd, Silne — *Gift, The*   40:109
    — *Retrospect*   41:123
Keats, American Brother of the Poet, The —
    Felix J. Koch   17C: 97
Keats and Browning: Ideals of Beauty — Alice Groff   5:247
Keats, Boyhood of, The — Agnes Lee   18:122
Keats, Color Element in "Eve of St. Agnes," The —
    M. S. Anderson   8: 84
Keats, Grave of, The — J. Homer Caskey   35:622
Keats: "Lamia" Contrasted with Coleridge's "Christa-
    bel" — Charlotte Porter   6: 32
Keats: Sense Epithets — Mary Grace Caldwell   10:573
Keats' Treatment of Nature — Edward Payson Morton 12: 58
Kedrov, V. — *Mad Dog, The*   58: 55
Keegan, Celia — *Evening Memory*   46:191
    — *Legend from the Arabic*   47:176
    — *Summer Twilight*   49:146
    — *Three Poems*   48:254
Keene, Frances, Translator —
    America and Her Intellectuals   45:210
    — *Rude Awakening*   45:231
Keikentveld, Jeannette, Translator — *Arabesque, An*   31:467
    — *Nameless*   31:363
    — *Where the Low Borderland Rises*   31:615

138

Keller, Carl T. — *Miguel de Cervantes*   44:265
Keller, Gottfried —
     Little Meret: Green Coat Henry's Story   17C: 50
     — *Village Romeo and Juliet, A*   9:498
Kemble, Fanny — *Poem to Shakespeare*   10:630
Kendall, Jean — *Atlantic, The*   49:320
Kendall, Joshua —
     Theocritus: Father of Pastoral Poetry   7:307
Kendall, Kathyra — *Two Poems*   44:183
Kennedy, William Sloan — *Browsings in "Hamlet"*   9:376
     — *Browsings in Shakespeare*   15C: 70
     — *Browsings in "The Tempest"*   9:577
     — *Clews to Emerson's Mystic Verse*   11:243; 12:71, 270
     — *Friendship of Whitman and Emerson, The*   7: 71
     — *Note*   10:451
     — *Renan's "Caliban"*   12:145
     — *Shakespeare's Astronomy*   13:366
     — *Tennyson and Other Debtors to Spenser's*
     "Fairie Queene"   10:492
     — *Tennyson Biography, The*   10:114
     — *To the Rose-Breasted Grosbeak*   12:346
Kent, Charles W. — *A Note or So on Tennyson*   9:629
Kent, Marion — *Midsummer*   52:194
     — *Question*   52:174
Kenyon, James Benjamin — *Sketch of Life*   14C:123
Kerley, Rosialee — *Wedding Guest, The*   33:232
Kester, Katharine — *Rondo Capriccioso*   37:458
Ketchum, Arthur — *Maid's Prologue, The*   25:206
     — *Song Before Twilight, A*   25:612
Ketrick, Paul J. — *Arabian Night*   40:316
Khuri, Professor A. E. —
     Arabic Poetry Before and After Islam   36:200
Kiddall, Arne (with Louis J. Bailey), Translator —
     New Letters of Henrik Ibsen   19:420
Kidder, Louis Winslow, Translator —
     Dithyramb — d'Annunzio   14C: 40
     — *Group of Verse from the Italian*   17A:133
Kiekintveld, Jeannette, Translator —
     Around My Portrait — Jens Peter Jacobsen   30:411
     — *Greece* — Jens Peter Jacobsen   30:474
     — *Hour of Meeting Strikes, The* —
     Jens Peter Jacobsen   30:309
     — *My Thoughts Name You* —
     Jens Peter Jacobsen   30:376
Kielland, Alexander — *Faded Leaves*   3:311
     — *For Green is Hope*   3:315
     — *Karen*   4:385

139

Kielland, Alexander — Scandinavian Author   3: 35
Kilbourne, Frederick W. —
  Some Curious Versions of Shakespeare   16C:132
  — Stage Versions of Shakespeare before 1800   15B:116
                15D:111
Kimball, Hannah Parker — After the Storm   9:477
  — Aspiration   13:533
  — Beauty Lovers   17C: 68
  — Consummation   7:453
  — In Present Day Poets   13:533
  — Kind Gray Day, The   11:356
  — Merlin Revivified and the Hermit   12:537
  — Reaction   10:336
  — Saving of Judas, The   9:161
  — Song of the Workers   13:535
  — They Dreamed   13:535
  — Under the Open Sky   9:475
Kimball, Helen Joy — Strange Harmonies   37:314
Kimberly, Robert — Pastoral   49:176
Kind Gray Day, The — Hannah Parker Kimball   11:356
Kind Policeman, The — Anne Murray Larned   28: 54
Kinder, Elizabeth — Need   55:162
Kindliness, as an Element of Faith —
  Emily S. Hamblen   10: 85
"King and No King" (Beaumont and Fletcher): Shakes-
  pearian Qualities of — L. M. Griffiths   3:169
King Coustans, The Tale of —
  William Morris, from the French   11:465
King David's Harp — Robert P. Tristram Coffin   34:471
King, Ethel — Calendar of Poets, The   51: 59
King, Harold — Modern Epic, The   40:407
King Hunger — Andreyev   22:401
King, John Charles —
  Shakespeare at the Paris Exposition   1:560
"King John" — Moral Proportion and Fatalism in
  Shakespeare's — Ella Adams Moore   8:139
"King John": Philosophical Note on — L. W. Elder   22:314
"King John": Study Program — P. A. C.   8:218
King, Julius B. — Spring Offensive   49: 77
King, L. A. — Shakespeare at the Paris Salon   2:554
"King Lear" at the Court Theatre in Munich   1:376
"King Lear": Study Program — P. A. C.   16B:127
King Lear's Wife — August Strindberg —
  Translated by Arthur Helgé Swan   24:108
King Philip IV — Manuel Machado   30:615
"King Robert of Sicily," Antecedents of Longfellow's —
  Hjalmer Edgren   14B:127

ing, the Greatest Alcalde, The —
Lope Felix De Vega Carpio   29:379
King Victor and King Charles" — P. A. C.   2:198
'ing Who Scoffed, The —
Oscar Williams and Jack Brnady   34:139
'ing's Choice, The —
Translated by Abraham Yarmolinsky   27:440
ing-Fisher, Edith E. — *Broken Vase, The*   51:268
— *Sonnets*   55:268
— *Three Poems*   53:157
— *Two Poems*   54: 70
ingdom of God — Ellery H. Clark   50: 26
ingsland, William G. — *Browning's Rarities*   6:264
— *Christmas Greeting, A*   12: 41
— *Clematis and Ivy: Unpublished Letters of
George Eliot*   6:1, 57, 182
— *Early Romances of Charlotte Brontë*   9:169, 479
— *Excerpts from a Sheaf of Browning's Letters*   4:233
— *Extracts from a Hitherto Unpublished Version of "Jenny"*   7: 1
— *"Forster's" Life of Strafford: Is It Forster's
or Browning's?*   6:555
— *Letters by Browning*   9: 83
— *Letters by Ruskin*   5:123; 8:410, 553
— *Literary Dilettantism*   6:512
— *Literary Treasures Unearthed*   8: 23
— *London Browning Union*   5: 53
— *London Letters*   1:389, 441, 491, 542, 589;
2:283, 386, 493, 609
— *London Literaria* 3:47, 154, 376, 649;
4:105, 524, 591, 643; 5:104, 534, 587, 644;
6:56, 167, 222, 374; 7:48, 469, 581;
8:466; 9:632; 10:149, 618
— *New Browning Letters from Mrs. Orr's Life*   3:522
— *Notes*   8:53, 109
— *Personal Recollections of Browning*   2:130
— *Poet's Politics, A*   7:473, 543
— *Rare Poems of Elizabeth B. Browning*   4: 46
— *Robert Browning as a Letter Writer*   8:78, 225
— *Robert Browning — The Man*   5:229
— *Ruskin as a Letter Writer*   6: 67
— *Ruskin: Unpublished Letter*   6:123
— *Ruskin as an Art Teacher*   5:405
— *Ruskin on "Gold": A Treasure Trove*   4:113
— *Ruskin on Wages: Unpublished Letters*   3:360
— *Ruskin's Letters to Chesneau*   7:123, 255, 349
— *Shelley and Godwin*   10:389

— *Shelley's Letters to Elizabeth Hitchener*   4:304
— *Unknown Poem of Mrs. Browning*   3:281
— *Unreported Speech by Ruskin*   8:222
Kingsley, Maude Elmer —
    Quaker Poet in Puritan New England, A   21:330
Kinney, Muriel — *My Friend, the Catbird*   28:376
— *My Soul and I*   26:774
— *Type, The*   28:373
Kinnosuki, Adache — *Japanese Garden, The*   10:321
Kinship of Blake, Vachel Lindsay, and D. H. Lawrence,
    The — Alice McGuffey Ruggles   46: 88
Kiper, Florence — *Hymn to the Winged Niké*   18:402
Kipling, Rudyard: Echoes and Growth in —
    Benjamin A. Heydrick   14A: 84
Kipling, Rudyard:" The Seven Seas an Atavism —P.   9:291
Kirby, Inez Barclay — *Two Poems*   50:361
— *Two Sonnets*   48: 71
Kirker, Katherine — *Lady Compassionate, The*   33:239
Klančar, Anthony —
    Dramatic Literature of Jugoslavia, The   48:305
— *Note on the Contemporary Catholic Theatre, A*   50:371
— *Survey of Yugoslav Literature, A*   50: 37
Klančar, Anthony J., Translator — *Napoleon's Samovar*   48:195
Klauber, Amy Josephine — *Exile, The*   33:246
Klein, Manfred, Translator — *Two Speeches* —
    Franz Werfel   45:334
Klenze, Camillo von — *Sigfrid Stories in the Nibelungen-*
— *Feud of the Schroffensteins, The*   27:457
Kleist, Heinrich von — Lawrence Marsden Price   27:577
Klenze, Camillo von, — *Sigfrid Stories in the Nibelungen*
    lied and Elsewhere, The   10:543
Klephtic Folk Songs of Modern Greece —
    Carrie C. Dulakis   53:222
Knape, Ernst Viktor — *On the Way*   45:351
Knapp, Juliet Lee — *Symbolistic Drama of Today*   32:201
Knister, Raymond — *Youth Goes West*   39:582
Knorr, Helena — *Athenaeum Press Series*   10:436
— *Henrik Ibsen and the Ethical Drama of the*
    Nineteenth Century   10: 49
— *Ibsen's "Masterbuilder" in New York*   12: 95
— *Introduction to American Literature, An*   10:587
— *Literary Studies*   11:435
— *"Morte d'Arthur"*   10:439
— *Pre-Shakespearean Drama*   10:436
— *Richard Hovey's Promise and Work*   12:436
— *Selections from Prose and Poetry of Walt*
    Whitman   10:586

142

Knowledge — Rainer Maria Rilke 30:466
Knowles, Frederic Lawrence — *Last Tryst, The* 15A: 1
— *Modern Poet, A* 14C: 63
— *Sketch of Life* 15A:134
Knowlton, E. C. — *Poetry of Dafydd Ab Gwilym* 36:415
Koch, Felix J. —
  American Brother of the Poet Keats, The 17C: 97
Koehler, Martha Peterson — *Return* 55: 82
Koenig, George A. — *Browning's Scientific Allusions* 2:137
Kokoscha, The Plays of Oskar — Barrett H. Clark 35:522
Komateekay — Alice Carter Cook 43:151
Korner, Sinclair — *"Hamlet" as a Solar Myth* 3:214
— *Shakespeare's Inheritance from the Four-
    teenth Century* 1:551; 2:410
— *Solar Myths in "Midsummer Night's Dream"* 3: 17
Korvin-Kroukovsky, Eugenia, Translator —
  Last Sacrifice, A — Alexander Ostrovsky 39:317
Kosor, Josip — *Passion's Furnace* 41:459
— *Woman, The* 41:317
Kotouc, Otto, Translator — *Evening Songs* —
  Viteslav Hálek 27:716
— *Songs of the Slave* — Svatopluk Cech 27:114
Kotzebue, August von — *Man Who Couldn't Talk* 40:223
— *Nightcap of the Prophet Elias* —
    Translated by Beatrice B. Beebe 40:391
— *Seven One-Act Dramas* —
    Translated by Beatrice B. Beebe 38:159
— *Turkish Ambassador, The* 38:192
Kral, Josef Jiri —
  Modern Bohemian Novelist: Jakub Arbes, A 4: 1
— *Shakespeare in Bohemia* 4:231
— *Under a Bush of Lilacs* 4:318
Kral, Josef Jiri, Translator —
  "Hamlet" and "Don Quixote" 4:169
— *Newton's Brain* 4:429, 511, 569, 616
Kramer, Aaron — *Four Poems* 58:287
Krarup, Miriam H. — *Home of Love* 45:219
Krarup, Miriam H., Translator — *On the Way* 45:351
Kresensky, Raymond — *Taps* 51: 81
Krishna to Nysoumba — Frances Fletcher 37:515
Krudy, Gyule — Joseph Remenyi 54:334
Krumpelmann, John T., Translator —
  Beloved Hedgerose, The — Andreas Gryphius 39:544
— *Broken Jug, The* — von Kleist 45:146
Kueffner, L. M., Translator —
  Seventh Solitude, The — Nietzsche 27:228
— *Song, The* — Arno Holz 27:231

143

— *To the Prince of Morocco* —
 Else Lasker Schueler   27:708
Kurlandzik, Schöne Charlotte, Translator —
 Bondswomen — Alexander Ostrovsky   36:475
Kvapil, Jaroslav — Sárka B. Hrbkova   27: 76
Kvapil, Jaroslav — *Clouds, The*   21:417
 — *Princess Pampelishka, The*   54: 3
 — *Will o' the Wisp, The*   27: 1
Kvaran, Einar H. — *Governor Lenhard* —
 Translated by Jakobina Johnson   43: 3

L'Anson, Caroline —
 To One Who Said He Cared Too Much   53:142
L'Envoi — Alison Hastings   29:330
L'Eroica — Cesare Lodovicis —
 Translated by Petronelle Sombart   34:159
La Chinita — Rafael M. Saavedra Y Bessey —
 Translated by Lilian Saunders   37:107
La Commedia Finita — William Cranston Morton   7:600
La Farge, David Linden — *Lilith, Mistress of Satan*   53:152
La Monte, Carolyn B. — *Brief Defense of Criticism, A*   6:332
La Pelée — Richard Butler Glaenzer   7:477
 — *Critical Work of Margaret Fuller, The*   28:456
La Pluie dans la Nuit — Sydney Barlow Brown   40:460
Labé, Louise, La Belle Cordière de Lyon — John Heard   42:151
Labé, Louise — *Selected Poems* —
 Translated by John Heard   42:160
*La Saisfiaz, The Real Significance of "The Brand
 Flamboyant"* — Charles Malloy   8:256
Labiche, Eugene — *Leghorn Hat,A*   28: 1
Labiche, Eugene, Vaudevillist Member of the Academy
 — Clair Vincent Chesley   28: 55
Laboratory Experiment in Poetry, A —
 Florence Mary Bennett   33:537
Laborer, The — Richard Dehmel   55:338
Lacrimae Rerum — Anthero de Quental   29:627
Lacrimae Rerum — Ruth Lambert Jones   42:185
Lady Hosokawa — Kido Okamato —
 Translated by Asatoro Miyameri   37: 1
Lady in the Library — Charlotte F. Myers   54:352
Lady of Gardineer, The — Henry Wadsworth Longfellow   48:176
Lady of Tripoli, The — Curtis Hidden Page   18:278
Lady of Wistfulness, Our — William Force Stead   29:373
Lady with the Dagger — Arthur Schnitzler —
 Translated by Helen Tracy Porter   15B: 1
Laforgue, Jules — *Another Complaint of Lord Pierrot* —
 Translated by William A. Drake   34:460

— *Our Little Helpmeet* —
Translated by Joseph T. Shipley   36:626
agerlöf, Selma — *Hatto, the Hermit*   11:348
— *"It" a Love Story*   11:321
aird, Caroll N. — *Revery*   49:176
ake, George G., Translator — *Cossack Prisoner, The* —
Mikhail Lermontov   34:158
— *Night* — Afanasiy Fiet   34:309
— *Unseasonable Song, An* — Nicolai Shtreiter   34:253
ake Morning — Belle Chapman Morrill   57:491
ake Winnepesaukee — Albert Edmund Trombly   29:357
amandé, André — *Attack, The*   33:474
— *Unknown Hero*   33:438
amb and Hogarth — Ella K. Jelliffe   39:411
amb, Charles, Dream Craft of —
Lewis Worthington Smith   8:233
amb, Charles, Literary Critic — Lu Emily Pearson   40:567
ambrith, David Kelley — *"Pippa Passes" on the Stage*   18:107
Lamia" in Contrast with "Christabel"   6: 32
ammas Eve — Edith Randolph   32:288
amp of Heaven, The — Leconte de Lisle —
Translated by C. L. Crittenton   20:158
ampman, Archibald, and the Sonnet —
Louis Untermeyer   20:432
amy, Cammie, H., Translator — *Attack, The* —
André Lamandé   33:474
— *Enamel* — José Maria de Heredia   34:293
— *Unknown Hero* — André Lamandé   33:438
— *Viole, La Belle* — José Maria de Heredia   34:282
ancaster, C. M., Translator —
Prologue to the Lays of Marie de France   54: 86
— *Three Poems*   54:270
ancaster, C. M., and Paul T. Manchester —
Conquistador's Song of Freedom, A   52: 49
ancaster, Charles Maxwell —
Breath of Feudal Romance, The   51:138
— *Dumas the Younger and French Dramatic
Forms Existing in 1850*   51:345
— *Freedom's Muscles*   50:290
ancaster, Charles Maxwell, Translator —
Arauco Tamed   49: 41
— *Selection from the History of the Holy War*   50:259
— *Tristan and Isolde*   49:301
— *Two Poems*   50: 74
andis, Esther L. — *"Pleasant Dreams"*   51: 58
ang, Erwin Paul — *Prayer, The*   41:453
angbell, Maryon — *Interference*   48: 60

145

Langtry's, Lillian, "As You Like It"   1:194
Language, The Music of — S. E. Bengough   4:562
Lanier, Sidney, Color and Motion in   12:558
   — *Last Words from*   19:482
   — *Poet of Sunrise, The*   15D: 89
   — *Singers of Sunrise*   9:407
Lansing, Ruth — *Robert Louis Stevenson's French Reading as Shown in His Correspondence*   29:218
Lansing, Ruth, Translator — *Madman or Saint* — Echegaray   23: 16
Lantern, The — Alois Jirasek — Translated by Zdenka Buben and George Rapall Noyes   36:317
Larger Realism, The — Hilda Ridley   24:353
Larissa, Capture of, and Trinova   9: 35
Lark in Legend and Song, The — Ida Prentice Whitcomb   15B: 81
Larmandie, Comte Leonce de — *Story of J. G. N., called "Humilis"*   25:576
Larned, Anna Murray — *Child Verses*   28: 54
Larra, Mariano José de — *Quitting Business* — Translated by Kenneth C. Kaufman   35:159
Lashley, Loraine — *Lighting Candles*   48:262
Last Crusade, The — Richard Butler Glaenzer   29:363
Last Day, The — Jorgensen   13:484
Last Encore, The — A. L. Mearkle   12:334
Last Farewell, The — Don José Rizal   26:393
Last Letters — Andrzej Strug   30: 36
Last Man In — Vera I. Arlett   41:410
Last Sacrifice, A — Alexander Ostrovsky — Translated by Eugena Korvin-Kroukovsky and George Rapall Noyes   39:317
Last Tenant — Winifred Adams Burr   55:373
Last Thought — Joseph W. Moorhead, Jr.   51:194
Last Tryst, The — Frederic Lawrence Knowles   15A: 1
Last Will and Testament — Robert Bernhard   50:261
Late Bird, The — Eleanor Stevens   54: 98
Later Thoughts on Shelley — J. C. Wright, F. R. S. L.   30:377
Latimer, George Dimmick — Study of Browning's "Ixion," A   4:243
Latest Tendencies in German Drama — Barrett H. Clark   26: 72
Lathe, Agnes M. — *Six Weeks with Chaucer*   3:630
Lavédan, Henri — *Afternoon Walk, The*   28:403
   — *Five Little Dramas*   28:385
   — *Along the Quays*   28:385
   — *Sunday on Sunday Goes By*   27:185
   — *Their Heart* — Translated by William V. Silverberg   30: 1

— *Two Husbands* 19:207
Lavédan's Little Dramas — Sibyl Collar Holbrook 28:414
Lawhead, H. D. — *Molière, Dramatist* 8:197
Lawhead, L. D. — *"All's Well That Ends Well"* 3:537
— *Was Falstaff Immoral?* 2:142
Lawrence, Edith — *On the Cliffs* 48:304
Lawrence, Jean Mitchell — *Fragments* 44: 47
Lawrence, Ida Eckert — *Sketch of Life* 15A:136
Lawson, L. — *"Lear"* 3:538
Lawton, William Cranston —
    Accretions to the Troy Myth After Homer 8: 14
    — *Commedia Finita, La* 7:600
    — *Environment of Literature in Ancient Rome,*
    The 7:113
Lay of the Honeysuckle — Marie de France 54:272
Lay of the War Ride of Igor —
    Translated by Alexander Petrunkevitch 30:289
Layman's Impression of "Pelléas and Mélisande" —
    Mary Evelyn Collar 23:158
Lazarus, Emma, Women, Poet, Patriot — Mary M. Cohen 5:320
Lazarus, The Resurrection of — Ivo Vojnovich —
    Translated by John J. Batistich and George
    Rapall Noyes 37:317
Le Blanc, Maurice — *She Who Waits* 16A: 36
Le Brez, Anatole — *Song of the Blowing Wind, The* 27:357
Le Cimetière Marin — Paul Valery —
    Translated by John F. Mathews 40:456
Le Gear, Laura Lourene — *Calves of Gold* 53: 75
    — *Flowering Althaea* 51: 82
    — *Flowering Althea* 53:153
    — *Lupine Dream* 52:362
Le Prade, Ruth — *When April Comes* 44: 80
Le Reveur — Joseph Upper 36:279
Leadership, Autocratic, Ubiquitous, Fraternal —
    Charles Fleischer 14B:133
Leaf from an Unopened Volume, A —
    William G. Kingsland 9:169
'Lear' 9:102
'Lear' and His Daughters — Eleanor P. Hammond 24:110
'Lear,' Moral Proportion and Fatalism —
    Ella Adams Moore 7:487
'Lear' Study Program — The Editors 10: 95
Leave of Absence — C. E. Freybe 26:499
Leaves from a Lesson Book — Althea Bass 43: 64
Leavitt, Charlotte M. —
    Odcombian Legge-Stretcher, The 34:210

147

Leconte de Lisle — *Birds of Prey*   17D: 89
— *Fall of the Stars, The*   17D: 88
— *Heart of Hjalmar, The*   28:479
— *In Excelsis*   28:478
— *In the Soft Air*   27:700
— *Lamp of Heaven, The*   20:158
— *Moonlight*   17D: 87
— *Noon*   24:332
— *Noon*   53: 58
— *Prairie, The*   19: 89
— *Red Star, The*   19:292
— *Secret of Life, The*   20: 80
— *Selections*   54:250
— *Tre Fila d'Oro*   53:172
Leconte de Lisle, For the Monument of — Pierre Louys   28:481
Lee, Agnes — *Boyhood of Keats, The*   18:122
Lee, Gabrielle — *Sonnet CXXVIII*   5:433
Lee, M. E. — *Honor Cross, The*   27:702
— *Taün, or The Black Death*   28:691
Lee, M. Hollander, Translator — "Renaissance" —
    Drachmann   19:369
Lee, Marion — *Mountain and Sea*   49:265
— *Poem*   49:265
Legacy, The — Arthur Schnitzler —
    Translated by Mary L. Stephanson   22:241
Legend from the Arabic — Celia Keegan   47:176
Legend from the Talmud, A — Hugo Salus —
    Adapted by Roy Temple House   24:348
Legend of Morris Gest, The — Arthur William Row   36:142
Legend of Sainte Cariberte des Ois, The —
    Gertrude Hall   14D: 1
Legend of Saint Nicholas, A — Beulah Marie Dix   25:473
Legends of the American Indian —
    Edna Wahlert McCourt   28:470
Leghorn Hat, A — Eugene Labiche and Marc Michel   28: 1
Lehman, Robert S. — *Edgar Hating*   48: 84
Lehner, Frederick — *Paul Claudel*   51:257
Leigh, A. B. — *At Versailles* — *In the Hall of Mirrors*   33:156
Leir, King, and Cordoille — Layamon's "Brut" —
    Translated by Anna Robertson Brown   4: 19
Leivick, H. — *Golem, The* —
    Translated by J. C. Augenlicht   39:159
Leivick, H., Poet and Playwright — Aaron Schmuller   53: 43
Lemaître, Jules — *Forgiveness*   24:209
Leman, The — Leonard Lanson Cline   28:105
Lemont, Jessie, Translator — *Between Daylight and
    Dream* — Rainer Maria Rilke   30:355

— *Blossoming* — Rainer Maria Rilke   30:445
— *Cloud* — Rainer Maria Rilke   30:468
— *From the Prayers of the Maidens to Mary* —
   Rainer Maria Rilke   30:207
— *He Who Visions* — Rainer Maria Rilke   34:157
— *Knowledge* — Rainer Maria Rilke   30:466
— *Miracle* — Rainer Maria Rilke   30:416
Lengyel, Cornel — *Ady: A Hungarian Genius*   48:238
— *Proem to a New Psalm*   49:202
— *World's My Village, The*   55:195
Leon Felipe, Spanish War Poet — Willis Knapp Jones   47:263
Leonard, Lucile Price — *De Quinceys Dream Fugue*   28:680
— *To the Pines*   25:215
Leopardi, Giacomo — *Calm After Tempest* —
   Translated by Hattie M. Finlay   42: 92
— *Infinite, The*   47:370
— *On the Portrait of a Beautiful Lady Carved*
   on Her Tombstone   57:366
Leopardi, Giacomo — Gamaliel Bradford, Jr.   5:385
Leopardi, Giacomo — William A. Drake   34:614
Leopardi — Robert Levin   47:370
Lermontov, Mikhail — *Cossack Prisoner, The* —
   Translated by George G. Lake   34:158
Lermontov, Mikhail Yowievich — *Song of Tzar Ivan*
   Vasiljevich — *His Young Life Guardsman and*
   the Valiant Merchant Kalashnikov   21:278
Les Fleurs — Stephane Mallarmé   26:228
Lessing's "Dramaturgie" — J. W. Thomas   5:593
Lesson — Sarah Trousdale   41:446
Let Me Forget — Hazel Griffith Davis   53:169
"Let Me Grow Lovely" — Anonymous   48:194
Let the Wind — Florence Kerr Brownell   49:365
Let There Be Light — Dorothy Hobson   49:135
Let Us Be Friends — Haras Rengaw   53: 48
Letter, The — Ruth Lambert Jones   30:147
Letter from an Athenian Physician to His Patient
   Telesilla, a Maiden of Argos, and Her Reply —
   John Albee   11: 20
Letter from Lovelace, A — Richard Butler Glaenzer   28:250
Letter from Heinrich Heine, A — Nathan Rosenbaum   58:185
Letters in English Fiction — Ella Kirk Jelliffe   41:517
Letters to a Young Musician — Joseph Upper   40:313
Letters to Sadie, The — Edward Broderick   12:347
Leuconoe, To — Horace —
   Translated by Helen Leah Reed   10:491
Levin, Robert — *Leopardi*   47:370

149

Levy, Lora S., Translator — *Dame Care* — Heine   55: 17

Lewis, Edward H. — *Metrical Changes in "A Mid-summer Night's Dream"*   9:110

Lewis, Edward T. — *Day Has Passed, The*   58:170
   — *Offering, An*   58:122

Lewis, J. H. — *Difficulties of Henry James, The*   39:117

Libby, Walter — *Evolution of Hamlet Criticism, The*   15A: 87
   — *Shakespeare's Final Philosophy*   24:421

Libraries of Shakespeare's Day   1:150

Life and Art, Poetry and Prose in — Oscar W. Firkins   15C: 77

Life and Deeds of Dada, The — William A. Drake   33:497

Life and Letters   14B:1; 14C:1; 14D:104; 15A:104; 15B:144
     15C:108; 15D:132; 16A:132; 16B:135; 16C:152; 17A:135
     17B:139; 17C:117; 17D:119; 18:140, 414, 533; 19:491
     20:239

Life and Poetry of Richard Dehmel, The —
   Roy Temple House   38:264

Life is a Dream — Colin C. Clements   31:204

Life, Modern, Relation of Modern Poetry to —
   Josephine Preston Peabody   14A: 56

Life of the Bee — Isabella Howe Fiske   14C: 59

Life Unanimous — Jules Romains —
   Translated by Sasha Best   24:112

Life's a Song — Mary Thro Rauth   50:182

Light Sleeper, A — Edith M. Thomas   9:478

Light, The — Georges Duhamel —
   Translated by Sasha Best   25:161

Lighting Candles — Loraine Lashley   48:262

Lilac and Bronze — Joseph Cherwinski   58:172

Liliencron, Detlev von — *From Childhood*   26:650
   — *In a Large City*   26:117
   — *Mill, The*   26:277
   — *Victory* — Translated by Edwin H. Zeydel   32:200

Lilith — Remy de Gourmont   51:298

Limitations   11:477

Lincoln Loquitur — Edgar Fawcett   11:528

Lind, L. R., Translator — *Autumn Twilight*   54:167
   — *Sleeper in the Valley, The*   54:167

Lindon, Leslie Doe — *January Thaw*   51:165

Lines for June — William W. Chance   55:353

Lines for the New Year — Louise Crenshaw Ray   40:141

Lines Sent With a Copy of the Rubaiyat —
   George Germond   16C:115

Lines Written During Texas-Louisiana Maneuvers, 1943 — Edward Nehls   50:269

Link, Seymour G. — *Tanka Sequence*   42:186
Links — Herman Heijermans —
    Translated by Howard Peacey and W. R. Brandt   38: 1
Linker, Robert White, Translator — *Generation
    d'Apresguerre: Bourne and Psichari, The* —
    Gilberto Freyre   41:433
    — *Going After Rubber* — José Verissimo   39:154
Linus — *Lament at the Gathering of the Vintage, A* —
    Edith M. Thomas   16C:130
Liptzin, Sol — *Young Vienna*   47:337
Lisboa, Rosalina Coelho, Crowned Poetess of Brazil,
    — Ignatius Phayse   40:110
List, Jacob I. — *When This War Is Over*   27:667
Listening — John Redhead Froome, Jr.   28:422
Litanies of Love, The — Curtis Hidden Page   18:195
Litanies of the Rose — Remy de Gourmont —
    Translated by George Williamson   33:469
Litchfield, Gertrude — *Prescience*   25:592
"Literary Boston of Today" — W. G. K.   14B: 13
Literary Cookery — Charles A. Ingraham   35:471
Literary Dilettantism — William G. Kingsland   6:512
Literary Essays, New Volumes of — C.   7:625
Literary History of America, A — Charlotte Porter   13:439
Literary Impulse of Modern Greece —
    Aristides E. Phoutrides   26: 56
Literary Legacy — Una W. Harsen   53:172
Literary Note, A   39:632
Literary Studies — Helena Knorr   11:435
Literary Study, The Aims of — Hiram Corson   6:473
Literary Style: Must It Join the Dodo? —
    Stanton A. Coblentz   52:156
Literary Tendencies, Some   6:559
Literary Theatre, The Irish — Irene Dwen Andrews   39: 94
Literary Treasures Unearthed   8: 23
Literature and Philosophy, Characteristics of —
    Emil C. Wilm   24:122
Literature and the Pedagogue —
    Lewis Worthington Smith   21:311
Literature and the Scientific Spirit — Oscar L. Triggs   6:113, 323
*Literature, Eclipse of Seriousness in Contemporary,
    The* — Walter Blackburn Harte   9: 36
Literature, Effects of Contemporary Events on   9:622
Literature, German — Mary Harned   9:284
Literature, German-American — Amelia von Ende   17C:108
Literature, Best Be Taught, How May —
    Hiram Corson   6:377, 473, 536
Literature in Ancient Rome, Environment of, The —
    William Cranston Lawton   7:113

Literature, Italian: Fogazzaro — Pietro Isola   18:13:

Literature, Japanese Women in — Yone Noguchi   15C: 8&

Literature: Knowledge versus Feeling —
     Katharine Lee Bates   6:38:

Literature, Modern Armenian — Chahen Garo   9:12:

Literature, Modern German — John Scholte Noller   16C:127

Literature, New Ideas in Teaching — William C. Collar,
     Oscar L. Triggs, Katharine Lee Bates, Albert S.
     Cook, L. A. Sherman   8:432, 56:

Literature, New Studies on — P.   7:45!

Literature, Personality in Teaching — Oscar L. Triggs   6:38!

Literature of Iceland, Present-Day —
     Vilhjalmur Stefansson   15B:12(

Literature of Iceland, The Newer —
     Vilhjalmur Stefansson   15A: 62

Literature of Portugal, The — Isabel Moore   18:342

Literature, Socialism in — P.   11:41&

Literature, Specialized Teaching of — L. A. Sherman   6:381

Literature, Study of — Frederic Ives Carpenter   6:378

Literature, Talks on the Study of — P.   10:128

Literature of the World — P.   10:598

Lithuanian Folk Song — *The Daina* — Demie Jonaitis   47:322

Lithuanian Folk Songs — Translated by Demie Jonaitis   47:329

Little Blue Guinea-Hen, The — *Gyp*   30: 60

Little Brown Bird, The — Grace Shoup   38:158

Little Brown Eyes — Robert Powell   54:351

"Little Eyolf"   7: 99

Little Hill, A — Pauline Ogden   43:371

Little Meret, Green-Coat Henry's Story —
     Gottfried Keller — Translated by Lilaise R. Smith   17C: 50

Little Path, The — Anne Murray Larned   28: 54

Little Red Shoes — Helen E. Middleton   53: 76

Little Soldier Unknown, The — Ada Negri —
     Translated by Rudolph Altrocchi   28:476

Little Song, A — Ruby Hudson   44: 93

Little Theatre, The (New York)   23:291

Livesay, Florence Randall, Translator —
     Ukrainian Folk Songs   26:351

Living Hours — Arthur Schnitzler —
     Translated by Helen Tracy Porter   17A: 36

Llona's, Teresa Maria, Intersection —
     Marie Pope Wallis   49:323

Lloyd, Mary — *Chaucer Questions*   2:136
     — *Swinburne's Jonson*   2:323

Locke, Frederick — *Greek Way, The*   47: 63

Locke-Richardson Shakespeare Club, The —
     Charles Woodbury   1:181

Lockesley Hall," Note on — P. A. C.   5:107
,ockhart, Gordon — *Haiku, A*   57:356
    — *House Before Dawn, The*   58: 88
    — *Old Trees in Spring*   58: 89
    — *White Butterflies*   57:382
    — *Winter Wind*   54: 69
,oder, B. H., Translator — *Poems* —
    Rainer Maria Rilke   55: 78
,odge, Thomas, *An Elizabethan Lyrist* —
    James Buckham   3:601
,odovici, Cesare — *Idiot, The* —
    Translated by Petronelle Sombart   30:317
    — *L'Eroica* — Translated by Petronelle Sombart   34:159
    — *Woman of No One, The* —
    Translated by Petronelle Sombart   32:159
,oft's Wish — Johann Sigurjonsson   46: 99
,ofty Motives — Albert Weinberg   38:603
,ogistics — Noel Jordan   51:150
,oin du Bal (Waltz) — Louis James Block   12: 17
,ondon Bore Me — Frederick Vanson   55:262
,ondon Letters   1:389, 441, 491, 542, 589; 2:283, 386, 493, 609
,ondon Literaria   3:47, 154, 376; 4:105, 524, 591, 643; 5:104, 534,
    587, 644; 6:56, 167, 222, 374; 7:48, 469, 581;
    8:466; 9:632; 10:149, 618
,oneliness — James Meagher   39:410
,onely Dream, The — Ruth Morehouse   51: 77
,ongfellow, Henry Wadsworth, and German Romance —
    Fred Lewis Pattee   17A: 59
,ongfellow, Henry Wadsworth — *Lady of Gardiner, The*   48:176
    — *Unpublished Letter on Evangeline, An* —
    Henry C. Warnack   14A:108
,ongfellow's "Evangeline," A Product of Swedish
    Influence? Is — Edward Thostenberg   19:301
,ongfellow's "Golden Legend" and Its Analogues —
    P. A. C.   4: 91
,ongfellow's "Hiawatha": Study Program   7:520, 576, 632
,ongfellow's "King Robert of Sicily," Antecedents of —
    Hjalmer Edgren   14B:127
,ongfellow's "Michael Angelo" —
    Charlotte Porter and Helen A. Clarke   13:427
,ongfellow's "Spanish Student"   6:161
,onging — Richard Dehmel —
    Translated by Paul H. Grummann   24:200
,onging — Florence Earle Coates   10: 25
,onging — Kathryn Evans McKay   56:378
,ook Well at This Fair Hostess, Friends —
    Dorothy Cowles Pinkney   55:183

Looking Back — Blanche Yvonne Mosler 45:11

Loomis, Laura Hibbard — *Chinese Sappho, A,* With
    Translations by Wan Ying Hsieh 41:517

"Lord Ormont and His Aminta," A Glance at —
    Louise Cann Ranum 22:137

Lord's Will, The — Paul Greene 33:366

Lorenz, Charlotte M., Translator — *Idyll* —
    Martinez Sierra 37: 63

Lorraine, A Claude — Camille Fairchild 27:600

Loss — Mary Thro Rauth 50:180

Loss and Gain — John Robert Quinn 57: 83

Lost and the Not Lost, The — Burnham Eaton 55: 35

Lost Lilacs — Esther Judkins 53:290

Lost Lover, The — Edna Wahlert McCourt 28:473

Lost Prophet — Zoe A. Tilghman 51:115

Lot's Wife — Katharine Strelsky 57: 8

Lotus Magic — Winifred Adams Burr 55:180

Lotus Symbolism in Homer, etc. —
    Anna Robertson Brown 2:620

Lotus, The — Julia Hall Bartholomew 29:490

Louis, Louise — *First Born* 53:159

Louise Labé, La Belle Cordière de Lyon — John Heard 42:15

Louisiana Purchase Exposition Ode —
    Ida Echert Lawrence 15C:113

Lounsbury, Charles — *Will, A* 50:262

Love — Leonard Lanson Cline 30:45

Love and Bread — August Strindberg —
    Translated by H. C. P. and C. P. 6:50

Love and Death — Margaret Cooper McGiffert 10:33

Love at First Sight — Nathan Haskell Dole 10:62

Love, Best, The 8:280

Love, Browning's Idea of 1:153

Love Drama of the Tenth Century, A —
    William Henry Hudson 3:485

Love, Facettes of: From Browning —
    Daniel G. Brinton 1:

Love Has No Coat of Mail — Madeleine Burch Cole 56:36

Love in a French Kitchen — Transcribed by Colin C.
    Clements and John Saunders 28:72

"Love in a Life" (Browning Study Hints) 3:52

"Love in Idlenesse" — Charlotte Porter 17A: 8

Love is Like That — Anne Morriss 53:17

Love Letter — Kathryn Evans McKay 56:37

Love Looked Back — Virginia Woodward Cloud 16B: 6

Love of the Natural — Villiers de l'Isle Adam 7:38

Love, Poetry, and Civic Service — Alexander Blok 57: 9

Love Song — Rainer Maria Rilke 55: 7

Love Triumphant — Sara Perry   57:495
Love Verses From the Hindoo —
        Translated by A. M. Wergeland   14C: 53
Love, What Is? — Elizabeth Hazelton Haight   14D: 66
Love's Banquet — Robert Iphys Everett   15B: facing 18
Love's Bitter Cup — Ronald Walker Barr   53: 78
Love's Dwelling — Isabel Francis Bellows   17A: 93
'Love's Labors Lost" —
        Charlotte Porter and Helen A. Clarke   14A:117; 14B:151
'Love's Labors Lost," Questions and Notes on: Study
        Program   1: 84
"Lover's Complaint, A" — The Meaning of "Talents"
        in — Horace Howard Furness   3:196
Lover's Fancy, A — Giraldo Forbes   53:309
Lovers, The — Edna Wahlert McCourt   28:474
Lowe, Lucy — Bitterly Reviled, The   33:300
Lowell, James Russell — C.   11:425
Lowell, James Russell and Whitman: A Contrast —
        Horace L. Traubel   4: 22
Lowell, Maria — Africa   10: 19
        — Song   9:461
Lowell's "Columbus"   7:161, 218, 275
Lowell's "Vision of Sir Launfal"   6: 47
Lowell's "Vision of Sir Launfal": Study Program —
        Charlotte Porter and Helen A. Clarke   15A: 97
Lower, Henry Eastman — Shadow-Hunter, The   9: 6
Lowlands vs. Highlands: Effects of Environment on
        Poets — E. Vicars   6: 83
'Lowly" Poets: Dunbar — C.   9:298
Lowry, Robert — Violent Wedding, The   58: 3
Loyal Daughter in Literature, The —
        Charlotte Porter and Helen A. Clarke   9:100
Lozano y Lozano, Juan — Evening Sonnet   54:185
Lubimov, Nicholas, Translator — Mozart and Salieri —
        Pushkin   31:297
Lucero, Juan Draghi — Sorceress of the Andes, The   53:168
Lucretius, the Poet, and Tennyson's Poem "Lucretius" —
        Katharine Allen   11:529
Lucretius, The Poet — Katharine Allen   11:529
Ludlow, Clara Southmayd — November   8:112
Ludwig, Otto — Forest Warden, The   24:129
Ludwig, Paula — To the Obscure God   58:326
Lullaby for Miriam — Richard Beer Hofmann   47:290
Lullaby for My Boy — Richard Dehmel   55:341
Lullaby in a Night That is Everywhere —
        Richard Lyons   51:137

Lunacy — Alvina Martine Cobanks   56:23!
Lund, B. C. — *Return*   49:17?
Lundt, Dorothy — *At Inspection*   5:30?
Lupine Dream — Laura Lourene Le Gear   52:36?
Luquiens, Frederick Bliss, Translator —
    Fabliau of the Three Hunchbacks — Durand   24:33?
Luria, Browning's — John White Chadwick   6:25!
"Luria" — Henry S. Pancoast   1:553; 2: 1?
"Luria" and Othello, Types and Arts Compared   6:58!
"Luria": Its Story and Motive — Henry S. Pancoast   1:553, 2:1?
Lutz, Gertrude May — *Chenku* — *Well of Sacrifice*   57: 5?
Lyly, (and Shakespeare) — Horace Davis   5:17?
Lyly's Plot of "Sapho and Phao" —
    Frederick John Teggart   8: 2?
Lyman, Anne Mary — *Weasel's Holiday, The*   32:30?
Lynn, Herrick — *There is Something of Beauty*   46:28?
Lyon, Carrie Ward — *Three Poems*   56:23?
Lyon Pass — René Char   57:48?
Lyons, Richard —
    Lullaby in a Night That is Everywhere   51:13?
Lyric France in English Verse — Lilian White Spencer   36:24?
Lyric, Oldest English, The — Richard Burton   5: 5?
Lyric Origins of Swinburne, The — Van Tyne Brooks   18:46?
"Lyric Poets" Series   8:15?
Lyric Year, The — Charlotte Porter   24: 6?
Lyrics, Four — William Stanley Braithwaite   25:25?
Lyrics from the Russian — Translated by Marjorie E.
    Farber, with an Introductory Note by Samuel
    Hazard Cross   44:27?
Lyrics of China, Old and New — Kay De Bard Hall   54:16?
M., H., Lieutenant — *"Call Me"*   47:37?
Macaulay, T. B. — *Unpublished Poem*   1:59?
"Macbeth" and "Lady Macbeth"   1:14?
"Macbeth," Arabic Vision of "Moving Wood"   2:24?
"Macbeth," Banquo, a Study in   11: 8?
"Macbeth," Character Studies in   1:24?
"Macbeth," Complexity in "Lady" — Ethel G. Skeat   2:44?
"Macbeth," Concerning a Passage in — W. J. Rolfe   15C: 9?
"Macbeth," Fear in — Fred Lewis Pattee   10: 9?
"Macbeth," Hecate in — Mary E. Cardwill   10:53?
"Macbeth," Irving's   1: 4?
"Macbeth," Modjeska's Lady — P.   4: 4?
"Macbeth," Moot Points —
    Charlotte Porter and Helen A. Clarke   2:58?
"Macbeth," Moral Proportion and Fatalism in   7:13?
"Macbeth," Moving Wood — Morris Jastrow, Jr.   2:24?
"Macbeth," Part of Hecate, The — W. J. Rolfe   11:60?

"Macbeth," *Stage Types of Lady* — Morris Ross   5: 90
"Macbeth": *Study Programs*   12:430; 20:229
"Macbeth," *Supernatural in* — Annie Russell Wall   5:490
MacCampbell, Donald — *Squaring the Family Circle*   43: 71
Macedon Road, The — David P. Berenberg   37:631
MacFarlane, Anne — *Slippers*   32:425
Machado, Antonio — *Twenty Poems*   58:159
Machado, Manuel — *King Philip IV*   30:615
Machar, J. S. — *On Golgotha*   28:485
Machiavelli, Niccolo — *Three Canzoni*   53:366
Macintire, Elizabeth, and Colin Clements —
    Ivory Tower, The   30:127
Macintire, Elizabeth J., Translator —
    Four Fairy Plays — Topelius   28:567
MacKay, H. W. Boyd — *English Hexameter*   23:139
Mackenzie, Constance — *Caliban and Cleon*   3:294
MacMechan, Archibald — *Idyll of a Northern River, The*   6:299
  — *"In Great Eliza's Golden Time"*   5:431
  — *Mistress of the Red Lamp, The*   5:488
MacMillan, Mary — *Gate of Wishes, The*   22:469
MacReady, Browning and   1:138
Mad Dog, The — V. Kedrov   58: 55
Madame Major — Ippolit Vasilievich Shapazhinsky   28:257
Madelon, Translated by Elizabeth S. Dickerman   30:469
Madison, C. — *Yiddish Theatre, The*   32:497
Madison, Charles A. — *Abraham Raisen*   35:210
  — *David Pinski, The Dramatist*   35:562
  — *Isaak Loeb Peretz*   37: 73
  — *Mendele: The Foremost of Ghetto Satirists*   33:255
  — *Peretz Hirschbein*   38:106
  — *Sholom Aleichem*   33:563
  — *Sholom Asch*   34:524
  — *Sholom Asch*   46:303
  — *William Hazlitt: Man and Critic*   40:373
  — *Yehoash-Solomon Bloomgarden*   37:537
Madman Divine, The — José Echégaray —
    Translated by Elizabeth Howard West   19: 1
Madman or Saint — José Echégaray —
    Translated by Ruth Lansing   23:161
Madman's Skull, The — Juan Ramon Molina   55:129
Madonna and the Scarecrow, The — De Witte Kaplan   34:254
Madrigal — Gutierre de Cetina   30:470
Maeterlinck, Maurice — *Aglavaine and Selysette*   14D: 11
  — *Alladine and Palomides*   7:281
Maeterlinck and Emerson   10: 76
Maeterlinck and Sharp — C.   7:157

157

Maeterlinck: Dramatist of a New Method — P. 5:151
— *Joyzelle, The* 16B: 1
— *Life of the Bee* 14C: 59
— *Monna Vanna* 15C: 1
— *Pélléas and Mélisande* 6:413
— *Seven Princesses* 6:29, 87, 150
— *Sightless, The* 5:159, 218, 273, 442
Maeterlinck, Impressions of — Richard Hovey 7:446
*Maeterlinck's "The Blind": A Cursory Review of the
Symbolism in* 13:554
— *"Bluebird," The Significance of* —
Emily S. Hamblen 22:460
Magaret, Helene — *Horses of Paradise* 40:452
Magda, Sudermann's and Duse's 8:557
Magic and Prodigy in the East — Morris Jastrow, Jr. 4:118
*Magic Characteristics in Eastern and Western Litera-
ture* — Talcott Williams 4:126
Magic of Love — William Pennance Church 37: 23
Mahoney, David — *Old Road, The* 46:285
Maid's Prologue, The — Arthur Ketchum 25:206
Major, Montgomery — *Spadassin* 36:265
Makers, The — Mary Carolyn Davies 27:110
Mallan, Lloyd, Translator — *Poems from Latin America* 51: 74
Mallarmé, Stéphane — Alfred Himwich 35:621
Mallarmé Stéphane — Federico Olivero 28:327
Mallarmé Stéphane — *Anguish* 50: 24
— *Herodiade* —
Translated by Joseph Twadell Shipley 32:458
— *L'Après-Midi d'un Faune* 31:305
— *Les Fleurs* 26:228
Mallory, Robert Allen — To One Most Beautiful 44:181
Malloy, Charles — *"La Saisiaz," The Real Significance of
"The Brand Flamboyant"* 8:256
— *Poem to Honor Emerson, A* 14C: 19
— *What Bearing upon Emerson's Poems Have
Their Titles?* 14C: 65
Malloy, Charles, Rondel to — Louise Chandler Moulton 9:458
Man and His Wife, A — Colin C. Clements 31:197
Man as an Environed Animal 6: 40
Man of the West, The — Fred Lewis Pattee 24:248
Man of the World, A — Marie von Ebner-Eschenbach —
Translated by Roy Temple House 22:128
Man Speaks — Robert J. Shores 27:449
Man Who Couldn't Talk, The — August Von Kotzebue 40:223
"Man with the Hoe, The" — Edwin Markham 11:157
Manchester, Paul T. —
Conquistador's Song of Freedom, A 52: 49

158

Manchester Players — A. E. F. Horniman   25:210
Mann, Walter H. — *Rose, The*   18:528
Mansfield, Mrs. Richard, Translator — *Hello* —
    Edmond Rostand   32:155
Mansfield, Richard: An Appreciation — Arthur Row   19:367
Mansfield, Richard, as Richard III — Charlotte Porter   2: 30
Many a Night — Richard Dehmel —
    Translated by Paul H. Grummann   24:125
Map, Walter, The First English Essayist   5:537
Maple Seed — Harriet Plimpton   50: 45
Maraba — A. Goncalves Dias. —
    Translated by Agnes Blake Poor   15A: 43
Marah of Shadowtown — Anne Throop   12:234
Marble, Annie Russell — *Josephine Preston Peabody*
    as a Lyricist and Dramatist   15B:149
"Marble Faun": Study Program   13:433
March, George I. — *World of Arthur Schnitzler, The*   39:573
March, Sidney — *Minnesingers, The*   20:457
Marcus, Shirley A. — *Warning*   46:285
Margot Asquith: An Impression — Arthur William Row   35:314
Margot-Parle, Delina — *Alien Singer, The*   54:269
Maria Magdalena — Friedrich Hebbel —
    Translated by Paula Green   25: 81
Marimba — Francisco P. Figueroa   49:368
Marinetti, F. T. — *Poems* — Translated by Anne Simon   25:439
Marinetti, F. T. — *Poems*   26:707
Marinetti, F. T., and Some Principles of Futurism —
    Anne Simon   26:738
Marinetti, F. T., Appreciation of, An — Anne Simon   25:453
Marivaux, Pierre Chamblain de — *Test, The* —
    Translated by Willis K. Jones   35:533
Mark Bennett on Roanoke — H. K. Russell   48: 3
Mark Twain Goes West — Thelma Cash   52:256
Markham, Edwin — *Joy of the Hills, The*   13:537
    — *Kyka*   13:538
    — *Look into the Gulf, A*   13:536
    — *Man with the Hoe, The*   11:157
    — *Muse of Labor, The*   13:539
Marks, Jeannette — *Forgotten Art, A*   19:488
    — *Passing of the Green, The*   18:393
Marlowe: A Note on His Plots   1: 54
Marlowe: A Poetic Drama — Charlotte Porter   14A:128
Marlowe, Note on — Saintsbury   1:213
Marlowe's Julia, Rosalind   1:141
Marquis, Cleon — *Backwaters*   56:360
    — *Binnacle and Compass*   57:492
    — *Hour, The*   57:493
    — *O Celia*   57:493

Marquis, T. G. — *Sidney's "Astrophel and Stella"*   8:57(

Marr, Harriett Webster — *By the Little Finger* — Botrel   53:27'

— *Mass on the Sea, The* — Botrel   55:26(

Marriage — Patricia Daniel   58:38

Marriage Is So Difficult — Lillian Harris   38:45:

"Marriage of Heaven and Hell" — William Blake   11: 2?

Marriage of Tristram, The — John Heard   48: 7:

Marriage, The — Douglas Hyde   20:13!

Marriage, The Destiny of — Portia and the Caskets —
    John Phelps Fruit   3: 6?

Marriott, Ann — *Morning*   46:18:

Marshall, Donald Worth — *Walter Pater: Some of His
    Imaginary Portraits*   32:431

Marston's "Antonio's Revenge" — L. M. Griffiths   2:414

Marston's Shakespeareanisms — L. M. Griffiths   2:289, 360

Martha of Sillen — *Old Clavichord, An* —
    Translated by Charles W. Stork   34:314

Martial, The Epigram and Its Greatest Master —
    F. B. R. Hellems   16D: 67

Martin, Blanche Rucker — *Clock Replies, The*   33:624

— *Dowager to the Clock, The*   33:264

Martin, John Joseph — *Wife of Usher's Well, The*   30: 94

Martin, Margaret I. — *Old-Fashioned Roses*   52:362

Martin, Marian — *Phantoms*   53:118

Martin, Marion —
    My God Dwelleth Not Within a Church   52:176

Martin, Portia — *Songs of the Chippewa*   31:463

Martin, Rachel Pettit — *Two Poems*   50:194

Martinez, Enrique Gonzales — Edna Lue Furness   58:282

Marton, Carl — *Chapel Bells at Eventide*   47:283

Marvelous Romance of Wen Chin-Chun — C. C. Hsing   35:298

Marx, Olga — *Elizabeth*   30:578

Marx, Olga, Translator — *King Philip IV* —
    Manuel Machedo   30:615

— *Rendering from the Verse of Campo-Amor, A*   31:157

— *Translations from Manuel Machedo*   30:616

— *Two Hungarian Folk Songs*   30:587

Mary Anderson in "Winter's Tale" — S. A. R.   1: 92

"Mary in Heaven"   6:213

Masefield's First Reading, John — Lawrence Stuckey   38:312

Mason, Cheryl — If I Knew   53:158

Mass at Dawn — Luis G. Urbina — Rendered into
    English Verse by Alice Stone Blackwell   24:312

Mass on the Sea — Theodore Botrel   55:266

Masson, David — *On Tennyson*   4:365

Master Hugues of Saxe-Gotha: Study Program —
    The Editors   10:288

Master of Palmyra — Adolf Wilbrandt —
    Translatey by Harriet S. Olive   13:161
Master Villon Offers Advice — J. Clarkson Miller   53:369
'Masterbuilder" in New York — Helena Knorr   12: 95
Matacotti, Franco — *Poems*   58:368
Matheus, John F., Translator — Le Cimetière Marin —
    Paul Valéry   40:456
Matron of Ephesus — Will J. Cunningham   46:258
Matson, Esther —
    Goblin versus "Hart-Easing" Words, Those   54:374
    — *In the Garden*   35:114
    — *Music in Flower Fragrance, The*   54:279
    — *Of Words that Are Winged*   38:307
    — *Ruskin's Tone Poems Anent Leaves*   40:443
    — *To All You Poets*   49: 80
    — *Triad of Symbols, A*   31:284
Matthew Beloved — Stanley Kauffman   44: 48
Mauclair, Camillo — *Daughter Mine* —
    Translated by Joseph T. Shipley   36:624
Maupassant, Guy de — *Peace at Home* — *at Any Price*   47:195
Maureen — Agnes I. Hanrahan   25: 59
Mauriac, François — *Perfume of Your Dress*   55: 50
Maury, Antonia C. de P. P. — *Friend of Emerson, A*   26:357
Mauton, Margaret — *Backward Lady, The*   53:291
Maxim The Bitter — Albert Phelps   15C: 53
Maxwell, Sue — *Robert Herrick, the Metrician*   52:353
May Night — Louis Aragon   57:194
May Night — Priscilla Flowers   37:551
Maynard, Laurens — *Ave Post Saecula*   28:745
Maynard, Laurens, Memorial to   28:744
Maze — Arthur Corning White   36:147
Mazuranic, Ivan — *Troop, The* — Translated by Bertha
    W. Clark and Luke Djurichich   34:294
McCann, William Spencer — *Postlude*   39:315
McClumpha, Charles Flint, Translator — *Ballade Ad-*
    dressed by Eustache Deschamps to Geoffrey Chau-
    cer on Sending Him His Works   3:349
McConnell, S. D. — *"Ferishtah's Fancies"*   3:379
McCook, Henry C. — *Answer to Query on "Sordello"*
    1:432, 486, 518
McCormack, Helen J. —
    Joseph Rodman Drake — *Keats' "Twin Spirit"*   38:531
McCracken, Elizabeth —
    Stage Productions of Browning's Plays   14C:115
McCourt, Edna Wahlert — *City Market Place, The*   27:353
McDermott, John Francis, Jr. —
    Queen Comes to Pray, The   36:450
    — *'Twas Well Done and Quickly*   39:415

McGiffert, Gertrude — *Hunting for Amiel's Garden*   17B:117
McGiffert, Margaret Cooper — *Love and Death*   10:333
McGill, Anna Blanche — *Henry James, Artist*   16D: 90
McIntyre, Clara F. —
    New Poets Judged by Old Standards   28:445
McKay, Kathryn Evans — *Five Poems*   56:376
McKinney, Isabel — *Mud*   30:417
McKnight, David A. — *Tragedy of Ophelia, The*   12:253
McKnight, Robert W. — *Monsieur Beaucaire*   33: 84
McKnight, Robert Wilson — *Pigeon, The*   30:596
    — *Voltaire, Shakespeare, and Billeting Area 18*   31:604
McNary, Sarah J. —
    Beowulf and Arthur as English Ideals   6:529
McVickar, D. — *Fool Who Lives Contentedly, The*   32:109
Meagher, James — *April Nights*   39:472
    — *Fragile Shell, The*   39:473
    — *Loneliness*   39:410
    — *My Father's God*   39:473
    — *Satan*   39:473
Mearkle, A. L. — *Last Encore, The*   12:334
"Measure for Measure"   3:538
Meditation — Lucy A. K. Adee   52:279
Meditation on a Hillside — Willson Osborne   42:164
Meditation on Tyranny — Ruby H. Simpson   56:290
"Meditations in Motley" — C.   7: 34
Meditations of Hujas, The   19:469
Meeting, A — Alvilde Prydz —
    Translated by Hester Coddington   25:498
Meeting of Odysseus and Nausicaa, The —
    Marjorie Burke   48: 87
Mehuse, C. O., Translator — *Christmas Eve*   49:355
Meister, Charles W. — *Comparative Drama* —
    Chekhov, Shaw, Odets   55:249
Mekota, Beatrice M., Translator — *Awakening, The*   33:159
    — *Four Bare Walls, The* —
    Frantisek Adolf Subert   28:497
    — *Great Freeholder, The* —
    Frantisek Adolf Subert   35:318
    — *Madame Major* — Ippolit Shpazhinsky   28:257
    — *Petr vok Rozmberk* —
    Frantisek Adolf Subert   31: 1
Mélançon-Dubuys, Kenneth — *Helen*   58:316
Mellon, Evelyn Emig — *Trains*   41:424
Mellon, Perikles — *Folk Songs of Greece under the Turk*   26: 47
Memento — Frances Beveridge Sydnor   55:264
Memories — Helene Picard   31:242
Memory of Robert Browning, The — Geraldine P. Dilla   37:120

Mendele: The Foremost of Ghetto Satirists —
    Charles A. Madison   33:255
Mendes, Catulle — *Fidelity*   18:413
    — *Tears*   21: 95
Mendoca, Anna Amelia Queiroz Carneiro de —
    Marie Pope Wallis   58: 45
Menefee, Edith L. — *Summer with George Meredith: In
    Particular, "Richard Feveral,"* A   7:505
Mendoza, Juan Draghi Lucero — *Inca Highway, The*   55:273
Meneses, Enrique de — *Glittering Highway, The* —
    Translated by Gustav Davidson   38:317
    — *Wasted Lives*   41:159
Mengers, Marie C., Translator — *Guardian, The*   46:290
Menocal, Esmé de — *What I Love*   42:288
Mentem Mortalia Tangunt — Beatrice Daw   29:468
Mercantini, Luigi — *Gleaner of Sapri, The*   27:712
Mercerized Folklore — Christabel F. Fiske   31:538
Merchant, Francis — *Interdependence*   47:287
'*Merchant of Venice*"   3: 69
'*Merchant of Venice*": Date of Composition   1:514
'*Merchant of Venice*" in Japan   1:467
'*Merchant of Venice*," Possant in   1:574
'*Merchant of Venice*": Study Program — W. J. Rolfe
        2:26, 82, 134, 195, 647
Meredith, George, A Summer with — Edith L. Menefee   7:505
Meredith, George, On the Source of Destiny —
    Emily G. Hooker   12:238
Meredith, George, "Story" in, The —
    Alma Brunt Sembower   23:360
Meredith, George: Vital Choice, The   13:459
Meredith's "Cecilia," The Woman-Egoist —
    Katharine Rolston Fisher   24:113
Merlin's Flight — Essay on Ralph Hodgson, An —
    George Brandon Saul   56:263
'*Mermaid Series*"   1:247
Mermaid Tavern in Fact and Fiction, The —
    Willis K. Jones   36:441
Merman and the Seraph, The   17C: 5
Merrick, Hyde Buxton — Drab Little Lady, The   27:355
Merrifield, Gladys — Poems   55:241
Merrill, Katharine — Use of the Ugly in Art, The   13:251
Merrill, William J. — Poetry of Ethna Carbery, The   19:225
Mesmerism from a Scientific Point of View, Browning's —
    Frances Emily White   4:261
Mesquite, The — Boyce House   43:360
Message of Hafiz, The — Nayerah Samsami   53:263
Metempsychosis — Campo-Amor   31:157

163

Mexican Landscape — Emery E. Petho   55:371

Mexico's Most Beloved Poet — Alice Stone Blackwell   30: 81

Meysenburg, Louise von, Translator — *Agony* —
    Sully-Prud'homme   22:400

Mezirka, Vera, Translator — *Diarmuid and Grainne* —
    Julius Zeyer   44:289

"Michael Angelo": Study Program —
    Charlotte Porter and Helen A. Clarke   13:427

Michael, Helen Abbott —
    Drama in Relation to Truth, The   7:149
    — *Woman and Freedom in Whitman*   9:216

"Michael": Study Program — The Editors   12:583

Michaelangelo — Emile Verhaeren —
    Translated by E. H. Pfeiffer   33:612

Michel, Marc — *Leghorn Hat, A*   28: 1

Mickiewicz, Adam — *Grazyna*   46: 3

Mid-Century 1950 — William W. Chance   55:352

Middleton, Helen E. — *Little Red Shoes, The*   53: 76

Midsummer — Marion Kent   52:194

"Midsummer Night's Dream" — Catherine Postell   18:522

"Midsummer Night's Dream": Fairy Lore in —
    Ethel G. Skeat   3:177

"Midsummer Night's Dream," Metrical Changes in —
    Edwin H. Lewis   9:110

"Midsummer Night's Dream": New Variorum Edition —
    P.   7:628

"Midsummer Night's Dream": Questions and Notes
    1:184, 232, 280

"Midsummer Night's Dream," Solar Myths in —
    Sinclair Korner   3: 17

"Midsummer Night's Dream: Study Program   8:578; 15C: 99

"Midsummer Night's Dream," Supernatural in   5:490

Mieler, Maria Ossipovana, Translator —
    Fortune Favors Fools — Narsdny   23:305

Mierow, Herbert Edward — *Alexander the Great*   55: 99
    — *Dream, The*   58:123
    — *Hill, The*   52: 3
    — *Portal, The*   56:238

Mifflin, Lloyd — *Sonnets*   11:133

Miguel Manara, a Mystery — O. W. Milosz   30:224

Mila Whendle — N. H. Musselman   13: 22

"Mildred," Browning's — J. J. Britton   5:266

Milians, Bernard D. — *Shadows*   49:275

Mill, The — Detlev von Liliencron   26:277

Mill, The — Vicente Huidobro   58: 76

Miller, J. Clarkson — *Master Villon Offers Advice*   53:369

Miller, J. Corson — *Forest-Moment*   56:344
    — *Moon-Mist*   56:364
    — *Nostalgia*   36:467
    — *Sunrise*   57: 2
Miller, L. — *Mr. Man* — Translated by S. K. Padover and
    Chasye Cooperman   40:475
Miller, Nellie Burget —
    In the Tents of the Shepherd Prince   53:232
Miller of Arcos, The — Willis Knapp Jones   58: 65
Miller, Paul Emile — *Speaking of Traditions*   52:268
Milosz, O. W. — *Miguel Manara* —
    Translated by Edward J. O'Brien   30:224
Milton and Shakespeare   1:396
*Milton, Astronomical Science of: As Shown in "Paradise
    Lost"* — Maria Mitchell   6:313
Milton, Cambridge Edition of — P.   11:438
Milton's Daughters — Villiers de l'Isle Adam   7:601
Ming-Y — Mario Collaci   44:160
Minot, Fanny E. — *The Avon Club*   1:321
Minnesingers, The — Sidney March   20:457
Minutiae — Louis Darcy   44: 86
Miracle — Nina Janes Webster   50:260
Miracle — Rainer Maria Rilke   30:416
Miracle, I Go on Tour with the — Arthur William Row   38:291
Miracle of Montserrat, The —
    Richard Butler Glaenzer   28:459
Mirage — Margaret Henry Gammon   39:100
Miranda and Ferdinand   3:190
Mirror — Winifred Adams Burr   55:372
Mirror, The — Pierre de Ronsard —
    Translated by Grace Wallace   32:415
Misconceptions Concerning Shaw, Some — Felix Grendon   20:376
Miserere, El — Becczner —
    Translated by Alice Gray Cowan   15B: 25
Miss Ariel's Paper Discussed — I. N. Cog   7:436
Miss Manda — Gladys Bagg Taber   38:412
Miss Marlowe's Rosalind — Charlotte Porter   1:141
Missal, The — Armand Sully-Prud'homme   55: 80
Mist — Lilian Saunders   36:629
Mist — Mabel Holmes Parsons   28:372
Mist on the Moor — Paul Scott Mowrer   28:483
Mistral, Frédéric — *Communion of Saints, The*   26:355
Mistral, Gabriela — *Dew*   57:160
    — *I Am Not Alone*   57:381
    — *My Discovery*   57:382
    — *Sensitive*   57:382
    — *Song, A*   56: 88

— *Statute of Earth, The*   57:38

— *Two Poems*   55: 3

— *You Were Mine*   57: 9

Mistress of the Red Lamp, The — Archibald MacMechan   5:48

Mistress Shakespeare — Conrad Seiler   43:11

Mitchell, Ellen M. — *"The Paradise" of Dante*   7:39

Mitchell, Grace W. — *Four Poems from the Korean*   47:26

Mitchell, Maria — *Astronomical Science of Milton as Shown in "Paradise Lost," The*   6:31

Mitchell, R. Marjorie — *To My Son*   54:19

"Mithradates" — Charles Malloy   14C: 6

Mitrisin, George — *Three Moments in a Life*   47:23

Mixon, Ada — *Peace on Earth*   28: 6

Miyameri Asatoro, Translator — *Lady Hosokawa* — Kido Okamato   37:

Miyoshi, Tatsuji — *Soil*   58: 8

Mobert, Helen L. — *Singing Pool, The*   30:27

Modern Apollo and The Fates, A — Helen A. Clarke   3:51

Modern Bohemian Novelist   4:

Modern Drama, Social Theories and Art in — Helen Cramp   22:14

Modern Dutch and Flemish Poets — Sipko Rederus   13:38

Modern Epic, The — Harold King   40:40

Modern European Dramatists:

— *Arthur Schnitzler*   23: 2

— *August Strindberg*   24: 4

— *Gerhart Hauptmann*   22:11

— *Hermann Sudermann*   22:19

— *Max Helbe*   23:12

Modern German Literature — John Scholte Noller   16C:12

Modern Harlequinade, A — Colin Campbell Clements   31:57

Modern Imperialism as Shown in Browning's Portrait of Napoleon III — Charlotte Porter   12: 8

Modern Poet, A — Frederic Lawrence Knowles   14C: 6

Modern Poetry and a Courageous Publisher — I. H. F.   15A:11

Modern Poetry, Womanhood in   1:44

Modern Short Story: Its Nature and Origin — T. E. Rankin   17A:10

Modern Spiritualism and "Mr. Sludge"   3: 7

Modern Tragedy, The Call of — Robert Iphys Everett   15A:13

Modjeska, Helen, A Chat with   1:52

Modjeska's Lady Macbeth   4: 4

Molière, Dramatist — H. D. Lawhead   8:19

Molière, A Devotee of — Paul Ginistry — Translated by H. Schnurer   34:42

Molin, Peele — *Story about Gunnel*   12:

Molina, Juan Ramon — *Madman's Skull, The*   55:12

Mombert, Alfred — *Heavenly Drinker, The*   26:396
Momento Mori — Evarts Scudder   30:471
Monck, Emily Christianna —
    Greek Traits in Walt Whitman   7:327
    — *Walt Whitman in Relation to Christianity*   7:607
Money Question, The — Alexandre Dumas, Fils   26:129
Monhegan — Charlotte Porter   16D: 96
Monna Vanna — Maurice Maeterlinck —
    Translated by Charlotte Porter   15C: 1
Monna Vanna in Japan   17B:141
Monnoye, Bernard de la —
    Imitation d'une Ode d'Anacreon   51: 76
Monotony — Justine L. Whitfield   33:365
Monroe, Harriet — *After All*   12:321
    — *Poe and Whistler*   21:391
Monsieur Beaucaire — Robert Wilson McKnight   33: 84
Monster, The — T. G. Schwartz   37:597
Montague, Clifford — *Comic Shillelagh, The*   57:114
    — *Credos for the Critics*   46:371
Montague, Clifford M. — *Grub Street Fights*
    — *Part I*   49: 25
    — *Part II*   49:147
    — *Part III*   49:248
    — *Part IV*   49:340
    — *Tropics*   40:414
    — *What is Wrong with Our Critics?*   48:246
    — *William Somerset Maugham: Dramatist*   47: 40
Monterde, Francisco — *She Who Returned to Life*   55:291
Montillon, H. G. — *Some Modern War Dramas*   28:600
Moock, Armando — *Don Juan's Women*   46: 45
    — *Songbook of the Baby Jesus*   45: 23
Mood — Joseph L. Freeman   33:623
Moon and "The Columbian Year" — D. G. Porter   5: 50
Moon Effect — Leconte de Lisle   54:254
Moon Festival — Kay De Bard Hall   54:164
Moon-Mist — J. Corson Miller   56:364
Moonlight   17D: 87
Moonlight — Lilian Saunders   36:628
Moonlight Sonata — Victor Perez Petit   51:353
Moore, Bessie Collins — *On Bayou La Batre*   37:576
Moore, Charlotte —
    Art Spirit in Browning's "Flight of the Duchess"   9:266
Moore, Ellen Adams — *Moral Proportion and Fatalism*
    as Exhibited in Shakespeare's Tragedies: —
    "Antony and Cleopatra,"   7:613
    — *"Coriolanus,"*   8: 86
    — *"Hamlet,"*   7:191

— "King John," 8:13

— "King Lear," 7:48

— "Macbeth," 7:13

— "Othello," 7:42

— "Romeo and Juliet" 7:55

Moore, G. — Drama Realistic 2: 3

Moore, Irene — Swinburne 16D:10

Moore, Isabel — Literature of Portugal, The 18:34

— Turquoise God, The 17C: 6

Moore, Isabella — Ice Dragon and the Sun God, The 19: 8

Moore, Lou Wall and Margaret F. Allen, Dramatisers —
The Happy Prince — Oscar Wilde 27:40

Moore, Margaret King — Penalty 36:15

Moore, William Dyer, Translator —
By the Light of the Moon 48: 9

Moorhead, Joseph W., Jr. — Last Thought 51:19

Mor Jokai, Hungarian Romancer — Joseph Remenyi 55:35

Moratin, José — Fanny's Consent —
Translated by Anna Emilia Bagstad 40:15

More about Apples — A. H. Phipps 40:14

Moreas, Jean — Remembrances 36:62

— Youth Speaks 53: 6

Morehouse, Ruth — Lonely Dream, The 51: 7

Moreland, John Richard — Blowing Sand 41:45

Morgan, Enid — Childhood 46:25

Morgan, Robert L. — Day Dreams 53:16

— Take Heart, Soul 53:17

— Tired Man's Prayer for Peace, A 52:26

Morgenlied — Allen E. Woodall 44: 9

Mörike, Eduard Wahlert — Erinna to Sappho 24:19

— Forsaken 27:23

— 'Tis She 27:10

Morituri: Teias — Hermann Sudermann 9:33

Morley, George — Shakespeare's Commemorations 2:252, 306, 60

3:20

Morley, S. Griswold — Ballade of Lost Youth, The 51: 9

— Eleven Pines 49: 4

— Mountain Minister 52:37

— Novels of A. Palacio Valdés, The 16C: 9

— Translator — "I Puritani" — Valdés 16D: 9

— Selections from Doctor Angelico's Manuscripts — Valdés 24:26

— Three Sonnets — Anthero de Quental 29:62

Morne Fortuné — Richard Butler Glaenzer 28:45

Morning — Ann Marriott 46:18

Morning — Nickels Walker Bird 30:13

Morning — Thomas Hornsby Ferril 34:24

Morning Song — Giosue Carducci —
    Translated by William A. Drake   35:117
Morrill, Belle Chapman — *Lake Morning*   57:491
    — *New England Poet's Dream*   57:290
    — *Two Poems*   57:482
Morris, Harrison S. — *Browning versus Browning*   1:408
    — *Poetic Symposium, A*   1:545
    — *Societies*   1: 32
Morris, William — *Gertha's Lovers*   10:337
    — *Night in a Cathedral, A*   10:473
    — *Story of Frithiof The Bold, The*   12:353
    — *Unpublished Letters on Socialism*   7:473, 543
Morris, William, Translator —
    Tale of King Coustans, The   11:465
Morris, William, Socialistic Trend in Life and Works
    of — Oscar L. Triggs   5:113, 210
Morris's "The Lady of the Land" — Genevieve Apgar   33:274
Morriss, Anne — *Love is Like That*   53:176
Morte d'Arthur, Malory's   10:439
Morton, Edward Payson — *Ruskin's "Pathetic Fallacy"*
    and Keats' Treatment of Nature   12: 58
Morton's Ships, David — Mabel Kingsley Richardson   34:278
Mosaic: Writing Spider — Frances Beveridge Sydnor   55:265
Mosler, Blanche Yvonne — *Looking Back*   45:113
    — *There Is But One*   48: 95
    — *Two Poems*   44:190
    — *Two Poems*   47: 64
Mother, The — Oscar Williams   45:114
Mother Cry, The — Edith M. Thomas   18:198
Mother Goose, A Yankee — E. F. R. Stitt   5:531
Mother of Confucius — Lucy Salamanca   45:350
Mother Superior, The — Roy Temple House   32:135
Mother's Jewel — Viola Conklin   53: 77
Mother's Prayer, A — Ruth E. Bradley   54: 2
Mothers — Nikolai Alekseyevich Nekrassov   26:278
Motherless Heroine, The — Louise Maunsell Field   17D: 99
Motherless Heroines in English Classics —
    Gertrude Withington   11:259
Motivation of "Parsifal," The — Paul H. Grummann   16C:123
Motokiyo's Kanawa — Translated by T. Ochiai   23:222
Mott, Emma Pratt — *Shakespeare and Rhythm*   4:212
Moulton, Louise Chandler — *I Wonder*   9:367
    — *If Once, Just Once*   15B: 18
    — *Life and Works of Arthur O'Shaughnessy*   7:211
    — *Rondel to Charles Malloy*   9:458
Moulton, Louise Chandler, in Present Day Poets   12:305
Moulton, Louise Chandler, Poetry of, The — H. A. C.   12:114;
    19:473

Moulton's, Mrs.: "O'Shaughnessy" — C.   7:21
Moulton, R. G. — *Wandering Jew Legend, The: Eugene
    Sue and Ebulea* — Evans   3:32
Mountain and Sea — Marion Lee   49:26
Mountain Minister — S. Griswold Morley   52:37
Mountain She-Devil, The — Translated by Yone Noguchi   29:44
Mountain Top, From The — Alvilde Prydz —
    Translated by Hester Coddington   25:45
Mountain, William E. — *City of the Heart's Desire, The*   17A: 9
    — *Dies Irae*   12:23
    — *Sonnet, Music*   9:47
    — *Turn from Me, Spirit*   10:33
    — *Walter Pater*   13:27
    — *Whitman's Letters to Doyle*   9:61
    — *Yucatan*   12: 1
Mountains of the Moon — Mary Glover Nettleton   56:14
"Moving Wood" — Charlotte Carmichael Stopes   7:18
Mowery, William Byron — *Election of the Roulette, The*   33:52
Mowrer, Paul Scott — *In Brittany*   28:48
    — *Mist on the Moor*   28:48
    — *Phantom Washerwoman, The*   28:48
    — *Voice of the Dead, The*   28:48
Moxom, Philip S. — *Does Browning's Alkestis Interpret
    Euripides Fairly?*   8:42
Mozart and Salieri — Alexander Pushkin   31:29
Mr. Enright Entertains — Avery Abbott   34:12
Mr. Man — L. Miller — Translated by S. K. Padover
    and Chasye Cooperman   40:47
Mrs. Browning's Sonnets from the Portuguese —
    Allen Eastman Cross   1:17
Mrs. Langtry's "As You Like It" — Charlotte Porter   1:19
"Much Ado about Nothing" — W. J. Rolfe   4:18
Much Ado about Nothing, Character in —
    C. A. Wurtzburg   6:12
Much Ado about Nothing, Dramatic Passion in —
    C. A. Wurtzburg   6:55
Mud — Isabel McKinney   30:41
Mughanniname   21:46
Mukeiji, Dhan Gopal (with Mary Carolyn Davies),
    Translator — *Chintamini* — Ghose   25:14
Mulhall, Helen A. — *I Shall Forgive*   38:60
Mullen, Elizabeth Lester, Translator — *Codicil, The* —
    Ferrier   19:19
Mullins, Helene — *Institutionalized*   58:11
    — *Successful Life, A*   47:18
    — *Truth about Liars, The*   34:14
Mummy Hand, The — Winifred Adams Burr   55:17

170

Murger, Henri — *Walt Whitman and Murger* 6:484
Murger, Whitman and — Horace L. Traubel 6:484
Munich, Shakespeare in 1: 47
Munson, Cecil La Rue — *Two Poems* 50:181
Münsterberg, Margarete, Translator —
    Glimpse of a Childhood — Rainer Maria Rilke 27:120
Murderer, The — Clarenden Ross 30:596
Murdoch, William J. — *Thief! Thief!* 56:220
Murnik, Radoslav — *Napoleon's Samovar* 48:195
Murphee, Charles Randall — *Diamonds That Fell, The* 58:279
Murphy, Ethel Allen —
    Some Essentials of Literary Appreciations 20:390
Murphy, Olive Frances, Translator — *Jubilee, The* —
    Anton Chekhov 31:616
    — *Tragedian in Spite of Himself, The* —
    Anton Chekhov 33:268
Murray, Eleanor Vinton — *Three Poems* 47:348
Musaeus' "Hero and Leander," A Greek Sea Idyl 20:449
Music — E. K. Herron 19:110
Music Apparitions — Helen A. Clarke 2:facing 288
Music, Browning's "One Way of Love" —
    Helen A. Clarke 4: facing 288
Music, "Come Live With Me" — Helen A. Clarke 2:532
Music for Browning's Poems 1:430
Music in Flower Fragrance, The — Esther Matson 54:279
Music-Lover's Calendar, The 17D:122
Music, "My Star" — Helen A. Clarke 1:340
Music, "New Willow Song" — Helen A. Clarke 1: 29
Music, Rosseau's "Willow Song" 1:175
Music, Shelley's Song from "Prometheus" —
    H. A. Clarke 4: facing 384
Music, Spenser's "Januarie" — Helen A Clarke 4: facing 1
Music, "Throstle Song" — Helen A. Clarke 1:510
Musical Settings — *Browning's "Ask Not One Least*
    Word of Praise" 3:258
    — *Shakespeare's "Come Away Death"* 3:212
Musical Symbolism in Browning — Helen A. Clarke 3:260
Musing on Camelot and Avelon — Gustav Davidson 33:552
Musselman, N. H. — *Mila Whendle* 13: 22
Musset, Alfred de — *Adieu Suzon!* —
    Translated by Richard Eldridge 44:182
    — *Caprice, A* — Translated by Anne Grace West 33:395
Muttering — René Char 57:484
My Battle Cry — Rainer Maria Rilke 26:274
My Broken Dream — Louis Bartlett Chace 53:144
My Discovery — Gabriela Mistral 57:382
My Dream — Anne Cleveland Cheney 17D:102

171

My Father — An American — Dorothy Kaucher   57:48

My Friend the Catbird — Muriel Kinney   28:37

My God Dwelleth Not Within a Church —
    Marion Martin   52:17

My Hills — Anna Elizabeth Bennett   45:11

My Honey Boy — Charlotte F. Myers   54:35

My Little Shop Window — Charles Ballard   37:50

My Love — Charlotte F. Myers   54:35

My Love Came Riding — Alma Robison Higbee   52:17

My Mayflower — Stephen Berrien Stanton   36:46

My School Days in Old Russia

My Soul — Charlotte F. Myers   54:35

My Soul and I — Muriel Kinney   26:77

"My Star" — Helen A. Clarke   1:349

My Thoughts Name You — Jens Peter Jacobsen   30:37

My Trees — J. Homer Caskey   35:63

My Unfinished Portrait — Ferdinand Voteur   56:

Myers, Charlotte F. — Art   54:35

    — Our Gothic Church   54:119

    — Poems   54:35

Mygatt, Tracy D. — His Son   39:60

Mykilati, Magus — "The American" as Seen by a Melancholy Dane and a Mystical Hindoo   11:237, 37

Myrick, Arthur B., Translator — Gringoire —
    Theodore de Banville   27:12

"Mystery of the West," Mr. Dodge's   17D:11

Mystic Image in Rainer M. Rilke, The —
    Federico Olivero   41:37

Mysticism of William Blake, The — Benedict S. Alper   44:34

Myth of Leda in Yeats and Dario, The —
    Howard T. Young   55:13

Myths of Mary, The — Henry Seidel Canby   20:14

Myths, Solar, in "A Midsummer Night's Dream" —
    Sinclair Korner   3: 1

Mythology and Its Interpretation — John L. Patterson   37:60

Nameless — Jens Peter Jacobsen   31:36

Nantucket Finale — Gerhard Friedrich   54:37

Napoleon III, Modern Imperialism Shown in Browning's
    Portrait of — Charlotte Porter   12: 80

Napoleon's Samovar — Radoslav Murnik   48:19

Narikin, The — May Folwell Hoisington   34:47

Narsdny, Ivan — Fortune Favors Fools   23:30

Nature and Humanity — Mary R. Baldwin   33:148

Nature Anthologies — Harriott S. Olive   12:45

Nature, Feeling for, The — Max Batt   18:25

Nature in the Elizabethan Poets —
    Gamaliel Bradford, Jr.   7:52

Nature, Poetic Interpretation of — C. A. Binkley   13: 53
Nature-Songs — Joseph Bovshover   56:372
Nautical Phrases   13:316
Navarro, Francisco — *City, The*   54: 71
Need — Elizabeth Kinder   55:162
Need of Poetry Today — Kitty Parsons   52:172
Neeff, G. A. — *Style According to Spenser and Browning*   8:469
Negri, Ada — *Little Soldier Unknown, The*   28:476
Negro Becomes a Literary Contributor, The —
    Gertrude C. Thornhill   39:431
Nehls, Edward — *Handcart Expeditions, The*   47:315
    — *Lines written during Texas-Lousiana*
      Maneuvres, 1943   50:269
Neill, Isabel — *Rooted*   40:152
    — *Wings of Remembrance*   39:309
Nekrassov, Nikolai Alekseyevich — *Mothers*   26:278
Nelson, Ernest W., Translator — *Heaven's Blue* —
    Victor Rydberg   27:356
Nephew, The Dead — August von Kotzebue —
    Translated by Beatrice B. Beebe   38:160
Nerval, Gerard de — *Avril* —
    — *Delfica*   54:176
    Translated by Frances Taylor   26:113
    — *Fantaisie* — Translated by Frances Taylor   35:379
    — *Les Chimères*   51: 54
    — *Three Poems*   54:176
    — *Two Chimeras*   53:371
Neserius, Philip George — *Folk Entertainment in Eng-*
    land, the Latter Years of the Reign of Elizabeth   38:141
Nesmith, H. E., Jr. — *Browning's Science*   2:287
Nethercot, Arthur H. —
    Funeral March of a Marionette, The   31:232
    — *Peter Gink*   35:118
Nettleship, John T. —
    Robert Browning: Essays and Thoughts   8:265
Nettleton, Mary Glover — *Mountains of the Moon*   56:147
Never the Twain — Lydia Glover Deseo   41:272
New Aspect of Shakespeare's Conception of Woman, A —
    Max Huhner, M.D.   32: 98
New Book on Shakespeare   7: 37
New Books   48:183, 276, 366; 49:86, 183, 279, 373; 50:80, 183,
      273, 379; 51:87, 180, 273, 369; 52:81, 177, 273, 370;
      53:82, 182, 280, 373; 54:376; 55:85, 281, 376; 56:89,
      182, 277, 379; 57: 180, 281
New Drama — Homer H. Howard   23:145, 290
New England Poet's Dream — Belle Chapman Morrill   57:290
New Letters of Henrik Ibsen —
    Translated by Louis Bailey and Arne Kildal   19:420

New Pirandello in "Diana e la Tuda," The —
    Fredericka Blankner —
    Translated by Beatrice B. Beebe   40:215
New Poetic Form as Shown in Browning   2:234
New Poetry, The — James Oppenheim   22:155
New Poets Judged by Old Standards —
    Clara F. McIntyre   28:445
New Star, The — Reinhold Fuchs —
    Translated by Max Batt   20:479
New Star — Gustav Davidson   33:617
New Willow Song, A — Helen A. Clarke   1: 27
New Year's Festival — Kay De Bard Hall   54:162
New York vs Chicago as a Dramatic Center —
    Arthur Row   22:151
Newberry, John Strong, Translator —
    Steamer Tenacity, The — Charles Vildrac   32:463
Newell, Charlotte — *Poets Laureate, The*   4:552, 599
Newman, Benjamin W. — *Salt Water*   36:232
    — *Underground*   38:571
Newton's Brain — Jakob Arbes   4: 429, 511, 569, 616
Nibelungenlied, Sigfried's Stories in the — ·
    Camillo von Klenze   10:543
Nibelungenlied, The — W. H. Carruth   17A:119
Nicholas, Donna — *I Bore a Son*   53: 69
Nielson, Harold — *Robert Herrick*   19:337
Nietzsche, Friedrich — *Dionysos Dithyrambs, The*
    — *Seventh Solitude From the*—
    Translated by L. M. Kueffner   27:228
    — *Trunkne Lied, Das*   16C:91; 21:416
    — *Venice*   23: 79
Night — Jane Dransfield Stone   24:277
Night — Afanasiy Fiet —
    Translated by George F. Lake   34:309
Night — Alcman   54: 70
Night — Nora Peters   52: 79
Night — Renato Fucini —
    Translated by Herbert King Stone   32:390
Night — William Allen Ward   50:263
Night in a Cathedral, A — William Morris   10:473
Night Piece — Louis A. Shaw II   56:276
Night Piece — William W. Chance   55:352
Night-School Song — Modern Greek Folk Song   9:355
Night Song — David Stacton   55:135
Night Song — Frances Crawford Orr   48:220
Night Train — Adele Kelley Thompson   46:207
Night's Lodging, A — Maxim Gorki   16D: 1

Nightcap of The Prophet Elias, The —
    August von Kotzebue —
    Translated by Beatrice B. Beebe   40:391
Nightfall — Wilhelmina K. Bailey   21: 96
Nightingale — Alice Henson Ernst   37:293
Ninth Night, The — Victor Dyk   29: 90
Nivens, Helen — Omega Waits   55: 84
    — Phoenix Eyes   55: 84
Nixon, John, Jr. — Going   57:167
    — Housekeeping   57:139
    — Northeast of Yesterday   55: 81
    — Town Lights   55:180
No More Fear — William R. Benet   24:119
No Sound of a Door — David R. Clark   58:181
No Tears — Hazel Griffith Davis   56:378
No Use — Esther M. Robidoux   52:270
Noa, Frederic M. — Theatrical Event in Havana, A   17B:118
Noailles, Comtesse de — In This Belated Twilight   45:226
    — To the Beloved — Translated by Felix Sper   38:446
Noarrieli, Jean de — Francis Jammes   50:362
Nobel Prize for Literature   16A:136
Noble, Edmund — Philosophy of Rhyme, A   7:585
Nocturn — José Asuncion Silva   53:360
Nocturne — F. T. Marinetti —
    Translated by Anne Simon   25:439
Nocturne — A. Rassato —
    Translated by Louise W. Kidder   17A:134
Noel, Marie — Poet's Prayer, The —
    Translated by Joseph T. Shipley   41:444
    — Delusion of a Human Cup, The   33:152
Noguchi, Yone — Demon's Shell, The   17C: 44
    — Japanese Hokku Poems   29:102
    — Japanese Women in Literature   15C: 88
    — Popular Songs of Japan   15B: 78
    — Translator — Melon Thief, The   15A: 40
    — Perfect Jewel Maiden, The   28:334
    — Sorrow of Yuya, The   28:338
    — Three Selections from the Noh Drama   29:447
Noh Drama, Three Translations from — Yone Noguchi   29:447
Noller, John Scholte — Modern German Literature   16C:127
Nomad Palaces, The — Gustav Kahn —
    Translated by Curtis Hidden Page   16D: 78
Noon — Leconte de Lisle —
    Translated by Mary Louise Dunbar   24:332
Noon — Leconte de Lisle   53: 58
Nooshich, Branislav — Prince of Semberia, The —
    Translated by Luka Djurichich and Bertha W.
    Clark   33: 85

Norlin, George — *Ancient Realist, An*   27:417
Norman, Henderson D. —
    Powers of Darkness and the Cock of Dawn, The   34:283
Norman, Hilda Laura — *Sensible Man, The*   32:580
Norris, J. Parker — *Editors of Shakespeare, The*   1: 64
    — *First American Editor of Shakespeare, The*   2:424
Northeast of Yesterday — John Nixon, Jr.   55: 81
Norther, The — Albert E. Trombly   31:465
Norton, Dan —
    All This I Know When Sounds the Chinese Lute   37:575
Norwegian Peasant Lad and His Dream-Tune, The —
    Björnstjerne Björnson —
    Translated by E. D. Girdlestone   5: 52
Nostalgia — Mana Willis Fisher   49:164
Not at Home — Henri Lavedan   28:407
Note on the Contemporary Catholic Theatre, A —
    Anthony J. Klančar   50:371
Novak, David — *City, The*   36:208
Novel, Earliest Known   8:168
Novels of A. Palacio Valdés, The — S. Griswold Morley   16C: 92
Novelette, Danish, Karen — Kielland   4:385
Noveletto — Mary Margaret Russell   41:418
Novelists and Poets, Current French —
    Curtis Hidden Page   18:113
November — Clara Southmayd Ludlow   8:112
November Bluebird — Louis Bartlett Chace   53:144
Novgorod the Great — Guber   49:366
Now Let Me Hasten — Jane Dransfield   46: 82
Noyes, Alfred, In Retrospect — Mabel Vincent   41:293
Noyes, George Rapall, Translator —
    — *At the Jolly Spot* — Alexander Ostrovsky   36: 1
    — *Bondwomen* — Alexander Ostrovsky   36:475
    — *Cat Has Not Always Carnival, A* —
    Alexander Ostrovsky   40:317
    — *Diarmuid and Grainne* — Julius Zeyer   44:289
    — *Dobromila Rettig* — Alois Jirasek   31:475
    — *Fairy Gold* — Alexander Ostrovsky   40: 1
    — *In the City* — Semen Yushkevich   47: 99
    — *Lantern, The* — Alois Jirasek   36:317
    — *Last Sacrifice, A* — Alexander Ostrovsky   39:317
    — *Novgorod the Great* — Guber   49:366
    — *Princess Pampelishka, The*   54: 3
    — *Resurrection of Lazarus, The* —
    Ivo Vojnovich   37:317
    — *Song of Fate, The* — Alexander Blok   44: 1
    — *Trilogy of Dubrovnik* — Ivo Vojnovich   56:195
    — *Wolves and Sheep* — Alexander Ostrovsky   37:159
    — *You Can't Just Live as You Please*   49:203

Noyes, Humphrey F. — *Family of My Heart, The*   52:175
"Numpholeptos," Browning's Science as Shown in   2:617
Nun, To a Beautiful — Nathan Haskell Dole   5:149
Nun's Reply, The — Anna Chapin Rey   5:478
Nut Brown Maid, The Authorship of the —
    Eugene C. Dolson   20:387
Nyerges, Anton N., Translator —
    Selections from Endre Ady   48:359
    — *Two Poems* — Alexander Petöfi   45:227
Nymph, The — Maxim Gorki — Translated by J. Vital
    de Porte and Roy Temple House   24:368

O'Brien, Edward J. — *Arthur Upson*   25:219
    — *Burden of Lost Prophets, The*   25:370
    — *Francis Thompson*   19:293
    — *Hosting of the Sidhe*   26:399
    — *Inspiration of Crashaw, The*   21:397
    — *Lionel Johnson*   26:405
O'Brien, Edward J., Translator — *Miguel Manara* —
    O. W. Milosz   30:224
    — *Poetry of the Epoch, The* — Beauduin   25:336
    — *Sancta Susanna* — Stramm   25:145
    — *Town in Me, The* — Beauduin   25:348
O'Brien, Francis — *For the Young Dead*   44:286
O'Brien, Nadine — *Your Son — and Mine*   51: 80
O'Brien, Seumas — *Wild Boar, The*   38:536
O Celia — Cleon Marquis   57:493
O'Connor, Evelyn —
    Possible Source of Shakespeare's Culture, A   23:114
O'Connor, Oleta Joan, Translator — *Song of Fate* — Blok   44: 1
O'Dair, Maud Murat — *Dower Rug, The*   36:468
O'Neill, Nance — Tragic Art of — C. P.   15A:104
O'Shaughnessy, Arthur, Life and Works of —
    Mrs. Moulton   7:211
O'Sheel, Shamus — *Isadora Duncan, Priestess*   21:480
"O When Will God Come as a Mighty Flood?" —
    Florence Kiper Frank   26:649
Obscure God, To the — Paula Ludwig   58:326
Obsession of Edgar Allan Poe   12: 42
Occident — Louis J. Block   9:474
Ochiai, T., Translator — *Kanawa* — Motokiyo   23:222
Odalisque — Thomas Rubino   51:167
Odcombian Legge-Stretcher, The — Charlotte M. Leavitt   34:210
Ode in Miniature — Henri de Regnier   45:349
Ode on the Heights — Arthur Franklin Johnson   15D: 95
"Ode to Duty"   8:106
Ode to the Parents of a Dead Babe — Haras Rengaw   53: 2

Odelette — Henri de Regnier   45:348
Odhner, Cyriel — *Base of Ching-Li, The* —
    Adapted from the Chinese   36:154
Oedipus Myth in Greek Literature: Study Program   11:102
Of One Most Beautiful — Richard Burdick Eldridge   47:349
Of Poetry as a Necessity — Esther Watson   30:138
Of Time and the Dry Heart — Ruth Forbes Sherry   44:176
Of Words That Are Winged — Esther Matson   38:307
Off the Road — Pauline Rodgers Young   36:300
Offering, An — Edward T. Lewis   58:122
Ogden, Pauline — *Little Hill, A*   43:371
Ogilvie, Mary Gould — *Before a Poem Is*   48:179
Okamato, Kido — *Lady Hosokawa* —
    Translated by Asataro Miyameri   37: 1
Old Clavichord, An — Martha of Sillen —
    Translated by Charles Wharton Stork   34:314
Old Cow Man, The — Charles Badger Clark   28:742
Old Earth — June R. Downey   11:354
Old-Fashioned Roses — Margaret I. Martin   52:362
Old Gaelic Tune of Hospitality — Anonymous   46: 2
Old Jake — Richard Butler Glaenzer   30:467
Old Love Affair, The — August von Kotzebue —
    Translated by Beatrice B. Beebe   38:220
Old Man — Curt Storm   47:189
Old Mother — Ruth M. Parks   57:225
Old Order, The — Evelyn Emig   32:586
Old Pictures in Florence —
    Charlotte Porter and Helen A. Clarke   8:586
Old Road, The — David Mahoney   46:285
Old Song, An — Russell W. Hendee   38:296
Old Trees in Spring — Gordon Lockhart   58: 89
Old Wash Lucas — Paul Green   35:254
Olive, Harriott S. —
    Berlin Stage during the Past Season, The   12:570
    — *Nature Anthologies*   12:459
    — *"Songs from the Ghetto" and "A Vision of
    Hellas"*   12:308
Olive, Harriott S., Translator —
    Master of Palmyra, The — Wilbrandt   13:161
Olives, The — Lope de Rueda —
    Translated by Willis Knapp Jones   39:310
Oliver, Katharine —
    Theatre of the French Revolution, The   30:608
Olivero, Federico — *Emile Verhaeren's Lyric Trilogy*   25: 63
    — *Francis Jammes*   34:177
    — *Georges Rodenbach*   27:652
    — *Mystic Image in Rainer M. Rilke*   41:379

— Paul Claudel 29:110
— Stéphane Mallarmé 28:327
Olmstead, E. W. (with F. D. Burnet), Translator —
  Fountain of the Satyr, The — De Castro 21: 88
Olympus and Kissivos — Modern Greek Folk Song ... 9:353
Omar Khayyam and Mysticism — Hereward Carrington ... 19:458
Omar Khayyam, New Renderings of —
  Nathan Haskell Dole 10:293
Omega Waits — Helen Nivens 55: 84
On a Figure of France Crucified — Gabriele d'Annunzio ... 27:111
On a Popular Poet — P. T. Hopkins 32:581
On a River — Caroline Henning Bair 48:335
On Bayou La Batre — Bessie Collins Moore 37:576
On Certain Uses of Apuleius' Story of Cupid and Psyche
  in English Literature —
  Elizabeth Hazelton Haight 26:744
On Female Poets — Percie Trowbridge Hopkins ... 30:588
On Golgotha — J. S. Machar 28:485
On Letters — Charles Ballard 53:350
On Past the Bars — Josephine Hawks 46:283
On Poetry — Read Bain 45:307
On Probation — Max Dreyer —
  Translated by Mary Harned 14B: 40
On Rate of Learning Our Mission — Don Geiger ... 57:355
On Reading the Greek Dramatists — Nathan Rosenbaum ... 57:386
On the Beach — Lilian Saunders 36:628
On the Breaking of the Bay Colt —
  Albert Edmund Trombly 29:605
On the Cliffs — Edith Lawrence 48:304
On the Death of a Child — Paul Heyse 26:279
On the Early English Anthologies —
  C. C. H. Williamson 44: 42
On the Highlands 13:335
On the Lonely Hallig — Detlev von Liliencron ... 27:232
On the Portrait of a Beautiful Lady Carved on Her
  Tombstone — Giacomo Leopardi 57:366
On the Sandy Shore — Henri de Regnier 54:221
On the Way — Ernst Viktor Knape 45:351
On Titles — Felix Spir 35:127
On Walking Wings — Paul Alexander Bartlett ... 52: 30
Ona, Pedro de — Arauco Tamed 49: 41
"One Man Escapes" —
  Joseph Auslander and Gustav Davidson 44:97, 193
"One Word More," Allusions in 3:533
"One Way of Love" — P. A. C. 3:588
"One Way of Love" (song) .... 4: facing 288
Onions, William E. — Coward 34:428

179

Only Fools Understand — Pierre Emmanuel   57:369
Opera in America — Julia Cline   41:239
Opera vs. Drama   23:302
Ophelia, A Brief for — Crane Walton   3:569
Ophelia, Tragedy of, The — David A. McKnight   12:253
Oppenheim, James — *New Poetry, The*   22:155
Ordinary Ones, The — Ellen Rogers   55:290
Orient, The — Lewis J. Block   9:473
Oriental Dream — Anthero de Quental   29:626
Oriental Shop, The — Julia Hall Bartholomew   30:473
Original of Wyatt's "Unmeasurable Mountains"
     Albert S. Cook   3: 97
Orleans, Charles d' — *Rondel* —
     Translated by Herman Salinger   39:595
     — *Spring*   55: 2
Orogo, Michael — *Turn Thou Thy Tears*   49: 81
Orr, Frances Crawford — *Night Song*   48:220
Orters, Mary Leighton — *Tonight*   51:156
Ortiz-Vargas, A — *Gabriela Mistral*   46:339
Ortlepp, Vivian — *Poems*   48:263
Osborne, Willson — *Meditation on a Hillside*   42:164
Oscar Wilde Fifteen Years After — F. G. H.   27:411
Oscar Wilde Still Lives — Arthur Row   30:433
Ostrovsky, Alexander — *At the Jolly Spot* — Translated
     by Jane Paxton Campbell and George Rapall
     Noyes   36: 1
     — *Bondwomen* — Translated by Schone Char-
     lotte Kurlandzik and George Rapall Noyes   36:475
     — *Cat Has Not Always Carnival, A* — Translated
     by Jane Paxton Campbell and George Rapall
     Noyes   40:317
     — *Fairy Gold* — Translated by Camilla Chapin
     and George Rapall Noyes   40: 1
     — *Last Sacrifice, A* — Translated by Eugenia
     Korvin Kronkovsky and George Rapall Noyes   39:317
     — *Wolves and Sheep* — Translated by Inez Sachs
     Colby and George Rapall Noyes   37:159
     — *You Can't Live Just as You Please*   49:203
Otello, Verdi's   1:444
Othello and Iago, The Characters of —
     Katherine G. Blake   18:236
Othello and "Luria," Types and Arts Compared —
     L. A. Sherman   6:585
Othello, Are the Rhymed Lines in, Shakespeare's? —
     W. J. Rolfe   10:416
Othello in Constantinople   1:576
"Othello" in Paris — Théodore Child   1:301, 362

Othello: Moral Proportion and Fatalism —
Ella Adams Moore   7:424
Othello: Study Programs —
Charlotte Porter and Helen A. Clarke   9:94; 20:394
Othello: Was He a Negro? — W. J. Rolfe   10:251
Other, The — Miguel de Unamuno   53: 3
Other Blind Man of Jericho, The — Earl W. Hildreth   37:512
Other Room, The — Frances Witherspoon   38:269
Other Side of the Door, The — Roland English Hartley   41:223
"Other's Bread" — Virginia Stait   34:316
Our Disillusioned Poets — Samuel D. Schamlhausen   38:401
Our Frank — August von Kotzebue —
Translated by Beatrice B. Beebe   38:206
Our Gothic Church — Charlotte F. Myers   54:119
Our Lady of Past Empires — Emile Verhaeren   51: 48
Our Lady of Wistfulness — William Force Stead   29:373
Our Little Helpmeet — Jules Laforge —
Translated by Joseph T. Shipley   36:626
Our Moribund Verse — Phyllis Ackerman   29:356
Our Poesy is as a Gum — Porter Sargent   42:329
Our Theatre in 1927 and the Point of View —
Arthur William Row   38:464
Our Trust — Ruth Lambert Jones   30: 80
Outcast, The — August Strindberg —
Translated by Mary Harned   17C: 8
Outcasts — E. R. Sammis   36:306
Overlooking the Dyke — Frances Barbara Grafe   53:165
Overman, E. L., Translator — *Bright Morning, A*   27:669
Overwhelmed — Richard Dehmel   55:340
*Ovid as a Short Story Writer in the Light of Modern
Technique* — Alexander Kadison   29:206
Owen, Elizabeth Leslie — *Two Poems*   54: 84
Owen, Louise — *Sonnet*   40: 91
Ox, The — Giosue Carducci —
Translated by William A. Drake   35:113

"P. A. C." (Charlotte Porter and Helen A. Clarke) —
  — *Aims of Literary Study, The*   7:270, 6
  — *Browning Study Hints*   3:521, 588, 637; 5:453
  — *"Julius Caesar" and "Strafford": A Compara-
tive Study*   4:148
  — *Longfellow's "Golden Legend"
and its Analogues*   4: 91
  — *Reading Course in Whitman*   6:644
  — *School of Literature*   6:47, 102, 161, 273, 520, 570;
7:41, 105, 161, 218, 275, 520,
576; 8:106, 158, 218, 272, 347,
454

— Study of *"Locksley Hall"* and *"Sixty Years
 After"*   5: 34
— Study of *Shakespeare's "Winter's Tale"*   4:51(
— Study of *"Strafford"*   1:190, 236, 282, 332, 372, 426,
                                                  511, 56:
Padover, S. K., Translator — *Mr. Man* — L. Miller   40:47:
Paesisti of the Nineteenth Century, The —
   Thomas D. Bergen   19:23:
Page, Curtis Hidden —
   Current French Poets and Novelists   18:11:
   — *Lady of Tripoli, The*   18:27:
   — *Litanies of Love, The*   18:19:
   — *Prayer of the Poet, The*   17C: :
Page, Curtis Hidden, Translator — *Chains, The* —
   Sully Prud'homme   16D: 7:
   — From *"The Nomad Palaces"* — Kahn   16D: 7:
Pailleron, Edouard — *Spark, The*   38:37:
Pain of Beauty, The — Ethel Pechin Dupuis   50:18:
Painted Legends — Christabel Fiske   35:38(
Palamas, Kostes, A Modern Greek World-Poet —
   Aristides E. Phoutrides   28: 7:
Palen, Jennie M. — *Heedless*   53:17:
   — *Victory*   53:17:
Panama, Off the Coast of — Annie Lake Townsend   2:624
Pancoast, Henry S. — *"Luria," Its Story and Motive*   1:553
                                                 2: 1:
   — *Old Age and Poets*   3: 5:
Pantheism — Giosue Carducci —
   Translated by William A. Drake   35: 9:
Paolo and Francesca Theme in Modern Drama, The —
   Gertrude Gardner Brainerd   27:39(
Papa and Mamma — Eduardo Barrios —
   Translated by Willis Knapp Jones   33:28(
Papá Juan, or The Centenarian —
   Serafin and Joaquin Alvarez Quintero   29:25:
Papers of the Browning Society in Boston —
   Alice Kent Robertson   1:26:
Papers of the Shakespeare Society of Philadelphia —
   Richard L. Ashhurst   1:36:
Parable and a Prophecy, A — Elizabeth Jacobi   34:45:
Parable of the Tree and the Wind — S. V. A. R.   3:37:
Paracelsus and Bombast — W. J. Rolfe   3:10:
Paracelsus and "The Data of Ethics" — Helen A. Clarke   1:117
Paradise, Horses of — Helena Magaret   40:45:
"Paradise" of Dante — Ellen M. Mitchell   7:39:
Paradox — Ruth Lambert Jones   30:55:
Paradoxical Ethics of Browning, The —
   Oscar W. Firkins   23:34:

arcell, Lillian — *Two Poems*   46: 75
aris Exposition   1:541
aris Letter — Charles Seymour   2:111, 222
aris, "Othello" in   1:301, 362
arisian Nocturnes — Paul Verlaine   30:461
arke, James H. — Atonement   41: 59
arks, Ruth M. — Old Mother   57:225
Parsifal": Motivation of, the — Paul H. Grummann   16C:123
Parsifal," On Staging of — George Turner Phelps   15D: 97
arsons, Eugene — Another Note on Tennyson   10:147
    — Symbolism of "Holy Grail" —
arsons, Kitty — Need of Poetry Today, The   52:172
arsons, Mabel Holmes — Beside the Road   30:460
    — Fantasy of Life, The   28:368
    — Mist   28:372
    — Strindberg, Reality and the Dream Play   26:763
arting — Jeanne Storm   47: 83
ascal, Floy — Facing Reality   33:451
aschall, Alma — When the Bugle Blows   55: 39
ascoli and Recent Italian Poetry —
    Gertrude E. T. Slaughter   18:501
ascoli, Giovanni — Anne Simon   27:190
asser-By, The Coppée — Translated by L. Dora   34:461
assing of Dana's People, The — Anna Throop Craig   35:605
assing of the Green, The — Jeannette Marks   18:393
assion's Furnace — Josip Kosor —
    Translated by F. S. Copeland   41:459
assover Eve — Judah M. Turkat   53:149
astel — Theophile Gautier —
    Translated by William A. Drake   36:243
astoral — Robert Kimberly   49:176
astoral for Easter: Opus 1 — Bruce P. Woodford   53: 50
astoral Landscape — Charlotte F. Myers   54:119
astoral Poetry — Mary Louise Dunbar   18:265
Pasvolsky, Leo, Translator — *Incident, An* —
    Leonid Andreyev   27:171
Pater, Walter — William Mountain   13:275
Pater, Walter: Some of His Imaginary Portraits —
    Donald Worth Marshall   32:431
Path of the Russian Theatre and "Le Coq d'Or," The —
    Alexander Bakshey   27:164
Pathetic Fallacy, Ruskin's — Edward Payson Morton   12: 58
Patience — Edna Becker   42:290
Patience of Li Po, The — Charles Farber   58:158
Paton, Lucy Allen — *Bit of Art from Matthew Arnold, A*   8:134
    — Phase of William Blake's Romanticism, A   5:481
Pattee, Fred Lewis — Fear in Macbeth   10: 92

— *Longfellow and German Romance*   17A: 5
— *Man of the West, The*   24:24
Pattee, Loueen, Translator — *Agnes Bernauer* — Hebbel 20:
Patten, E. M., Translator — *Abendfeier* — E. Ziel   27:70
— *Last Farewell, The* — Don José Rizal   26:39
Pattern for a Painted Screen — Lucy Salamanca   54:17
Patterson, John —
    Some Lyrics of Anacreon in Pseudo-Anacreon   9:40
Patterson, John L. — *Book of Praises*   43:28
— *Mythology and Its Interpretation*   37:60
Patton, Beatrice Ayer — *Hawaiian Pantheon*   47:17
— *Poet Lore of Hawaii*   44:25
Patton, Ruth Ellen — *Poems*   46: 8
Paul Claudel — Frederick Lehner   51:25
Paul Verlaine — Federico Olivero   31:26
Paulding, J. K. — *Björnson's "Beyond Human Strength"* 13:54
"Pauline," Allusion in   1: 8
"Pauline", Comparison of Old and New Editions   1:52
"Pauline," Reference Index to, A   1: 3
Pauvres, Les — Verhaeren   31:46
Payment Time — Paul Bourget   11:47
Payne, Iden — *Where Love Is*   37:59
Payne, Maidi — *Vow by a Star-Dropped Sky*   46: 4
Payro, Roberto — *Tragic Song, The*   50:
Peabody, Josephine Preston — *Caravans*   13:54
— *"Marlowe"*   14A:18
— *Modern Life and Modern Poetry*   14A: 5
— *Source, The*   13:54
— *Stay-at-Home, The*   13:54
— *Wings, The*   25:35
Peabody, Josephine Preston,
    As a Lyricist and Dramatist —
    Annie Russell Marble   15B:14
Peace at Home — Georges Courteline   29:33
Peace at Home — *At Any Price* — Guy de Maupassant 47:19
Peace on Earth — Ada Mixon   28: 6
Peacey, Howard Translator — *Links* —
    Herman Heijermans   38:
Peacock, Marjorie Beatrice, Translator —
    Novgorod The Great   49:36
Pearl, The — Translated by Anna Robertson Brown   5:43
"Pearl of Princesses, The" — John Andrew Hamilton 44:24
Pearson, L. E. — *John Muir, Prophet-Naturalist*   36: 4
Pearson, Lu Emily — *Charles Lamb, Literary Critic* 40:56
Pearson, P. H. —
    Bellman: The Swedish Poet of Native Romance   11:251
Peart, S. E. —
    Comradeship of Antony and Cleopatra, The   4:217

184

— *Portia vs the Lawyers*   2:658
Pechkoff, Alexis, A Study of the Work of —
    Albert Phelps   15C: 53
Pedio, E. — *Human Ecstasy*   17A:133
Peeling Apples — John Robert Quinn   57:269
Peer Gynt: An Intepretation — Jane Dransfield Stone   18:383
Pegasus Club
Péguy, Charles — *Saint Geneviève*   28:246
Peguy, Charles — Elizabeth S. Dickerman   28:246
Pelée, Lillian Sutton — *At the Little Pipe*   31:422
    — *Stringing Beads*   39:295
    — *Ties of Blood*   32:572
Pélléas and Mélisande — Maurice Maeterlinck   6:413
Pena, Martins — *Rural Justice of the Peace, A*   54: 99
Penalty — Margaret King Moore   36:153
Pence, J. A. — *Extracts from Letters on "Hamlet" from*
    Prest. Adams and J. H. Hackett   10:459
Pendelton, Charlotte — *Browning's Memorial*   1: facing 400
    — *From the "Roman de la Rose"*   1:549
    — *Spring Song, A*   1:511
    — *Study in Shakespeare's Fairy Rhythms, A*   1: 30
Pendergrass, Jean —
    To You Who Scoff at Makers of Verse   37:596
Perennial Witticism vs a Shakespearean Crux —
    Louis N. Feipel   23:341
Peretz Hirschbein — Charles A. Madison   38:106
Peretz, I. L. — *Amnon and Tamar*   48:149
Peretz, Isaak Loeb — Charles A. Madison   37: 73
Perez, J. L. — *Eighth Circle of Gehenna, The* —
    Translated by Jerome Roman   30:436
Perfect Jewel Maiden, The —
    Translated by Yone Noguchi   28:334
Perfect Rose, The — Emma D. Babcock   54:183
Performance of Peabody's "Marlowe" at Agassiz Home,
    Radcliffe College   16C:155
Perfumed Thorns — Juan Ramon Jimenez —
    Translated by Herbert King Stone   32:374
Perry, Grace — *Three Poems*   58: 44
Perry, Jeannette Barbour — *Is Blank Verse Lawless?*   8:528
Perry, Sara — *Immortality*   57:495
    — *Love Triumphant*   57:494
    — *Wonder*   57:494
Persian Poetry, Some Characteristics of   3: 1
Personalia — Matthew Arnold   8:100
Pessimism of the Ring of the Nibelungen, The —
    Paul H. Grummann   26:258
Pessimist Poet, A   5:385

185

Petals — Gwen Halvosa   58:370
Peter Gink — Arthur H. Nethercot   35:118
Peters, Nora — *Night*   52: 79
Peterson, Gordon E. — *Autumn*   43:362
Petho, Emery E. — *Harvest Refrain*   51:155
Petit, Victor Perez — *Moonlight Sonata*   51:353
Petite Vierge, La — Verhaeren   31:460
Petöfi, Alexander — *Fairy Dream*   48:112
— *Two Poems*   45:227
Petr Vok Rozmberk — Frantisek Adolf Subert   31: 1
Petrova, Olga — *Refuge*   58:195
Petrunkevich, Alexander, Translator —
    Lay of the War Ride of Igor, The   30:289
Pettinella, D. M., Translator — *Poems* — Murillo Araujo   58:367
— *Poems* — *Franco Mattacotti*   58:368
Pfeiffer, Edward H., Translator — *Prayer* —
    Guy Charles Cros   32:315
    — *Sonnet à Hélène* — Pierre de Ronsard   34:151
    — *Statue, A (The Apostle)*   47: 98
Phantasms — Robert Bracco —
    Translated by Dirce St. Cyr   19:241
Phantom Washerwoman, The — Paul Scott Mowrer   28:483
Phantoms — Marian Martin   53:118
Pharaoh's Daughter — Jon Trausti   57: 3
Pharr, Emory C. — *For You Who Have Been To Sea*   47:384
Phayre, Ignatius — *Crowned Poetess of Brazil: Rosalina
    Cuelho Lisboa*   40:110
Phèdre   17C: 59
Phelan, Lawrence — *Summer's End*   48:141
Phelps, Albert — *Later Work of Maurice Maeterlinck*   11:357
    — *Maxim The Bitter*:
    A Study of the Work of Alexis Pechkoff   15C: 53
Phelps, C. E. D. — *Browning*   5:288
Phelps, George Turner — *On The Staging of Parsifal*   15D: 97
Phelps, Mary — *Joy Element of Browning, The*   15B: 95
Phillippine Poetry — Hadwin Williams   40:288
Phillips, A. L., Translator — *Christmas Eve*.   49:355
Phillips, Addison Leroy — *Chaucer's Good Counsel*   48:268
Phillips, Stephen   10:430, 448
Phillips' "Paolo and Francesca" — C. P.   12:126
Phillips' "Ulysses" — Charlotte Porter   14A:128
Philology and Literature, Studies in — P.   9:143
Philosophical Note on "King John", A — L. W. Elder   22:314
Philosophy and Literature, Characteristics of —
    Emil C. Wilm   24:122
Philosophy and Poetry Again — Norman Hapgood   8:471
Philosophy of Balzac — Catherine Beech Ely   30:381

186

Philosophy of The Tooth Brush, The —
    Anita and Albert Weinberg   36:615
Phipps, A. H. — *More About Apples* 40:144
Phoenix, The — August Strindberg —
    Translated by H. C. P. and C. P.   6:611
Phoenix, The, Cynewulf — Anna Robertson Brown   2:523
Phoenix Eyes — Helen Nivens   55: 84
Phoenix Feather — Carrie Ward Lyon   56:236
Phosphorescence — Lilian Saunders   36:628
Phoutrides, Aristides E. —
    Literary Impulse of Modern Greece, The   26: 56
Picard, Hélène — *Memories*   31:242
Pico, Pedro E. — *You Can't Fool With Love*   49:107
Pierre Louys and The Songs of Bilitis — Ernest S. Bates
    and Gladys C. Graham   32:562
Pierre Louys of Hellas — Joseph T. Shipley   37:584
Pierrot Dead   16D: 81
Pierrot, Cult of, The   19:318
"Pietro of Albano" Variants of Browning's —
    Charlotte Porter   3:577
Pifer, Alan J. — *Poems*   46:380
Pigeon, The — Robert Wilson McKnight   30:579
Pigeonneau's Inadvertent Romance — Anatole France   11: 28
Pilgrim — Gladys Marriefield   55:242
Pilgrim's Way, The — Gretchen Warren   26:403
Pinder, Frances Dickenson — *Wind of April*   33:117
Pine Music — Genevieve Stephens   49:382
Pines That Forever Dream — Louis Bartlett Chace   56:223
Pines, To The — Lucille Price Leonard   25:215
Pinkney, Dorothy Cowles — *Casualty Between Wars*   56:219
    Look Well at This Fair Hostess, Friends   55:183
    — *Three Poems*   55:238
Piper, The — Thomas S. Jones, Jr.   15C: 76
"Pippa Passes" — Isabel Francis Bellows   6:133
"Pippa Passes" and "Pippa Dances" — Helen A. Clarke   20:122
"Pippa Passes" on the Stage — David Kelly Lambuth   18:107
Pippa's Power, Secret of, The — Charles J. Woodbury   3:350
Pirandello, Luigi — *Doctor's Duty, The*   48:291
Pistol of the Beg, — K. M. Capek
    Translated by Schonberger   34:475
Place We Loved, The — Isla Paschal Richardson   40:112
Plaint — Oscar C. Williams   31:274
Planet Home — Gustav Davidson   45:350
Plastic Word, The — Anna Cox Stephens   12:384
Plato as a Literary School for Writers —
    Janet Payne Bowles   17D: 90
Platt, Isaac Hull — *Shelley and Whitman*:
    A Comparison and a Contrast   8:332

187

Plays of Oskar Kokoschka, The — Barrett H. Clark   35:522
Playfarer, The — Homer H. Howard   23:145
Playhouse, The — Charlotte Porter   23:153, 294
Playreader — Helen A. Clarke   23:155, 300
Pleasant Evening, The — Theophile Gautier —
    Translated by Emanuel Eisenberg   36:462
Plight of Dramatic Criticism, The — Arthur Swan   24:201
Plimpton, Harriet — *Catalog of Joys, A*   44:184
    — *Dark Window*   48:336
    — *"I Will Not Have It So"*   46:213
    — *Maple Seed*   50: 45
    — *Rain Making Clear, The*   53:349
    — *Rest?*   53:347
    — *So Much of Light*   51: 3
Pliny's Authors — G. S. Bryan   18:519
Plosky, Anna — Two Poems   47:260
Plutarch's "Virtuous Deeds of Women" — John Albee   11: 20
Pluto Meditates — Mary Willis Shelburne   44: 98
Podesta, José J. —*First Argentine Gaucho Drama, The*   51: 99
Poe, Edgar Allan and Whistler   20:391
Poe, Edgar Allan, Grave of — Jennie Bard Dugdale   11:583
Poe, Edgar Allan, New Edition of — C.   7:519
Poe, Edgar Allan, Obsession of, The — *John Phelps Fruit*   12: 42
Poe. Edgar Allan, On Happiness — Danske Dandridge   15D:108
Poe, Edgar Allan, Plea for, A — G. L. Swiggett   13:379
Poe, Edgar Allen: Rationale of the Short Story, The
    — John Phelps Fruit   16A: 57
Poem for A Little Girl — A. Wilber Stevens   55:263
Poem Translations from the Symphonies of Beethoven —
    Sara De Ford   54:291
Poems — F. T. Marinetti, Translated by Anne Simon   25:439
Poems by Arno Holz — Translated by Lucille E. Hein   48: 92
Poems from Latin America —
    Translated by Lloyd Mallan   51: 74
Poems From the Yiddish — Aaron Schmuller   58: 80
Poems of Leprosy, Two — Arthur Fremont Rider   17C:104
Poems, Use of Alliteration in Shakespeare's, The   5:190
Poema de la Niebla Ciudadana — Joaquin Gomez Bas   53:154
Poet, A Canadian, Isabella V. Crawford —
    — Lawrence J. Burpee   13:575
Poet, A Tory — P.   3:530
Poet and Poetry, The — Yevgeni Vinekurov   58:317
Poet: Can (He) Be Democratic — "Mr. Breeze"   7:610
Poet Lore of Hawaii — Beatrice Ayer Patton   44:252
"Poet Lore" Prize Competition — The Editors   17C: 1
"Poet Lore" What It Means —   3:645
Poet of Italy: An Appreciation of Giosue Carducci, A
    — Milo Arms   16B: 67

Poet of Sunrise, The, Sidney Lanier — James S. Snoddy   15D. 89
Poet, The — Gerhardt Hauptmann   27:103
Poet Who Dwells in "The Valley Nis", The
    — Lorena M. Gary   47: 59
Poet, Young, Reading Course for a — C.   9:118
Poet's Politics, A — William G. Kingsland   7:473, 543
Poet's Prayer, The — Marie Noel —
    Translated by Joseph T. Shipley   41:444
Poets and Novelists, Current French —
    Curtis Hidden Page   18:113
Poets and Old Age — Henry Pancoast   3: 57
Poets, Choice of Subject Matter in — "Miss Ariel" —
    I. N. Cog   7:356
Poets, Effects of Environment on — E. Vicars   6: 83
Poets, Glimpses of Present Day —   13:527, 14D:113, 15A:131
Poets in School, The — W. J. Rolfe   6:592
Poets Laureate, The — Charlotte Newell   4:552, 599
Poets, Life of the Spirit in The Modern English — C.   7:455
Poets of America, Some Early Women —   4:332
Poets, Old Age and — Henry S. Pancoast   3: 57
Poets, Summer Outing With, A   9:411
Poets, Tombs of   —   1:251
Poetic Characteristics of Matthew Arnold —
    Clara G. Barnard   6: 76
Poetic Criticism: Horace to Stedman — P.   5: 43
Poetic Expression, Nature of, The — D. Dorchester, Jr.   5: 81
Poetic Interpretation of Nature — C. A. Binkley   13: 53
Poetic Language — Ivan Calvin Waterbury   21:241
Poetic Personifications of Evil — Arthur F. Agard   9:206
Poetic Symposium — Harrison S. Morris   1:545
Poetry — Agnes Armstrong   48:175
Poetry, American   3:639, 4:580, 11:129
Poetry — American Style — Robert Rutherford   51:151
Poetry and Drama, Recent German — Amelia von Ende   18:123
Poetry — Louis J. Block   18:224
Poetry and Philosophy, Old Quarrel Between, The
    — R. M. Wenley   10:365
Poetry and Prose from William Blake   11: 25
Poetry and Prose in Life and Art — Oscar W. Firkins   15C: 77
Poetry and the Common Man — Virginia Rohr   53:308
Poetry and Science — Harrison Allen   3:233
Poetry and the Emotionalisms of Evolution —
    F. B. R. Hellems   20:113
Poetry and The Radio — John Williams Andrews   52:261
Poetry, Beginnings of, The — W. H. J.   13:598
Poetry, British   3:363, 10:123
Poetry, Cathedral Imagery In   6:279

189

Poetry, *Ethics vs. Beauty in*   5:353
Poetry, *Immortality as a Motive in* —
    Francis Howard Williams   9:367
Poetry *in Chile* — Willis K. Jones   32:403
Poetry *in the Doldrums* — Stanton A. Coblentz   48:221
Poetry, *Japanese* — Elizabeth Balch   14C: 91, 14D: 83, 16B: 94
Poetry, *Latin*   7:453
Poetry, *Magic in*   4:109, 119:126
Poetry, *Modern, Relation of Modern Life to* —
    Josephine Preston Peabody   14A: 56
Poetry, *Music and Life* — Claude C. H. Williamson   35:587
Poetry, *New, The* — James Oppenheim   22:155
Poetry *of Brick, The* — Arthur Bacon Ruhl   10:381
Poetry *of Dafydd ab Girlynn, The* — E. C. Knowlton   36:415
Poetry *of Ethna Carbery, The* — William J. Merrill   19:225
Poetry *of Louise Chandler Moulton, The* —
    Arthur Franklin Johnson   19:473
Poetry *of Richard Dehmel, Life and, The* —
    Roy Temple House   38:264
Poetry *of Robert Louis Stevenson* — Alexander Jessop   18:396
Poetry *of The Better Kind* — Henry T. Schnittkind   26:523
Poetry *of the Epoch, The* — Nicolas Beauduin   25:336
Poetry, *Oldest English Lyric, The*   5: 57
Poetry, *Persian*   3: 1
Poetry, *Philosophy and* — Norman Hapgood   8:471
Poetry, *Primitive American*   4:329
Poetry, *Prometheus Myths in*   4:141
Poetry, *Propaganda for, A* — Ferris Greenslet   11: 41
Poetry, *Recent American* — Helen A. Clarke   2:427, 3:639
Poetry, *Study of from Standpoint of Aesthetics*   6:536
Poetry: *What It Has Done for The World?* —
    Louise S. Baker   8:145
Poetry — *When This War Is Over* — Jacob I. List   27:667
Poetry, *Whitman on*   1:129
Poetry's *Genii* — Cale Young Rice   43:193
Pohl, Frederich J. — *Varnishing Day*   38:128
Point Bridge — Peter D. Zivkovic   58:280
Pompilia — Alice Kent Robertson   1:263
Pool, The — Annette von Droste-Hülshoff —
    Translated by P. H. Thomson   27:229
Poor, Agnes Blake, Translator — *Maraba* — Dias   15A: 43
Pope, The — Charles Chauncey Shackford   1:309
Popular Songs of Japan   15B: 78
Porras, Antonio — *Adam and Eve* — Translated by
    Willis Knapp Jones and Glenn Barr   41: 1
Portage — Blanche A. Sherman   47:367
Portal, The — Herbert Edward Mierow   56:238

Porte, J. Vital de (with Roy Temple House),
  Translator — *Nymph, The* — *Gorki*   24:368
Porter, Charlotte — *Ariel*   25:217
— *Beat of the Wing, The*   19:234
— *Berdoe's "Browning's Message"*   2:374
— *Books on Whitman*   6:95; 9:131
— *British Verse: George Meredith and Watts-*
  Dunton   10:123
— *Browning Books of the Year*   5:277
— *Browning's "Strafford," Dramatic Motive in*   5:515
— *Browning's Tribute to Shakespeare*   3:216
— *Browning's Love Letters, The*   11:301
— *Cambridge Edition of Milton, The*   11:438
— *Chat with Modjeska, A*   1:524
— *Child by the Sea, The*   16B: 46
— *Classical Greek Poetry*   6: 43
— *Contemporary French Novelists*   11:431
— *Corson's Introduction to Shakespeare*   2:155
— *Course in Shakespeare, A*   14A:117
— *"Cyrano de Bergerac": What It Is and Is Not*   11:118
— *Day of Deliverance, Browning's, Return of the*
  Druse in Lyric Form   16A: 23
— *Dowden's Ballads*   2:325
— *Elizabethan Lyrics*   7:213
— *Emerson and Sterling Letters, The*   10:143
— *Essays*   1:635
— *Furness' "As You Like It"*   2:270
— *Fate: A Parable*   17C:103
— *Gosse's Northern Studies*   3: 93
— *Hearth Fire, The*   20:155
— *Higginson's "Cheerful Yesterdays"*   10:440
— *Holmes' Life and Letters*   8:608
— *Holy Day Prayers*   17B:117
— *Ibsen's New Play "John Gabriel Borkman"*   11:102
— *Ibsen's New Play, "Little Eyolf"*   7: 99
— *Ideals of Womanhood by Browning and the*
  Greek Dramatists   9:385
— *In Portia's Gardens*   10:305
— *Irish Players in Philadelphia, The*   23:159
— *Kalidasa's Masterpiece*   8: 35
— *Keats' "Lamia" Contrasted with Coleridge's*
  "Christabel"   5: 32
— *Kipling's "Seven Seas," An Atavism*   9:291
— *Langtry in "Rosalind"*   1:194
— *Latin Poetry*   7:453
— *Leo's "Shakespeare Yearbook"*   2:486
— *"Literary History of America," A*   13:439

— Literatures of the World   10:598
— "Love in Idleness"   17A: 86
— Lyric Poets' Series   8:150
— Lyric Year, The   24: 60
— Mansfield as Richard III   2: 30
— Margaret Fuller and Her Friends   8:155
— Marlowe in "Rosalind"   1:141
— Maurice Maeterlinck: Dramatist of a New
    Method   5:151
— Modern Imperialism as Shown in Browning's
    Napoleon III   12: 80
— Modernism of Hafiz, The   7:516
— Modjeska's Lady Macbeth   4: 42
— Monhegan   16D: 96
— New Book on Shakespeare, A   7: 37
— New Books of the Season: Anthologies 6:620
— New Editions   10:140
— New Shakesperean Books   4:222
— New Studies in Literature   7:459
— Notes on Recent Fiction   8:457, 617
— Old English Ballads   6:565
— Old and New Ideals of Womanhood   3:269
— Old Friends with New Faces   6:639
— "One Way of Love"   2: 37
— Our Anglo-Saxon Epic   6:563
— Our So-Called Copyright Law   4:155
— Personalia: Coleridge, Arnold, Stevenson 8:100
— Phillips' "Paolo and Francesca" and
    Swinburne's Rosamond   12:126
— Playhouse, The   23:153, 294
— Poetic Criticism: Horace to Stedman 5: 43
— Pursuit of Happiness, The   5:582
— Quoth the Duck   27:719
— Recent British Verse   3:363; 5:459; 6:366; 7:366;
                     8:38, 147; 9:440
— Recent Browning Books   4:276
— Recent Poetic Dramas: Phillips' "Ulysses;"
    Peabody's "Marlowe"   14A:128
— Recent Shakespearean Books 5:221; 8:215; 9:610
— Religio Poetae   6:269
— Rehan, A. — Open Letter to   2:591
— Richard Mansfield as Richard III   2: 30
— Robinson's "Early English Literature" 2:548
— Smith's Troubadours at Home   12:596
— Socialism in Literature   11:418
— Story of Poet Lore, A   37:432
— Studies in Philology and Literature 9:143

— *Sudermann's "Magda" and Duse's*   8:557
— *Talk on American Patriotic Poems, A*   5:342
— *Talk on Study of Literature*   10:128
— *Technique of the Drama*   7:214
— *Ten Brink's Shakespeare Lectures*   7:216
— *Tennyson's "Demeter"*   2:201
— *Tennyson's Last Book*   4:640
— *Tory Poet, A*   3:530
— *Valuable Stage History, A*   3:148
— *Variants of Browning's "Pietro of Albano"*   3:577
— *Variorum Editions of Shakespeare*   7:628; 10:430;
                    13:141
— *What It Is to Be Dramatic*   2:140
— *What Loneliness*   37:457
    Also Contributions to *Life and Letters, Notes,*
    The Library, Study Programs, Translations,
    Etc.
Porter, Charlotte, Translator — *Daughter of Joria* —
    d'Annunzio   18: 1
— *Monna Vanna* — Maeterlinck   15C: 1
— (With Helen T. Porter) —
    Saint John's Fire — Sudermann   15D: 1
Porter, D. G. — *Moon and the Columbian Year*   5: 50
Porter, Helen Tracy — *Characteristics of the Work of*
    Louise Imogen Guiney   13:287
— *Higginson's "Contemporaries"*   12:311
— *Julia Ward Howe's Reminiscences*   12:313
Porter, Helen Tracy, Translator —
    Lady with the Dagger, The — Schnitzler   15B: 1
— (With Helen A. Clarke) —
    "Love's Labor's Lost," Study Program   14B:151
— *Loving Hours* — Schnitzler   17A: 36
— (With Charlotte Porter) —
    Saint John's Fire — Sudermann   15D: 1
— *Three Heron's Feathers, The* — Sudermann   12:161
Porter, John Elmoran — *Summer Passes*   48:237
Portia and the Caskets   3: 69
Portia's Gardens, In — P.   10:305
Portrait Gallery — Carrie Ward Lyon   56:237
Portrait of a Hand — Irma Wassall   46:281
Portrait of the Artist's Wife —
    Roland English Hartley   48:121
Portraits — Thomas Hornsby Ferrill   33:131
Portugal, The Literature of — Isabel Moore   18:342
Portuguese Sonnets, Some Modern — C.   6:518
Posin, J. A., Translator — *In the City* —
    Semen Yushkevich   47: 99

Positive Science and Positive Ignorance — Gino Bonola 58: 88
Possant, Ernst, as Shylock 1:574
Possible Source of Shakespeare's Culture —
  Evelyn O'Connor 23:114
Postell, Catherine — *Midsummer Night's Dream, The* 18:522
Posthumous Coquetry — Théophile Gautier —
  Translated by Emanuel Eisenberg 36:460
Postlude — William Spencer McCann 39:315
Pot of Gold, The — Joseph T. Shipley 34:111
Pott, Mrs. Henry Bacon — *Shakespeare's Circular* 1:155
Powell, Clarence Alva — *Prefatorial II: The Source* 58:351
Powell, Robert — *Little Brown Eyes* 54:351
Power Almighty — Don Geiger 57:354
Powers of Darkness and the Cock of Dawn, The —
  Henderson D. Norman 34:283
Prairie, The — Leconte de Lisle —
  Translated by C. L. Crittenton 19: 89
Prayer — Betty Fisher 46:257
Prayer — Fredericka Blankner 40:425
Prayer — Guy Charles Cros —
  Translated by Edward H. Pfeiffer 32:315
Prayer — Mary Ellen Stelling 53:164
Prayer, A — Carrie C. Taylor 49:164
Prayer, A — Francis Jammes —
  Translated by John Heard 42:265
Prayer Against Falling in Love in Spring —
  Rosalie Berman 39:131
Prayer for a Child — Charles James 13:605
Prayer for Courage, A — Hugh Brodie 51: 2
Prayer of Altunis — Translated by P. L. Sarkans, Jr. 34:156
Prayer of the Poet, The — Curtis Hidden Page 17C: 3
Prayer, The — Erwin Paul Lang 41:453
Prayers — Francis Jammes —
  Translated by John Heard 44:363
Prayer Meeting — Andrew Kafka 56:176
Prayer-Meeting, The — Paul Green 35:232
Pre-Shakespearean Drama — Helena Knorr 10:436
Precious — Frances Ruth Davidson 38:425
Precious Secret, My — Vanjna de Vellio 17A:134
Preface for Critics, A — Read Bain 51: 67
Prefatorial II: The Source —
  Clarence Alva Powell 58:351
Presbrey, Isabella Anna, Translator — *Clocks* 55: 83
Prescience — Gertrude Litchfield 25:592
Present Hour, The — Gabriela Mistral 55: 36
Presser, Freda Lillian — *I Want to Hide* 53: 75
Preston, Janet — *Interlude* 36: 75
  — *Victory* 35:586

194

Price, Lawrence — *Ford Madox Hueffer*   31:432
Price, Lawrence Marsden — *Heinrich von Kleist*   27:577
Price, Mary J., and Lawrence M., Translators —
    Feud of the Schroffensteins, The — von Kleist   27:457
Price of Sight, The — Edward Broderick   13:354
Price, William R., Translator — *Eventide* — Verlaine   23:368
Pride of Stupidity, The —   7:155
Priests and Prayers in Literature — Ella Kirk Jelliffe   41:261
Primitive American Poetry — D. G. Brinton   4:329
Primitive Man in Modern Fiction — Hilda Ridley   19:212
Primitive Spanish Epic and Ballad Origins —
    George H. Daugherty, Jr.   54:222
Prince of Semberia, The — Branislav Nooshich — Trans-
    lated by Luka Djurichich and Bertha W. Clark   33: 85
Prince Who Learned Everything out of Books, The —
    Jacinto Benavente   29:505
"Princess Has Her Lovers, The" — Sara Teasdale   21:466
Princess Pampelishka, The — Jaroslav Kvapil   54: 3
Princess Weaver of the Skies, The —
    Ysabel DeWitte Kaplan   32:267
Principal Tones of Arnold's Poetry, The —
    Geraldine P. Dilla   32:279
Printed Page — Helena Sidis   48:365
Prison in Spring, The — Georges Duhamel —
    Translated by Sasha Best   25:460
Prisoner, The — Bruce P. Woodford   57:195
Prisoner, The — Clarendon Ross   29:590
Prize, Early English Study   1:154
Problem and Thesis — Clarendon Ross   36:457
Problem of Individualism in Relation to Society in Ibsen,
    Maeterlinck, and Hauptmann, The —
    Genevieve M. Allen   32:262
Problem, The   14C: 65
Problems of the Elizabethan Poets — Joseph Shipley   38:359
Prockter, Maxine — *To a Hospital*   50:186
Proem to a New Psalm — Cornel Lengyel   49:202
Progress — Anna Grosse   58: 79
Prolegomena to "Henry IV" — Richard L. Ashurst   1:367
Prologue — Carl Glick   33:553
Prologue to the Lays — Marie de France   54: 86
Prometheus Myth in Poetry — Helen A. Clarke   4:135
Prometheus Stories in Literature — The Editors   9:589
Promise Unfulfilled, The — Modern Greek Folk Song   9:354
Pronunciation, Early English   1: 54
Proverbs of Hell — William Blake   11: 27
Prud'homme, Sully — *Agony*   22:400
    — *Chains, The*   16D: 78

— *Faithless, The* 18:53?
— *Ty My Reader* 15B:13?
Prydz, Alvilde — *From the Mountain Top* 25:45?
— *He Is Coming* 25:23(
— *Meeting, A* 25:49?
Pshibishevsky, Stanislav — *For Happiness* 23: 8?
Pshibishevsky, Stanislav — Lucille Baron 23:11?
Psychological Basis of Swinburne's Convictions, The —
    A. E. Freeman 38:57?
Psychologist Among Poets, A — Herbert L. Stewart 31:27?
Publicity — Lillian Harris 38:59(
Publisher, A Courageous, and Modern Poetry — I. H. F. 15A:11?
Puerto Rican Peasant Song — Charles Edward Eaton 45:35?
Pulse in Verbal Rhythm — Mary Hallock-Greenewalt 16B: 7?
Pulse of Spring: A Story of an Artist —
    Eleanor B. Caldwell 13:32?
Purple Cobwebs — Frank Dougall Crane 43:37?
Purport of Browning's and Whitman's Democracy,
    The — "Mr. Breeze" — I. N. Cog 7:55(
"Pursuit of Happiness, The" 5:58?
Pushkin, Alexander — *Two Poems* 50: 7?
Pushkin — Nathan Haskell Dole 2:113, 56(
Putnam, Samuel — *Criticism and Decadence* 34:40?
Putt, Eileen — *Ballet of the Red Shoes, The* 55:23?

Quaker Poet in Puritan New England, A —
    Maud-Elma Kingsley 21:33(
Quakers, The — August von Kotzebue —
    Translated by Beatrice B. Beebe 38:17?
Quartos, Shakespeare 1:56, 39?
Queen Comes to Pray, The —
    John Francis McDermott, Jr. 36:45(
Queen Jezebel — Edith Lombard Squires 40:61?
Queen Ysabeau's Hunting — Mary Eleanor Roberts 17B: 8?
Quel Che So (What I Know) — Felice Cavallotti 26:11?
Quellien, Narcisse — *Backward Thoughts* 30:61?
Quental, Anthero De — *In God's Hand* 29:62?
— *Lacrimae Rerum* 29:62?
— *Oriental Dream* 29:62(
— *Three Sonnets* —
    Translated by S. Griswold Morley 29:62(
Query — Clarice Short 50:37?
Quest of Summer, The — Richard Burton 9: ?
Question — Lyra Lu Vaile 53:16(
Question — Wilfred Rand 37:62?
Question Unasked, The — Modern Greek Folk Song 9:35?
Questioner — Marguerite Walbridge Truslow 56:14?

Questions and Notes on "Love's Labour's Lost" —
    W. J. Rolfe   1: 84
Quick, Dorothy — *Sailor Speaks, The*   51:166
    — *Underground*   49:384
Quinn, John Robert — *Fair Exchange*   56:375
    — *Four Poems*   57:279
    — *Loss and Gain*   57: 83
    — *Peeling Apples*   57:269
Quintero, Serafin and Joaquin Alvarez —
    Bright Morning, A   27:669
    — *By the Light of the Moon*   48: 99
    — *Grief*   41:391
    — *Papá Juan* or *The Centenarian*   29:253
    — *Widows' Eyes* — Translated by Ana Lee Utt   40:552
Quirk, E. P. — Shakespeare's *"Less Greeke"*   2:526
Quitting Business — Mariano José de Larra —
    Translated by Kenneth C. Kaufman   35:159
Quoth the Duck — Charlotte Porter   27:719

R. G. White's Depreciation of Shakespeare —
    Ignatius Donnelly   1:586
Rabbi Ben Ezra, Remarks on Some Passages in   1: 57
"Rabbi Ben Ezra": Study Program — The Editors   10:103
Radin, Dorothea Prall, Translator — *Grazyna*   46: 3
    — *Princess Pampelishka, The*   54: 3
Raduz and Mahulena — Julius Zeyer   34: 1
Raege, Lois — *Poems*   47:250
Rain — Gladys Merrifield   55:241
Rain — Sully Prud'homme   53:145
Rain in Poetry — Teresa Hooley   30:412
Rain Making Clear, The — Harriet Plimpton   53:349
Raindrops — Rosemary Harris   52:155
Raisen, Abraham — Charles E. Madison   35:210
Raising the Devil — Emelyn E. Gardner   39:134
Rand, Wilfred — *Question*   37:622
    — *Sonnet*   37:474
Randolph, Edith — *Lammas Eve*   32:288
Random Recollections of Brothers in Fiction —
    Ella Kirk Jelliffe   41: 50
Rankin, Thomas Ernest —
    Character Writing in English Literature   23: 42
    — *Modern Short Story: Nature and Origin*   17A:100
Rann of the Burning — J. Patrick Byrne   46:256
Ranum, Louise Carr —
    Glance at "Lord Ormont and His Aminta," A   22:137
Rapport — Ann Dimock   53: 2
Rassato, A. — *Nocturne*   17A:134

197

Rationale of the Short Story According to Poe —
    John Phelps Fruit   16A: 57
Rats — M. J. Fruchter   37:154
Rauth, Mary Thro — *Life's a Song*   50:182
    — *Loss*   50:180
    — *Portrait*   52:290
    — *Rose-Colored Dress*   53:167
    — *Step-Children of Fate*   53:176
Ray, Anna Chapin — *Nun's Reply, The*   5:478
Ray, Louise Crenshaw — *Lines for the New Year*   40:141
Raymond, Dora Neill — *Femme Qui Rit, La*   31:392
    — *Florizel to Fiametta*   31:469
Raymund, Bernard, Translator — *As an Aeolian Harp* —
    Gerhart Hauptmann   26:402
    — *From Childhood* — Detlev von Liliencron 26:650
    — *On the Death of a Child* — Paul Heyse 26:279
    — *Wisdom* — Paul Verlaine   27:439
Reaction — Hannah Parker Kimball   10:336
Reader, The — Maxim Gorki   15B: 33
Reading Course for a Young Poet — C.   9:118
Ready? — Gwen Halvosa   58:149
Realism in American Fiction of Today —
    Irving Wilson Voorhees   17C: 76
Realist, An Ancient — George Norlin   27:417
Realization — Elizabeth Jordan Gray   44:286
Recent Bacon-Shakespeare Literature   1: 69
Recent Progress in Community Music and Drama —
    Cecil Fanning   32:149
Recent Stories — C.   10:132
Recht, Charles — *Jaroslav Vrchlicky and His Place in
    Bohemian Drama*   25:534
Recht, Charles, Translator — *At the Chasm* —
    Vrchlicky   24:289
    — *Clouds, The* — Kvapil   21:417
    — *Whom the Gods Destroy* —
    Jaroslav Hilbert   27:361
Reconciliation   21:337
Reconsiderations — Clarendon Ross   30:596
Red Star, The — Leconte de Lisle —
    Translated by C. R. Crittenden   19:292
Redden, Eunice V. — *Domesticity*   52:267
    — *Speech of the Wind, The*   52: 98
Redentin Easter Play, The — From the Low German 47: 3
Redheaded Boy and a Dog, A — F. C. Schallenberger 54:240
Redondillas — Juana Inez de la Cruz   53: 66
Read, Helen Leah
    — *Aristophanes' Philosophy of Poetry
    According to Browning*   5:237

— *Browning's Pictures of Chivalry*   11:588
— *To Leuconöe*   10:491
Reflection — Marion Conger   56:361
Reflection of The Bible in Early English Literature, The
    — Christabel F. Fiske   30:208
Reference Index to Strafford, A — P. A. C.   1:190, 236, 280
Reform — Mary Carolyn Davies   27:110
Refuge — Olga Petrova   58:195
Regelson, Abraham, — *Son of The Stars, A*   57:375
Regeneration — Barbara Hollis   29:609
Regina, A Poem of 1910 — Lilian M. Anderson   35:209
Regions of Wizardry — Martin Chesley   49:180
Regional Theatre of San Juan Teotihuacan, The —
    Lilian Saunders   37:468
Regnier, Henri de — *Autumn Twilight*   54:167
— *For The Gate of Exiles*   52: 80
— *Guardian, The*   46:291
— *Ode in Miniature*   45:349
— *Odelette*   45:348
— *Poems*   53:179
— *Two Poems*   54:220
— *Voice, The*   53: 49
Reid, Dorothy E. — *Golden Wedding, The*   38:155
Reincarnation Ring, A — Edith M. Thomas   20: 77
Relativity of Spring — Vincente Huidobro   58: 87
Released — Mary Willis Shelburne   47:286
Religio Poetae — P.   6:269
Religion of Schiller, The — Elizabeth Kingsbury   16A: 87
Relonde, Maurice, Transcriber —
    Farce of The Worthy Master Pierre Patelin,
    the Lawyer, The   28:343
Remarks on Some Passages in Rabbi Ben Ezra —
    H. L. Wayland   1: 57
Remembering — Louise Morgan Sill   27:360
Remembrance — Albert E. Trombly   28:251
Remembrances — Jean Moréas —
    Translated by Joseph T. Shipley   36:624
Remenyi, Joseph
— *Frygyes Karinsky, Hungarian Humorist*   52: 69
— *Mor Jokai, Hungarian Romancer*   55:355
— *Two Hungarian Romanticists*   54:334
Reminiscences — Delia Bacon   3:593
Remy de Gourmont's "Lilith," A. Critique —
    Marcel Francon   51:291
'Renaissance" — Holger Drachmann
    Translated by Lee M. Hollander   19:369
Renaissance Pictures in Browning — Richard Burton   10: 66

Renaissance, Recent A — Maria Lesserts Elmendorf   2:401, 44
Renan's "Caliban" — W. S. Kennedy   12:14
Rencontre — Gustav Davidson   29:20
Renderings from the Verse of Campo-Amor —
     Olga Marx   31:15
Rendervo, Sipko — Modern Dutch and Flemish Poets   13:38
Rengaw, Haras — Let Us Be Friends   53: 4
     — Ode to the Parents of a Dead Babe   53:
Renunciation — Isabelle Schwartz   27:12
Repetition and Parallelism in English Verse — C.   7:45
Repose — Ione Morrison Rider   39:29
Requiem — Helen Carson Janssen   55: 9
Required English, A Suggestion in — The Editors   9:58
Response — Gustav Davidson   27:70
Responses — Gustav Davidson   29:63
Rest? — Harriet Plimpton   53:34
Rest Thee as on Thy April Bed —
     William Stanley Braithwaite   25:14
Restlessness — Joseph Bovshover   56:37
Resurrection of Lazarus, The — Ivo Vojnovich —
     Translated by John J. Batistich and
     George Rapall Noyes   37:31
Retreat — Edith Lawrence   47:33
Retrograde — Ila Crank Smith   51:27
Retrospect — Silne Kayrd   41:12
Return — B. C. Lund   49:17
Return — Martha Peterson Koehler   55: 8
Return No More — Loraine Lashley   51:17
Return of Harlequin, The — Colin Campbell Clements   31:59
Return of the Closet Drama, The — Arthur Swan   26:36
Return — Thomas Hornsby Farril   36:47
Return, The — Mavis C. Barnett   35:12
Returned, The — Marcia Miller   51:17
Returning from Rubber Gathering — José Verrissimo —
     Translated by Bob White Linker and
     Francis Simkins   39:467
Reunion — F. C. Schallenberger   56:274
Revelation — David P. Berenberg   34:472
Revelations in an Empty Rooming House — H. R. Gillis 53: 60
Reverberation in Crystal — Nelly Baxter   47:75
Revery — Caroll N. Laird   49:176
Reynolds, G. F. — Art of Play Interpretation, The   27: 91
Reynolds, Marion L., Translator — Rimas
     — Gustavo Becquer: 32:157
     — Numero I   32:157
     — Numero IX   34:138
     — Numero LIII   31:158

200

— *Numero LV*   32-158
— *Numero LVIII*   32:139
— *Numero LXII*   33: 96
— *Numero LXIV*   34:153
Reynolds, Ruth — *Small Size*   55: 77
Rhodes, S. A., Translator — *Les Chimères*   51: 54
Rhyme, A Philosophy of — Edmund Noble   7:585
Ribner, Irving, Translator — *Three Poems by de Nerval* 54:176
Rice, Cale Young — *Poetry's Genii*   43:193
Richard Dehmel — Edwin H. Zeydel   31:393
Richard II: Study Program — Charlotte Porter and
        Helen A. Clarke   13:586
Richard III: Short Story of, A — Katherine G. Blake   16A: 80
Richards, John — *Dreamer, A*   37:106
Richardson, Isla Paschal — *Afterward*   40:118
        — *Place We Loved, The*   40:112
Richardson, Mabel K. — *David Morton's Ship*   34:278
Richman, Donald — *Clouds*   49: 76
Richter, Jean Paul   5:551
Richter, Margaret R. — *These for Fragonard*   48:274
Ride on Air, A — Camille Fairchild   27:448
Rider, Arthur Freemont — *Two Poems of Leprosy*   17C:104
Rider, Ione Morrison — *Reprose*   39:294
Riders to The Sea — J. M. Synge   16A: 1
Riders to The Sea: Performance of by The
        Twentieth Century Club
        — Charlotte Porter and Helen A. Clarke   16A:132
Ridley, Hilda — *Larger Realism, The*   24:353
        — *Primitive Man in Modern Fiction*   19:212
Reidel, Beatrix M., Translator
        — *A Cassandre* — Ronsard   44:181
        — *A Quoi Bon Entendre* — Hugo   42:190
        — *Imitation d'une Ode d' Anacreon*   51: 76
Rihani, Ameen — *Andalusion Love Songs*   15B: 74
        — *Attar and Sanai*   16D: 87
Rilke, Rainer M., Mystic Image in, The —
        Federico Olivero   41:370
        Translated by Jessie Lemont   30:355
Rilke, Rainer Maria — *Autumn Day*   55: 78
        — *Between Daylight and Dream* —
        — *Blossoming* — Translated by Jessie Lemont   30:445
        — *Book of the Hours, The* —
        Translated by Sasha Best   26:121
        — *Child's Spring Song* —
        Translated by Alice Very   58:290
        — *Cloud* — Translated by Jessie Lemont   30:468
        — *Death is Great*   56:173

201

— *From The Prayers of The Maidens to Mary* —
Translated by Jessie Lemont   30:207
— *Glimpse of a Child* —
Translated by Margarete Münsterberg   27:120
— *He Who Visions* —
Translated by Jessie Lemont   34:157
— *Knowledge* — Translated by Jessie Lemont 30:466
— *Miracle* — Translated by Jessie Lemont   30:416
— *My Battle Cry* — Translated by Sasha Best 26:274
— *Poems*   55: 78
— *You, My Adorable Solitude*   53:148
Rimas — Gustavo Becquer —
Translated by Marion Lee Reynolds
— *Numero* I   32:157
— *Numero* IX   34:138
— *Numero* LIII   31:158
— *Numero* LV   32:158
— *Numero* LVIII   32:139
— *Numero* LXII   33: 96
— *Numero* LXIV   34:153
Rimbaud, Arthur — *Sleeper in The Valley, The* 54:166
Rime — Gustavo Adolfo Becquer — Translated by
Ina Duvall Singleton   30:303
"Ring and The Book" — *Grammatical Form* 1:291
— *Original of*   5:285
— *Some of The Teachings*   1:314
— *Study Program* —
Charlotte Porter and Helen A. Clark 10:569
— *Symposium*   1:263. 309
Rising Moon, The — Gustave Kahn —
Translated by William A. Drake   34:444
Ristori in America — Thomas Dickinson 18:243
Ritter, Margaret Tod — *Tablet in Bronze* 37:536
— *Violin Concerto*   34:310
Ritual — Irene Stewart   40:141
Rivera, José Eustasio — *Condor*   55:132
Rizal, Don José — *Last Farewell, The*   26:393
Road House, At The — Bliss Carman   7:397
Robert Frost, The Classical in — George O. Aykroyd 40:610
Robert Herrick, The Metrician — Sue Maxwell 52:353
Robert Louis Stevenson's French Reading as Shown
in His Correspondence — Ruth Lansing 29:218
Roberts, Hortense Roberta — *Wind in The Wheat* 50: 88
Roberts, Mary Eleanor — *Queen Ysabeau's Hunting* 17B: 88
Roberts, Theodore — *Failure*   10:234
Robertson, Alice Kent — *Browning Memorial*
Services — *Boston*   2:152

— *"In A Balcony"*	2:310
— *Pompilia*	2:263
— *Tragic Motive of "In A Balcony"*	2:310
Robertson, Clyde — *Dry River*	41:304
— *Heloïse to Abelard*	36:158
Robidoux, Esther M. — *No Use*	52:270
Robinson, Frances — *Creative Writing*	50:271
— *Two Poems*	48:181
Robinson, Harriet H. — *Pompilia Sonnets*	4:284
— *Sonnet Sonnetized, The*	3:551
Robinson, Jane — *We Made A Vow in Autumn*	48:180
— *Shakespeare Family Annals*	2:258, 315
Robinson, W. Clarke — *Greene Entries, The*	2:221
Robison, Alberta — *Five Lyrics from The German*	53:147
Roche, Loretta — *Poems*	48:333
Roche-Guyon, G. — *Dizaino* —	
From The Verse of the Duchess	19:478
Rod, Edward — *Golden Wedding, A*	10:483
Rodenbach, Georges — Federico Olivero	27:652
Roelvink, Herman C. J., (Pseudonym,	
Donaert van Elben) — *Stormbird, The*	24: 65
Rogers, Ellen — *Ordinary Ones, The*	55:290
Rogue's Treasure — Alma Robison Higbee	51: 66
Rohr, Virginia — *Modern and Traditional Poetry*	53: 36
— *Poetry and The Common Man*	53:308
Rolfe, W. J. — *"As You Like It"*	9:552
— *Blue Eyes in Shakespeare*	1:479
— *Browning: Mastery of Rhyme*	5:258
— *Browning: A Musical Query*	5: 48
— *"In Memoriam" and Other Tennysonia*	8: 90
— *In Memoriam: The Christmases of*	13:151
— *"Julius Caeser"*	5:169, 424, 6:7
— *Magic and Prospero*	3:144
— *Merchant of Venice, Date of*	1:514
— *Merchant of Venice: Study*	2:26, 82, 134, 195, 647
— *Miranda and Ferdinand, Caliban and Ariel*	3:190
— *"Much Ado About Nothing"*	4:184
— *Note on Halliwell — Phillips*	1:107
— *Note on "In Memoriam"*	7:428
— *Note on "Locksley Hall"*	5:107
— *Paracelsus and Bombast*	3:103
— *Poets in School, The*	6:592
— *Questions and Notes on "A Midsummer*	
Night's Dream"	1:184, 232, 280
— *Questions and Notes on "Love's Labor Lost"*	1: 84
— *Riccardi Palace of "The Statue and*	
The Bust", The	3:284

203

— Shakespeare's Town — 11:446
— Shakespearean Questions: Are The Rhymed
Lines in "Othello" Shakespeare's? — 10:416
— Shakesperaean Questions Concerning
a Passage in "Macbeth" — 15C...93
— Shakespearean Questions Concerning Claudio
in "Much Ado About Nothing" — 12:551
— Shakespearean Questions Concerning
Touchstone — 14A: 95
— Shakespearean Question: Is the Part of
Hecate in "Macbeth" Shakespeare's? — 11:602
— Shakespearean Question: Was Banquo Bad? — 11:396
— Shakespearean Questions: Was Malvolio a
Puritan? Was Othello a Negro? — 10:251
— "Taming of the Shrew" — 8:182
— "Tempest, The": Magic and Prospero — 3:144
— "Tempest, The": Notes on — 3: 23
— Tennyson's Quotation — 1:375
— Tom Hood — 8:535
— "Two Gentlemen of Verona" — Study — 1:130
Romains, Jules — I Am Seeking — 24:350
— It is Not in Vain That I Have Been Seeking — 24:351
— Life Unanimous — 24:112
Roman Advocate of the Simple Life, A —
— Elizabeth Hazelton Haight — 17A: 78
"Roman de la Rose," A Note on — 1:550
"Roman de la Rose," From the — 1:549
Roman, Jerome, Translator —
Eighth Circle of Gehenna, The — J. L. Perez — 30:436
Romance de la Tardecita — Silva Valdes — 52:359
Romancers, The — Edmond Rostand —
Translated by Anna E. Bagstad — 32:520
Romanticism, A Phase of William Blake's — 5:481
Romanticism Is Still in Flower, Where — O. H. Rystad — 19:332
Romanticism of Rostand, The — Eleanor W. Thomas — 32: 64
Romany Quest, The — Julia Hall Bartholomew — 29:630
Romberg, V., Translator — Dangerous Desire for Growth
in a Glass House — Garshin — 12:327
"Romeo and Juliet" in French — Charles Seymour — 3: 27
"Romeo and Juliet" in Japan — 1:469
"Romeo and Juliet": Juliet's Runaway — Once More — 4: 14
"Romeo and Juliet": Moral Proportion and Fatalism
in — Ella Adams Moore — 7:551
Romeo and Rosaline — L. M. Griffiths — 1:205
Romeo to Juliet — Virginia Stait — 41:524
"Romola": Study Program — The Editors — 13:281
Rondel — Charles d'Orleans —
Translated by Herman Salinger — 39:595

204

Rondo Capricioso — Katherine Kester   37:458
Ronsard, Pierre de — *A Cassandre* —
    Translated by Beatrice M. Riedel   44:181
    — *For Helen*   53:174
    — *Mirror, The* — Translated by Grace Wallace   32:415
    — *Sonnet à Hélène* —
        Translated by Edward H. Pfeiffer   34:151
Roof, Katharine Metcalf — *Stone Venus, The*   37:124
Room 226 — Mary Fagin   36:610
Room, The Other — Frances Witherspoon   38:269
Room with the Black Door, The — Hinson Stiles   39:101
Rooted — Isabel Neill   40:152
Roots of Magic — J. Patrick Byrne   48:231
Rosalind — Miss Faucit   1:145
    — Mrs. Langtry   1:194
    — Miss Marlowe   1:141
'Rosamond" — C. P.   12:126
Rosamund at the Tracks —
    Anita Ryttenberg and Albert Weinberg   39:436
Rosarivo, Raul Mario — *Sonnet for Friend Toad, A*   54:184
Rose, The — Walter H. Mann   18:528
Rose and Red Wine, The — Lorena M. Gary   54:317
Rose-Breasted Grosbeak, To the —
    William Sloane Kennedy   12:346
Rose-Colored Dress — Mary Thro Rauth   53:167
Roses — Agnes I. Hanrahan   25: 58
Roses Three — Richard Butler Glaenzer   28:117
Rosenbaum, Nathan — *Letter from Heinrich Heine, A*   58:185
    — *On Reading the Greek Dramatists*   57:386
Rosenbaum, Sidonia C. —
    Contemporary Women Poets of Spanish America   52:133
Rosenberg, Robert K. — *Chrysalis*   54:276
Rosenburg, Robert R. — *Full Many a Flower*   52:163
Rosenhagens, The   21: 1
Rosmer, Ernst — *John Herkner*   22:321
    — *Twilight*   23:369
Rosny, I. H. — *Temptress, The*   10: 26
Ross, Clarendon — *Derelict, The*   30:601
    — *Murderer, The*   30:596
    — *Prisoner, The*   29:590
    — *Problem and Thesis*   36:457
    — *Reconsiderations*   30:596
    — *Spiritual History of Modern Drama*   33:128
Ross, Morris — *Deterioration of the Stage, A*   3:353
    — *Stage Types of Lady Macbeth*   5: 90
Rossetti, Dante Gabriel — *First Picture*   1:204
Rossetti, Dante Gabriel — *Word for, A* —
    Nancy K. Foster   21:322

Rossetti's "Jenny" — William G. Kingsland   7: 1
Rossetti's Treatment of Love — Emma L. Hellings   16A: 76
Rossettis, The — C.   10:298
Rostand, Edmond — *Hello* —
     Translated by Mrs. Richard Mansfield   32:155
     — *Romancers, The* —
     Translated by Anna E. Bagstad   32:520
Rostand and Chantecler — Caroline Sheldon   23: 74
Roumanille, Josef — Maria Lesserts Elmendorf   2:408
Row, Arthur — *Great Moments in Great Acting*   29:358
     — *New York vs. Chicago as a Dramatic Center*   22:151
     — *Oscar Wilde Still Lives*   30:433
     — *Richard Mansfield: An Appreciation*   19:367
     — *Sarah Bernhardt, The Great Lover of the Century*   29:606
     — *Shakespeare and Yvette Guilbert*   30:144
     — *Sir Herbert Beerbohm Tree: A Memory and an Appreciation*   29:241
     — *Star Who Is a Luminary, A* (Blanche Yurka)   39:132
Row, Arthur W. — *Arthur Wontner* —
     Another Forbes-Robertson   40:150
Row, Arthur William — *Acting in Tents in Chautauqua*   36:222
     — *Home as the Root of All Evil*   35:623
     — *I Go on Tour with the Miracle*   38:291
     — *Kate Douglas Wiggin Garden Party, A*   36:188
     — *Legend of Morris Gest, The*   36:142
     — *Margot Asquith: An Impression*   35:314
     — *Our Theatre in 1927 and the Point of View*   38:464
Rowell, Adelaide C. — *Beloved, It is Morn*   36:101
Royster, Salibelle — *Autumn Coquetry*   47:367
Rubaiyat of Titus Lucretius Corus — G. S. Bryan   19:467
Rubber Gathering, Returning from — José Verissimo —
     Translated by Bob White Linker and Francis Simkins   39:467
Rubber, Going after — José Verissimo — Translated by
     Bob White Linker and Francis Simkins   39:154
Rubino, Thomas — *Odalisque*   51:167
Rude Awakening (Pêcheur d'Ombres) — Jean Sarment   45:231
Rueda, Julio J. — *Unforeseen, The* —
     Translated by Gino V. M. de Solenni   35: 1
Rueda, Lope de — *Cuckolds Go to Heaven*   46:208
Rug, To an Old Persian — Madge Sutherland Clarke   39: 93
Rug Market, The — Julia Hall Bartholomew   29:628
Ruggles, Alice McGuffey — *Kinship of Blake, Vachel Lindsay, and D. H. Lawrence*   46: 83
Ruggles, Alice Morrill — *"La Très Sage Heloïse"*   43: 88
Ruhl, Arthur Bacon — *Poetry of Brick, The*   10:381

Rummons, Constance —
    Ballad Imitations of Swinburne, The   33: 58
Rural Justice of the Peace, A — Martins Pena   54: 99
Ruskin, John — *As a Letter Writer: Unpublished*
    Letters — William G. Kingsland   5:1, 67, 123
    — *As an Art Teacher* — William G. Kingsland   5:405
    — *Letters By* — William G. Kingsland   8:420
    — *Letters to Chesneau* — William G. Kingsland   7:123,
                      255, 343

    — *On Gold: A Treasure Trove* —
      William G. Kingsland   4:119
    — *On Wages: Unpublished Letters* —
      William G. Kingsland   3:363
    — *Unreported Speech by, An*   8:222
Ruskin's Pathetic Fallacy — Edward Payson Morton   12: 58
Ruskin's Tone Poems Anent Leaves — Esther Matson   40:443
Russell, Bayka — *Two Poems*   51:256
Russell, Bayka, Translator — *Anguish* — Mallarmé   50: 24
Russell, H. K. — *Mark Bennett on Roanoke*   48: 3
Russell, H. K., Translator (with Mary Margaret Russell)
    — *Redentin Easter Play, The*   47: 3
Russell, Mary Margaret — *Devil's Doll, The*   42:338
Russell, Mary Margaret, Translator (with H. K. Russell)
    — *Redentin Easter Play, The*   47: 3
Russian Dramas   2:113, 566
Russian Players   16C:156
Russian Theatre, The Story of — Susan Karpova   38: 77
Russian Writers, Goethe and — Otto Harnack   2:572
Rust of Unused Powers, The — R. D. Huger   26:279
Ruthenberg, Grace Hutchinson — *Solomon*   36:600
Rutherford, Jane — *Undesirables*   33:420
Rydberg, Victor — *Heaven's Blue*   27:356
Rystad, O. H. — *Where Romanticism is Still in Flower*   19:332
Ryttenberg, Anita — *Rosamund at the Tracks*   39:436

Saavedra, Miguel de Cervantes — *Entremes of the Cave*
    of Salamanca, The — (See also Cervantes)   39:120
Sachs, Hans — *Brooding Calves*   38:435
Sacrifice — Gretchen Warren   27:124
Sacrifice, A Last — Alexander Ostrovsky — Translated
    by Eugenie Korvin-Kroukovsky and George Rapall
    Noyes   39:317
Sacrifice, The — Ellery H. Clark   51:168
Sadler, Cora G. — *Sapphics*   37:630
Sadler, Eva May — *Three Translations from Verhaeren*   31:460
Saga, A Present Day — Holger Drachmann —
    Translated by Johannes H. Wisby   6:394

Saga Literature — Johannes H. Wisby   6:281
Saga of Thornstein Staff-Stroke   6:290
Saga, Sigfrid, The Enchanted Garden —
     Homer N. Dunning   22:319
Sahler, Emma F. — *Impetuous Angel, An*   14A: 46
Sailor Speaks, The — Dorothy Quick   51: 66
Saint Chamarand, Maurice — *Art of Humilis, The*   25:572
Saint George o'Dreams — Richard Butler Glaenzer   29:365
Saint-Jean, La — Verhaeren   31:461
Saint John's Fire — Hermann Sudermann   15D: 1
Saint Nicholas, A Legend of — Beulah Marie Dix   25:473
Saintsbury, George — *Note on Marlowe, A*   1:213
Sakinàme — Hafiz —
     Translated by Edna Worthley Underwood   21:471
Salamanca, Lucy — *Mother of Confucius*   45:350
     — *Pattern for a Painted Screen*   54:173
Salamanca, The Entremes of the Cave of — Cervantes   39:120
Salana, Rafael — *Crop of Dreams*   55:129
Saleski, R. E. — *What is Eternal?*   26:651
Salinas, Pedro — *Three Poems*   45:220
Salinger, Herman, Translator — *Child Cried at Night, A*   45:352
     — *Death is Great* — Rilke   56:173
     — *It is Going to Snow* — Jammes   51:290
     — *Perfume of Your Dress, The* — Mauriac   55: 50
     — *Rondel* — Charles d'Orleans   39:595
Salisbury Cathedral — Dorothy Berry Hughes   55:247
Salmon, Arthur L. — *Chatterton*   4:593
     — *Modern Stoic, A* — *Emily Bronte*   4: 64
     — *Russian Pietist, A* — *Feodor Dostoyevski*   6:309
Salome   18:199
Salt Water — Benjamin W. Newman   36:232
Salus, Hugo — *Legend from the Talmud, A*   24:348
Salute to Norway — Richard Beck   49: 2
Salve — Charlotte Pendleton   1:401
Sam Tucker — Paul Green   34:220
Samain, Albert — *Visions*   26:277
Sammis, E. R. — *Outcasts*   36:306
     — *Poet's Paradise, The*   36:569
Samsami, Nayerah — *Message of Hafiz, The*   53:263
San Francisco under Stress — Harry Cowell   17C: 73
Sancta Susanna — August Stramm —
     Translated by Edward J. O'Brien   25:514
Sanchez, Florencio, *A Great Uruguayan Dramatist* —
     Roy Temple House   34:279
Sand — Mary Willis Shelburne   45:112
Sandor, Petöfi — *Songs of the Alfold*   51:157
Saneness of George Giffard, The — Christabel F. Fiske   31:210

Santayana on Browning — Helen Dryer Woodard   13: 97
"Sapho and Phao," Plot of   8: 29
Saphro, Frances Arno, Translator — *Uncle Vanya* —
    Chekhov   33:317
Sapphics — Cora G. Sadler   37:630
Sappho — Poem by   10:626
Sarah Bernhardt, The Great Lover of the Century —
    Arthur Row   29:606
Sarcels — Bernard Baum   57:268
Sardou's Cleopatra   2:654
Sargent, Cecil Clayton — *Beasts, The*   51:167
    — *Doctor Praying for Prayer, A*   48:182
    — *God to a Tired Mother*   46:286
Sargent, Irene, Translator —
    To the White Cross of Savoy — Giosue Carducci   32:454
Sargent, Porter — *Our Poetry is as a Gum*   42:329
Sarkans, P. L., Translator — *Prayer of Altunis*   34:156
Sarment, Jean — *Rude Awakening (Pecheur d'Ombres)*   45:231
Sarogini Naidu: New Hindu Poetess — Milton Bronner   20: 61
Sarogini Naidu of Hyderabad — Edith M. Thomas   25: 60
Satan — James Meagher   39:473
Saturday Night — Jacinto Benavente   29:127
Saturnalia, The — Arthur Colton   19: 90
Saul, George Brandon — *Felim's Daughter*   58:291
    — *Merlin's Flight: An Essay on Ralph Hodgson*   56:263
    — *Short Stories of Daniel Corkery, The*   58:118
    — *Short Stories of William Butler Yeats, The*   57:371
    — *Silver Daughter of the Puritans*   48: 47
    — *Trial by Fable, The*   50:175
    — *Willow Remains*   58: 2
Saunders, Lilian — *On the Beach*   36:628
    — *Regional Theatre of San Juan Teotihuacan,*
    The   37:468
    — *Seven O'Clock*   37:431
Saunders, Lilian, Translator — *La Chinita* —
    Saavedra y Bessey   37:107
Saunders, John M., Translator —
    Love in a French Kitchen   28:722
Savage, Elizabeth J. — *Gesture*   47:382
    — *Poems*   46:382
    — *Poems*   47:261
Savage, John J. — *Three Songs from the Gaelic*   25:140
Sawin, Theophilus Parsons — *Browning's "Childe*
    Roland" and Tennyson's "Vision of Sin"   9:256
Sawyer, Ruth — *Sidhe of Ben-Mor, The*   21:300
Scandinavian Authors, Modern —
    C. Sadakichi Hartmann   3: 33

Scandinavian Book Market, News from The —
    Ernst Brausewetter, Translated by M. H.   8:601
Scarlet Slippers, The — Hildegarde Walls Johnson   49:179
Scarlet Wings — Edna Wahlert McCourt   28:471
Scarpa, Roque Esteban — *Dead in Time*   56:226
Scars — Barbara Hollis   34:457
Scatori, Stephen and Roy Temple House, Translators —
    Zaragueta — Carrion and Aza   33: 1
Schackford, Charles Chauncey — *Pope, The*   1:309
Schamlhausen, Samuel D. — *Our Disillusioned Poets*   38:401
Scharrelmann, Wilhelm (with J. Weigand) —
    Wages of War, The   19:129
Schaukal — *Epigram: Life*   23: 79
Schelling, Felix E. — *On Browning*   2: 48
    — *Word on English Literature in America, A* —   1:210
Schenk, Anna, Translator —
    Dream of a Spring Morning, A — d'Annunzio   14A: 6
    — *Dream of an Autumn Sunset, The* —
        d'Annunzio   15A: 6
    — *Story of Greece, A* — Serago   15:B19
Schiller, The Religion of — Elizabeth Kingsbury   16A: 87
*Schiller's "Jungfrau von Orleans": Its Point of Contact
With Shakespeare* — J. N. Willan   7:169
Schlauch, Margaret, Translator — *Chimpanzee Farce* —
    Franz Werfel   37:627
Schmidt, F. G. G. — *Ibsen's Influence upon German
    Literature*   17A:112
Schmidt, Godfrey P., Jr. — *I Did But Jest*   35:130
Schmuller, Aaron — *Four Poems*   58:179
    — *H. Leivick, Poet and Playwright*   53: 43
    — *Poems from the Yiddish*   58: 80
Schmuller, Aaron Translator — *Group of Poems A* —
    — Joseph Bovshover   56:365
Schnittkind, Henry T. — *Poetry of The Better Kind*   26:523
    — *Shambles*   25:559
Schnitzler, A. — *Gallant Cassian* —
    Translated by Moritz A. Jagendorf   33:507
Schnitzler, Arthur — *Duke and the Actress, The*   21:257
    — *Lady with the Dagger, The*   15B: 1
    — *Legacy, The*   22:241
    — *Living Hours*   17A: 36
    — *Son, The*   57:357
    — *Vast Domain, The* — Translated by
        Woticky and Caro   34:317
Schmitzler, Arthur — Paul H. Grummann   23: 25
Schnitzler, Dr. Herman, Translator — *Wasted Lives*
    — de Lezama and de Meneses   41:159

Schnurer, H., Translator — *Devotee of Molière, A*
    — Paul Ginistry   34:426
Scholl, John William, Translator —
    Heavenly Drinker, The — Mombert   26:396
Scholom Asch — Charles A. Madison   34:524
Scholz, William von — *Souls Exchanged*   52:195, 291
    — *Horse Inoue, The*   58:150
    — *Inscription on a Spring*   58: 84
    — *Jew of Coustance, The*   57:387
Schonberger, E. D. Translator — *Pistol of The Beg, The*
    — Capek   34:475
    — *Solstice, The* — Capek   35:475
School of Literature   6:47, 102, 213, 273
    520, 570, 661
Schoolroom Genius — Dorothy Cowles Pinkney   55:239
Schreiber, Flora Rheta — *Emily is in the House*   46: 76
Schueler, Else Lasker — *To The Prince of Morrocco*   27:708
Schwabenland, Ruth — *Poems*   48:236
Schwartz, Isabelle — *Renunciation*   27:121
Schwartz, T. G. — *Monster, The*   37:597
Science, Poetry and — Harrison Allan   3:233
Scientific Vein — Mary Tookey   58: 92
Scientist's Argument for the Infinite, A — C.   11:309
Scott, Mariana — *Tragedy, The*   53:195
    — *Being Mostly The Early Morning Meditations*   58:146
    — *Greek Impressions*   58:332
Scott, Mariana, Translator — *Idyl*   52:141
    — *White Fan, The*   54:120
Scott of Buccleugh Clan — Christabel F. Fiske   37: 24
Scott, Virginia — *Chanson du Coeur Brisé*   36:100
Scratch Club Papers   1:441
Screw, The — Sara De Ford   57: 60
Scudder, Evarts — *Enigma*   30: 34
    — *Momento Mori*   30:471
Scudder, Vida D. — *Comparative Study of Wordsworth's*
    "Michael," Tennyson's "Enoch Arden," Browning's
    "Andrea del Sarto," A   3: 87
    — *Irish Literary Drama, The*   16A: 40
    — *Womanhood in Modern Poetry*   1:449
Scyld, Passing of, Beonwulf — Anna Robertson Brown   2:133
Sea Fog, The — Patten Beard   26:776
Sea Gardens — Stanton A. Coblentz   55:374
Sea Gull, The — Chekhov —
    Translated by Fred Eisemann   24: 1
Sea Jewels — Lilian Saunders   36:628
Sea Poems, A Group of   8:476
Sea-Trove — William Hester   48: 91

211

Seacoast of Bohemia, The — Alice Williams Brotherton   20:159
Seaman, Owen — *From the Provençal of Sordello,*
    Troubadour   5:236
Season's Suspense, The — Stephen Berrien Stanton   36:449
Second Life, The — George Hirschfeld — Adapted by
    Mary L. Stephenson   39:475
Secret of Life, The — Leconte de Lisle —
    Translated by C. R. Crittenden   20: 80
Secreting, The — William Stanley Braithwaite   25:255
Secular Trilogy — Gertrude May Lutz   55:275
See, Edmund — *Friend of His Youth, A*   36:159
Seidensticken, Oswald — *English and German*
    Literature in the Eighteenth Century   2: 57, 169
Seiler, Conrad — *Mistress Shakespeare*   43:119
Seize on Tragic Time — Ruth Forbes Sherry   58: 99
Select Books — W. H. J.   13:595
Select Book Notes — W. J. Rolfe   13:148, 302, 451
Selected Poems of Louise Labé —
    Translated by John Heard   42:160
Selection from The History of The Holy War, A. —
    Ambroise   50:259
Selections — LeConte de Lisle   54:250
Selections from "Cantaro Fresco" —
    Juana de Ibarbourou   56:148
Selections from "Doctor Angelico's Manuscripts" —
    A. Palacio Valdés — Translated by
    S. Griswold Morley   24:268
Self-Culture — Richard Dehmel —
    Translated by Paul H. Grummann   24: 58
"Self Reliance" — *Study Program* — Charlotte Porter
    and Helen A. Clarke   14A:111
Sellars, Charles C. — *Garland of Brickbats, A*   37:396
Selver, P., Translator — *Woman, The* — Josip Kosor   41:317
Sembower, Acta Brunt — *Story in George Meridith, The*   23:360
Sensible Man, The — Hilda Laura Norman   32:580
Sensitive — Gabriela Mistral   57:382
Sentimental Voyage, A Little — Louis Delattre —
    Translated by the Editors   9:186
Separateness — Helena Sharpsteen   24:128
Sequel — Irene M. Estep   52:369
Sequence, From an Unpublished — Frederic Hunter   25:226
Serao, Matilda — *Story of Greece, A*   15B: 19
Serb Hero Songs — Translated by Abraham Yarmolinsky   27:440
Serbian Poet, A, Miloutin Boitch — Jean Dornis   30:356
Serpent — Gustav Davidson   38:421
Serpent of Old Nile, The — Gamaliel Bradford, Jr.   10:514
Seterberg, Ruth — *Black Lambs*   52:126
    — *Brick Red Steeds*   53:370

212

Seven Choruses: *Summer 1950* — R. T. Taylor   56:341
Seven O'Clock — Lilian Saunders   37:431
Seven One-Act Dramas — August von Kotzebue —
    Translated by Beatrice B. Beebe   38:159
Seven Plays of Old Japan — Colin C. Clements   31:159
Seven Poems — Mildred Boie   44:376
Seven Poems and Translations — Eleanor L. Turnbull   44:372
Seven Poems of Stefan George — Edwin H. Zeydel   34:288
Seven Princesses, The — Maurice Maeterlinck   6:29, 87, 150
Seven Songs — Randolph Shaffer, Jr.   46:150
Seventeen Love Sonnets — Gaspara Stampa   57:473
Seventh Solitude, The — From Nietzsche's
    Dionysus - Dithyrambs   27:228
"*Sewing the Silken Seam*" *in the English and Scottish*
    Traditional Ballads — Lowry C. Wimberley   30:567
Seymour, Charles —
    "*Hamlet*" *at the Comedie-Francaise*   1:571
    — *Notes from Paris on the Death of Browning*   2:111
    — "*Romeo and Juliet*" *in French*   3: 27
    — *Sardou's "Cleopatra"*   2:654
    — *Shylock in Paris*   2:139
Shadow Guest — Gladys Thein   56:224
Shadow Hunter, The — Henry Eastman Lower   9: 6
Shadow of a Woman, The — Remy de Gourmont   55: 3
Shadow of Statues, In The — Georges Duhamel
    — Translated by Sasha Best   25:371
Shadows — Bernard D. Milians   49:275
Shaffer, Randolph, Jr. — *Seven Songs*   46:150
Shafts from a Carib Bow — Richard Butler Glaenzer   28:456
Shakespeare — Alice Williams Brotherton   5: 81
Shakespeare and Lyly — Horace Davis   5:177
Shakespeare and the Greek Tragedians — Paul Stapfer   6:187
Shakespeare and the Speaking Line —
    Lewis Worthington Smith   48: 61
Shakespeare and Yvette Guilbert — Arthur Row   30:144
Shakespeare, William — Harold Willard Gleason   39:289
Shakespeare, William, Actor in, The   5:589
Shakespeare, William, Alliteration in — S. S. Bengough   5:190
Shakespeare, William, Anniversary at Stratford
    on Avon, The — George Bryden   1:286
Shakespeare, William, and Bacon Controversy
    — Henry M. Hugunin   1:151, 4:200
Shakespeare, William, and Bacon, Recent Literature on   1: 69
Shakespeare, William, and Ben Jonson   5:431
Shakespeare, William, and Destiny — Emily G. Hooker   12:247
Shakespeare, William and Hauptmann — J. H. Beckmann   23: 56
Shakespeare, William, and Schiller   7:169

213

Shakespeare, William, and the Greek Tragedians   6:187
Shakespeare, William, and the Russian Drama —
    Nathan Haskell Dole   1:497, 2:113
Shakespeare, William, Anniversary at
    Stratford-on-Avon, The   1:286
Shakespeare, William, Anniversary Performance at
    Stratford-on-Avon   5:227
Shakespeare, William, Anniversary Plays 3:226
Shakespeare, William, Appreciation of, in France   16C:157
Shakespeare, William, Art of   1: 31
Shakespeare, William, As a Citizen —
    J. S. Stuart Glennie   2: 1
Shakespeare, William, As a Clinician   1:428
Shakespeare, William, As Critic of the Ballad Drama,
    Etc. — J. W. Bray   9:242, 250
Shakespeare, William, At The Paris Exposition
    John Charles King   1:560
Shakespeare, William, Birthday   1:252, 286
Shakespeare, William, Birthplace   1:295, 399, 3:229
Shakespeare, William, Books   3:231
Shakespeare, William, Boydell's Edition of   1:203
Shakespeare, William, Ten Brink's Lectures of   7:216
Shakespeare William, Browning's Tribute to   3:213, 216
Shakespeare, William, Browsings in —
    William Sloane Kennedy   15C: 70
Shakespeare, William, Characters in "As You Like It" —
    C. A. Wurtzburg   4:31, 81
Shakeseare, William, Characters in "Much Ado About
    Nothing"   6:126, 491
Shakespeare, William — Come Away, Death (Song)   3:212
Shakespeare, William, Commemorations —
    George Morley   2:252, 306, 607, 3:356, 37
Shakespeare, William, Commemorative Feasting   3:371
Shakespeare, William, Commemorative Festivals   8:167, 340
Shakespeare, William, Commemorative Week, Stratford,
    Letters on — Charlotte Carmichael Stopes   3:356
Shakespeare, William, Compliment to Brautôme —
    Charles Hugh Hunton   4:446
Shakespeare, William, Comradeship of Antony and
    Cleopatra   4:217
Shakespeare, William, Course in "Love's Labors Lost," A
    — Charlotte Porter and Helen A. Clarke   14A:117;
    14B:151
Shakespeare, William, Critical Study of, A   1: 38
Shakespeare, William, Date of Birth and Death   4:380
Shakespeare, William, Dutch Version of   1:259
Shakespeare, William, Early Mutilators of —
    William Henry Hudson   4:360

Shakespeare, William, Editor of the First American
  Edition of   4:287
Shakespeare, William, Editors of, The   1: 64
Shakespeare, William, Egoism   1:406
Shakespeare, William, Evenings With — Helen A. Clarke 2:376
Shakespeare, William, Eyes in   1:479
Shakespeare, William, Face — A. H. Wall   2:634
Shakespeare, William, Fairy Rhythms of   1: 30
Shakespeare, William, Family Annals —
  W. Clarke Robinson   2:258, 315
Shakespeare, William, Favorite Latin Author   1:323
Shakespeare, William, Final Philosophy of —
  Walter Libby   24:421
Shakespeare, William, First American Edition of —
  E. H. Wall   3:228
Shakespeare, William, First American Editor —
  J. Parker Norris   2.424
Shakespeare, William, Folios (1623), Auction Sale of   1:247
Shakespeare, William, "Fragmenta Aurea" of Sir John
  Suckling   14C: 54
Shakespeare, William, Furness' Variorum Edition of   1:439;
                                                    13:141
Shakespeare, William, German Jahrbuch   1:382, 439
Shakespeare, William, "Greeke" — E. P. Quirk   2:526
Shakespeare, William, Hamilton Mabie's Biography of —
  H. S. O. and H. T. P.   12:612
Shakespeare, William, "Hamlet" as a Solar Myth —
  Sinclair Korner   3:214
Shakespeare, William, History of [his] Stage Life:
  Gentle Will, Our Fellow   5:7, 72, 129, 183, 254, 414,
                                               505, 564, 612
Shakespeare, William, Ignorance Concerning the Coast
  of Bohemia — Charlotte Porter   6:196
Shakespeare, William, in Dutch — Taco H. de Beer   1:259
Shakespeare, William, in Japan — Emil Hansknecht —
  Translated by Mary Harned   1:466
Shakespeare, William, Inheritance from the Fourteenth
  Century — Sinclair Korner   1:551; 2:410
Shakespeare, William, Is Caesar Ignoble? —
  Annie Russell Wall   4:191
Shakespeare, William, "John-A-Combe," The Moving
  Wood, and a Forgotten Estimate of Bacon   7:185
Shakespeare, William, Juliet's Runaway —
  Edmund C. Stedman   4: 14
Shakespeare, William, "Julius Caesar"   5:169; 13:560
Shakespeare, William, King Lear at the Court Theatre
  in Munich   1:376

Shakespeare, William, Land of .... 1:15]

Shakespeare, William, Libraries of .... 1:15(

Shakespeare, William, Lyly and .... 5:17'

Shakespeare, William, Manual 3:22:

Shakespeare, William, Manuscripts, Earliest 6:22:

Shakespeare, William, Memorial .... 8:46(

Shakespeare, William, Memorial Plays —
    George Boyden .... 2:32(

Shakespeare, William, "Midsummer Night's Dream",
    Solar Myths in — Sinclair Korner .... 3: 1'

Shakespeare, William, Milton Compared with .... 1:39(

Shakespeare, William, Motherless Heroines in 10:62:

Shakespeare, William, "Much Ado about Nothing" —
    W. J. Rolfe 4:18:

Shakespeare, William, Music 1:29:

Shakespeare, William, New Word on Sonnets —
    J. Goodlet 3:50:

Shakespeare, William, On the Text of —
    Horace Howard Furness 3:33:

Shakespeare, William, Opening Scenes, The Keynote of
    Action and Motive of — Charles W. Hodell   6:169, 337
    45:

Shakespeare, William, "Othello" in Paris 1:301, 36:

Shakespeare, William, Owners of First Folios of 10:15:

Shakespeare, William, Peculiarity of, A .... 7:52'

Shakespeare, William, Portia and the Caskets of —
    John Phelps Fruit 3: 6:

Shakespeare, William, Quartos 1:56, 39:

Shakespeare, William, Quotes Spenser 3:10:

Shakespeare, William, Recent Books on — P. .... 9:61(

Shakespeare, William, Recent Editions —P. 8:21:

Shakespeare, William, Reproduction of the First Folio of 13:46:

Shakespeare, William, Rhythm and —
    Emma Pratt Mott 4:21:

Shakespeare, William, Rolfe's Edition of 8:15:

Shakespeare, William, "Romeo and Juliet" in French —
    Charles Seymour .... 3: 2'

Shakespeare, William, Skull, etc. .... 1:24(

Shakespeare, William, Some Curious Versions of —
    Frederick W. Kilbourne 16C:13:

Shakespeare, William, Sonnets 3:505; 4:223; 5:18

Shakespeare, William, Sonnets: "W. H." and the "Dark
    Lady" — Charlotte C. Stopes .... 2:46(

Shakespeare, William, Spring Pilgrimmage to —
    Charlotte Carmichael Stopes 4:37

Shakespeare, William, Stage Versions before 1800 of —
    Frederick W. Kilbourne 15B:116; 15D:11

216

Shakespeare, William, Statues   2:288, 466
Shakespeare, William, Stratford-on-Avon —
    J. F. Furnivall   3:229
Shakespeare, William, Study of   1:109
Shakespeare, William, Summary of Books on   3:231
Shakespeare, William, Supernatural in —
    Annie Russell Wall   5:490, 557, 620
Shakespeare, William, "Tempest": Magic and Prospero
    — W. J. Rolfe   3:144
Shakespeare, William, "Tempest," Notes on —
    W. J. Rolfe   3: 23
Shakespeare, William, Temple's Edition of   8:215
Shakespeare, William, Tercentenary, London —
    Isabella Banks   3:201
Shakespeare, William, Text of —
    Horace Howard Furness   3:335
Shakespeare, William, Use of Life as a Dramatic
    Material — C. A. Wurtzburg   6: 70
Shakespeare, William, Victorian Commemorations —
    George Morley   3:204
Shakespeare, William, Whitman's View of —
    Jonathan Trumbull   2:368; 3:626
Shakespeare's Astronomy — William Sloane Kennedy   13:366
Shakespeare's Boys — Sarah Bridges Stebbins   2:445
Shakespeare's Birthday in Concord, N. H. —
    Frances M. Abbott   1:274
Shakespeare's Clownery — Charles W. Hodell   17D:113
Shakespeare's Culture, A Possible Source of —
    Evelyn O'Connor   23:114
Shakespeare's Development as Shown in His Songs   11:549
Shakespeare's Egoism — John Phelps Fruit   1:406
Shakespeare's "Fellow," Robert Armin, Annals of   1:507
Shakespeare's Fidelity to History — Talcott Williams   13: 91
Shakespeare's Girls — Sarah Bridges Stebbins   2:445
Shakespeare's Influence on Goethe —
    Edwin Watts Chubb   16A: 65
Shakespeare's Inheritance from the Fourteenth Century
    Sinclair Korner   1:551
Shakespeare's "John-a-Combe" —
    Charlotte Carmichael Stopes   7:185
Shakespeare's Legerdemain with Time in Julius Caeser   11:276
Shakespeare's Miranda and Tennyson's Elaine —
    Samuel G. Davies   5: 15
Shakespeare's Opening Scenes, the Keynote of Action
    and Motive — Charles W. Hodell   6:169, 337, 452
Shakespeare's Phrasing, A Peculiarity of   7:527
Shakespeare's Political Philosophy — L. W. Elder   21:483

217

Shakespeare's Shrew, New Views of — Arthur S. Way,
W. J. Rolfe, Ella Crowell   8:169, 182, 192
Shakespeare's Stage in Munich   1: 47
Shakespeare's Time, Clowns and Fools of —
H. Ernest Borradaile   8:206
*Shakespeare's Tragedies, The Moral Proportion and the
Fatalism of Passion Exhibited in* —
Ella Adams Moore   7:75, 138, 191, 424, 487, 551, 613
*Shakespeare's "Winter's Tale" Considered in Connection
with Greene's "Pandosto" and "Alkestis" of
Euripides* —
Charlotte Porter and Helen A. Clarke   14C:132
Shakespearean Books — P.   4:222; 5:221; 11:293
Shakespearean Critics Disagree, Where   5:141
Shakespearean Crux, Perennial Witticism vs. A —
Louis N. Feipel   23:341
Shakespearean Questions — W. J. Rolfe   10:416; 11:396, 602;
                                  12:551; 14A:95; 15C: 93
"Shakuntula," Kalidasa's Masterpiece — P.   8: 35
Shallenberger, F. C. — *Redheaded Boy and a Dog, A*   54:250
— *Three Monologues*   58:173
— *Two Poems*   56:274
Shambles   25:559
Shank, Margery Ruebush — *Son at Sea, A*   49:370
— *Ways of the Wind*   49:370
Sharp, William, Maeterlinck and — C.   7:157
Sharphsteen, Helena — *Separateness*   24:128
— *Three Days*   18:395
— *Why?*   24:121
Shattuck Forest — S. Bert Cooksley   37:153
Shaun the Tinker — John Casey   25:251
Shaw, Bernard and His Critics — Winifred Smith   47: 76
Shaw, Bernard, Some Misconceptions Concerning —
Felix Grendon   20:376
Shaw, Charles B. — *This Fellow of Infinite Jest*   40:265
Shaw, Louis A., II — *Poems*   56:276
She Has a Body — Remy de Gourmont —
Translated by George Williamson   34:302
She Who Returned to Life — Francisco Monterde   55:291
She Who Waits — Maurice Le Blanc —
Translated by Clarence Stratton   16A: 36
Shelbourne, Mary Willis — *Cypress Swamp*   53:367
— *Devotee of Grief*   48:334
— *Pluto Meditates*   44: 88
— *Released*   47:286
— *Sand*   45:112
— *Unwilling Sojourn*   46:184

218

Sheldon, Caroline — *Rostand and Chantecler*   23: 74
Sheldon, William L. — *Antigone of Sophocles, The, and*
    Shakespeare's Isabel   4:609
Shell, The Fragile — James Meagher   39:473
Shelley, Clare — *Four Poems*   55:336
Shelley, Percy Bysshe, and Verlaine —
    Alice L. Wilson   8:406
Shelley, Percy Bysshe and Whitman — Isaac Hull Platt   7:332
Shelley, Percy Bysshe, at Essex Hall — Jane H. Simpson   2: 78
Shelley, Percy Bysshe, Centenary —
    William G. Kingsland   3:650; 4:527
Shelley, Percy Bysshe, Comparison and Contrast with
    Whitman   8:332
Shelley, Percy Bysshe, Forged Letters   1:592
Shelley, Percy Bysshe, In Memoriam — G. W. Alger   4:315
Shelley, Percy Bysshe, Letters of Godwin and —
    William G. Kingsland   10:389
Shelley, Percy Bysshe, Letters to Elizabeth Hitchener —
    William G. Kingsland   4:304
Shelley, Percy Bysshe, Life in "Epipsychidion" —
    F. G. Fleay   2:225
Shelley, Percy Bysshe, Memorial   5:103
Shelley, Percy Bysshe, Sense Epithets —
    Mary Grace Caldwell   10:573
Shelley, Percy Bysshe, Society — William G. Kingsland   3:650
Shelley, Percy Bysshe, Unpublished Letters —
    William G. Kingsland   3:155
Shelley's Faith — Kineton Parkes   4:289, 397
Shelley's Influence on Browning — Florence Converse   7: 18
Shelton, A. J. — *Dark Halls of Maldane, The*   55:258
Shepard, Elizabeth Alsop — *Captain's Walk, The*   57:265
Sheriff and His Son, The — Nicolai Gogol   48:311
Sherman, Blanche A. — *Portage*   47:367
Sherman, L. A. — *Literature and the Scientific Spirit:*
    May There Be a Science of Aesthetics?   6:323
    — *"Luria" and "Othello": Types and Art*
      Compared   6:585
    — *New Ideas in Teaching Literature*   7:563
    — *Specialized Teaching of Literature*   6:381
Sherry, Ruth Forbes — *Of Time and the Dry Heart*   44:176
    — *Seize on Tragic Time*   58: 99
Shillaber, Benjamin P. — *Poems*   26:269
Shinnecock Hills — Christine Liebeneck Swayne   23:221
Shipley, Joseph — *Problems of the Elizabethan Poets,*
    The   38:359
Shipley, Joseph T. — *First of the Moderns*   35:626
    — *Pierre Louys of Hellas*   37:584

219

— *Poets' War, The*   36: 76
— *Pot of Gold, The*   34:111
Shipley, Joseph T., Translator — *Poet's Prayer, The* —
    Marie Noel   41:444
— *Some Recent French Poetry*   36:624
Shipley, Joseph Twadell, Translator — *Herodiade* —
    Mallarmé   32:458
    — *L'Apres-Midi d'un Faune* — Mallarmé   31:305
Sholem Asch — Charles A. Madison   46:303
Sholom Aleichem — Charles A. Madison   33:563
Shores, Robert J. — *Man Speaks*   27:449
Short, Clarice — *Query*   50:378
Short Stories of William Butler Yeats, The —
    George Brandon Saul   57:271
Short Story of Richard III, A — Katharine G. Blake   16A: 80
Shoup, Grace — *Home*   41:369
    — *Little Brown Bird, The*   38:158
Shower: The Moon, The — Translated by Yone Noguchi   29:455
Shtreiter, Nicolai — *Unseasonable Song, An* —
    Translated by George G. Lake   34:253
Shylock in Paris — Charles Seymour   2:139
Siamanto, An Armenian Poet — Alice Stone Blackwell   28:231
Sidhe of Ben Mor — Ruth Sawyer   21:300
Sidis, Helena — *Printed Page*   48:365
    — *Stray*   48:332
    — *Tools*   49: 76
    — *Winter Landscape*   47:384
Sienkiewicz, Henrik — *Hindoo Legend, A*   15B: 48
Sierra, Gregorio Martinez — *Cradle Song, The*   28:265
Sierra, Martinez — *Idyll* —
    Translated by Charlotte M. Lorenz   37: 63
Sigfrid Stories in the Nibelungenlied and Elsewhere —
    Camillo von Klenze   10:543
Sightless, The — Maurice Maeterlinck   5:159, 218, 273, 442
Significance of Maeterlinck's "Bluebird", The —
    Emily S. Hamblen   22:460
Sigurjonsson, Johan — *Loft's Wish*   46: 99
Silberschlag, Eisig — *Eve Has Seven Faces*   49: 50
Silence — Sara Teasdale   18:401
Silent Listeners — Melba Williams   35:231
Silent Town, The — Richard Dehmel   55:342
Sill, Bird Anthology from, A — H. L. Graham   9:566
Sill, Louise Morgan — *Remembering*   27:360
Sillanpää — Richard Beck   46:358
Sillen, Martha of — *Old Clavichord, An* —
    Translated by Charles Wharton Stork   34:314
Silva, José Asuncion — *Nocturn*   53:360

Silvay, Challiss — *Three Epitaphs*   40:157
Silver Daughter of the Puritans —
    George Brandon Saul   48: 47
Silver Flute — Arthur Upson   18:187
Simkins, Francis, Translator — *Generation d'Apres-*
    guerre, The: Bourne and Psichari —
    Gilberto Freyre   41:433
Simmons, Laura — *Dream and the Business, The*   24:126
Simon, Anne — *Appreciation of Marinetti, An*   25:453
    — *F. T. Marinetti and Some Principles of*
    Futurism   26:738
    — *Giovanni Pascoli*   27:190
Simon, Anne, Translator — *Congedo* — Giosue Carducci   26:114
    — From *Elegie Romane* — Gabriele d'Annunzio   27:662
    — *Poems* — Marinetti   25:439
    — *Poems* — Marinetti   26:707
    — *Quel Che So (What I Know)* —
    Felice Cavallotti   26:118
Simon, Anne, In Memoriam to   27:660
Simonds, Mattie F. — *Grown-Up Children*   36:471
Simonson, Ethel Bunce — *Poems*   46: 93
Simoon — August Strindberg —
    Translated by Mary Harned   17C: 21
Simple Destiny, A — Seymour Gresser   58: 93
Simpson, Jane H. — *Shelley at Essex Hall*   2: 78
Simpson, Ruby H. — *Meditation on Tyranny*   56:290
Sinclair, Ida Lowry — *Bungalow, Six Rooms, Modern, A*   41:451
Singer, Frank James — *Journey to Bikini*   53:214
Singer, Frank, Translator — *Sheriff and His Son, The*   48:311
Singer, The — M. A. Worswick   5:331
Singh, Charan — *Stray Clouds*   55:272
Singing Things — Frances Ruth Davidson   38:290
Sir Herbert Beerbohm Tree, A Memory and an
    Appreciation — Arthur Row   29:241
"Sister Beatrice," Performance by Twentieth Century
    Club — Charlotte Porter and Helen A. Clarke   16A:132
Six Poets of Belgium — Clark Stillman   47:359
Sixteenth Century Garden or the Adventure of the
    Advised Eye, A — Christabel F. Fiske   29:565
Skeat, Ethel G. —
    Fairy Lore: "Midsummer Night's Dream   3:177
    — *Lady Macbeth's Complexity*   2:441
Skinner, Murray — *Etching*   49:367
Sky Above the Roof, The — Paul Verlaine   53:372
Sky's Veil — Catherine B. Gibson   46:283
Slam, The   23:304
Slaughter, Gertrude E. T. —
    Pascoli and Recent Italian Poetry   18:501

Sleep — E. K. Herron   11:478
Sleep — Catherine Ruth Smith   48:358
Sleep — De Maris Argo   49:322
Slippers — Anne MacFarlane   32:425
Slippers That Broke of Themselves — Marie Drennan   37:258
"Sludge, The Medium, Mr." — Francis B. Hornbrooke   7:240
"Sludge, The Medium" — Morris Jastrow, Jr.   3:75; 7:240
Slumber Song for Maria — Richard Burdick Eldridge   47:194
Small Size — Ruth Reynolds   55: 77
Smile, The — Willis Eberman   57:490
Smith, A. Tolman — *Browning's "Sordello": A Study in
    the Psychology of Childhood*   6:238
Smith, Alfred J. — *Poems*   46:254
Smith, Bess Foster — *Imprint*   56:181
Smith, C. Alphonso — *Dramatic Import of the Falling
    Sickness in Shakespeare's "Julius Caesar," The*   6:469
    — *Interpretation of Tennyson's "Break, Break,
    Break," An*   8: 33
    — *Mood of Browning's "Childe Roland," The*   11:626
Smith, Catherine Ruth — *Sleep*   48:358
    — *Wooing*   50:284
Smith, Edna Louise — *Two Women*   35:631
Smith, Elva A. — *Poems*   47:378
    — *Two Poems*   46:284
Smith, Frederick M. — *Stevenson's Essays*   14A: 70
Smith, George J. — *Whitman's Reading of Life*   17C: 79
Smith, Henry Bowen — *Tryst*   38:570
Smith, Hyacinth Stoddard — *Cordia*   19:165
Smith, Ingeborg, Translator — *Spring* —
    Charles d'Orleans   55: 2
Smith, James Duncan —
    On Spenser's "Faerie Queene"   10:492
Smith, James Edgar — *Chariot of Fire*   13: 1
Smith, Lewis Worthington — *Dearborn-Detroit*   53: 38
    — *In the Workshop*   24:365
    — *Literature and the Pedagogue*   21:311
    — *Literature of Dreams, The*   8:233
    — *Shakespeare and the Speaking Line*   48: 61
Smith, Lilaise R., Translator — *Little Meret* — *Keller*   17C: 50
Smith, Marion Couthouy —
    Flight and the Passing, The   27:102
Smith, Marion Spencer — *American Grandfather, An*   35:443
Smith, Nora Archibald — *Immune*   37:473
    — *José Echegaray*   20:218
Smith, Phoebe — *Two Poems*   46:251
Smith, Robert L. — *Ballads and Rhymes*   58:182
Smith, S. F. — *Poems*   26:269

Smith, William Benjamin — *Great American Poem, A*   7A:124
Smith, William Benjamin, Translator —
    Trunkne Lied, Das   16C: 91
    — *Merman and the Seraph, The*   17C: 5
Smith, Winifred —
    Bernard Shaw and His Critics (1892-1938)   47: 76
    — *Ghosts at First Nights in Italy*   33:114
Smoke — Theophile Gautier —
    Translated by Emanuel Eisenberg   36:462
Smug Citizen — Maxim Gorki —
    Translated by Edwin Hopkins   17D: 1
Smyth, Albert H. — *Art Poems of Browning*   2:145
    — *Development of Drama*   2:220
    — *Timmins' Warwickshire*   2: 52
    — *Greek Hamlet, A*   3: 38
    — *Letter*   3:593
Snail, The — Antoine-Vincent Arnault —
    Translated by William A. Drake   36:146
Snailtrack Metaphors — Antonio de Undurraga   55:133
Snoddy, James S. — *Color and Motion in Lanier*   12:558
    — *Sidney Lanier: The Poet of Sunrise* 15D: 89
Snow — Elinor Arguimbau   57:217
"*Snow Bound*"   6:102
Snow Crystal, A — Ethel Standish Woods   46: 87
Snow, Frances Haffkine, Translator — *Four Bare Walls,*
    The — Francis Adolf Subert   28:497
    — *Madam Major* — Ippolit Shpazhinsky   28:257
Snow Legend — August W. Derleth   43:338
Snowfall — Doris Wetzel   38:589
Snyder, Emily Eveleth — *Young Love*   50:378
So Many Wounded Words Without Sound —
    Angel Custodio Gonzales   56:227
So Much of Light — Harriet Plimpton   51: 3
So Near a Perfect Thing — Robert Avrett   55:271
Sobel, Bernard, and Carl Glick — *Immortal, The*   32:441
Social Tendencies — G. W. C.   14B:27; 14C:23
Social Theories and Art in Modern Drama —
    Helen Cramp   22:141
Socialism in Literature — P.   11:418
Societies — Harrison S. Morris   1:32, 82, 127
Society, Leit-Motiv, The   4:274
Sógard, Thyge — *Continental Literature*   4:286, 527
Sógard, Thyge, Translator — *Glove, A* — Björnson   4:7, 70
    — *Karen* — Kielland   4:385
Soil — Tatsuji Miyohi   58: 89
Soldier — *His Prayer, A* — Anonymous   51:149
Solitude — Cotton Noe   28: 77

Solitude — Siddie Joe Johnson   40:390
Solomon — Grace Hutchinson Ruthenberg   36:650
Solomon, Miriam — *In Praise of the Morn*   53:307
Solomon, Song of, The   18: 79
Solstice — K. M. Capek —
     Translated by E. D. Schönberger   35:475
Sombart, Petronelle, Translator — *Idiot, The* —
     Cesare Lodovici   30:317
     — *L'Eroica* — *Cesare Lodovici*   34:159
     — *Woman of No One, The* — Cesare Lodovici   32:159
Some Aspects of Contemporary Spanish Drama —
     Charles Alfred Turrell   29:319
Some Aspects of Echegaray — Katharine A. Graham   21:234
Some Curious Versions of Shakespeare —
     Frederick W. Kilbourne   16C:132
Some Husbands and Wives of Fiction — Ella K. Jellife   41:403
Some Modern Belgian Poets — Federico Olivero   31:364
Some Modern War Dramas — H. G. Montillon   28:600
Some Predecessors of Spenser — Sarah W. Brooks   1:214
Some Recent French Poetry —
     Translated by Joseph T. Shipley   36:624
Some Remarks on Verse Techniques —
     Robert Wood Clark   56: 76
Some Storied Parents — Ella K. Jellife   40: 81
Some Tendencies of the English Speaking Drama —
     Jennie M. Coustance   33:385
Some Thoughts on the Poetic Drama —
     Florence Mary Bennett   30:265
Some Troubadours of Province — Dorothy Anderson   38:473
Some Unpublished Housman Letters — Cyril Clemens   53:255
Somewhere I Chanced to Read — Gustav Davidson   33:155
Son at Sea, A — Margery Ruebush Shank   49:370
Son Left in the Plantation of Mulberry Trees, The —
     Chin Lin Cheu   33:595
Son of the Stars, A — Abraham Regelson   57:375
Son, The — Arthur Schnitzler   57:357
Sonata Eroica — Margaret Tod Ritter   35: 42
Sonatina — Ruben Dario   45:353
Song — David Stacton   55:134
Song, A — Gabriela Mistral   56: 88
Song, An Old — Russell W. Hendee   38:296
Song Before Night — Richard Dehmel   30:264
Song Before Twilight, A — Arthur Ketchum   25:612
Song — Maria Lowell   9:461
Song for David — Margaret Ward   43:286
Song for Lost Years — Beth Bishop   54:282
Song in My Heart, A — Gertrude Clarke Glover   54:290
Song of Battle — F. C. Shallenberger   56:275

Song of Drought, The — Agnes Cornell	37:274
Song of Freedom, A — Richard Dehmel	55:339
Song of Harvest — Richard Dehmel	55:338
Song of Man, A — Joseph Bovshover	56:373
Song of the Blood-Red Sun — Paula S. Filpus	53: 72
Song of the Blowing Wind, The — Anatole Le Braz	27:357
Song of the Stars — Camille Fairchild	27:706
Song of the Will-o-the Wisp — Norma Way	47:175
Song of Tzar Ivan Vasiljevich — Michael Yourevich Lermontov translated by Eugene M. Kayden	24:278
Song, The — Nathan Zimelman	51:271
Song to My Son — Richard Dehmel	26:652
Song, Topelius' — Translated by A. Louis Elmquist	24:207
Songs — Gilean Douglas	49:181
Songsfrom "Le Bon Chanson" — Paul Verlaine	16D: 80
Songs from Plato and Ptolomaeus — Translated by M. J. Hertzberg	19:438
Songs from the Gaelic, Three — John J. Savage	25:140
Songs from the Ghetto — Harriott S. Olive	12:308
Songs of Arab and Moor — Jeanne d'Ucel	38:447
Songs of Japan, Popular — Yone Noguchi	15B: 78
Songs of Naples, The — Thomas D. Bergen	21:152
Songs of the Alfold — Petöfi Sandor	51:157
Songs of the Chippewa — Portia Martin	31:463
Songs of the Gitanos — Christine Turner Curtis	47:350
Songs of the Slave — Svatopluk Cech	27:114
Songs of the Wilderness — George Germond	15D: 72
Songbook of the Baby Jesus — Armando Moock	45: 23
Sonnet — David Stacton	5:134
Sonnet A Hélène — Pierre de Ronsard — Translated by Edward H. Pfeiffer	34:151
Sonnet CXXVIII — Gabrielle Lee	5:433
Sonnet for Friend Toad — Raul Mario Rosarivo	54:184
Sonnet Literature, Curiosities in — E. B. Brownlow	3:545
Sonnet — Louise Owen	40:91
Sonnet on the Petrarchan — Mary Boole Hinton	14A:152
Sonnet Sonnetized, The — Harriet H. Robinson	3:551
Sonnet, Structure of the — E. B. Brownlow	8:593
Sonnet, Tailed, The — E. B. Brownlow	4:454
Sonnet to Beauty — Margaret Tod Ritter	35:620
Sonnet to Christ Crucified — Edith King-Fisher	55:269
Sonnet to Someone Young — Mary Webber	55:182
Sonnet — Wilfrid Rand	37:474
Sonnets, Ca Ira — Giosue Carducci	27:343
Sonnets — Edith King-Fisher	55:268
Sonnets — Willis Eberman	49:276
Sonnets from the Portuguese	1:172

Sonnets of Sir Thomas Wyatt — E. B. Brownlow 3: 44
Sonnets of the Holy Land — Mary Brent Whiteside 36:471
Sonnets on Separation — Helen J. Goede 47: 56
Sonnets, Three — Anthero de Quental 29:626
Sonnets to Delia 8:473
Sonnets to the Space Age Moon — Agnes C. Tucker 58:371
Sor Juana after Three Hundred Years —
    George Davenport Yantis 57:161
Soceress of the Andes, The — Juan Draghi Lucero 53:168
"Sordello"; Hero as Man, The — Charles Carroll Everett 8:313
"Sordello," Poet, The — Charles Carroll Everett 8:243
"Sordello," Plant in 1:485
"Sordello," Poetic Limitations of — George Willis Cooke 4:612
"Sordello," Spider in 1:432, 486, 518
"Sordello," Study in the Psychology of Childhood 6:238
"Sordello," Verse of — Owen Seaman, translator 5:236
Sorrow of Yuya — Yone Noguchi 28:338
Soubrette, The — Richard Burton 11: 13
Souls Exchanged — Wilhelm von Scholtz 52:195, 291
"Soul's Tragedy, A" — Edna Goodenow Willcox 13:411
Sound Magic in Poetry — Anne Throop Craig 29:596
Soup Stone, The — W. A. Stigler 35: 91
Southern Verse — Tom Sigismund Stribling 17D:103
Sowacki, Juliusz, In Switzerland —
    Translated by Vladyslaus Jarzembski 24: 59
Sowers, The — Gabriele d'Annunzio, translated by
    Rudolph Altrocchi 33:137
Spadassin — Montgomery Major 36:265
Spanish Drama, Some Aspects of Contemporary —
    Charles Alfred Turrell 29:319
"Spanish Student" 6:161
Spark, The — Edward Pailleron 38:373
Spaulding, Henry G. — *Caponsacchi* 1:269
Speaking of Traditions — Paul Emile Miller 52:268
Speech of the Wind, The — Eunice V. Redden 52: 98
Speirs, Russell — *Gilt Edges* 41:525
    — *Grave, The* 40:113
Spence, A. M. — *Iago's Conscience* 5:194
    — *Our Inherited Bad Grammar* 7:450
Spencer, Amy Lee — *Four Poems* 53:271
Spencer, Lillian White — *Lyric France in English Verse* 36:244
Spenser Died, When — Julia C. R. Dorr 7:183
Spenser, Some Predecessors of 1:214
Spenser's "Faerie Queen," Tennyson and Others
    Debtors to — William Sloane Kennedy 10:492
Sper, Felix — *Brood of Aesop, The* 34:271
    — *Byron of the Brush, A* 40:597

— *Confessions of an Erratic Reader*	35: 89
— *Cream of Conrad, The*	38:422
— *Germ of the Domestic Drama, The*	40:544
— *On Titles*	35:127
Sper, Felix, translator — *To the Beloved* —	
Comtesse de Noailles	38:446
Speyer, Leonora — *After*	32:148
Speyer, Leonora, translator — *Parisian Nocturnes*	
— Paul Verlaine	30:461
— *Song Before Night* — Richard Dehmel	30:264
Sphinx, The — Charles Malloy	14C: 65
Spiced Wine — Willis K. Jones	36: 84
Spider's Allusions	1:432, 486, 518
Spiegel, Moshe, translator — *He Lives* — A. Holdas	52:117
Spielhagen, Friedrich — *Veteran Novelist, The*	16D:131
Spiritual History of Modern Drama, The —	
Clarendon Ross	33:128
Spiritualism	3: 75
Spot on the Porch, The — Helen Gilbert	42: 81
Spring	49: 79
Spring — Ruth George	25:137
Spring and Autumn — Joseph Bovshover	56:368
Spring and Winter — Gretchen Warren	27:123
Spring in the City	9:462
Spring Offensive — Julius B. King	49: 77
Spring Snow — Willis Eberman	57:491
Spring Song — Lucy A. Adee	46:149
Spring Song, A — Charlotte Pendleton	1:511
Springtime in the Ozarks — Mary Salinda Foster	53:348
Squaring the Family Circle — Donald MacCampbell	43: 71
Squires, Edith Lombard — *Arabesque*	39:454
— *Earth Lover*	46:194
— *Galatea Wakes*	38:105
— *Queen Jezebel*	40:615
Squires, Vernon Purinton — *Influence of Milton on*	
Wordsworth	9:540
"St. Agnes Eve," *Literary Factors in*	3: 10
St. Christopher and Nevis — Richard Butler Glaenzer	28:456
St. Cyr, Dirce, Translator — *Hidden Spring, The* — Bracco	18:143
— *Phantasms* — Bracco	19:241
St. Francis — Sara De Ford	57:276
St. Genevieve — Charles Péguy	28:246
St. George's, Grenada — Richard Butler Glaenzer	28:457
St. John — Caroline Stern	32:153
Stacton, David — *Poems*	55:134
Stage, Deterioration of the — Morris Ross	3:353
Stage History, A Valuable — P.	3:148

227

Stage Performance of Browning's Plays —
    Elizabeth McCracken   14C:115
Stage Versions of Shakespeare before 1800 —
    Frederick W. Kilbourne   15B:116, 15D:111
Staging of "Parsifal," On The — George Turner Phelps   15D: 97
Stained Glass Window — Lorena Marsh Gary   58:311
Stairway's End — Madeline Burch Cole   56:363
Stait, Virginia — *Furrows*   36:157
    — *"Others Bread"*   34:316
    — *Romeo to Juliet*   41:524
    — *Unsephulchered*   34:287
Stampa, Gaspara — *Seventeen Love Sonnets*   57:473
Stanley, Marian C. — *Heloise to Abelard*   20:156
Stanley - Brown, Katherine —
    Haunts of Paul Scarron, The   35:569
Stanton, Stephen B. — *Concert on the Common*   38:400
Stanton, Stephen Berrien —*Fallen, The*   36:389
    — *My Mayflower*   36:464
    — *Season's Suspense, The*   36:449
Stanzas — Joseph Bovshover   56:370
Stapfer, Paul — *Shakespeare and the Greek Tragedians*   6:187
Star Dust Path, The — Colin C. Clements   31:181
Stars in Poetry — Teresa Hooley   34:445
Stark, Elva June — *Firing Squad*   50:267
Starling, Lirrel — *Gargoyles of Notre Dame: 1942*   49:359
Starlings — Gwen Halvosa   58:143
Statue, A (The Apostle) — Emile Verhaeren   47: 98
"Statue and the Bust" — W. J. Rolfe   3:284, 648
"Statue and the Bust": A Parable — Prentiss Cummings 10:397
Statute of Earth, The — Gabriela Mistral   57:381
Stauffer, Ruth M. — *Byron and Shelley in Italy*   28:554
Stead, William Force — *Burden of Babylon, The*   29:369
    — *Our Lady of Wistfulness*   29:373
Steadman, John Marcellus, III — *Two Poems*   45:356
Steamer Tenacity, The — Charles Vildrac —
    translated by John Strong Newberry   32:463
Stebbins, Sarah Bridges — *Shakespeare's Girls*   2:445
    — *Shakespeare's Boys*   2:445
Stedman, Edmund Clarence — *Falstaff's Song*   15:532
    — *Hand of Lincoln, The*   13:531
    — *Juliet's Runaway — Once More*   4: 14
    — *"Pan in Wall Street"*   13:528
    — *Present Day Poets, in*   12:305
Stedman's, Edmund Clarence — *American Anthology*   12:606
Stefansson, Vilhjalmer —
    Newer Literature of Iceland, The   15A: 62
    — *Present Day Literature of Iceland*   15B:126

Stelling, Mary Ellen Taylor — *Prayer*   53:164
Step-Children of Fate — Mary Thro Rauth   53:176
Stephens, Anna Cox — *Plastic Word, The*   12:384
Stephens, Charlotte W. — *Death*   46:290
Stephens, Genevieve — *Pine Music*   49:382
Stephens, Genevieve K. — *Tom Paine*   53:382
Stephenson, Mary L., translator — *Legacy, The* —
    Schnitzler   22:241
    — *Second Life, The* — George Hirschfeld   39:475
Steps Toward a Civic Theatre — James Platte White   23:320
Stern, Caroline — *St. John*   32:153
Sternlicht, Sanford — *Six Poems*   58: 85
Stetson, Charlotte Perkins, as a Social Philosopher
    and Poet — C.   11:124
Stetson, Nancy Pendleton — *Vignettes*   49:298
Stetson, A. Wilber — *For a Friend*   55:263
    — *Poem for a Little Girl*   55:263
Stevens, Eleanor — *Late Bird, The*   54: 98
Stevens, Helen Freeman — *Cape Cod Pictures*   43: 94
Stevenson, Robert Louis — *Advice to a Young Man*   16B:137
    — *Personalia*   8:100
    — *Poetry of*   18:396
    — *Verses in Memory of*   7:397
Stevenson's Essays — Frederick M. Smith   14A: 70
Stevenson's French Reading as Shown in
    His Correspondence — Ruth Lansing   29:218
Stewart, Herbert L. — *Psychologist among Poets, A*   31:275
Stewart, Irene — *Ritual*   40:149
Stewart, John L. — *G. I. Bread*   52: 2
Stigler, W. A. — *Soup Stone, The*   35: 91
Stiles, Hinson — *Room with the Black Door, The*   39:101
"Still it is Spring" — Sree Basudeb   42:364
Stillman, Clark — *Flemish Poet: — Karel van de -*
    Woestijne, The   47:274
    — *Six Poets of Belgium*   47:359
Stirrups of Eros, The — Isabella Howe Fiske   16B. 76
    The Six Poets of Belgium   47:359
Stitt, E. F. R. — *Love and Duty in Tennyson and*
    Browning   4:271
    — *Mother Goose's Claim to Yankee Blood*   5:531
Stock Traders — Stanton A. Coblentz   55:374
Stockley, W. F. P. — *Uncertainty in English Prosody*   41:204
Stolen Prince, The — Z. Topelius   28:567
Stone, Herbert King, translator — *Night* —
    Renato Fucini   32:390
    — *Perfumed Thorns* — Juan Ramos Jimenez   32:374
    — *Weariness from Suffering* —
    Juan Ramos Jimenez   32:430

229

Stone, Jane Dransfield — *Ibsen's "Brand"* 17C: 60
— *Night* 24:277
— *"Peer Gynt": An Interpretation* 18:383
Stone Venus, The — Katharine Metcalf Roof 37:124
Stopes, Charlotte Carmichael —
Edinburgh University and Women.
Professor David Masson on Tennyson 4:635
— *Shakespeare's Commemoration Week:*
Stratford Letters 3:356
— *Shakespeare's Commemorative Festival* 8:342
— *Shakespeare's "John-a-Combe"*
Moving Wood, The, and a Forgotten
Estimate of Bacon 7:185
— *Shakespeare's Sonnets, "W. H.," and the*
"Dark Lady" 2:460
— *Spring Pilgrimage to Shakespeare's Town, A* 4:371
Stork, C. N., translator — *Death* —
Hugo von Hofmannsthal 29:245
Stork, Charles W., translator — *Old Clavichord, An* —
Martha of Sillen 34:314
Stork, Charles Wharton, translator — *Epigram: Life* —
Schaukel 23:199
— *Erinna to Sappho* — Mörike 24:199
— *Two, The* — Hofmannsthal 23:444
— *Venice* — Nietzsche 23: 79
Storm, Curt — *City Prayer* 47:379
— *Old Man* 47:189
Storm in the Atlantic — Renee Tallentyre 55:175
Storm, Jeanne — *Parting* 47: 83
Storm, The — Gretchen Warren 26:404
Storm, Theodor — *Town, The* 27:225
— *Town Where the Wild Goose Calls* 53: 79
Story about Gunnel, The — Pelle Molin —
translated by Anna Cronhjelm Wallberg 12: 1
"Story" in George Meredith, The — Alto Brunt Sembower 23:360
Story of Greece, A — Matilda Serao 15B: 19
Story of Poet Lore, The — Charlotte E. Porter 37:432
Story of the Russian Theatre, The — Susan Karpova 38: 77
Stowe's, Harriet Beecher, Life and Letters —
Caroline Healey Dall 10:579
"Strafford" and "Julius Caesar" — P. A. C. 4:148, 5:384
"Strafford," Dramatic Motive in Browning's — 5:515
"Strafford," Prose Life of 4:524
"Strafford," Reference Index to 1:137, 236
"Strafford," Revision of 4:473
"Strafford," Suggestions to Study 1:190, 282, 332, 372
426, 511, 562

230

Stramm, August — *Bride of the Moor, The*   25:499
   — *Sancta Susanna*   25:514
Strange Harmonies — Helen Joy Kimball   37:314
Strassburg, Gottfried von — *Tristan and Isolde*   49:301
Stratford -on-Avon   1:252, 286, 296, 399
Stratton, Clarence, translator —
   Italian Landscape, An — d'Annunzio   16C:110
   — *Joyzelle* — Maeterlinck   16B: 1
   — *Pierrot Dead* — Verlaine   16D: 81
   — *She Who Waits* — Le Blanc   16A: 36
Stray — Helena Sidis   48:332
Stray Clouds — Charan Singh   55:272
"Stream of Consciousness" *Drama, The* —
   Sam E. Davidson   42: 71
Stream of Time — Gustav Davidson   33:594
Street, Charles M. — *"To Be or Not to Be"*   25:461
Street, James M. — *New Hamlet Query, A*   20:468
Street Light in the Rain, The — Richard Edwards   58:311
Street of David, The — Mary Brent Whiteside   36:471
Strelsky, Katharine — *Lot's Wife*   57: 81
Strelsky, Katharine, translator — *Consolation* —
   d'Annunzio   56:174
Stribling, Tom Sigismund — *Southern Verse*   17D:103
Strindberg, August — Axel J. Uppvall   31: 69
Strindberg, August — *Debit and Credit*   17C: 28
   — *Julie*   17:161
   — *King Lear'sWife*   24:108
   — *Love and Bread*   6:501
   — *Outcast*   17C: 8
   — *Phoenix, The*   6:611
   — *Simoon*   17C: 21
   — *Stronger, The*   17A: 47
   — *To Damascus* — Authorized translation by
     Sam E. Davidson
   — Part I   42: 1
   — Part II   42: 99
   — Part III   42:195
Strindberg, Scandinavian Author   3: 36
Strindberg's Influence on Eugene O'Neill —
   Ira N. Hayward   39:596
Stringing Beads — Lillian Sutton Pelee   39:295
Stronger, The — August Strindberg   17A: 47
Stronghold, The — Susan Whally Allison   10:491
Strug, Andrzej — *Last Letters* — translated by
   Sophia Corwin   30: 36
Stuart, Ruth McEnery — *April Dreaming*   25:611
Stuckey, Lawrence — *John Masefield's First Reading*   38:312

Study in Shakespeare's Fairy Rhythms, A —
Charlotte Pendleton   1: 30
Study in the Nude, A — June E. Downey   31:253
Study of Shakespeare, The — Horace Howard Furness   1:109
Stupid Lady, The — Lope de Vega   57:291
Suavity — Gabriela Mistral   55: 37
Subert, Francis Adolf — *Awakening, The* —
translated by Beatrice M. Mekota   33:159
    — *Four Bare Walls, The* — translated by
Beatrice M. Mekota and
Francis Haffkine Snow   28:497
Subert, Frantisèk Adolf — *Great Freeholder, The* —
translated by Beatrice M. Mekota   35:318
    — *Jan Vyrava* — translated by Sarka B. Hrbkova   26:281
    — *Peter vok Rozmberk* —
translated by Beatrice M. Mekota   31: 1
Successful Life, A — Helene Mullins   47:189
Suckling, Sir John — From the Fragmenta Aurea of   14C: 54
Sudermann, Hermann, and Hauptmann and Their Plays   14B:114
Sudermann, Hermann, and Recent German Criticisms   14C: 46
Sudermann, Hermann — *Johannes*   11:161
    — *Morituri: Teias*   9:330
    — *Saint John's Fire*   15D: 1
    — *Three Heron's Feathers, The*   12:161
Sudermann's "Magda" and Duse's — P.   8:557
Sue's Wandering Jew — R. G. Moulton   3:322
Suggested by a Bas-Relief of Victory —
Laura Marquand Walker   26:280
Sullivan, Virginia Irene — *Exchange*   46:370
Sully, Prud'homme, Armand — *Agony*   22:400
    — *Chains, The*   16D: 78
    — *Faithless, The*   18:533
    — *Ici-Bas*   53:171
    — *Missal, The*   55: 80
    — *Rain*   53:146
    — *To My Reader*   15B:139
Summer Folk — Gorki   16C: 1
Summer Folk, Singularity of Gorki's Art Illustrated in   16C:152
Summer Passes — John Elmoran Porter   48:237
Summer Rain — Leonard L. Tate   48:255
Summer Twilight — Celia Keegan   49:146
Summer's End — Lawrence Phelan   48:141
Summers, Edith, translator — *Faithless, The* —
Prud'homme   18:533
Summons — Richard Dehmel   55:343
Sumurün   23:292
Sun Symbolism in Browning   11: 55

Sunday on Sunday Goes By — Henri Lavedan   27:185
Sunken Bell, The — Gerhard Hauptmann —
    Translated by Mary Harned   10:161
Sunken Bell, The, Another Interpretation of —
    Jane Long Boulden   10:452
Sunken Bell, The, Symbolism of   10:312
Sunlight — Lilian Saunders   36:628
Sunrise — J. Corson Miller   57: 2
Sunrise, Two Singers of: Lanier, Gilder —
    Grace Duffield Goodwin   9:407
Sunset — Barbara Hollis   33:141
Sunset Down Mt. Vernon Street — Frances Avery Faunce   34: 62
Supernatural in Two Recent Plays — O. W. Firkins   20:438
Surrender — Vigiliano Zullo   43:185
Surrender — Silence Buck Bellows   44:188
Survey of Yugoslav Literature, A — Anthony J. Klančar   50: 37
Surville, Clotilde de — *Child, The* —
    Translated by William A. Drake   34:473
Survivors, The — Duane Valentry   50:272
Susanna, High Lights in the Story of — J. Warshaw   28:242
Sutcliffe, Donald R. — *Chansonne of the Lonely Heart*   53:166
Sutton, Kathleen — *Four Poems*   44: 82
Swan, Arthur — *Return of the Closet Drama, The*   26:368
    — *Typography of Plays, The*   27: 97
Swan, Arthur Helge — *Plight of Dramatic Criticism, The*   24:201
Swan, Arthur Helge, translator — *Julie* — Strindberg   22:161
    — *King Lear's Wife* — Strindberg   24:108
Swanson, Roy W., translator — *Criminals* —
    Gustav of Geijerstam   34:186
Swayne, Christine Liebeneck — *Shinnecock Hills*   23:221
    — *Tristram Forethoughtful*   24:358
Sweeney, Mildred McNeal — *In Delos in the Drifting Isle*   21:240
Swigart, Jessie A. — *Eviction*   53: 79
Swiggert, G. L. — *Plea for Poe, A*   13:379
Swinburne — *Rosamund*   12:126
Swinburne, Algernon Charles — Irene Moore   16D:108
Swinburne, Lyric Origins of, The — Van Tyne Brooks   18:468
Switzerland, In — Juliusz Sowacki —
    translated by Lee M. Hollander   23:225
Sydnor, Frances Beveridge — *Three Poems*   55:264
Symbolism of Tennyson's "Holy Grail" —
    Eugene Parsons   16B: 86
Symbolism of "The Flame of Life" — Florence Brooks   16C:112
Symbols for a Child's Interment —
    Dorothy Cowles Pinkney   55:238
Symbolistic Drama of Today — Juliet Lee Knapp   32:201
Synge, J. M. — *Riders to the Sea*   16A: 1

233

Synge, J. M., and the Playboy of the Western World
— Louis Untermeyer 19:364
Syrian Vignettes — Florence Mary Bennett 37:486
Szini, Gyula — Joseph Remenyi 54:345

T., J. — *Temple Steps, The* 27:104
Taber, Gladys Bagg — *Miss Mauda* 38:412
Tablet in Bronze — Margaret Tod Ritter 37:536
Tagore, Rabindranath — *Bayadére, The* 25: 61
Take Heart, Soul — Robert L. Morgan 53:170
Taliesin — Richard Hovey 8: 1, 63, 292
Talisman, The — Alice Williams Brotherton 40:153
Talisman, The — Lilian White Spencer 30:446
Tall Jew, The — Walter Heiby 46:364
Tallantyre, Renée — *Tropical Folio* 49: 84
Tallantyre, Renée, translator
— *Group of Latin-American Poems, A* 54:184
— *Marimba* 49:368
— *South American Poems* 55:129
— *Storm in the Atlantic* 55:175
Taming of the Shrew 8:169, 182, 192, 197, 346
Tanka Sequence — Seymour G. Link 42:186
Tannenforst, Ursula — *Divided* 2:193
Taps — Raymond Kresensky 51: 81
Tarn of the Mad Student, The 13:465
Tate, Leonard L. — *Summer Rain* 48:255
Taün, The Black Death — M. E. Lee 28:691
Taunt — Charles H. Toll, Jr. 47:381
Tavaststgerna, Karl — *Without Words* 12: 12
Taylor, Carrie C. — *Autumn* 49:354
— *Prayer, A* 49:164
— *Three Poems* 47:335
Taylor, Charles M., translator — *Why Men Shudder* —
Archag Tchobanian 30:444
Taylor, Elizabeth — *Tale of Arion, A* 10: 8
— *Delfica* — Gerard de Nerval 26:113
Taylor, Frances, translator — *Fantaisie* —
Gerard de Nerval 35:379
Taylor, L. M. — *Cockcrow* 33:118
— *Fleurs, Les* — Stephane Mallarmé 26:228
Taylor, R. T. — *Seven Choruses: Summer 1950* 56:341
Tchekhov — See Chekhov
Tchermikovsky, Saul — *Baruch of Mayence* 54:139
Tchobanian, Archag — *Why Men Shudder* —
translated by Charles M. Taylor 30:444
Teachings of "The Ring and the Book" —
Francis B. Hornbrooke 1:309
Teacup — Mary Webber 55:181

234

Tears — Catulle Mendés — traslated by Roy Temple House   21: 95
Tears of Dawn — Faith Van Valkenburgh Vilas   33:105
Tears of the Birds — translated by Yone Noguchi   29:451
Teasdale, Sara A. — *Ballad of Two Knights, A*   22: 78
   — *Princess Has Her Lovers, The*   21:466
   — *Silence*   18:401
Teggart, Frederick John —
   Plot of Lyly's "Sapho and Phao," The   8: 29
Telephone, A Prophecy of the — K. S. S.   3: 98
"Tempest," Browsings in the — William Sloane Kennedy   9:577
"Tempest," Characters in the   3:144, 190
"Tempest," Magic of the — W. J. Rolfe   3:144
"Tempest," Notes on the — W. J. Rolfe   3: 23
"Tempest," Study Programs   8:347, 15D.123
Temple Gate, The — Helen Archibald Clarke   37:456
Temple Steps, The — J. T.   27:104
Temptress, The — J. H. Rosny —
   translated by the Editors   10: 26
Ten Brink's Shakespeare Lectures — P.   7:216
Tendencies of English and French Literature During
   the Elizabethan Period — Morton W. Easton   1:157
Tennyson, Alfred, and Browning   2:101, 447, 628
Tennyson, Alfred, as Poet of the English People —
   George W. Alger   8:325
Tennyson, Alfred, at Eighty   1:442
Tennyson, Alfred, Biography of, The — W. S. Kennedy   10:114
Tennyson, Alfred, Books on — C.   5:630, 9:138
Tennyson, Alfred, Dream Craft of —
   Lewis Worthington Smith   8:233
Tennyson, Alfred, Debtor to Spenser's Faerie Queene —
   William Sloane Kennedy   10:492
Tennyson, Alfred, E. B. Browning on —
   William G. Kingsland   8: 23
Tennyson, Alfred, Love and Duty in — E. F. R. Stitt   4:271
Tennyson, Alfred, Note on — Eugene Parsons   10:147
Tennyson, Alfred, Professor Masson on —
   Charlotte C. Stopes   4:635
Tennyson, Frederick, and His Poetry — W. Winthrop   10:258
Tennysonia, "In Memoriam" and Other   8: 90
Tennysons, Arthur Henry Hallam on the   8: 27
Tennyson's "Break break, break," an Interpretation —
   C. Alphonso Smith   8: 33
Tennyson's "Demeter" — Charlotte Porter   2:201
Tennyson's Elaine and Shakespeare's Miranda —
   Samuel D. Davies   5: 15
Tennyson's "Enoch Arden": Study Program —
   Vida D. Scudder   3: 87

Tennyson's "Holy Grail," Symbolism of, The —
Eugene Parsons   16B: 86
Tennyson's "Idylls of the King"   8:592
Tennyson's "Idylls of the King": Study Programs —
William Channing Gannett   13:588
Tennyson's "In Memoriam," Notes on — W. J. Rolfe   7:428
Tennyson's "In Memoriam": Study Programs   5:574, 13:284
Tennyson's "Lady of Shalott" — Anna Robertson Brown   4:408
Tennyson's Last Book — P.   4:640
Tennyson's Literary Factors in "St. Agnes' Eve" —
Albert S. Cook   3: 10
Tennyson's "Locksley Hall' and "Sixty Years After,"
A Study of — P. A. C.   5: 34
Tennyson's "Lucretius" — Katharine Allen   11:529
Tennyson's Lyrics, Outline Studies of — P. and C.   9:421
Tennyson's Memorial — William G. Kingsland   9:632
Tennyson's Parallels   1:395
Tennyson's Plays, The Dramatic Sentiment of —
Louis J. Block   8:512
Tennyson's Princess   2:237
Tennyson's Songs — Louis James Block   7:127
Tennyson's "Ulysses," Literary Geneology of —
Albert S. Cook   3:499
Tennyson's Use of Homeric Material —
Elizabeth Hazelton Haight   12:541
Tennyson's "Vision of Sin" and Browning's
"Childe Roland" — Theophilus Parsons Sawin   9:256
Tennysons, The, Arthur Henry Hallam on —
William G. Kingsland   8: 27
Teresa Maria Llona's Intersection — Marie Pope Wallis   49:323
Test, The — Pierre Chamblain de Marivaux —
translated by Willis K. Jones   35:533
Testament — Georgie Starbuck Galbraith   50:267
Testament — Nelly Browne   45:219
Testing of Phaeton, The — Joseph Warren Beach   24:361
Texan Sketches — Albert E. Trombly   31:465
Thackeray — *Unpublished Letters*   3: 50
"Thanatopsis": Study Program   6:520
Thanks to a Fruit Shop — Richard Butler Glaenzer   29:366
That Music in Flower Fragrance — Esther Matson   54:374
Thaxter, Levi Lincoln: Inscription on Tomb   1:398
Theatre, De l'Oeuvre — Richard Hovey   7:446
Theatre for Poetry, A   28:748
Theatre, Irish Literary, The — Irene Dwen Andrews   39: 94
Theatre of the French Revolution, The —
Katharine Oliver   30:608
Theatre, Story of the Russian, The — Susan Karpova 38: 77

Theatrical Event in Havana, A — Frederic M. Noa   17B: 118
Thee Only — J. Giuffre, translated by Louise W. Kidder   17A: 134
Thein, Gladys — *Shadow Guest*   56: 224
Their Heart — Henri Lavedan   30: 1
Theis, O. F. — *Frank Wedekind*   24: 237
Theocritus, Father of Pastoral Poetry — Joshua Kendall   7: 307
Theology of Robert Browning, The — H. White   12: 417
There Is but One — Blanche Yvonne Mosler   48: 95
There Is Something of Beauty — Herrick Lynn   46: 287
These for Fragonard — Margaret R. Richter   48: 274
These Sudden Stars — Ruth Brandes de Bedts   47: 314
They'll Not Return — William Stanley Braithwaite   25: 254
They Were All Young Once — Robert C. Francis   39: 290
Thief! Thief! — William J. Murdoch   56: 220
Things Singing — Frances Ruth Davidson   38: 290
Things That Grow — Hazel Hall   32: 152
This Fellow of Infinite Jest — Charles B. Shaw   40: 265
This Soft Brown Dust — Stanton A. Coblentz   47: 234
Thomas, Edith M. — *"Bird of Time, The"*   24: 204
   — *Golden Bough, The*   18: 277
   — *In Muscovy*   16D: 65
   — *Light Sleeper, A*   9: 475
   — *Mother Cry, The*   18: 198
   — *Reincarnation Ring, A*   20: 77
   — *Sarojini of Hyderabad*   25: 60
Thomas, Edith M., translator — *Dizaino* —
   Duchesse de Rochefort-Gueyon   19: 478
   — *Folk Songs of Greece under the Turk* —
   Perikles Mellon   26: 47
   — *Lament at the Gathering of the Vintage, A* —
   Linus   16C: 130
Thomas, Eleanor W. — *Romanticism of Rostand, The*   32: 64
Thomas, Helen Douglas — *Hidden Memory*   58: 93
Thomas, Helen Sterling — *Tarn of the Mad Student, The*   13: 465
Thomas, J. W. — *Lessing's "Dramaturgie"*   5: 593
Thompson, Adele Kelley — *Night Train*   46: 207
Thompson, Francis — Edward J. O'Brien   19: 293
Thompson, Francis — Glady Wolcott Barnes   26: 229
Thompson, Kate V. (with Julia Ellsworth Ford) —
   Neo-Celtic Poet William Butler Yeats, The   15D. 83
Thompson, Nesta M., translator — *Poems* — Arno Holz   34: 154
Thompson, Tollet B. — *Ibsen's "When We Dead Awaken"*   20: 201
Thompson, Virginia Spicer — *Poems*   47: 84
Thomsen, T. Christian — *If Life Were a Dance on Roses*   53: 231
Thomson, Alison — *Vision*   55: 194
   — *Wounded Pelican*   55: 233
Thomson, P. H., translator — *Fair Rohtraut* —   27: 227

— *Forsaken* — Edward Mörike   27:230
— *On the Lonely Hallig* — Detlev von Liliencron   27:232
— *Pool The* — Annette von Droste-Hülshoff   27:229
— *Town, The* — Theodor Storm   27:225
— *'Tis She* — Edward Mörike   27:109
Thorn in The Flesh, A — Kate Douglas Wiggin   36:191
Thorn Tree, The — Lucy A. K. Adee   49:359
Thornhill, Gertrude C. — *Negro Becomes a Literary
    Contributor, The*   39:431
Those Goblin Versus "Heart-Easing" Words —
    Esther Matson   54:374
*Those Who Sleep beneath the Cross: Elegies of the
    Soldier-Priest* — J. Bellouard   30:148
Thou Shalt Not Pass — Felice Cavalotti   27:122
Thought, A — Dorothy Coleman   47: 85
Thoughts and Fancies — W. E. M.   7:467
Thoughts in World Darkness — Charles Ballard   52:271
Three Canzoni — Niccolo Machiavelli   53:366
Three Days — Helen Sharpsteen   18:395
Three Epitaphs — Challis Silvay   40:157
Three French Poems — Gerard de Nerval   54:176
Three Heron's Feathers — Hermann Sudermann   12:161
Three Men, A Triptych — Henry Bellamann   35:148
Three Moments in a Life — George Mitrisin   47:235
Three New French Novelists — Jesse Lee Bennett   27:591
Three Old French Lyrics — Henry Clinton Hutchins   27:597
Three One-Act Plays — August Strindberg
    — Translated by Mary Harned   17C: 8
Three Prayers — Louise Goodson   55: 64
Three Songs from "Buch der Lieder" —
    Rainer Maria Rilke   27:714
Three Songs from the Gaelic — John J. Savage   25:140
Three Sonnets — Anthero de Quental   29:626
Three Translated Selections from the Noh Drama —
    Yone Noguchi   29:447
Three Translations from Verhaeren — Eva May Sadler   31:460
Thresher, Mary Colby — *To a Japanese Print*   24:419
Throstle Song, The — Helen A. Clarke   1:510
Throop, Anne — *Marah of Shadowtown*   12:234
Throstle Song, The (*Music*)   1:510
"Through the Metidja" — E. Boudinot Stockton   3:101
Thurnbull, Bell — *Variations on a Japanese Theme*   34:416
Tide Tale — René Char   57:485
Ties of Blood — Lillian Sutton Pelée   32:572
Tiger Lilies — Lorena M. Gary   58:171
Tilghman, Zoe A. — *Lost Prophet*   51:119
Time and Space — Dorothy Marie Davis   56:143

Time for Laughter — John Russell McCarthy   55: 50
Time Turns Under — Florence Crocker Comfort   48:290
Timon of Athens   3:539
Tired Man's Prayer for Peace, A — Robert L. Morgan   52:260
'Tis She — Edward Mörike   27:109
Titan — Leonard Lanson Cline   29:486
Tito the Unresisting — Gilbert Cosulich   24:339
"Titus Andronicus"   3:539
To a Bleak Young Man of Today — Julia Cooley Altrocchi   58:271
To a Child — Isabella Howe Fiske   17C: 96
To a Contemptuous Chinese Camel —
    Celinda Bishoprick Abbot   41:131
To a Crocus — Erich Hardt   48: 46
To a Japanese Print — Mary Colby Thresher   24:419
To a Little Girl — Charles Angoff   47:262
To a Mother Who Lost Her Son in the War —
    Harris Downey   55:236
To a Pink Gown — Theopile Gautier* —
    Translated by Emanuel Eisenberg
To a Violinist — Jean Cross Hansen   53:174
To a Young Poet — Gerhard Friedrich   54: 83
To All You Poets — Esther Matson   49: 80
To Be Continued — Ramona G. Yarmy   53:178
To Be or Not to Be — Charles M. Street   25:461
To Be or Not to Be — *Again* — Morris Le Roy Arnold   27: 81
To Damascus — August Strindberg —
    Authorized translation by Sam E. Davidson:
    Part I   42: 1
    Part II   42: 99
    Part III   42:195
To François Rabelais — Abraham Feldman   52:290
To John — Lewis Colwell   42:275
To My Brothers — Joseph Bovshover   56:367
To My Reader — Sully Prud'homme   15B:139
To My Son — R. Marjorie Mitchell   54:194
To One Contemplating the Lyric Route —
    Ames Blanchard   31:252
To One Most Beautiful — Robert Allen Mallory   44:181
To One Who Said He Cared too Much — Caroline l'Anson   53:142
To Peter Short, Aged Five — Margaret Fuller   53: 80
To Resume — René Char   57:484
To the Beloved — Comtesse de Noailles —
    translated by Felix Sper   38:446
To the Dark Water — Irene Holt Albert   58: 64
To the Obscure God — Paula Ludwig   58:326
To the Pines — Lucille Price Leonard   25:215
To the Poet — John Lee Higgins   38:472

To the Prince of Morocco — Else Läsker Schueler   27:708
To the Stars — Andreyev   18:417
To the White Cross of Savoy — Giosue Carducci —
    translated by Irene Sargent   32:454
To the Wind — Joseph Bovshover   56:368
To Vienna — Nathan Zimelman   52:116
To You Who Scoff at Makers of Verse —
    Jean Pendergrass   37:596
To Youth — Albert E. Trombly   27:359
Tobey, Frances — *Two Ancient Festival Survivals in
    "Wordsworthshire"*   27:326
"Toccata of Galuppi": Study Program — The Editors   10:288
Toll, Charles H., Jr. — *Taunt*   47:381
Tolstoi, Leo — C.   11:425
Tom Paine — Genevieve K. Stephens   53:221
Tonight — Mary Leighton Orters   51:156
Tonsberg, Carl — *Dawn, The*   57:168
Tookey, Mary — *Scientific View*   58: 92
Tools — Helena Sidis   49: 76
Topelius, Z. — *Four Fairy Plays*   28:567
Topelius' Song — Translated by A. Louis Elmquist
    (with Robert Finney)   24:207
Toro, Julio del, translator — *Truth Suspected, The* —
    D. Juan Ruiz de Alaron   38:475
Torture by Hope, The — Villiers de l' Isle-Adam   6:303
Tory Poet, A   3:530
Totheroh, Dan W. — *While the Mushrooms Bubble*   32:251
Touchstone, Concerning: Shakespearean Questions —
    W. J. Rolfe   14A: 95
Town in Me, The — Nicolas Beauduin   25:348
Town Lights — John Nixon, Jr.   55:180
Town, The — Theodor Storm   27:225
Town Where the Wild Goose Calls — Theodor Storm   53: 79
Towne, Frank, translator —
    Selections from Leconte de Lisle   54:250
Townsend, Anna Lake — *Off the Coast of Panama*   2:624
Toy Theatre Plays — *Hilarion* — Josephine Howell-Carter   26:374
    — *Leave of Absence* — C. E. Freybe   26:499
    — *Legend of Saint Nicholas* — Dix   25:473
    — *Victoria* — Jane Winsor Gale   26: 78
    — *War* — Fillmore   25:523
    — *Wings, The* — Peabody   25:352
Tragedian in Spite of Himself, The — Anton Chekhov   33:268
Tragedy, The — Mariana Scott   53:195
Tragic Songs, The — Roberto Payro   50: 3
Trains — Evelyn Emig Mellon   41:424
Transformation — Frances M. Frost   37:514

Transformation — Louis F. Urbana   54:184
Transient, The — Grace Strickler Dawson   41:447
Translated — Grace Wilcox   41:251
Translation from the Spanish of Manuel Machado —
    Olga Marx   30:616
Translations from Endre Ady — Anton N. Nyerges   48:359
Trask, Katrina, Sketch of the Life of   14D:1,18
Traubel, Horace L. — *Freedom to Write and to Print*   2:529
    — *Lowell-Whitman: A Contrast*   4: 22
    — *Walt Whitman and Murger*   6:484
    — *Walt Whitman's Artistic Atheism*   5:498
Trausti, Jon — *Pharaoh's Daughter*   57: 3
Travail — Grace Edith Garratt   53: 81
Traveler, The — André Germain —
    translated by Joseph T. Shipley   36:624
Tre Fila d'Oro — Leconte de Lisle   53:172
Tree, In the Heart of a — Sydney Barlow Brown   40:442
Tree, Sir Herbert Beerbohm: A Memory and an
    Appreciation — Arthur Row   29:241
"Très Sage Héloise, La" — Alice Morrill Ruggles   43: 88
Triad of Symbols, A — Esther Matson   31:284
Trial by Fable, The — George Brandon Saul   50:175
Tributes to Helen Archibald Clarke   37:315
Triess, E. W., translator — *Harvest Song* —
    Richard Dehmel   26:498
    — *Renunciation* — Isabelle Schwartz   27:121
Triggs, Oscar Lovell — *"Colombe's Birthday" by*
    Julia Marlowe - Tabor Company   7: 32
    — *In Re Caliban*   17D: 76
    — *Literature and the Scientific Spirit*   6:113
    — *New Ideas in Teaching Literature*   6:389
    — *Robert Browning as the Poet of Democracy*   4:481
    — *Socialistic Thread in the Life and Works of*
        William Morris   5:113, 210
    — *Syllabus for Study of Aesthetics*   9:281
    — *Walt Whitman*   5:289
Trilogy, A — Rose Drake   43:189
Triology of Dubrovnik, A — Ivo Vojnovich:
    I. *Allons Enfants!*   56: 99
    II. *The Twilight*   56:195
    III. *On the Terrace*   56:291
Triolet — Beth Bishop   54:360
Triolet Nocturne — Everett Gillis   45:114
Tristan and Isolde — Gottfried von Strassburg   49:301
Tristan Forethoughtful — Christine Liebeneck Swayne   24:358

241

Tristam the Jester — Ernst Hardt —
    Adapted and tranlated by John Heard:
        Part 1   43:229
        Part II   43:289
Troll King's Breakfast, The — Z. Topelius   28:589
Trombly, Albert Edmund — *Ad Una Cantate*   32:618
    — *Chipmunk, The*   29:633
    — *Dante's Rejected Canto*   27:446
    — *I Hung My Heart to the Wind*   29:109
    — *Jack's Later Beanstalk*   29:638
    — *Lake Winnepesaukee*   29:357
    — *On the Breaking of the Bay Colt*   29:605
    — *Remembrance*   28:251
    — *Texan Sketches*   31:465
Trombly, Albert E., translator — *Unhappy Love* —
    Guiseppe Giacosa   27:601
Troop, The — Ivan Mazuranic, translated by
    Bertha W. Clarke and Luke Djurichich   34:294
Tropics — Clifford M. Montague   40:414
Tropical Folio — Renée Tallantyre   49: 84
Troubadours at Home, The — C. P.   12:596
Trousdale, Sarah — *Lesson*   41:446
Trowbridge, John T., Birthday of   17C:117
Troy, Robert H. — *Why Falstaff Dies in "Henry V"*   8:330
Truant — Oliver W. Evans   49: 83
True, Barbara — *Four Poems*   51:176
True Character of Chivalry, The — J. S. Stuart Glennie   1:583
True Greatness of Browning, The — Alice Groff   1:470
True History of the London Shakespeare Tercentenary —
    Isabella Banks   3:201
Truitt, Warren — *Who Wrote "Venus and Adonis"?*   7: 28
Trusman, H. J. — *"Pietro of Abano"*   3:577
Trumbull, Jonathan — *Walt Whitman's View of
    Shakespeare*   2:368
    — *Whitman-Shakespeare Question*   3:626
Trunbull, Mrs. Lawrence — *Study of William Watson, A*   9: 64
Trunkne Lied, Das — Friedrich Nietzsche —
    translated by William Benjamin Smith   16C: 91
Truslow, Marguerite Wallbridge — *Hotel Room*   56:146
    — *Questioner*   56:145
Truth about Liars, The — Hélène Mullins   34:145
Truth about Negro Poetry, The — Elizabeth Eldridge   43:183
Truth Suspected, The — D. Juan Ruiz de Alaron —
    translated by Julio del Toro and Robert V. Finney   38:475
Tryst — Henry Bowen Smith   38:570
Tsanoff, Radoslav — *Ivan Vazoff, Balkan Poet
    and Novelist*   19: 98

Tucker, Agnes C. — *Late Harvest*   53: 99
— *Sonnets to the Space-Age Moon*   58:371
Tufts, Kingsley — *Frustration*   47:280
Tumbler, The — Everett Glass   37:516
Turcios, Froylan — *Country Girl*   54:185
Turgenieff, Ivan — *Hamlet and Don Quixote*   4:169
Turkat, Judah M. — *Passover Eve*   53:149
Turkish Ambassador, The — August von Kotzebue —
      translated by Beatrice B. Beebe   38:192
Turn from Me, Spirit — William E. Mountain   10:335
Turn Thou Thy Tears — Michael Orogo   49: 81
Turnbull, Eleanor L. — *Jorge Guillen*   48:151
— *Seven Poems and Translations*   44:372
Turnbull, Eleanor L., translator — *Three Poems* —
      Pedro Salinas   45:220
Turpin, Georges — *Two Poems*   25:606
Turquoise God, The — Isabel Moore   17C: 69
Turrell, Charles Alfred — *Some Aspects of Contemporary*
      Spanish Drama   29:319
'Twas Well Done and Quickly —
      John Francis McDermott, Jr.
"Twelfth Night": Study Programs —
      Charlotte Porter and Helen A. Clarke   8: 44; 16A:124
Twilight — Ernst Rosmer (Else Bernstein)
      translated by Paul H. Grummann   23:369
Twilight, A Song before — Arthur Ketchum   25:612
Twilight in Ireland — Helen Coale Crew   22:150
Twilight Lullaby — Rose Madeline Harris   50: 76
Twilight of the Arts — Van Wyck Brooks   24:322
Twisting of the Rope — Douglas Hyde   16A: 12
Twisting of the Rope: Performance of, by
      Twentieth Century Club — Charlotte Porter and
      Helen A. Clarke   16A:132
Two. The — von Hoffmansthal —
      Translated by Charles Wharton Stork
Two Ancient Festival Survivals in "Wordsworthshire" —
      Frances Tobey   27:326
Two Bay Horses — Louis Bartlett Chace   56:177
Two Black Sheep — Arthur Corning White   35:464
Two Blind Men and a Donkey — Mathurin M. Dondo   32:391
Two Chimeras — Gerard de Nerval   53:371
Two Dreams — Frances Barber   20: 68
Two Gentlemen of Verona:
      Questions and Notes on   1:130, 3:513
Two Haiku — Daniel Hemenway   57:495
Two Hungarian Folk Songs — translated by Olga Marx   30:587
Two Hungarian Romanticists — Joseph Remenyi   54:334

243

Two Husbands — Henri Lavédan —
 translated by R. T. House   19:207
Two Noble Kinsmen   1:585
Two Papers a Day — Lewis Colwell   42:382
Two Poems of Leprosy — Arthur Fremont Rider   17C:104
Two Poets of Croisic — Herbert Ernest Cushman   11:382
Two Rooms — Belle Chapman Morrill .   57:482
Two Sonnets for One Lately Dead —
 Sister Mary Aquinas   55: 38
Two Sonnets of Ronsard — Edith King-Fisher   55:268
Two Speeches — Franz Werfel   45:334
Two Thousand A. D. — *A Prophecy* —
 Joseph Herbert Bean   52:173
Two Translations from Catullus — Sarah Ruth Watson   53: 82
Two Translations, Mughanniname — Hafiz —
 translated by Edna Worthley Underwood   21:467
Two Women — Edna Louise Smith   35:631
Type, The — Muriel Kinney   28:373
Typography of Plays, The — Arthur Swan   27: 97
Tyson, Reba Jane — *Three Poems*   44: 85

Ukrainian Folk Songs   26:351
Ullman, Margaret — *Children of Homer, The*   24:338
Ulysses — Charlotte Porter   14A:128
Umphrey, G. W., translator — *Sonatina* — Dario   45:353
Unamuno, Miguel de — *Other, The*   53: 3
Unbidden Guest, The — O. W. Firkins   35:276
Uncertainty in English Prosody — W. F. P. Stockley   41:204
Uncle Vania — Chekhov —
 translated by Frances Arno Saphro   33:317
Uncritical Appreciation, An — Marie Emilie Gilchrist   30:304
Under a Bush of Lilacs — Jakub Arbes   4:318
Under the Open Sky — Hannah Parker Kimball   9:475
Underground — Benjamin W. Newman   38:571
Underground — Dorothy Quick   49:384
Underhill, John Garrett — *Benavente as a Modern*   29:194
Underhill, John Garrett translator — *Cradle Song, The*
 — Sierra   28:625
 — *Governor's Wife, The* — Benavente   29: 1
 — *King, the Greatest Alcalde, The* —
 De Vega Carpio   29:379
 — *Prince who Learned Everything*
 out of Books, The — Benavente   29:505
 — *Saturday Night* — Benavente   29:127
Underwood, Edna Worthley —
 Two Translations from Hafiz:
 — *Mughanniname*   21:471

— *Sakiname*   21:471
Undesirables — Jane Rutherford   33:420
Unforeseen, The — Julio J. Rueda —
    Translated by Gino V. M. de Solenni   35: 1
Unhappy Love — Guisseppe Giacosa   27:601
Unknown Hero — André Lamandé   33:438
Unpublished Letters of Emerson —
    George Willis Cooke   14A:104
Unquiet Warriors — Kay de Bard Hall   53:111
Unreason of a She-Intelligence   3: 45
Unreasonable Song — Nicolai Shtreiter —
    translated by George G. Lake   34:253
Unscpulchered — Virginia Stait   34:287
Untermeyer, Louis — *Archibald Lampman and the Sonnet*   20:432
    — *J. M. Synge and the Playboy of the*
      Western World   19:364
Untimely Death — Hazel Griffith Davis   56:364
Untouchable — Ester Velig Cuevas   56:224
Unwilling Sojourn — Mary Willis Shelburne   46:184
Upon Reading a New Edition of Chaucer —
    Gerhard Friedrich   54:373
Upon the Death of My Father — Delia Doole   48:271
Upper, Joseph — *Approaching Spring*   33:151
    — *Disinherited*   36:576
    — *Dissolution*   36:609
    — *Grace after Beauty*   39:314
    — *Inventory*   37:474
    — *Journey, The*   36:465
    — *Letters to a Young Musician*   40:313
    — *Reveur, Le*   36:279
    — *We*   37:467
Uppvall, Axel J. — *August Strindberg*   31: 69
Upson, Arthur — *Phedre*   17C: 59
    — *Silver Flute, The*   18:187
Upson, Arthur — Edward J. O'Brien   25:219
Upton, Ruth — *Poems*   48:244
Urbina, Luis G. — *Mass at Dawn, The*   24:312
    — *Transformation*   54:184
Uriel Acosta — Karl Gützkow - Translated by
    Richard Hovey and François Stewart Jones
        7: 6, 83, 140, 198, 263, 333
"Uriel," Emerson's — Charles Malloy   14C: 65
Use of Imagery, The — Clara Edmunds-Hemingway   50: 34
Utt, Ana Lee, translator — *Grief* — Quintero   41:391
    — *Widow's Eyes* — Quintero   40:552

Vagabond, The — Edith C. Bates   28:485
Vaile, Lyra Lu — *Answer*   53:160
  — *Question*   53:160
Val, Monta du — *"Here's to the Little Gentleman in
    Black Velvet"*   16A: 56
Valdés, A. Palacio — *I Puritani*   16D: 97
  — *Novels of*   16C: 92
  — *Selections from Doctor Angelico's Manuscripts*   24:268
Valdes Fernan Silva — Willis Knapp Jones   47:352
Valdes, Silva — *Romance de la Tardecita*   52:359
Valencia, Guillermo — *White Storks* —
    Translated by Alice Stone Blackwell   37:616
Valentry, Duane — *Survivors, The*   50:272
Valéry, Paul — *Cimetière Marin, Le* —
    translated by John F. Mathews   40:456
Valle Inclan, Don Ramon del — *Dragon's Head, The* —
    Translated by May Heywood Brown   29:531
Valley of Gloom, The — Marie Drennan   34:449
Valley Slumber Song — Lucy A. K. Adee   48: 58
Valliope, C. North, translator — *Ten Poems* —
    Stefan George   45:343
Value — *Per Se* — Lorena M. Gary   46:377
Van Delden, Egbert H. — *Alice in Everydayland*   38: 96
  — *Guy Upstairs, The*   40:251
Van Doren, Carl, translator — *Judith* — Hebbel   25:257
Van Kaathoven, Alice, translator—
    Beat of the Wing, The — De Curel   20:321
Van Lerberghe, Charles — *In an Orient Barque*   36:627
Vanson, Frederic —*London Bore Me*   55:262
Vargas, A. Ortiz — *Guillermo Valencia,
    Colombia's Master Poet*   47:419
Variations on a Japanese Theme — Bell Thurnbull   34:416
Variations on an Old Theme — Hazel E. Hutchins   41:455
Variorum Edition of Shakespeare — C. P.   13:141
Varnishing Day — Frederick J. Pohl   38:128
Vase, The — Winifred Adams Burr   55:179
Vase of Ching-Li, The — Cyril Odhner   36:154
Vast Domain, The — Arthur Schnitzler   34:317
Vazoff, Ivan, Balkan Poet and Novelist —
    Radoslav A. Tsanoff   19: 98
Vazquez, Jose Andres — *With Chains of Gold* —
    translated by Willis Knapp Jones   34:417
Vega Carpio, Lope Felix de — *King, the Greatest
    Alcalde, The* — translated by John Garret Underhill   29:379
  — *Stupid Lady, The*   57:291
Vellio, Vanjna de — *My Precious Secret*   17A:134
Vengeance of Catullus, The — Charles Recht   25:536

Venice — Nietzsche —
    translated by Charles Wharton Stork   23: 79
Venice Preserved — Hugo von Hofmannsthal   26:529
"Ventia Victrix"   1:379
"Venus and Adonis," Music of the Language of —
    S. E. Bengough   4:562
"Venus and Adonis," Who Wrote? — Warren Truitt   7: 28
Venus - Madonna — Richard Dehmel —
    translated by Paul H. Grummann   24: 64
Verdi's "Otello"   1:444
Verhaeren, Emile — *Clocks*   55: 83
    — *Michaelangelo* — translated by E. H. Pfeiffer   33:612
    — *Our Lady of Past Empires*   51: 48
    — *Statue, A (The Apostle)*   47: 98
    — *Three Translations from* — Eva M. Sadler   31:460
Verhaeren's Emile, Lyrical Trilogy — Federico Olivero   25: 63
Verissimo, Jose — *Going after Rubber* — translated by
    Bob White Linker and Francis Simkins   39:154
    — *Returning from Rubber Gathering* —
    translated by Bob White Linker and
    Francis Simkins   30:467
Verlaine, Paul — *Autumn Song* — translated by
    William A. Drake   36:199
    — *Eventide*   23:368
    — *Favorable Moment, The*   56:194
    — *Group of Poems, A* — translated by
    William A. Drake   33:458
    — *Parisian Nocturnes* — translated by
    Leonora Speyer   30:461
    — *Pierrot Dead*   16D: 81
    — *Songs from "La Bonne Chanson"*   16D: 80
    — *Wisdom*   27:439
Verlaine, Shelley and — Alice L. Watson   8:406
Verlaine, Paul — Federico Olivero   31:268
Verplanck, Gulian C. — *Shakespeare's First
    American Editor* — G. Parker Norris   2:424
Verse, American — C.   4:580; 5:375; 6:204, 620; 7:566,
    8: 95; 9:126; 10:134
Verse, British — P.   5:549; 6:368; 7:366; 8: 95; 9:440;
    10:123, 430
Verse, New and Old British   8:147
Verse, Notes on American — C.   9:445
Verse, Our Moribund — Phyllis Ackerman   29:356
Verse, Repetition and Parallelism in English   7:458
Verse, Some Recent — William Stanley Braithwaite   22:223
Verse Techniques, Some Remarks on —
    Robert Wood Clark   56: 76

Verse, Two Volumes of American   6:620
Verses for My Friends — Beatrice Daw   29:595
Very, Alice — *Eight Poems*   43: 84
Via Cruciata — Robert P. Tristram Coffin   33:608
Vicars, E. — *Lowlands vs. Highlands*:
   Effects of Environment on Poets   6: 83
Vickner, Edwin Johan and Glenn Hughes, transuators —
   Balcony, The — Gunnar Heiberg   33:475
Victoria — Jane Winsor Gale   26: 78
Victorian Anthology, Stedman's — C.   7:630
Victory — Detlev von Liliencron, translated by
   Edwin H. Zeydel   32:200
Victory — Janet Preston   35:586
Viele, Guffin Francis — *Dawn The*   22:398
Vignettes — Nancy Pendleton Stetson   49:298
Vilas, Faith van Valkenburgh — *Tears of Dawn*   33:105
Vildrac, Charles — *After Marriage*   22:399
   — *Great White Bird, The*   25:228
   — *Spring*   25:137
   — *Steamer Tenacity, The* — translated by
     John Strong Newberry   32:463
   — *Those There Are*   25:139
Village Romeo and Juliet, A — Gottfried Keller   9:498
Villanelle of the Guignol — Margaret Lewis Albanese   48:253
Villon, François — *Ballade*   52: 67
   — *Ballad of the Ladyes of Lang Syne*   1:548
Villon's Last Rondeau — Albert Edward Johansson   53: 81
Vincent, Leon H. — *Elizabethan Novelist, An*   9: 47
Vincent Mabel— *Alfred Noyes in Retrospect*   41:293
Vinecurov, Yevgeni — *Poet and Poetry, The*   58:317
Viole, La Belle — José Maria de Heredia —
   translated by Cammie H. Lamy   34:282
Violent Wedding, The — Robert Lowry   58: 3
Violets in the Fall — Albert E. Trombly   31:466
Violin Concerto — Margaret Tod Ritter   34:310
Virgil's Art — John Albee   12:306
Vishnu and Goethe's "World Spirit"   1:401
Vision — Alison Thomson   55:194
Vision —Murray Beskin   53: 47
"Vision of Hellas, A"   12:308
"Vision of Sir Launfal": *Study Programs*   6: 47; 15A: 97
Visions — Albert Samain   26:275
Visions, From the Book of — John Casey   25:251
Visit, The   14C: 65
Visitant — William W. Chance   55:354
Visitor at the Temple — A. H. Ware   33:113
Visitors — Stanton A. Coblentz   46:357

248

Vittorelli, Jacopo — *Anacreontics*   27:709
Voeu — Henri de Regnier   54:220
Voice, The — Henri de Regnier   53: 49
Voice of the Dead, The — Paul Scott Mowrer   28:484
Voice of the Devil   11: 28
Voice of the Woman, The — F. T. Marinetti —
   translated by Anne Simon   25:440
Vojnovich, Ivo — *Resurrection of Lazarus, The* —
   translated by John J. Batistich and
     George Rapall Noyes   37:317
   — *Trilogy of Dubrovnik, A*   56: 99, 195, 291
Voltaire — Anna E. Bagstad   32:519
Voltaire, Shakespeare, and Billeting Area 18 —
   Robert Wilson McKnight   31:604
Voorhees, Irving Wilson — *Realism in American Fiction
   of Today*   17C: 76
Voteur, Ferdinand — *My Unfinshed Portrait*   56: 3
Vow by a Star-Dropped Sky — Maidi Payne   46: 43
Vrchlicky, Jaroslav — *At the Chasm*   24:289
   — *Vengenance of Catullus*   25:536
   — *Witness, The*   25:546
Vrchlicky, Jaroslav — Charles Recht   24:309
Vrchlicky, Jaroslav, and His Place in Bohemian Drama   25:534

Wadleigh, Ursella — *Farmer's Wife*   50: 78
Wages of War — J. Wiegand and Wilhelm Scharrelmann   19:129
Wagner's Parsifal, The Motivation of —
   Paul H. Grummann   16C:123
Waiting Till You Come — Tom T. Errilla   46:338
Walberg, Anna Cronhjelm, translator —
   Hatto the Hermit, A Legend of — Selma Lagerlöf   11:348
   — *It: A Love Story* — Selma Lagerlöf   11:321
   — *Story about Gunnel, The* — Molin   12: 1
   — *Without Words* — Tavatstjerna   12: 12
Walker, Laura Marquand — *Suggested by a Bas-Relief
   of Victory*   26:280
   — *Why Go Ye to the Sphinx*   27:445
Walker, Marion Sinclair — *Fog-Bound*   47: 95
Walking Wings, On — Paul Alexander Bartlett   52: 30
Wall, A. H. — *Shakespeare's Face*   2:634
Wall, Annie Russell — *Answer to Query*   1:184
   — *Authorship of De Tribus, The*   6:471
   — *Dante's Imperialism*   2:501
   — *Is Shakespeare's Caesar Ignoble?*   4:191
   — *Sordello Club Paper*   1:424
   — *Supernatural in Shakespeare*   5:490, 557, 620
Wallace, Elizabeth, translator —*Grandfather, The* —
   Galdos   21:161

Wallace, Grace, translator — *Backward Thoughts* —
    Narcisse Quellien   30:614
    — *Mirror, The* — Pierre de Ronsard   32:415
Wallace, J. F. — *Jean Paul Richter*   5:551
Walled-up Window, The — August von Kotzebue —
    translated by Beatrice B. Beebe   38:246
Wallin, Elvira B. — *Wanderers of the Winds*   46:376
Wallis Marie Pope — *Anna Amelia Queiroz*
    Carneiro de Mendoca   58: 45
    — *Contemporary Brazilian Poet: Adalgisa Neri, A*   55: 51
    — *Teresa Maria Llona's Intersection*   49:323
Wally, Haya, translator — *By Ourselves* — Fulda   23: 1
Walsh Thomas, translator —
    Fray Louis De Leon to His Pupil   22: 79
    — *Julio Herrer y Reissig*   33:601
    — *Papa Juan or the Centenarian* — Quintero   29:253
Walsh, Walter — *Religion of Robert Burns, The*   7: 57
Walter, Elizabeth — *Hugo von Hofmannsthal,*
    Neo-Romanticist   26:644
Walter, Elizabeth, translator — *Venice Preserved* —
    von Hofmannsthal   26:529
Walter, Nina Willis — *In His Honor*   50:360
    — *In What Alembic*   58:331
    — *Remembering*   54:311
    — *Three Poems*   58: 91
    — *Young Poet*   58:270
Walter Pater, Some of His Imaginary Portraits —
    Donald Worth Marshall   32:431
Walton, Crane — *Brief for Ophelia, A*   3:569
Wanderer (Anglo-Saxon)   17D: 96
Wanderer, The — translated by Albert W. Haley, Jr.   58:352
Wanderer of the Winds — Elvira B. Wallin   46:376
Wanderer's Lament (Old English Lyric) —
    translated by Anna Robertson Brown   3:140
Wanderer's Song — Karl-Erik Forsslund   51: 79
Wanderers, The — Maurice Ferber   43:364
Wandering Jew Legend, The — R. G. Moulton   3:323
War — J. E. Fillmore   25:523
War — Robert Beloof   56: 2
War — Turpin   25:606
Ward, H. Glynn — *Aftermath, The*   37:501
Ward, Margaret — *Amber of Koenibsberg*   43:228
    — *Song for David*   43:286
    — *Stranger by the Lake, The*   43:188
    — *Two Poems*   43:327
Ward, Ruth H. — *Four Triolets in a Garden*   44: 84
Ward, William Allen — *Night*   50:263

Ware, A. H. —*Beyond*   35:527
   — *Day of Dreams*   33:267
   — *In Memoriam*   35:575
   — *Visitor at the Temple, The*   33:113
Warnack, Henry C. — *Unpublished Letter from*
   Longfellow on Evangeline   14A:108
Warning — Clarissa Hall   48:273
Warning — Shirley A. Marcus   46:285
Warren Gretchen — *Pilgrim's Way, The*   26:403
   — *Sacrifice*   27:124
   — *Spring and Winter*   27:123
   — *Storm, The*   26:404
Warshaw, J. — *High Lights in the Story of Susanna*   28:242
Was Ibsen Original — A. Alexander Enna   40:420
Washington — Charlotte F. Myers   54:352
Wassall, Irma — *Portrait of a Hand*   46:281
Wasted Lives — Antonio de Lezama and
   Enrique de Meneses — Authorized translation by
   Dr. Herman Schnitzler — Adapted for the English
   Stage by Gustav Davidson   41:159
Watch and the Almond Tart, The — August von Kotzebue
   translated by Beatrice B. Beebe   38:240
Water Lily, The — Edna Wahlert McCourt   28:472
Water Whimsies — Mary Webber   55:181
Waterbury, Ivan Calvin — *Poetic Language*   21:241
Watson, Esther — *Of Poetry as Necessity*   30:138
Watson, Sara Ruth — *Two Translations from Catullus*   53: 82
Watson, Warren — *Libraries in Shakespeare' Day*   1:150
Watson, William, A Study of   9: 64
Watts-Dunton — *In British Verse*   10:123
Way, Arthur S. — *New Views of Shakespeare's Shrew*   8:169
Way, Norma — *Song of the Will-o-the-Wisp*   47:175
Wayland, H. L. — *Remarks on Some Passages in*
   "*Rabbi Ben Ezra*"   1: 57
Ways of the Wind — Margery Ruebush Shank   49:370
We — Joseph Upper   37:467
We Made a Vow in Autumn — Jane Robinson   48:180
We the Occupied — Gilean Douglas   51:148
We Will Not Ask — Hazel Griffith Davis   56:359
Weariness from Suffering — Juan Ramon Jiminez —
   translated by Herbert King Stone   32:430
Weary Black — Yvonne A. Freund   58:194
Weasel's Holiday, The — Anne Mary Lyman   32:307
Weaving, The — John Towner Frederick   30:607
Webber, Mary — *Poems*   55:181
Webster, Nina James — *Miracle*   50:260
Wedded Husband, The — Shen Hung   32:110

Wedding Guest, The — Rosialee Kerley	33:232
Wedding, The Golden — Dorothy E. Reid	38:155
Wedekind, Frank — O. F. Theis	24:237
Weeks, Ricardo — *Brothers*	48:358
Wehrfritz, Margaret — *Poems*	46:281
Weinberg, Albert — *Lofty Motives*	38:603
— *Rosamund at the Tracks*	39:436
Weinberg, Albert and Anita — *Philosophy of the*	
Tooth Brush, The	36:615
Weinberger, Mildred — *Elaine*	34: 72
Weingarten, Joseph A., translator —	
Amnon and Tamar — Peretz	48:149
Weisburd, Melvin Irving — *The Appointment*	57: 61
Well of Hazels — Anne Throop Craig	34:429
Wenewelir — Edna Wahlert McCourt	28:471
Wenig, Adolph — *Evenfall*	46:282
Wenley, R. M. —*Old Quarrel between Poetry*	
and Philosophy	10:365
Werfel, Franz — *Chimpanzee Farce* — translated by	
Margaret Schlauch	37:627
— *Two Speeches*	45:334
Wergeland, A. M., translator —	
Love Verses from the Hindoo	14C: 53
Wergeland, Henrik — *Christmas Eve*	49:355
Wesley, Cecil Cobb — *Indian's Last Dream, The*	55:176
West, Elizabeth Howard, translator —	
Madman Divine, The — Echegaray	19: 1
West, Kenyon — *Margaret Fuller's Permanent Influence*	7:377
Wetzel, Doris — *Snowfall*	38:589
Weysz, Hans, translator — *Duke and the Actress, The* —	
Schnitzler	21:257
What Fun it Was — Claire Shelley	55:336
What I Know — *Quel Che So* — Felice Cavallotti	26:118
What I Love — Esmé de Menocal	42:288
What Is Eternal — R. E. Saleski	26:651
What Is Love? — Elizabeth Hazelton Haight	14D: 66
What Is Wrong with our Critics? — Clifford M. Montague	48:246
What Loneliness — Charlotte E. Porter	37:457
What Poetry Has Done for the World — Louis T. Baker	8:145
What's Right — Roland English Hartley	43:169
What Should Be the Poet's Attitude towards His Critics	5:135
What Will You Bring Me — William G. Angermann	53:164
Wheel of Fortune, The — From "Morte d' Arthur" —	
translated by Anna Robertson Brown	5: 25
"Wheels ob de Human Chariot" — Anne Frierson	41:458
When — Alwyn Coristine	51:117
When a Man Wanders — Hazel Harper Harris	40:602

When April Comes — Ruth Le Prade 44: 80
When Evening Comes — Ronald Walker Barr 53:194
When I Have Fear — Oscar C. Williams 30:432
When Spring Has Lengthened out the Day —
    Claire Shelley 55:337
When the Bugle Blows — Alma Paschall 55: 39
When the New Wine Blooms — Björnstjerne Björnson —
    translated by Lee M. Hollander 22: 1
When the World is October Yellow — Richard Edwards 58:355
When You Are Gone — Mary Buirgy 53:170
Where Eons March — Winifred Adams Burr 55:373
Where Love Is — Iden Payne 37:475
Where Romanticism Is Still in Flower — O. H. Rystad 19:332
Where Shall We Go? — Henri Lavédan 28:397
Whicher, George Frisbie, translator —
    Five Medieval Latin Lyrics 49:165
While the Mushrooms Bubble — Dan W. Totheroh 32:251
Whipkey, Stella Dunaway — *Door Mats* 40: 92
Whirling Wind Exults in the Storm — Portia Martin 31:463
Whistler, and, Poe — Harriet Monroe 21:391
Whitcomb, Ida Prentice —
    Lark in Legend and Song, The 15B: 81
    — *Maze* 36:147
White, Arthur Corning — *Two Black Sheep* 35:464
White Butterflies — Gordon Lockhart 57:382
White Fan, The — Hugo von Hofmansthal 54:120
White, Florence Donnell and Edith Fahnstock, translators
    — *Magic Theatre, The* — Cervantes 32:234
White, Frances Emily — *Browning's Mesmerism from a
    Scientific Point of View* 4:261
White, Hal S. — *God Speaks to Travelers* 35:156
White, Henry — *Theology of Robert Browning, The* 12:417
White, James Platt — *Caldron, The* 23:302
    — *Civic Theatre, The* 23:320
    — *Dramas of M. Paul Hervieu, The* 14C: 79; 15A: 77
White, J. Blanco — *A Letter from* 10:624
White, Richard Grant — *On Donnelly's Cipher* 1:586
White Storks — Guilliermo Valencia —
    translated by Alice Stone Blackwell 37:616
White Water Man — Amanda Benjamin Hall 49: 3
White Wolves, The — John Heard 47:368
Whitehouse, Josephine Henry — *Canary, The* 37:589
    — *Daily Bread* 40:129
    — *Indian Summer* 39:455
Whiteside, Mary Brent — *Sonnets of the Holy Land* 36:471
Whitfield, Justine L. — *Monotony* 33:365
Whither — Alice Mary M. Griffith 35:140

Whiting, Eleanor — *Common Ground*   32:140
Whiting, Eleanor Curtis — *Ashes*   33:423
Whitman, Walt — *Shakespeare, for America*   2:492
Whitman, Walt — Oscar L. Triggs   5:289
Whitman, Walt, and Arno Holz — Amelia von Ende   16B: 61
Whitman, Walt and Browning   4:482
Whitman, Walt, and His Art — John Burroughs   6: 63
Whitman, Walt, and Murger — Horace L. Traubel   6:484
Whitman, Walt "Artistic Atheism" of — Horace L. Traubel   6:484
Whitman, Walt, "Artistic Atheism" of —
        Horace L. Traubel   5:498
Whitman, Walt, Books on — P.   6: 95; 9:131
Whitman, Walt, Boston Criticism of, A —
        John Burroughs   4:392
Whitman, Walt, Comparison and Contrast with Shelley   8:332
Whitman, Walt Contrasted with Lowell —
        Horace L. Traubel   4: 22
Whitman, Walt, Criticism of — C. B. Wright   9:154, 311
Whitman, Walt, English Edition of   7:376
Whitman, Walt, Friendship of Emerson and —
        William Sloane Kennedy   7: 71
Whitman, Walt, Greek Traits in —
        Emily Christiana Monck   7:327
Whitman, Walt, Human Brotherhood in — P.   10:421
Whitman, Walt, In Relation to Christianity —
        Emily Christiana Monck   7:607
Whitman, Walt, Letters to Doyle — W. E. M.   9:617
Whitman, Walt, New Edition of   9:626
Whitman, Walt, Personality in   10:113
Whitman, Walt, Poem to — Louis James Block   5:422
Whitman, Walt, Poetry   1:129
Whitman, Walt, Prose and Poetry — Helena Knorr   10:586
Whitman, Walt, Reading Course   6:644
Whitman, Walt, Shakespeare for America   2:492
Whitman, Walt, Shakespeare Question, The —
        Jonathan Trumbull   3:626
Whitman, Walt, Shelley and — Isaac Hull Platt   8:332
Whitman, Walt, Testimonial   1:348
Whitman, Walt, Woman and Freedom in —
        Helen Abbott Michael   9:216
Whitman's Graveside, At —   4:461
Whitman's Ideal Democracy — Helena Born   11:569
Whitman's, Walt, Imagery   4:229
Whitman's Message   4:229
Whitman's "Prayer of Columbus"   7:161, 218, 275
Whitman's Reading of Life   17C: 79
Whitman's Views of Shakespeare — Jonathan Trumbull   2:368

Whitman's "Wound Dresser" — W. E. M.   10:307
Whitsunday Fight, The — Holgar Drachmann —
    translated by Johannes H. Wisby   7:405
Whittemore, Margaret — Woodcut   42: 98
   — Woodcut   42:194
   — Woodcut   42:290
Whittier's, John Greenleaf, "Mabel Martin" — P. A. C.   8:158
Whittier's, John Greenleaf, "Snowbound' Study Program   6:102
What Is There to Say — Edith Hope   55:230
"Whom God Hath Joined" — translated and adapted from
    the French by John Heard   44:232
Whom the Gods Destroy — Jaroslav Hilbert   27:361
Why? — Helena Sharpsteen   24:121
Why Go Ye to the Sphinx — Laura Marquand Walker   27:445
Why Men Shudder — Archag Tchobanian   30:444
Widows' Eyes — Serafin and Joaquin Alvarez Quintero —
    translated by Ana Lee Utt   40:552
Wiechart, Ernst, Child Cried at Night, A   45:352
Wiegand, Charmion von — Jasmine and the Poet   37:418
Wiegand, J. and Wilhelm Scharrelmann —
    Wages of War, The   19:129
Wife of Usher's Well, The — John Joseph Martin   30: 94
Wiggin, Kate Douglas — Fragments of a Play   40:281
   — Thorn in the Flesh, A   36:191
Wiggin, Pauline G. — Shakespearean Books   11:293
Wilbrandt, Adolf — Master of Palmyra, The   13:161
Wilcox, Grace — Translated   41:251
Wild Asters — Danske Dandridge   13:357
Wild Boar, The — Seumas O'Brien   38:536
Wild Roses — Lucy A. K. Adee   54:372
Wild Wind — Donna Lois Gideon   47:287
Wild Wind, The — Louis Bartlett Chace   56:237
Wilde, Oscar, as a Poet — Homer E. Woodbridge   19:439
Wilde, Oscar, Fifteeen Years After — F. G. H.   27:411
Wilde, Oscar — Happy Prince, The   27:406
   — "Salome"   18:199
Wildenbruch, Ernst Harold von Biography —   3:481
    Otto Heller and Hugh A. Clarke   3:393
Wildenbruch, Ernst Harold von — Claudia's Garden   8:478
   — Portrait and Autograph   3 :facing 393
Wilkinson, Maude — Objection to Browning's Caliban
    Considered, An   5:562
Will, A — Charles Lounsbury   50:262
Will-o-the-Wisp — Jaroslav Kvapil   27: 1
Willan, J. N. — Schiller's Jungfrau von Orleans   7:169
Willcox, Ella Goodenow — Browning's "A Soul Tragedy"   13:411
Willcox, Louise Collier — Deed Foreborne, A   15A: 30

William Shakespeare — Harold Willard Gleason   39:289
William Somerset Maugham: Dramatist —
    Clifford M. Montague   47: 40
Williams, Francis Howard
    — *Beatrice and Numpholeptis*   3:163
    — *Browning's Form*   2:301
    — *Chanson*   1:547
    — *Clough and Emerson: The Metaphysical*
      Significance of "Dipsychus" and "The World
      Soul"   6:348
    — *Immortality as a Motive in Poetry*   9:367
    — *Relation of Nature to Man in Browning, The*   4:238
    — *Tennyson Memorial Address*   5: 55
Williams, H. Isabelle, translator —
    Pitiless Policeman, The — Georges Courteline   28:217
Williams, Hadwen — *Philippine Poetry*   40:288
Williams, Melba — *Silent Listeners*   35:231
Williams, Oscar — *Mother, The*   45:114
Williams, Oscar C. — *Down on the East Side*   36:641
    — *Dusk*   32:287
    — *Fires of Youth, The*   30:443
    — *Gold*   32:306
    — *Plaint*   31:274
    — *When I Have Fear*   30:432
Williams, Oscar, and Jack Brady —
    King Who Scoffed, The   34:139
Williams, Talcott — *Characteristics of Magic in Eastern*
    and Western Literature   4:126
    — *On Browning*   2: 47
    — *Shakespeare's Fidelity to History*   13: 91
Williamson, C. C. H. — *On the Early English Anthologies*   44:286
Williamson, C. H. — *Joy of Poetry, The*   43:136
Williamson, Claude C. H. — *Poetry, Music, and Life*   35:587
Williamson, George, Translator — *Litanies of the Rose* —
    de Gourmont
    — *She Has a Body* — de Gourmont   34:302
Willow Remains — George Brandon Saul   58: 2
"Willow Song", A New   1: 27
Wilm, Emil C. — *Characteristics of Philosophy and*
    Literature   24:122
Wilson, Alice L. — *Shelley and Verlaine*   8:406
Wilson, Margaret Adelaide — *Bee Tender, The*   19: 86
Wimberly, Lowry Charles — *Ideas of the Soul in English*
    and Scottish Popular Ballads   36:542
Wind in the Wheat — Hortense Roberta Roberts   50: 88
Wind of April — Frances Dickenson Pinder   33:117
Windblown — Edna M. Harris   38:426

Windcraft — Martin Chesley 51: 47
Windeler, B. Cyril — *Daniel* 45: 49
— *Two Poems* 44:368
Wings, The — Josephine Preston Peabody 25:352
Wings of Remembrance — Isabel Neill 39:309
Winningstad, Philip, translator — *You Can't Live Just as You Please* — Ostrovsky 49:203
Winsett Marvin Davis — *The Game* 58:366
Winter, Doryll — *Infidelity?* 47: 72
Winter — Hazel Griffith Davis 50:258
Winter Bloom — Bridget T. Hayes 30:385
Winter Landscape — Helena Sidis 47:384
Winter Night — Julian Ziegler 47: 94
Winter Scene — Frances Westgate Butterfield 50: 36
Winter Sunset — Gladys Merrifield 55:242
Winter Swamp-Meadow Nocturne — Louis Bartlett Chace 53:145
Winter Weariness — Giosue Carducci — Translated by William A. Drake 35: 88
Winter Wind — Gordon Lockhart 54: 69
"Winter's Tale" Considered in Connection with Green's "Pandosto" and the "Alkestis" of Euripides 14C:132
"Winter's Tale", Miss Anderson in 1: 92
"Winter's Tale": Study Program 4:516
"Winter's Tale": Variorum — P. 10:300
Winthrop, W. — *Frederick Tennyson and His Poetry* 10:258
Wisby, Johannes H. — *American as Seen by a Melancholy Dane and a Mystical Hindoo* 11:237, 373
— *Saga Literature* 6:281
Wisby, Johannes H., translator — *Present Day Saga, A* — Drachmann 6:394
— *Whitsunday Fight, The* — Drachmann 7:405
Wisby, Thor Horlf — *Epitaph* 10:629
Wisdom — Paul Verlaine 27:439
Wisdom of Nichette, The — Harriet L. Huntington 16A: 28
Wish of Aucassin, The — C. Maxwell Lancaster, translator 54:270
Wiseman, J. — *Country Ramble, A* 13:355
Wister, Owen — *Henrik Ibsen* 2:338
With Chains of Gold — José Andres Vazquez 34:417
Witherspoon, Frances — *Other Room, The* 38:269
Withington, Gertrude — *Motherless Heroines in English Classics* 11:259
Without Words — Karl Tavaststjerma — translated by Anna Gronheljm Wallberg 12: 12
Witness, The — Charles Recht 25:546
Wolfe, Archibald John, translator — *Children of the Sun, The* — Gorki 17B: 1

257

Wolves and Sheep — Alexander Ostrovsky — translated by
    Inez Sachs Colby and George Rapall Noyes   37:159
Women, The — Josip Kosor — Authorized translation
    from the Serbo-Croatian by P. Salver   41:317
Woman and Freedom in Whitman —
    Helen Abbott Michael   9:216
Woman-Egoist: Meredith's Cecilia —
    Katharine Rolston Fisher   24:113
Woman of No One, The — Cesare Lodovici —
    translated by Petronelle Sombart   32:159
Woman's Way, A — Marion Dorothy Hermer   47:288
Womanhood, Ideals of, The — Charlotte Porter   9:385
Womanhood in Modern Poetry — Vida D. Scudder   1:449
Womanhood, Old and New Ideals of   3:269
Women at Edinburgh University — Charlotte C. Stopes   4:635
Women, Dramatic Ability of   7:512
Women in Music   1:292
Women Poets, Early American — Mary Harned   5:332
Women, Shakespeare's   1:453
Wonder — Sara Perry   57:494
Wondership, The — Leon Cunningham   30:363
Wontner, Arthur: Another Forbes Robertson —
    Arthur W. Row   40:150
Wood, Mildred C. — *Jephthah's Daughter*   48:142
Woodall, Allen E. — *Edwin Arlington Robinson*   43:363
    — *Morgenlied*   44: 93
Woodbridge, Homer E. — *Oscar Wilde as a Poet*   19:439
Woodbury, Charles J. — *Secret of Pippa's Power, The*   3:350
Woodford, Bruce P. — *Pastoral for Easter — Opus I*   53: 50
    — *Prisoner, The*   57:195
Woodlands, The — Julia Wickham Greenwood   27:342
Woodman, L. C. — *Gustavo Adolfo Becquer,*
    Spanish Romanticist   26:512
Woods, Ethel Standish — *Bulbs in Water*   46: 94
    — *Snow Crystal, A*   46: 87
Woodward, Helen Dryer — *Santayana on Robert*
    Browning: A Pessimistic Criticism   13: 97
Wooing — Catherine Ruth Smith   50:284
Wooing of Damayanti, The — From the Sanskrit —
    Amy H. W. Bullock   16B: 51
Word about Aunt Lasmi, A — Sree Basudeb   35:100
Word for Rossetti, A — Nancy K. Foster   21:322
Word on English Literature in America, A —
    Felix E. Schelling   1:210
Words that are Winged, Of — Esther Matson   38:307
Wordsworth, William — C.   11:425
Wordsworth, William, Influence of Milton on —
    Vernon Purington Squires   9:540

Wordsworth, William, "Intimations of Immortality":
    Study Program   8:454
Wordsworth, William, Literary Democracy of —
    J. W. Bray   8:306
Wordsworth, William, "Ode to Duty": Study Program —
    P. A. C.   8:106
Wordsworth's "Michael" — The Editors   12:583
Wordsworth's "Michael": Comparative Study —
    Vida D. Scudder   3: 87
Workshop, In the — Lewis Worthington Smith   24:365
World of Arthur Schnitzler, The — George I. March   39:573
World's My Village, The — Cornel Lengyel   55:195
Worn Steps — Charles Angoff   48:266
Worswick, M. A. — Singer, The   5:331
Worth, Kathryn — Dead Dreams   30:465
Woticky, Edward, translator with Alexander Caro —
    Vast Domain, The — Arthur Schnitzler   34:317
Wounded Pelican — Alison Thomson   55:233
Wright, Alfred J., Jr. — Goblins   57:136
Wright, Charles B. — Browning Mistaken by Boyesen   10:461
    — Browning Right Again   9:312
    — Two Felicities, The   9:472
Wright, J. C. — Gardens and the English Poets   29:346
Wright, J. C., F. R. S. L. — Later Thoughts on Shelley   30:377
Wright, Jean A. — Fool on a Roof, A   25: 53
Wright, L. — Browning's Standpoint   2:604
Wright, Margaret — Colin Clements   31:576
Wurtzburg, C. A. — "Alkestis" of Euripides and of
    Browning   2:345
    — "As You Like It":
    An Inductive Study   3:341; 4: 31, 81, 498
    — Characters in "Much Ado about Nothing"   6:126, 491
    — Passion in "Much Ado about Nothing"   6:550
    — Shakespeare's Use of Life as a Dramatic
    Material   6: 70
Wyatt, Sir Thomas: Sonnets — E. B. Brownlow   3: 44, 97, 127
Wyman, W. H. — Bacon - Shakespeare Literature   1: 69; 2:613

Yantis, George Davenport — Sor Juana after Three
    Hundred Years   57:161
Yarmolinsky, Abraham, translator — Serb Hero Songs   27:440
Yarmy, Ramona G. — To Be Continued   53:178
Yeatman, Jennette H., translator— Missal, The   55: 80
Yeats in the Making — Charles Johnston   17B:102
Yeats, William Butler, Neo-Celtic Poet, The —
    Julia Ellsworth Ford and Kate V. Thompson   15D: 83
Yeats, William Butler, — Portrait   15D:facing

Yehoash: *Solomon Bloomgarden* — Charles Madison 37:537
Yelton, DeWitt — *Cigarette* 49:354
Yesterday — Helen M. Francis 35:270
Yiddish Theatre, The — C. Madison 32:497
You — Charlotte F. Myers 54:356
You — Colin C. Clements 29:472
You Can't Fool with Love — Pedro E. Pico 49:107
You Can't Live Just as You Please —
    Alexander Ostrovsky 49:203
You Were Mine — Gabriela Mistral 57: 98
Young Dead, The — Francis O'Brien 44:286
Young, Howard T. — *Myth of Leda in*
    Yeats and Dario, The 55:136
Young Love — Emily Eveleth Snyder 50:378
Young, Pauline Rodgers — *Off the Road* 36:300
Young Poet — Nina Willis Walter 58:270
Young Poet Considers, The — Charles Ballard 40:158
Young Poet, Reading Course for a — C. 9:118
Young Vienna — Sol Liptzin 47:337
Young, Zoola — *Autumn Longing* 47:358
Your Gift — William Pennance Church 37:152
Your Son — *and Mine* — Nadine O'Brien 51: 80
Your Vivid Touch — Claire Shelley 55:336
Youth Goes West — Raymond Knister 39:582
Youth Speaks — Jean Moreas 53: 60
Yucatan — William Mountain 12: 10
Yugoslav Literature, A Survey of —
    Anthony J. Klançar 50: 37
Yushkevich, Semen — *In the City* 47: 99

Zaragüeta — Miguel Ramos Carrion and Vital Aza —
    translated by Stephen Scatori and
    Roy Temple House 33: 1
Zeigler, Francis I. — *August Strindberg* 17A: 46
Zeigler, Francis I., translator — *Stronger, The* —
    Strindberg 17A: 47
Zelson, Louis G., translator —
    She Who Returned to Life — Monterde 55:291
Zeydel, Edwin H. — *Expressionism in Germany* 36:399
    — *Richard Dehmel* 31:393
    — *Seven Poems of Stefan George* 34:288
Zeydel, Edwin H., translator — *Victory* — von Liliencron 32:200
Zeyer, Julius — *Diarmuid and Grainne* — translated by
    George Rapall Noyes and Vera Mezirka 44:289
    — *Raduz and Mahulena* — Translated by
    Zdenka Buben and George Rappall Noyes;
    songs by Dorothea Prall 34: 1

Ziegler, Julian — *Winter Night*   47: 94
Ziel, E. — *Abendfeier*   27:707
Zimelman, Nathan — *Song, The*   51:271
   — *To Vienna*   52:116
Zivkovic, Peter D. — *Point Bridge*   58:280
Zone Libre — Louis Aragon   57: 80
Zoology, Literary Influence of Mediaeval, The —
      Oscar Kuhns   11: 73
Zorrilla, José — *Dagger of the Goth, The* —
      translated by Willis Knapp Jones   40:426
Zorrilla, José, A Spanish Poet-Lauriate —
      Fanny Hale Gardiner   10:506
Zucker, A. E., translator — *Redentin Easter Play, The*   47: 3
Zullo, Vigiliano — *Change, The*   43:135
   — *Group of Poems, A*   42:356
   — *Surrender*   43:185